The Beatles Digest 2nd Edition

Published in the United States by

An F&W Publications Company

COPYRIGHT 2002 by KRAUSE PUBLICATIONS, INC.
Library of Congress Catalog Card Number: 00-104627
International Standard Book Number: 0-87349-512-8

Printed in the United States of America

All sheet music provided by Orpheus

Contents

Why The Beatles Still Matter

By Robin Platts

Early 1973. I'm 5 years old and my parents have just arrived home after visiting a friend of the family, Dr. Binless. The doctor has given them a couple of old LPs he no longer listens to. One of my parents walks over to the turntable, takes off the Disney LP I've been listening to and replaces it with one of the new acquisitions. A collection of Beatles oldies.

The needle makes contact with the vinyl. After a second of crackle, the drums kick in and the sound explodes.

"She Loves You, YEAH, YEAH, YEAH..."

My life will never be the same. What I am hearing sounds like something from another world. It sounds ancient, even though it is barely 10 years old. Everything I hear will somehow be shaped by, or forced to measure up, to this sound.

Why are the Beatles still important?

Why do the Beatles still matter?

> " My life will never be the same. What I am hearing sounds like something from another world. "

"For a start, the Beatles invented rock and roll."

For a start, the Beatles invented rock and roll. Yeah, I know, rock and roll was really invented by an assortment of people in the '40s and '50s. Ike Turner's in there somewhere, Elvis, Bill Haley and all that. But rock and roll as we know it, and certainly the idea of rock and the rock group, was invented by the Beatles.

Four guys, two guitars, bass and drums. The sheer coolness. Sure, Elvis was cool, but to take that and multiply it by four? That was something. And how many other groups were made up of members who all seemed equally important to the equation? Not many, and certainly none where each of the elements was so fully defined. Not just in terms of musical contributions, but in terms of the myth and the image. The witty one, the cute one, the quiet/mystical one and the... Well, Ringo was always just Ringo, and that was enough.

As far as I'm concerned, the Beatles were the first rock and roll group, and every group that has come after them has, in some way, however obscure, tried to live up to what they did. And no one has quite succeeded, but the results have made for some spectacular bands and some great records.

The Beatles didn't come up with everything first, but they fused it all together so perfectly and they took it, pushed it to places that no one could have imagined. The Who was louder, the Stones were raunchier, maybe the Kinks were wittier. But no one else seemed to be able to be all things to all people like the Beatles were.

Just by being who they were and playing the music that they wanted to play, just by being curious and wanting to try new things, they created the blueprint for everything that rock and roll has been since then, everything rock and roll has tried to be. They still cast a long shadow over rock and roll, rock, pop – whatever it's called these days.

It's been 33 years since they split up and, since that day, no one has done anything that takes away even a small piece of the Beatles myth.

Nothing.

Can you remember the last time you heard someone use the phrase "better than the Beatles?" I can't ever remember hearing it and I've had a lot of conversations about rock and roll with a lot of different people. If you've heard it, I suggest that the person was either drunk or caught up in a temporary fervor of the kind that grips true music lovers. But I challenge anyone, in a sober, objective moment, to point to anything that has improved on what the Beatles did.

There have been plenty of "new Beatles" contenders over the years, some brilliant (Squeeze), some just pretty decent (Oasis). But there has never been a "new Beatles," really, just like there's never been a new Dylan.

No one has made a record better than (insert your favorite Beatles record title here) and, for all the technological advances of the last three decades, no producer has figured out a way to make records that sound better than the ones George Martin cut for the Beatles almost 40 years ago. It didn't sound like the kind of music that could be made by mere mortals. It sounded like it came from somewhere else, from outer space, or some musical heaven, like it had always been there.

Even at their worst, their sloppiest, the Beatles are still great. The endless Twickenham rehearsals from January '69 are often charming ("What Do You Want to Make Those Eyes at Me For" is a hoot, for example); Magical Mystery Tour, the film, has some great moments ("I Am the Walrus," "Jessie's Dream"); and some of the tracks on

Just by being who they were.

the Decca audition tape really rock ("Money," "Memphis").

The records are universal. Few acts, if any, in the history of popular music have created something for everyone. Even in the '60s, grannies could be found tapping their toes to the Fabs' hits along with teens, parents and just about everyone else. And they are still winning new fans over, even now, 33 years after they stopped making records together. Just last week, I overheard two adolescent guys talking enthusiastically as they flipped through the "B" section of the local CD store:

"Have you heard *Rubber Soul* yet? You should get it — it's really good!"

"I haven't heard of this one. *Revolver*. The cover's cool — I'm gonna get this one. What're you gonna get?"

"*Abbey Road.*"

"Good choice."

And with that they wandered off to the till with their purchases — each about to discover an album that had blown a million minds over the last three-and-a-half decades.

And so it goes. You didn't have to be there in the '60s to fall under the Beatles' spell. It seems that no subsequent generation is immune to Beatlemania. When the *Anthology* series came out it created a huge media buzz. When the Beatles 1 CD came out, it was a huge hit, even though it consisted entirely of songs that almost any self-respecting rock fan would already have in their collection. So it was obviously selling for the most part to people who didn't want to get all the albums on CD and didn't even want to spring for the double-disc "Red" and "Blue" albums. I can only assume that the 1 CD weeded out and eliminated the last

holdouts, the remaining people on the planet who actually didn't own a Beatles album.

And it's not about to stop. McCartney's latest tour is massive and his repertoire is, not surprisingly, heavy on the Beatles stuff. The soundtrack to the Sean Penn film *I Am Sam* consists of nothing but Beatles covers, and there's another Fabs tribute album on the way. More DVD and CD reissues are in the pipeline — *Let It Be, A Hard Day's Night* and who knows what else. When George Harrison passed away in 2001 there was a huge worldwide outpouring of grief, just has there had been two decades earlier when we lost John Lennon. Both times, it felt like we had lost a part of ourselves, like a part of the collective consciousness was gone.

And, just in case the Beatles needed the royal seal of approval, Queen Elizabeth will reportedly lead her subjects in a sing-along of "All You Need Is Love" at her Jubilee.

In other words, the Beatles are still, as they have been since 1964, an unstoppable force. The myth of the Beatles is all-powerful, but it wouldn't mean that much if the music wasn't so good. But it is. It is absolutely, tremendously f&*$ing brilliant. For all the other things they were, the Beatles were a brilliant rock and roll band who made records so good that nothing else before or since can compare.

I've listened to each of their albums numerous times. I'll go through phases where I won't listen to them for months at a time, convinced that I've heard them too much, that there's no further joy or revelation to be found in those grooves. Then somebody puts on *Abbey Road* or "Strawberry Fields Forever" or the *Anthology* video. Or I hear a bootleg track I've somehow never heard before. And the magic is still there. That force that grabbed me in the opening bars of "She Loves You" 30 years ago is still as powerful as it ever was. And I know that if, God willing, I hear it 30 years from now, it won't have changed. ■

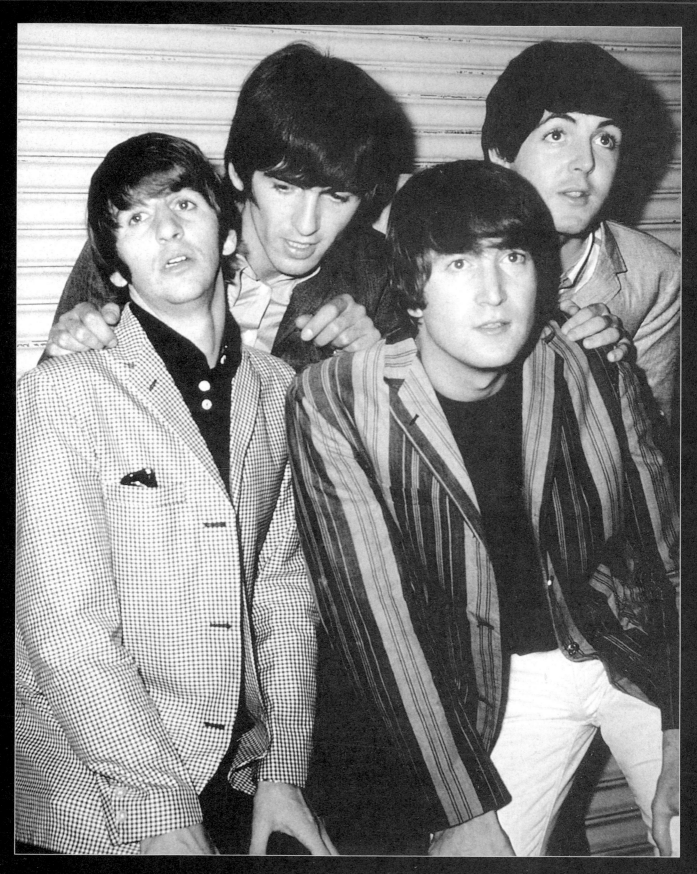

Ranking The Beatles Music

By Chris Nickson

More than anyone else, the Beatles made us grow up. While they reigned musically, we slowly cast off the youthful garb of the 45, and struggled into the more adult LP. From the callow, pimply kid behind "Love Me Do" (a very tentative, eyes-to-the-ground beginning) to the assured completeness of *Abbey Road* (which seems made to hang together) is a long distance in a short time, but we followed them blindly. They, and we, had no idea where they were going, but the journey itself was riotous and beautiful. Oh, and along the way they made some pretty good music.

That's with an emphasis on some. For all the deification of the Beatles, not everything they did — not every one of the singles or albums — is worthy of worship. And that's hardly surprising. Given the rate at which they had to produce new material, not everything could be touched with genius. Perhaps the truly remarkable thing is that their percentage of quality songs was so high.

No musical artists, before or since (and there were a lot more before than since), have defined their time the way the Beatles did. Maybe the bands of San Francisco — Jefferson Airplane, Big Brother and the Holding Company, the Grateful Dead — captured the hippie ethos more perfectly. Maybe the Kinks, the Who, and the Small Faces had a better understanding of Britain's mod scene. But no one came close to touching the global Zeitgeist of a decade the ways the Fab Four did. Or maybe it was a case of the global Zeitgeist catching up with them.

> *"No musical artists, before or since (and there were a lot more before than since), have defined their time the way the Beatles did."*

"Their percentage of quality songs was so high."

■ *Glenn A. Baker Archives*

They were schooled in the '50s, their hearts were in rock and roll. They covered Chuck and Jerry Lee, Carl, and Elvis, along with anything else they could think of, in Hamburg. And what came out when Lennon and McCartney sat down to write was a distillation of the essence, refracted through a peculiarly English — and decidedly Liverpudlian — prism. It wasn't rock as everyone had known it, but rock as it would become, tinged with an urban, even cosmopolitan, experience.

However, that didn't mean it was good yet. Take the first three proper singles (we'll discount that January 1962 issue of "My Bonnie" b/w "The Saints" as something best forgotten) – "Love Me Do" b/w "P.S. I Love You," "Please Please Me" b/w "Ask Me Why," and "From Me To You" b/w "Thank You Girl" — and it's apparent they're the sound of a band in search of itself, and slowly getting there. There are notable moments in there, but nowhere does it really all come together. The first really great Beatles single is "She Loves You" (and who but the hardcore remember the B side?) if only because of that "yeah, yeah, yeah," but even that pales next to "I Want To Hold Your Hand," with the U.S. version getting the nod, for its B side of "I Saw Her Standing There," some great one-chord rock and roll.

This was their first defining moment, when they arrived as a major musical force and more than another pop group on the trail from the '50s into the '60s when London swung. George's guitar solo might not have quite caught up with the times, but everything else was in place. The harmonies have evolved from the Everly Brothers into something richer and more complex, but with a harder edge than, say, the Beach Boys. The roots might have been in America, but the branches were ineffably English. It was, really, like nothing that had been heard before, particularly in America. And in Britain, it was light years ahead of people like Cliff Richard, who

"They were schooled in the '50s,

had never been more than a diluted rocker, and Tommy Steele, rapidly heading to the West End stage.

Skipping over "Can't Buy Me Love," an experiment that didn't really work because none of the lads had a jazzy bone in their bodies, you get to "A Hard Day's Night," with its Lennon-esque wordplay in the title. Call this one (not "Help!") the grandfather of folk-rock with its chiming electric-acoustic chords and complex lyrical jiggery-pokery, upending clichés in a manner that probably made Bob Dylan realize that other musicians had been listening to him.

With "I Feel Fine" and "Ticket To Ride" (November '64 and April '65) they invented riff rock, albeit in a way unrecognizable a few years down the line. But in both it's the riffs which are the frame around which the songs are built, rather than the chord sequences, which meant that George was suddenly of full importance in the sound, instead of just adding his trills, frills, and solos. "Day Tripper" was along the same lines, but like the Borg on "Star Trek: The Next Generation," they'd assimilated this new element into the whole so it fit seamlessly, rather than stood out.

Of course, this jumps over the wonderful "Help!" — more Lennon does Dylan, the relatively lightweight "Eight Days A Week," and the god awful "Yesterday." It might have been covered more than any song in history, but that doesn't make "Yesterday" a great song — merely that it appeals to the lowest common denominator of emotions. It's maudlin, a sort of very early dry run for the far more accomplished "Eleanor Rigby." If history were

rewritten, and it suddenly vanished forever from human consciousness, Paul would be poorer, but the rest of us would be much better off.

However, it's part of the course that leads up to June 1966. From there until November 1967 one can only surmise the Beatles were working on another plane altogether. There was more space between the releases, allowing them to be more creative. They were using the studio as another instrument, thanks to the capabilities and open mind of George Martin and his engineers. And, obviously, their Muse wasn't taking any holidays. How else do you explain "Paperback Writer" b/w "Rain," "Penny Lane" b/w "Strawberry Fields Forever," "All You Need Is Love" b/w "Baby You're A Rich Man," and "Hello Goodbye" b/w "I Am The Walrus." Yes, there were a couple of other singles in there, too, but they were filler (as was "Hello Goodbye," really). In 17 months this group expanded the whole definition of pop music, adding levels of complexity that still resonate — notably when a group is described as "Beatlesque" these days, it's this period the word evokes.

While they'd been edging away from the standard form of the pop song, the blueprint that had been laid down years before (as had Dylan, although he came to it from folk, bringing in a completely different, and far more socially conscious, element), it wasn't until "Paperback Writer" that they'd made the jump. *Rubber Soul*, their first real album, a disc that was a whole in feel and execution rather than a collection of tracks, had been the first step in the direction, and *Revolver* was the giant leap. But "Paperback Writer" and "Rain" told us what was happening. They were disturbing, not comforting as pop music had always been.

> " *In 17 months... they expanded the whole definition of pop music.* "

their hearts were in rock and roll."

They weren't love songs. In fact, at the time, you'd have been hard pressed to really understand the subject matter of the "A" side.

"Paperback Writer" pointed rock in a whole new direction, one which others would pick up on soon enough, while "Rain" was intriguing for its comments on England and sonically for its use of the new possibilities of the studio. And it's worth mentioning that they were superb songs; Lennon and McCartney now had enough confidence in themselves to really let go, and stopping touring would give them the time and freedom to experiment further.

While some of the results of that are songs like "Yellow Submarine" b/w "Eleanor Rigby" there was much stronger fruit, like the precursor to *Sgt. Pepper's Lonely Hearts Club Band*, "Penny Lane" b/w "Strawberry Fields Forever." While "Penny Lane" seems conventional (as do all Paul's songs, really), it's McCartney pushing his own envelope in a lyrical masterpiece, a wonderful sketch of a place, while the arrangement evokes the very British institution of a Salvation Army band.

But it's the other side where the Beatles reach their musical zenith. If John Lennon had only written "Strawberry Fields Forever" it would be enough to qualify him for genius status, even if it's really two songs. Full credit to George Martin, too, but ultimately   it's about the Beatles themselves — just listen   to

Anthology for the way the song develops through the process of trial and error. Maybe none of them knew exactly what they were groping for, but they understood when they'd found it.

From there, "All You Need Is Love" actually pulls back a little, a knock-off full of self-referential humor. But it's still light years ahead of the singles other groups were releasing. It was certainly more than "just" a single. The theme was ideal for the summer of love, and that live broadcast between 21 countries (although it was deflating to understand the track wasn't being recorded live for the 45 which appeared in shops the following Friday).

It's the flip that makes it something special, with George's "Baby You're A Rich Man," one of the most accessible of his Indian-flavored songs, and one of the best, with a recognizable, even singable chorus. No one had put a song like that on a single before — but they soon would. It might not have been a musical high point for the Beatles, or even for George, but it showed they were still looking around, still breaking down barriers, if only because they didn't see the barriers there in the first place. In this brave new world, anything was possible.

And it was. "Hello Goodbye" might have been a throwaway, but the flip side, taken from *Magical Mystery Tour* was "Strawberry Fields" taken five or six stops down the line. "I Am The Walrus" was archetypal Lennon, with its clever wordplay, and some very disturbing, graphic images. And by utilizing the electric piano as the main instrument it put the group in a very different place. Soaked in psychedelia, yes, but also something which stands completely alone, in many ways apart from the Beatles canon as a twisted, but beautiful piece of music.

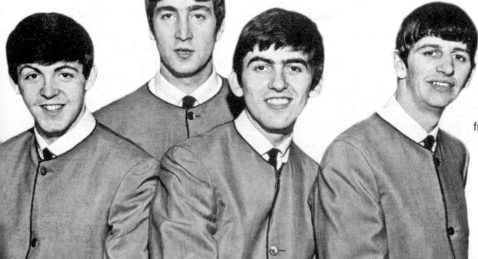

Like any good run, it had to come to an end, however. And when they re-emerged with "Lady Madonna" in March '68, it was apparent that they'd moved back, which would be reflected in The Beatles later that year. "Lady Madonna" was McCartney's tribute to Fats Domino, but why? Fats was still around, and capable of doing that piano thing much better than Paul ever could. It was a fun little party piece, but that was all, and certainly not worthy of release, which can also be said for "Hey Jude," which was, at best, half a song and an ending that lasted forever. Even "Revolution" didn't exactly storm the musical barricades, based on the kind of 12-bar structure they'd all played forever. So, after the daring adventures of '67 came the retreat of '68 (the same thing which would lead the Band into Music from Big Pink), and the end of good Beatles singles. "Get Back"? Nice little live number, but not worth the vinyl. "Something"? Great song. Wonderful George

Harrison single. But it's not really the Beatles, is it? It even seems out of place on the nearly perfect album that's *Abbey Road.* "Let It Be"? Put it on McCartney and it would have been perfectly at home. "The Long And Winding Road"? An embarrassment to all concerned.

Which makes a total of six essential, need-to-be-in-every-record-collection singles ("She Loves You," "I Want to Hold Your Hand," "I Saw Her Standing There," "A Hard Day's Night," "Eleanor Rigby, and "Strawberry Fields Forever." Harsh, you say? Not by the standards the Beatles unconsciously set themselves. And it's six more than most bands ever manage. The best singles were more than songs, they were mini-albums, rich in content, far beyond the three- or four-chord trick which had started the decade (and the band's career). They'd brought us to a complexity undreamed of in 1960, and given a depth to popular music.

■ *Glenn A. Baker Archives*

forever." There was this whole battle going on, and I'm just trying to drum away.

But they got over it, and then we went down to make a record. I'm not sure about this, but one of the reasons they also asked Pete to leave was George Martin, the producer, didn't like Pete's drumming. So then, when I went down to play, he didn't like me either, so he called a drummer named Andy White, a professional session man to play the session. But George has repented since [laughs]. He did come out one day saying it, only when he said it it was 10 years later. In the end, I didn't play that session. I played every session since, but the first session, he brought in a studio drummer.

Goldmine: There were two versions of the first tune ["Love Me Do"], one where Andy White plays and one where you play.

Ringo Starr: You're right. There are two versions. I'm on the album, and he's on the single. You can't spot the difference, though, because all I did was what he did, because that's what they wanted for the song.

Goldmine: I heard that Martin handed you a tambourine.

Ringo Starr: Yeah, and told me to get lost. I was really brought down. I mean, the idea of making a record was real heavy. You just wanted a piece of plastic. That was the most exciting period of records — the first couple of records. Every time it moved into the '50s on the charts we'd go out and have dinner and celebrate. Then when it was in the '40s, we'd celebrate. And we knew every time it was coming on the radio and we'd all be waiting for it in cars or in someone's house. We wouldn't move for that three minutes.

And then, of course, the first gold disc and the first #1! But

like everything else, when you've had five #1s, one after the other and as many gold discs as you can eat, it's not boring, but it's just that the first couple of records were so exciting. I think they are for everybody. It's like sweets every day, though. You get used to it.

So I was really brought down when he had this other drummer, but the record came out and made it quite well, and from then on I was on all the other records, with my silly style and silly fills. They used to call it "silly fills."

Goldmine: Who?

Ringo Starr: Everyone used to sort of say, "Those silly fills he does."

Goldmine: And yet, it turned drumming around for a lot of people.

Ringo Starr: But we didn't know that then. Everyone put me down — said that I couldn't play. They didn't realize that was my style and I wasn't playing like anyone else — that I couldn't play like anyone else.

Goldmine: How did it come to be that George Martin allowed you to play the second session?

Ringo Starr: I think I drove him mad, because we rehearsed for the next record and I had a tambourine in one hand and maracas in the other and played the kit with them. George was just flabbergasted. I didn't have a stick in my hand; I just had a tambourine and maracas, and I was hitting the cymbals and smashing the tom with the maracas, so he thought he'd better do something about it. So he said, "Well, if you use sticks, I'll let you play."

He never said that really, but I think he just thought I'd

"Those *silly fills* he does."

gone mad, so he'd better please me and let me play on the next record. And from then on, I played, except for "Back In The U.S.S.R.," which Paul played on because I wasn't there. We just carried on from there, and then it got to where John and Paul were always the writers and the bass player and rhythm guitar, and George was getting some notice as a lead guitarist, but I was still getting, "He's all right," so it was a bit of a putdown at the time.

Goldmine: Let's talk about sessions. How much creative input were you allowed, and how much did George Martin dictate?

Ringo Starr: Well, at the beginning, George Martin dictated a certain amount, and then it was John and Paul's writing to consider. See, what helped me a lot was that I had three frustrated drummers around, because everyone wants to be a drummer for some reason. John could play and Paul could play and George could play, but they each had one standard style. We all have one standard style, but they only had one sort of groove, where I have two or three.

John and I used to have, not arguments, but discussions, because we'd be playing all these records and he'd say, "Like that," and I'm saying, "But John, there's two drummers on there," and he could never hear there were two drummers. They'd play stuff with two drummers on it and the three of them each had their own idea of what the drummer should do, and then I had my idea. So all I would do was combine my idea, their three ideas, and the ideas of the two drummers on a record. They got what they were given, and it worked. But that helped me to play. Also, the

long hours in Germany, you know, you soon get your act together.

So we were playing and making these records, and then we sort of got free-form rock in our own way, though it was a lot tighter than acid rock because we had songwriters and we did songs and didn't just jam. We went through a lot of changes on records. Then in '68, I got the kit with the calf skins and that changed everything. Then it really became tom-tom city because of the calf and wood.

When you're touring, everyone thanks God that the plastic heads were invented because you're playing outside in the heat, or the wet, or whatever, and skins are very hard to handle. But since '66, we were in a controlled environment, in the studio, so the temperature was always the same and you could deal with calf. You can't deal with them outside, although drummers have for thousands of years. So plastic heads were a godsend on the road, but then when we were just in the studio, I ordered this kit and I had calf skins put on.

To backtrack even further: I'd had this kit that my stepfather got for £12. It was a great old kit, but it was old-fashioned. I joined a band when I was 18, and in my silliness, thought, "I want a new kit." So I bought an Ajax kit, which is an English company. It was a black pearl kit, about £47. roughly $125, complete with a pair of sticks. "You can take it away and play it"; it was one of those. You had everything you needed.

Then one of the band members got a car so we could carry the kit, because in the old days, as I was saying, we were on the bus, so you couldn't take a kit. I would only take a

> *"They got what they were given and it worked."*

snare drum, a hi-hat and cymbal and beg all the other drummers for their kits. Some of them wouldn't give them to me, so I'd just have to play with a snare. I never like to let the kit out, either, unless I know the person. You never let anyone use the snare. The only two times I ever lent a snare, it was broken. And it takes a long time to get it to how you want it to sound. I would understand others not lending the kit, but I thought they were real mean.

One time, I remember a guy asking me if he could use my kit and I said, "Well, can you play?" And he said, "Yeah, I've been playing for years," and if you can imagine, a guy gets on your kit and puts his foot on the beater of the bass drum pedal and thinks it's a motorbike starter, kick starting. So I just went over and grabbed him off the kit and threw him offstage. It blew me away! The man never played in his life, and he thought it was a motor bike. That was one time I lent the kit out.

Goldmine: So you had this Ajax set.

Ringo Starr: Right up to The Beatles, and then we were getting new instruments and things and I wanted a new kit. I wanted a Ludwig kit. It was good, for their own good and my good, because while we were touring, of course, they would give me a couple of free kits because I was a Ludwig drummer. I used to play that mini-kit on stage. Couldn't hear a thing! But it was good for me to get behind because I'm not that tall, so I looked bigger with a small kit, so at least you could see me.

Goldmine: But it didn't matter much what you sounded like in concert, did it?

Ringo Starr: No. That's why we stopped.

Goldmine: George Harrison said that he felt the response to The Beatles was some sort of hysterical outlet for people. The four of you must have sat around and conjectured as to what the hell was going on. That had to be mind blowing.

Ringo Starr: Well, we enjoyed them getting their hysterical needs out because no one came to listen to our gigs. They bought records to listen to. They just came to scream and shout, which was fine, but after four years, I was becoming such a bad player because I couldn't hear anything. Because of the noise going on, all I had to do was just constantly keep the time, so we'd have something to follow.

> " *It was pointless playing on stage anymore.* "

If you look at films, you'll see I'm looking at their mouths — I'm lip-reading where we're up to in the song because I couldn't hear the amps or anything. We were becoming bad musicians, so we had the discussion about it. Besides, we could play in any town or country in the world and get the same response, but only the four of us would know if we played any good, and that was very seldom because we couldn't hear. So you're getting the same response for a bad gig and it wasn't any help. You only wanted applause if you did something that worked, so we decided to go into the studio. It was pointless playing on stage anymore.

Goldmine: I guess I wonder what you thought. I mean, that response had never happened before.

Ringo Starr: I don't know. The media and the madness of the time, I guess. Things were very dead just up to when we came out and that was just part of what we did.

Goldmine: So on stage, you were absolutely reading lips at that point?

Ringo Starr: Yeah, just to find out where we were up to in the song, and just carrying a beat. So then we went back into the studio where we could get back to playing with each other again, because we'd do the same 12 numbers every night and we'd do a 30-minute show. That seems amazing now, because Bruce Springsteen does four hours. He still has the best show I've seen in the last 10 years, and I only watched two hours of that, and it was enough. But every group does at least an hour and a half, and Bruce, who is the extreme, does four hours.

We did a 30-minute show, and if we didn't like the place, we'd play a bit fast and do it in 25 minutes. We were getting real despondent playing live, so we went into the studio for months and months. It got us playing again and exploring a lot of avenues of the technology of the studio, which compared to now, was Mickey Mouse.

Goldmine: Eight-track was a big deal then.

Ringo Starr: And we didn't have one. We begged for one because we did everything on four-track up to Pepper [*Sgt. Pepper's Lonely Hearts Club Band*] and four-to-four, but EMI was technically a very, very good studio with their engineers and electronic wizards. When we went four-to-four, to go tape-to-tape, there's usually a loss, but the loss was so slight, because their engineers were technically so good that no one missed it. You can't miss it anyway because the public didn't know what they were missing, so they only got what they got. But we put the drums through phasers and things like that.

Goldmine: How did you feel about all that?

Ringo Starr: It was great, because it worked with the tracks we were doing and it was magic. Just like magic. And we put it through the Hammond speaker and it goes 'round and 'round, whatever that's called, and just tricks like that. We put the guitar through something going backwards and it was all experimental madness to us, but it was in the form of a song. It wasn't us just freaking out, playing, which we did quite a lot, but we never released any tapes like that.

Goldmine: And you knew you wouldn't have to reproduce it on stage anyway.

Ringo Starr: We knew we weren't going out on stage and it ended up, like on Pepper, that if we wanted to go out, we'd have to take an orchestra with us. But no one was interested in going out. We were only interested in making records. So that was exciting, the sound we could get. And then the group broke up. So I started playing with a lot of other people. One year I did Leon Russell, Stephen Stills, B.B. King, and Howlin' Wolf, which was good for my head. After being in one band so long, suddenly playing with such a diverse group of people was good for me.

Goldmine: I wondered if during The Beatles, you ever felt you wanted to get out and do something else.

Ringo Starr: No, never did. That was always good enough for me. I never played any other sessions. I only did a few, like Jackie Lomax and a couple of other people. But then it was exciting when the group had split and I just started playing with a lot of people. In 1970, England was the place everyone wanted to make albums, so I played a lot of

"I left for two weeks

different sessions, like with Jimmy Webb and Harry Nilsson.

Goldmine: After The Beatles, I heard that you really felt that you didn't want to play drums anymore, for a while at least.

Ringo Starr: It wasn't that I didn't want to play drums; I didn't know what to do with my life. I'd been playing with the band for so long and suddenly it ended. I just sat there wondering what to do with my life, because I wasn't a producer and I wasn't a writer.

Goldmine: To backtrack for a second: The White Album. *I read that you left for about a week.*

Ringo Starr: I left for two weeks. I felt I wasn't part of the group. I felt that the other three were really together and close and I wasn't part of the group, so because of that feeling, I felt I wasn't playing well. I went around to John, knocked on the door and said, "I'm leaving the band, man. You three are really close and I'm getting out." And he said, "I thought it was you three." So I went around to Paul and said the same thing: "I'm leaving; I'm not playing well because you three are real close and I'm not in the band anymore." And he said, "I thought it was you three." I said, "Well, I don't know who it is, but I'm going on holiday," and I went to Sardinia for a couple of weeks to clear my head. That's when they made "U.S.S.R.," which I wasn't on. Then I came back to *The White Album*, which I felt, for me, was a better album than Pepper for the group.

Goldmine: Why do you say that?

Ringo Starr: Well, we were much more like a band. We're like session players on Pepper, using all those orchestras and sound effects. I mean it was good fun, but I felt we were getting more like a group on *The White Album* again, though it was a double album, and double albums give too much

information for me, anyway. But that and *Abbey Road*, besides *Rubber Soul*, are a few of the finest albums.

Goldmine: The music became a lot more sophisticated, and I'm sure you were called on to do more sophisticated kinds of things.

Ringo Starr: Never. You got what you got. I don't know if it got more sophisticated. I don't think you'd call *The White Album* sophisticated, but I enjoyed it more than Pepper, which you could call sophisticated. But you'd only call that sophisticated because of what you put on top; the brass section and such. The idea behind Pepper, which never got fully realized, was that it was going to be a whole show, but we only got into two tracks and then we made it just a regular album.

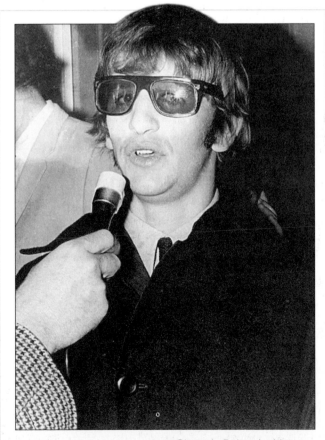

■ *Glenn A. Baker Archives*

"I don't think you'd call The White Album sophisticated."

...I felt I wasn't part of the band."

Goldmine: A show as far as a concept album, or something to take on the road?

Ringo Starr: Just a concept album of a show, and we segued from *Sgt. Pepper* into the next track with the cheer, and there's Billy Shears, and then we did it for two tracks and we got bored with that and just made another album. *The White Album* was not to do tricks; it was for us to get together, I felt, and play together as a group, which is what we were, and best at.

Goldmine: I read that Paul had been very critical of your playing on The White Album *before you left for two weeks, and that's one of the reasons you left.*

Ringo Starr: No, I left for the very reason I told you. I thought I just had to go away and straighten my head out because it was getting too silly. And while I was away, I got telegrams from John saying, "The best rock 'n' roll drummer in the world," and when I came back, George had the whole studio decorated with flowers. So Paul may have been pissed off. I don't know; he never did anything. But he never actually said to me, "That's not good," or whatever, so I don't know where that rumor came from. He was never that critical.

Goldmine: Dispelled that rumor.

Ringo Starr: I've never read that one, even [laughs]. I've read most of them. There was a guy in New York who said he played on everything. All that bull has gone down. You have to let those things pass. Some drummer in New York wanted to make a name for himself and said he played on everything, and I never played on anything. So what was I doing? I know on some sessions I wasn't all there, but I wasn't off completely away.

Goldmine: Obviously, John and Paul were the most integral portion of what went on in the studio.

Ringo Starr: It was their songs.

Goldmine: But what would happen? Take us through a typical session, or even a song.

Ringo Starr: Well, what would happen is that someone would say, "Well, I've got this," because it was very early on that John and Paul didn't write together. It was their own songs, and then a lot of them would start as jams and someone would put lyrics to them; like "Helter Skelter" was a full-on jam, and "Birthday," just to mention jams where we had nothing when we went in. Other songs would have a verse and a chorus and they'd finish them, or anyone could shout a line and if the line was good, they'd use it. The roadies, the tea lady, if anyone had a line, it would be used.

It was always open like that, and always the best line would be used. It wouldn't matter who said it. No one had the ego big enough to say, "I have to write this," Not all the time; I mean, they wrote 90 percent finished songs, but not musically, because they could only use what we could play. "Birthday" was one case. "They say it's your birthday," do you know that track?

Goldmine: Of course.

Ringo Starr: We went over to Paul's and came back and wanted to do a sort of rowdy rock 'n' roll track because Little Richard had freaked us out yet again, so we just took a couple of chord sequences and played them sort of raucous and loud and there was a newspaper on the floor and it was about someone's birthday. So Paul started singing and we all just hopped on behind him. That's how that came about, but we never went in with anything. We just went in and I sat behind the kit and they stood behind their instruments and that came about like that.

it would be used."

Ringo Star The Fab 4/4

Goldmine: On the finished tunes, would you get called into the session, come in and listen to the tune, and just supply what you felt was right?

Ringo Starr: No. On the finished tunes, they'd sit at the piano and play them. Then we'd go through several different changes of how we all felt it should be done. Mainly, the writer had the definite idea, but if anyone did anything to change it and it was good and moved into a place they enjoyed, that's how it would be. There was a lot of open-mindedness. There were very few tracks with the definite idea "This is how it has to be." Mostly, if someone came up with anything that was different and worked, then everyone would go along with it.

Goldmine: In those days, for a drummer to have that kind of creative allowance was somewhat unusual.

Ringo Starr: Well, I was allowed to create anything I could as long as it worked, and it was the same with the guitar or the bass or the piano. It was all the same, but the difference was that it had to fit around their song.

Goldmine: What about when you began to write?

Ringo Starr: First of all, I used to rewrite Jerry Lee Lewis B-sides and not really know it. I just put new words to all the songs. It took me years to fetch a song in because I, as much as anyone else, was in awe of our two writers, who I felt were the best writers around. So I'd write my little songs and I'd be embarrassed to fetch them in because of John and Paul.

So then I started fetching them in and they'd all be laughing on the floor, "Oh, you've rewritten 'Crazy Arms,'" or something.

> " *Some days you really feel like you'd like to be there.* "

So then I started writing a bit more, like, "I listen for your footsteps coming up the drive," some song I wrote, don't know the title any more ["Don't Pass Me By"]. That was the first one that we did of mine. But they used to write songs for me, tailor made, because they knew my range and it was like a personality thing I used to put across. Or then I'd pick the country song, because I always liked country 'n' western: "Boys" I had done for years, then they started writing songs just for me. Then I started writing my own, and then I wrote "Octopus' Garden." I always mention "Octopus' Garden."

Goldmine: That was the first one you were proud of, really, wasn't it?

Ringo Starr: Well, it was so silly.

Goldmine: That was written on your holiday in Sardinia?

Ringo Starr: Yeah. We were on this boat and they offered us this meal and we'd ordered fish and chips, and the fish came and I said, "What's that?" There were legs and things. And the guy said, "Oh, it's octopus," and being English and food-wise, that blew me away. "Are you kidding? Octopus? You've got be to crazy. Nobody eats that. Tentacles? It's not fish; it's jet-propelled."

Then I got talking to the captain, and he was telling me the story of octopuses building gardens under the sea. They find shiny rocks and tins and whatever and they build these gardens, and I found it fascinating. I was just sitting on the pier one day and I wrote "Octopus's Garden" for me and the children. And some days you really feel like you'd like to be there, under the sea, in an octopus's garden, because it gets a bit tough out here, and it was as a tough period then. So I felt it would be very nice to be real quiet under the ocean.

...I felt it would be very nice to be real quiet under the ocean."

"I was just sitting on the pier one day...

Goldmine: Was the breakup gradual? I presume it didn't happen in just one day.

Ringo Starr: No, the breakup came because everyone had ideas of what he wanted to do, whereas everyone used to have ideas of what we would do, as a group. Then we weren't really fulfilling John's musical ambitions or Paul's or George's, or my own, in the end, because it was separate. We weren't working for one aim, just the one band. Everyone wanted to do other things as well. So you could see it coming but like everything else, we all held it off for a while.

Then it just got too silly and we had a meeting about what everyone wanted to do. You can't keep a band together. We never did it for the money; we did it for the playing. I mean, the money is very nice, but we were players first. As anyone will tell you, if we had wanted, we could have just carried on and made fortunes, but that was not our game. Our game was actually making music. So it became too strange, because there was a lot of stuff I didn't want to play on that I felt just wasn't exciting anymore.

Goldmine: Can you be specific?

Ringo Starr: Well, John is the easiest to talk about. He wanted to do stuff which was avant-garde in its way. Besides, I had no place being on it and I wasn't on some of it. He wanted to do that more than play with the group, and Paul wanted to do another thing, and George was wanting something else.

Goldmine: What did you want?

Ringo Starr: Well, I just wanted to play really good music — not that any of it is bad. I enjoyed the group thing, and then people wanted to do other things, which could have included

us if we had wanted to. But half the time, we didn't want to get involved with certain tracks because it just wasn't what we were there to do as a group. We were there to do it individually, but not as a group. So the regression started about '68 and it was over by '70. So that was the end of that, and I did feel lost, as we talked about before.

Goldmine: I would imagine it was an adjustment personally, but did you feel lost musically?

Ringo Starr: Well, I'd never played with a better band, you see, so I think that's the loss I felt.

Goldmine: Where does one go from the best?

Ringo Starr: It's not even just the best. A lot of it was telepathy. We all felt so close. We knew each other so well that we'd know when any of us would make a move up or down within the music, and we'd all make it. No one would say anything or look at each other; we'd just know. The easiest word is telepathy. The band worked so well, and we were four good friends a lot of the time. But like any four friends, we had rows and shouted and disliked each other for a moment.

Then it ended, and I started playing sessions and had a really good time, but I was just playing. You can play with any band, but that band was something special to me, and it's never been like that again. I've had great sessions, great tracks, but it's never been like that, and you can't expect that if you walk into a studio and play someone's session. You're strangers.

We had all lived together so close; we knew each other so well that it crossed over into the music. We knew exactly what the other was doing. That's even the wrong way to explain it. We just knew that the chemistry worked! The excitement! If things were just jogging along and one of us felt, "I'm going to lift it here," it was just a feeling that went through the four of us and everyone lifted it, or everyone lowered it, or whatever. It was just telepathy. When I do sessions now, I'm playing the best I can, and some sessions are really great. But I've never played on anyone's album all the way through, because I always felt it was boring, so I'd do three or four tracks.

Goldmine: Can you define what you think is a good drummer?

Ringo Starr: Yeah, me. It took me a long time to think of myself like that, but I am probably the best rock drummer.

Goldmine: Why do you say that?

Ringo Starr: Because I play with emotion and feeling, and that's what rock is. Rock is not reading, and I'm not putting reading down, although it's something that I don't do and something I never wanted to do. I did have one lesson in the old days and the guy wrote all those dots on the paper, but I felt it wasn't the way I wanted to play. I only wanted to play, and some days it's a real bummer for people, because if I'm on a downer, I still have to play, and you only get what's in my soul at the time. But that's life. We all make a choice. A lot of session guys can go in and read and play five different sessions a day, totally different types of music. He just reads it and plays it, but that's a different musician to me.

Goldmine: There was never a time where you felt you should have lessons or you'd like to take lessons?

Ringo Starr: Only in the very early days when I first got the

kit, because you think that's what you should do. So I had one lesson and realized that wasn't what I should be doing.

Goldmine: Did you play along with records?

Ringo Starr: No, I never practiced in my life. I just practiced one day and then joined a band and made every mistake I could on stage.

Goldmine: That's incredible.

Ringo Starr: Well, it was easier then. I don't know if it was easier then, but it seems like it was. Now, you've got to be an amazing player to get a job, even in the local band that plays a Bar Mitzvah. You've got to read and play.

As I told you before, back then if you had an instrument, you were in a band. That was how easy it was when I started. And a month after I had the kit, I had one lesson, gave that up, practiced once in the back room and joined a group and I've played with groups ever since. I think it's better for you. Well, I don't know if it's better for you, but it was for me.

I have a son who is a drummer, who played for three years, three hours a day, practicing with headphones on to records and to himself, but that's his style. He plays a totally different style from me, and he plays, not better, but technically he can do more than I can do. And he's interested in all those words they keep mentioning like flams and paradidtiles and things like that, which I never understood.

Goldmine: So you really feel that what made you special

> " *I am probably the best rock drummer.* "

...really good music."

was that you worked from your gut emotion?

Ringo Starr: Well, I think that the drums are an emotional instrument and there's no melody. It's not like you can sit in a room with a guitar or piano and play. It's only "boom-boom-boom" or "ratta-tat-tat," and there's no real melody there. That's why I dislike solos. I don't care which drummer does a solo; it's not melodic, and he just has an ego problem.

Goldmine: When did you decide to make your first solo album?

Ringo Starr: After the breakup, I was sitting around, wondering what to do with myself. I had done a few sessions, but it was the end of that gig and I was wondering what to do next. I realized I had to do something, so I ran and did a standard album. I did all tracks I was brought up with at the parties at the house: "Sentimental Journey" and "Stardust" and all those '40s tunes.

Goldmine: Was Sentimental Journey *really a gift to your mother?*

Ringo Starr: Yeah. It was a gift for her, and it got me off my ass. So I did that, and then I was working on George's album and he flew Pete Drake in because Pete had done something with Dylan's album and they were friends. I lent Pete my car, and he noticed I had a lot of country cassettes in the car. I told him I liked country music. So he said, "Well, why don't you do a country album?"

And I said, "I'm not going to live in Nashville for six months," which was how long The Beatles would be there to make an album. He said, "Are you kidding? We did Bob's album in two days." I was blown away, even though

The Beatles' first album took 12 hours, but it had been so long ago my memory had failed. So I said, "Okay, I'll come over next week and we'll do an album." And we did the album in three days. It was just all to get me moving.

I did the *Sentimental Journey* album and then the Nashville album [*Beaucoups Of Blues*], and then Harry Nilsson called me. Harry and I had been invited to present some Grammy awards, so I thought, "I'm not going to fly all the way to America just to present a Grammy award and then go home. Why don't I do some sessions in Nashville again?" So I phoned Richard Perry, who I had met in England while playing on some sessions for Harry, and said, "Why don't we do some sessions while we're in Nashville?" Then he called back saying, "Well, why don't you leave Nashville and fly to L.A. and we'll do some sessions there?"

So I figured I'd make two weeks out of it, and that's how the *Ringo* album came about. I came into L.A. just to do the album, and it just happened that John had flown into L.A. and George was in L.A. I was making an album, and we're all friends even if we had split up, so I said, "Have you got any songs, boys?" and John said, "Yeah, I've got a song," so I said, "Well, come and play." So he came down, and I asked George if he had one and he came down, and then I called Paul in England and said, "You can't be left out of this" — like it was the big deal of his life — so we came to England and did the track. That's how that came about. It was all accidental, not planned.

Goldmine: How did you feel, suddenly becoming the focal point of a project in an album that revolved around you?

Ringo Starr: It was really good. Before that, we had had the two singles, which George had produced, "It Don't Come Easy" and "Back Off Boogaloo," which were #1. I had written them and George finished them. So that was exciting, and I was getting excited about the business again as a solo career, so I was back in the music trade as a solo. It just took time for me to get used to the idea, because I had never been a solo artist. I had always been in a band, since drummers are usually in the band.

Goldmine: Are there specific recordings you are particularly proud of?

Ringo Starr: There's different styles, though it's the one attitude. I still think the finest stuff I did was on "Rain." "Rain" is, to me, my all-time favorite drum track.

Goldmine: Why?

Ringo Starr: Because of what I did; wherever my head was at the time. It is a vague departure for me. And Abbey Road, and there's lots of things in between; bits here and bits there. "Get A Woman," by B.B. King; I felt I played some real solid drums on that. "A Day In The Life"; I felt the drums were as colorful as the song and the guitars. There's one, "It's been a long time..." ["Wait"]. That has really fine tom-tom work on it.

It's fine on everything, really, but some of them knock me out. And it took me a while to listen to Beatle records without going through the emotions of the day: how we felt, what was going on, who was saying hello to who.

After we broke up, it took me a couple of years to really listen. You know, you'd make the record and really enjoy making it, and when it was finished, you'd enjoy

> *" I was getting excited about the business again as a solo career. "*

listening to it in the studio and enjoy having it at home as a piece of plastic in a sleeve, but then I would never play them again. Only in the last several years could I listen to them as tracks. And you can also look back and see the stages you were going through or you went through.

Goldmine: What about highlights, playing or personal?

Ringo Starr: There's too many. Well, there's high and high. How high do you want to get? You know what I'm saying? As an act, which we were, the Palladium or the "Ed Sullivan Show," because they were definite moves in a career. I always thought, though we played music, we still wanted to be the biggest band in the world. Not that we knew it would be a monster, but we knew we were aiming somewhere, and the only degree of saying it is popularity. And we did become the most popular group on Earth, so there's all those moves.

But like the "Rain" session, where something just comes out of the bag; that just arrives, that's exciting. It's not a conscious thing; it just happens, and some sessions can get exciting. Musically, sometimes you would be blown away with what came out, but not every time. Other times you did the best you could and if it worked, great. But sometimes a lot of magic, a lot of magic, just came out of the blue, and it comes out for everybody. To play with three other people, any other people, when it works is when everyone is hitting it together; no one is racing, no one's dragging, the song is good or the track is good and the music is good, and you're all just hitting it together.

...without going through the emotions of the day."

If you're not a musician, I don't know if you'll understand that, when just three, four, 10 of you, a 100-piece orchestra, hit it together for as much time as you can — because there's very few times it goes through the whole track, never mind the whole album. There's magic in that that is unexplainable. I can't explain what I get from that. It's getting high for me. Just a pure musical high.

Goldmine: How does someone maintain his perspective on being a human being when the world has made him larger than life?

Ringo Starr: I think you're born with it. Also, at certain periods, I did go over the edge and believe the myth, but I had three great friends who told me, "You're fooling yourself."

Goldmine: But weren't they going over the edge as well?

Ringo Starr: Yes, but they had three friends, too, to tell them they're fooling themselves. It's not that we actually all did it at once.

Goldmine: During all the talk about a Beatles reunion and all of that, was there ever a time when you thought if you got together for a night that...

Ringo Starr: Well, we did. The four of us never got together, but at certain times after the breakup, three of us got together.

Goldmine: Was that magic still there?

Ringo Starr: Well, we looked at each other and smiled. It was interesting. Now, it's impossible to put it all back

together, of course, but I don't think any of us really thought we'd get back together. Everyone got too busy. No matter how much money they offered us, we never did it for the money, then or now. Then, when we were doing it in the '60s, and when they were offering us $50 million in the '70s, it wasn't an incentive to play. Money is no incentive for musicians. It's nice to have, but it's not enough.

Goldmine: I think it was John and Paul who said they felt that spark couldn't be re-created. I wondered whether you agreed or how you felt.

Ringo Starr: I don't believe that. I think, had the four of us gotten down and played, that spark would have been there. But the reasons would have been different, and that was the difference.

Goldmine: What kind of effect would you say The Beatles, the fame, all that, has had on you today?

Ringo Starr: I don't know. It's hard to say where I'd be if it hadn't happened. But it did, so I'm exactly where I feel I should be. Does anybody know what he would have done if he hadn't been doing what he did do at the time he was doing something? It's impossible to tell.

The difference would be that you wouldn't be interested in talking to me if I had just been playing some little club somewhere. But whether I would have been a different human being ... it's hard to tell. I'm sure I must have changed, but would I have changed had I gone through a whole different type of life? I don't know. The effect it all had from being born to today and everything that went on in between is that we're here in the garden, trying to say hello. ■

> " *I had three great friends who told me, 'You're fooling yourself.'* "

■ *Glenn A. Baker Archives*

"I'm exactly where I feel I should be."

■ *Glenn A. Baker Archives*

Conversation w/Ringo

By Allen J. Weiner

While his distinctive backbeat on Beatles records is legendary—always on time; never a beat ahead or behind—the bulk of Ringo Starr's solo work is not generally well known. Most of it has been critically maligned, sometimes brutally so. To be sure, Ringo's solo career has had its share of ups and downs. He has scored a total of seven Billboard Top 10 singles, five of them in the Top 5 and two #1s. Three more reached the Top 40. He has had five Top 40 albums, including 1973's *Ringo*, which reached #2 in *Billboard* (#1 in Cash Box and Record World), and on which all four Beatles appeared.

Unfortunately, all of his subsequent efforts have been measured against that mega-hit. While none of them ever matched it, a few were given less credit than they deserved. That is particularly true of his 1983 release *Old Wave*, largely a collaboration with Joe Walsh. It was not released in England or the United States but did appear in many other countries, including Canada and Germany.

Starr would be the first to admit that several of his solo efforts were just plain lousy, lacking originality or inspiration. How much of the blame can be placed on Ringo's long bout with alcoholism is difficult to judge, but it clearly played a significant part in his professional undoing.

He had begun his solo career with two off-beat albums. *Sentimental Journey* (Apple, 1970) was a collection of cover versions of standards, mostly from the

> **" Ringo's solo career has had its share of ups and downs."**

1940s. *Beaucoups Of Blues* (Apple, 1970), cut in Nashville, was a venture into country 'n' western music, long a favorite form of his and a project that must have been dear to his heart. Neither effort was very successful among rock enthusiasts, although *Sentimental Journey* reached #22 in *Billboard*. His landmark *Ringo* album came next (Apple, 1973), followed by the successful and entertaining *Goodnight Vienna* (Apple, 1974).

Things began going wrong with *Ringo's Rotogravure* (Atlantic, 1976), a weak imitation of the previous two albums and the first under his new contract with Atlantic. The bottom really fell out with *Ringo The 4th* (Atlantic, 1977), a bizarre misfire aimed at the disco market. Bad Boy (Portrait, 1978) was a slight improvement with a few good songs, but far more weak ones. The album even includes "A Man Like Me," a simple rewrite of "A Mouse Like Me" from the children's album *Scouse The Mouse*, released only in England in 1977.

Starr seemed to bounce back with *Stop And Smell The Roses* (Boardwalk, 1981), cut mostly in 1980 and including contributions by former Beatles Paul McCartney and George Harrison. The album was not well received critically and barely cracked *Billboard's* Top 100, reaching only as far as #98. Then came *Old Wave* (RCA and Boardwalk, 1983). Then came nothing but scattered guest appearances.

A new album was recorded early in 1987 with Chips Moman at that producer's 3 Alarm Studio in Memphis. Two years later Ringo blocked release of the album, claiming that his work was of inferior quality due to excessive use of alcohol during the sessions. Starr noted that he had not played drums on the album

himself, and that he viewed Moman's planned release as an attempt to cash in on the then-successful "All-Starrs" tour.

In October 1988 Ringo and his wife, actress Barbara Bach, checked into an Arizona alcohol rehabilitation center for six weeks. After completing treatment, Ringo publicly admitted that he had wasted a good chunk of his life and squandered much of his career due to a virtual lifetime of alcohol dependency. Although a number of things worked against a revitalization of his career, he was determined to get back to work any way he could.

Lacking a record deal, he assembled a supergroup comprising Clarence Clemons, Joe Walsh, Dr. John, Levon Heim, Rick Danko, Billy Preston, Jim Keltner, and Nils Lofgren and took his show on the road. Fronting his own group for the first time, "Ringo Starr and His All-Starr Band" played 32 North American dates before enthusiastic crowds during July-September 1989. A short seven-show swing through Japan followed.

Despite the release of an entertaining live concert album and video, a new record contract eluded Starr until March 1991, when he signed with the Private Music label. Working with four producers (Jeff Lynne, Don Was, Phil Ramone, and Peter Asher), Starr cut 16 songs during 1991, culling 10 of them for *Time Takes Time*, his first studio album to be released in nine years. More than a little reminiscent of *Ringo*, *Time Takes Time* is both infectious pop-rock and gentle message about the hard knocks life inevitably has in store and the foolishness of wasting time crying over them.

The album is supported by a new tour of North America and Europe beginning in June, with Ringo heading up a new "All-Starr" band. The new lineup includes Nils Lofgren and Joe Walsh, both holdovers from the 1989 tour, and new additions Dave Edmunds, Todd Rundgren, Burton Cummings, Tim Cappello, Timothy B. Schmit, and Ringo's son, Zak Starkey.

The following interview with Ringo took place in his New York hotel suite following a lively press conference at Radio City Music Hall. Before the press, Ringo had displayed the same wit, charm and humor that disarmed America early in 1964 when he shared the platform with his three former bandmates. Although suffering from a slight cold, he remained equally good humored throughout the interview.

Goldmine: Did you have any specific objective in mind when you entered the studio to begin work on Time Takes Time?

Ringo Starr: Initially, it was, "Let's go and make an album. Let's do some songs." I went in with Jeff [Lynne] and we did four tracks. Then I went in with Phil Ramone and did three tracks with him. The tracks were good, but it didn't make any real sense.

Goldmine: Nothing to really hold it together?

Ringo Starr: No. So then we did some tracks with Don Was, and that sort of helped straighten it out a bit because then there were three attitudes. Then the record company [Private Music] actually sent Peter Asher in and I said, "Sure," because he's done some really great stuff. And then it started to feel that we were really making a record. Then we went back in with Don and did some more tracks. Then we remixed the other stuff so that it then felt like an album.

Goldmine: Since you did work with four producers, was there a lot of shifting of gears because you suddenly had a new producer who did things differently than the last one? You've mentioned that Phil Ramone brought a "New York approach" to his sessions.

Ringo Starr: Well, I loved that with Phil. I mean, I never worked with him before, though we've bumped into each other. Actually, every producer I worked with I loved. [Laughing] You know, "Let's do it like this, let's do it like that." We sort of had to straighten it out in the end, but I had a lot of fun with everybody.

Goldmine: And it plays through as a unified piece now.

Ringo Starr: It does now because of the remixes on

■ *Glenn A. Baker Archives*

Phil's and Peter's, and Jeff mixed his own.

Goldmine: Is there anything symbolic in the title?

Ringo Starr: Just that it's really good for me to hear. Just that time takes time, and you have to learn if you want to do anything.

Goldmine: A line from the first song on the album, "Weight Of The World" [also the first single], jumped out at me: "You either kiss...

Ringo Starr: [Reciting along] the future or the past goodbye." All of the songs have something in them for me, even if I didn't write them.

Goldmine: There seems to be several points where that theme reappears, like "Don't Go Where The Road Don't Go."

Ringo Starr: Well, that's one that I wrote, so it certainly says what it says.

Goldmine: I think it says, "Now those friends have all disappeared."

Ringo Starr: We have a lot of fair-weather friends, you know. And that song, because I wrote it, was relating to me because there's been a mighty change in me, thank God, from being totally derelict. But it's not heavy, you know?

Goldmine: Things do change; rock 'n' roll has changed. This is the first time that we have a generation of rock 'n' roll stars who are over 40.

Ringo Starr: Well, we're the only ones who were there.

I think that the kids now are not playing rock 'n' roll; they're playing smash 'n grab [laughs].

Goldmine: There seems to be two markets divided by age.

Ringo Starr: I found with my kids, though, that they all went through their own situation, then they played everything I'd listened to. And then they keep that, and then play their own situation again. I don't know if I was the same because I don't think that I had the choices they have. Johnnie Ray was my first real hero, after Gene Autry. The singing cowboy. What a great voice.

Goldmine: But I think it changed when Bill Haley came out.

Ringo Starr: Well, that's what I was getting to. Bill Haley: I was a fan of his because of his rock 'n' roll. I was 14 at the time. But even he seemed like your dad when Elvis came. Elvis was the one who actually turned my head around. I knew Chuck Berry, and Carl [Perkins], and all of those guys as well. They were coming through. And I was into the blues and all of that. But Elvis actually did it for me.

Goldmine: You mentioned at the press conference announcing your new record and tour that there were 15 or 16 songs in all that were cut for this album, so there's some stuff that got left out, including "Don't Be Cruel."

Ringo Starr: "Don't Be Cruel" is out on the CD5, so there'll be a few bonus tracks along the way.

Goldmine: Can you give a little background on "Angel In Disguise"? Did Paul [McCartney] start it?

"Elvis was the one who actually

Ringo Starr: Paul wrote it and then gave it to me to finish, which I did, and I recorded it with Peter Asher. And it just needed something. I didn't know what it was, and I don't know if Peter knew what it was. We have to say no to some tracks, you know? One that I wrote isn't on the album, "Everyone Wins," the most positive song. But, it didn't make it for the album. It just didn't happen.

Goldmine: You've said that you're not interested in putting out leftover tracks, and that if they weren't good enough at the time they won't get better with age. Sometimes they're omitted for that reason, other times you just don't have room.

Ringo Starr: There's none of these that I would absolutely say never comes out. In fact, up to two-and-a-half weeks ago, "Everyone Wins" was on the album. And we changed it. You know, you're putting your best shot out here. It's my best shot, so I even have to take myself off if I want to be honest. But, it may sneak back later.

Goldmine: Was that the first time you'd ever written anything with Paul?

Ringo Starr: Well, we didn't really write it together. He'd sent me the tape with his two verses and a chorus, and I just did the last verse in my own way.

Goldmine: You're listed as the author of [The Beatles'] "Don't Pass Me By."

Ringo Starr: I am the author of "Don't Pass Me By."

Goldmine: But there's a tape of a BBC interview [recorded July 14, 1964 for Top Gear] where you and Paul noted that the two of you were working on your song "Don't Pass Me By."

Ringo Starr: You sure that wasn't George?

Goldmine: No, I'm pretty sure it was Paul.

Ringo Starr: OK. Well, I don't remember Paul working on it. Paul would have said that as the band were working on it; he wasn't working on it as the writer. {Author's note: The actual radio dialogue was comic banter typical of the group at that time, with Ringo being asked about his songwriting. The following is an excerpt from that interview:

Ringo: I've written a good one, ya see, but no one seems to want to record it.

Paul: No.

Ringo: Oh, Paul may record it on a...

Paul: No.

Ringo: Yes, Paul, you promised!

Paul: No, the thing is, I was doing the tune for you to sing it.

Ringo: No, I don't want to sing it. You sing it.

Paul: [begins reciting lyrics to "Don't Pass Me By."]}

Goldmine: It's funny. That title keeps coming up. On the day that The Beatles were actually recording that in the studio [June 1968], Kenny Everett taped a very famous interview that actually was released by Apple in Italy, and John is saying, "We're working on Ringo's track."

Ringo Starr: [laughs] Yeah, but that's when we were

turned my head around."

working on the tracks, not writing it. They didn't help me at all writing it.

Goldmine: How did you get to do the song "You Never Know" [from the film Curly Sue]? It wasn't part of the album, but you did it during those sessions.

Ringo Starr: Somebody called and said, "We've got this song that's to go with this movie. We've spoken to the director, John Hughes, and he thinks it's a great idea. Would Ringo do this song?" And I said yes. I'm in the studio, I'm working again, I was off that Sunday. They put it together and I went in and did it. But they did tell me it was going to be at the beginning of the movie, not right at the end. I've not seen the movie, but I think the song was actually to set up the movie, but they didn't use it [until the end]. I don't know what happened. But those things happen, you know. You do it and then things change. I'm not going to cry about it; it's on to the next round.

Goldmine: A lot of people were really struck by your remake of "I Call Your Name," recently done as a video [videotaped for May 5, 1990, Liverpool Lennon benefit concert]. That's not out on a record. Any chance?

Ringo Starr: I don't own it. I did it for that specific reason and I gave it to the charity and that was it. I don't know if they'll ever do anything with it. I might do it on tour, though.

Goldmine: Speaking of the tour, Joe Walsh is in the band again. When I saw your show last time [1989], I expected you guys to do "In My Car." Both of you recorded it and you wrote it together.

Ringo Starr: We felt we might. You've got so much material to choose from. Everyone I've been doing the interviews with says, "Why didn't you do that?" "Why didn't you do

this?" So they're just picking one track that they actually like, but we have to do it the way we feel it will be great for the show and, in my case, what I want to do.

Goldmine: Will you hold some songs in readiness in case you want to change the song lineup?

Ringo Starr: Up to now we're saying the rest of the boys get three songs, possibly four, and I'll get the bulk again, about eight to 10. But it depends on how long they go. Until we get to the rehearsals, we can't shape it in any way. So, what we've done for each other — like Todd [Rundgren] put four songs on a tape, Burton [Cummings] put four on a tape, and everyone's done that. So, at least we'll have heard them.

We'll practice at home, not that I ever do, but, sure, some people do. And when we get to the show, we'll see what actually works. One of the most amazing trips on the last tour was that we tried "Back Off Boogaloo" [during some early shows on the tour]. We tried it this way and that way, but it just did not work live. We even had Dr. John on a snare drum. It just didn't happen. I mean, things don't happen. That was one of them. Now, we might try it this time and it clicks. We don't know. It's funny what happens out there.

Goldmine: How will you get the songs together?

Ringo Starr: We've just passed each other the [demo] tapes [of the songs each band member will do]. Todd knows the four songs Burton, Nils [Lofgren] and Dave [Edmunds] are thinking about, so it's not like we hit rehearsal the first day and "this is it." We all have some sort of idea, so that's why we can rehearse in two weeks. Possibly Todd has the most complicated of any of the songs, and that's not that complicated.

Goldmine: In 1985 EMI was set to put out an album of unreleased Beatles songs called Sessions.

Ringo Starr: What songs are they? They're not songs. There's no songs.

Goldmine: Well, there are some titles that were never released. Some sounded like they had probably never been finished.

Ringo Starr: Well, it's like putting "Yesterday" out with its original title, "Scrambled Egg." I don't understand that these are songs. As far as I know, there are no songs that didn't come out.

Goldmine: Well, there's one of yours, "If You've Got Trouble."

Ringo Starr: [singing] "You've got your trouble, then do-do-da-do."

Goldmine: Right. You got it.

Ringo Starr: Yeah, well that's a song that we just didn't do; didn't finish it.

Goldmine: Fans are obsessed with this. You just can't ignore the fact we want to know, "What's that one? And that one."

Ringo Starr: Well, after me screaming, "There's no songs," there is that one. But what else is there?

Goldmine: Well, there are some others, like "How Do You Do It?," which the group apparently didn't want to do and did it reluctantly because George Martin insisted. There's "That Means A Lot," done during Help!

Ringo Starr: Well, you've made an absolute liar out of me. And you're right!

Goldmine: This is what you get from collecting.

Ringo Starr: This will stop me being a "know-all."

Goldmine: Now that the lawsuit between EMI and Apple has been settled there are reports that the way is finally clear for this stuff to come out; the BBC tracks, for example.

Ringo Starr: I like the BBC tracks because I think they're really worthwhile. They're live and we were playing really well because that's when we were playing every night.

Goldmine: And there are lots of unreleased songs there.

Ringo Starr: Sure. We had to do eight tracks a night, including ones we hadn't done.

Goldmine: So we might see those come out?

Ringo Starr: I believe the problem with the BBC tracks is that they've only got a second generation tape. They're still looking for the first generation.

Goldmine: There was a recent report that George Martin is trying to work with the original tapes.

Ringo Starr: George Harrison is trying to work with them also. We're waiting for the tape. I like my cassette [laughs]. It's cool.

Goldmine: What do you think of Beatles songs or any rock 'n' roll standards being used in television commercials?

...because I think they're really worthwhile."

Ringo Starr: I don't particularly like to hear the Nike one. But I had nothing to do with that. Talk to Yoko.

Goldmine: That's actually John's recording [of "Instant Karma"] on that.

Ringo Starr: Yes, but I'm not on it. And he's not here to discuss it anymore.

Goldmine: I was also appalled to see that there is now a line of John Lennon eye glasses.

Ringo Starr: I know nothing about that. I'm trying to get in charge of my own life.

Goldmine: It doesn't sound like you're very strongly in favor of it.

Ringo Starr: No, I'm not, really.

Goldmine: What about censorship and putting labels on records warning parents about lyrics?

Ringo Starr: This happens every 10 years. This madness happens where people try to sue people saying that their children jumped out the window because this record said something. I just think that it's totally silly. The kids will get it anyway. If your parents are censoring you, your pals parents aren't censoring him. It goes down. It's like, "Rock 'n' roll is the devil's music!" And you had all that madness. It's gone on forever. I take very little notice of it, actually. Everyone wants to censor somebody. It just gets on my nerves.

Goldmine: Back in 1980 when you were working on Stop And Smell The Roses, George [Harrison] produced a couple of tracks for you: "Wrack My Brain" and "You Belong To Me." The story is that there was an early version of the song that later became "All Those Years Ago," which was George's tribute to John, and your drum track is on that. Was there an earlier version of the song entirely? Perhaps with a different title and different lyrics?

Ringo Starr: Not that I recall. No. You'll have to talk to [George]. I don't know.

Goldmine: Similarly, John apparently made demos of four songs that he gave to you shortly before he died that he thought would be good for you.

Ringo Starr: Yeah, they gave me some of John's songs after he died. But I couldn't do them. I was not interested then. I mean, if he had given them to me it would be a different situation. But he did not give them to me. They were given to me later and I couldn't deal with it at that time. They said, "John felt these would be good for you."

Goldmine: You can hear John say, "This is for Ringo" on the demos. I think they were "Life Begins At Forty," "Nobody Told Me" and "I Don't Wanna Face It."

Ringo Starr: Sure. But it was too late for me to do them.

Goldmine: You've cowritten three songs on Time Takes Time, all with Johnny Warman, who was responsible for the "Spirit Of The Forest" charity single. You hooked up with him through Ring-O Records?

Ringo Starr: Yeah, because he used to be on the label. We've kept in contact ever since. Besides being a writer and a rock 'n' roll musician he's also a health freak. So, we'd work out and write. He'd come and stay with me in Monte Carlo. In the mornings we'd get up and go running and stretching and working out. In the afternoons and evenings we'd sit around writing, then

"Everyone wants to censor somebody."

go and have dinner, and we'd start the whole thing again the next day.

Goldmine: "Runaways" really stands out on the album. It's a change of pace: What were you trying to say in that?

Ringo Starr: I watched a program on kids who'd run away. But, it was mainly a program on the parents trying to find them and just how devastated they are. And the dreams that the kids have, like to go to London and it's all going to be cool, and I'll be free. So many of them end up raped, pillaged and burned. They just want to run away from home. I wanted to do that too when I was 16. And hundreds and hundreds of them are doing it today. They run away to Hollywood, they run away to New York. And these are the caves of steel. I just put it in this science fiction form. It's still about runaways, but in a science fiction attitude.

Goldmine: How do you write? Do you play the piano or guitar?

Ringo Starr: I still play three chords on the piano and I still play three chords on the guitar. That's how I do it. With Johnny, he was holding the guitar. In the early days when I would write "Photograph," or whatever, then I would give it to George [Harrison], who would actually put the real chords in. But I would have written it on the three chords, and he would put the passing chords in.

Goldmine: You knew where you wanted to go.

Ringo Starr: Sure. You just make it real. Not that we couldn't have done it on those three chords [laughs], but he knows a few more, which makes it sound better.

Goldmine: Do you write from time to time when inspiration hits you?

Ringo Starr: It's just started again. I've written very little. I've got a couple of pieces — I call it "bits" — of me just on my own with the guitar, I just sit down, and if it comes, it comes.

Goldmine: It's not just because you've got an album coming up and you have to sit down and do a couple of songs? It might happen any time?

Ringo Starr: Any time. It's not just because I'm working. It's not like I'm never going to write now until the next album. If anything happens, it happens.

Goldmine: Record collectors are frequently surprised at how many records are issued in one country but don't come out in others.

Ringo Starr: Well, you know, Amsterdam is the capital of bootleg records.

Goldmine: That's a different matter entirely. I'm talking about things that are issued.

Ringo Starr: Oh, you're talking about real stuff.

Goldmine: Yeah. Like, The White Album [The Beatles; 1968] *only came out in mono in England, never here. If you listen to it, it's like listening to a different album.*

Ringo Starr: Of course it is. It's a mono mix.

Goldmine: "Don't Pass Me By," for example, plays through much faster. Or maybe it was slowed down on the stereo. The question is, were you guys aware at the time that this sort of thing was going on?

Ringo Starr: I wasn't. I was not aware. I don't know if the others were aware.

"We made it totally separate."

Goldmine: In preparing the *Sgt. Pepper* album The Beatles themselves worked on the mono mix but reportedly were not even there when the stereo version was mixed.

Ringo Starr: Well, that's not true. I remember being there for a lot of the stereo mixes. Because we were having fun making the horses gallop across the room. Things like that.

Goldmine: *There's a report that during the '60s Paul made a special little Christmas album just for the other members of the group and gave one to each of you, with only four copies ever pressed. Do you remember receiving one?*

Ringo Starr: No. I don't have mine. But I do have some acetates that just have The Beatles playing the blues on them that no one else has.

Goldmine: *Some people think that it was a mistake to ever make albums in the first place. In the '50s, stars seemed to want to get one great song recorded that might have a shot at the Top 10. Now you have to record an entire album, and singles are pulled off the album.*

Ringo Starr: Yes, but you've forgotten that period in between when you made the single and you made the album. That's what we did. We made it totally separate. We always ended up with more tracks over in America, so that's how they could make these compilation crazy albums.

Goldmine: *But do you think the music has suffered because artists have to do a whole album, whereas they might have had a great single?*

Ringo Starr: Yeah, but who would put the money behind the

great single? The return is not enough. It's economics again. It's nothing to do with music.

Goldmine: *Things have changed. In those days, kids had enough money to buy the 50-cent single.*

Ringo Starr: Most of them only had enough to buy the single. And when you toured, you only toured to sell records. You didn't go on the road to make any money. They paid your expenses and you got a few dollars, but the main aim was to keep promoting that record because people were buying lots of records in those days.

Goldmine: *The last time you went on tour [1989] you didn't have an album to promote, which is very unusual these days. Why did you opt for the tour?*

Ringo Starr: I didn't opt for it. That was the actual situation of life. I didn't have anything, but I wanted to go out. [Promoter] David Fishof came up with this idea and asked, "Do you want to put a band together and go on tour?" And I said yes. And then I thought, "Shit, who would I go with?" That's how the concept came. We'll just go out and give them all the hits we can. With Levon [Helm], Dr. John, Billy [Preston] and Joe [Walsh] and everyone it just became the concept — let's go and give them the hits. It was a revue, really. As one promoter said, it was like listening to his past flash between his ears [laughs].

Goldmine: *How did you like playing in Japan? You did a short leg there.*

It was like listening to his past flash between his ears.

"You didn't go on the road

"Hank Williams was my hero."

Ringo Starr: A short leg of Japan; that's enough. It was good. The kids were good and the reaction was good, but that was enough, thank you.

Goldmine : Who were some of the early rockers, other than Elvis, who most influenced you? I know you've mentioned Jerry Lee Lewis.

Ringo Starr: Jerry Lee was my hero and Clyde McPhatter.

Goldmine: I always thought that you guys heard the Big Joe Turner songs or the Hank Williams soup through Jerry Lee Lewis's cover versions.

Ringo Starr: Hank Williams was my hero. We had the original records. We came from Liverpool, which was a port, and all those guys who went to sea used to bring all the records in. At one point Liverpool — maybe it still is — was the capital of country 'n' western music in England. ■

to make any money."

John Lennon

(1940-1980)

By Rick Whitesell

O ften it takes a great shock to jar us into reflection, into stopping long enough to take stock of what is really happening around us in the world. On December 8, 1980, a lot of us were certainly shocked and depressed to learn that John Lennon had been gunned down in front of the Dakota Hotel in New York City. And while the media sought to wrench every emotion (and dollar, of course) from us — with special programming, tributes, magazines, buttons, etc. — it seems that the public was not sidetracked from the main issue here.

The point of the Lennon murder, if a "point" can be derived from an act of such senselessness, is that no matter how talented, charismatic or legendary an artist becomes in the music field, they're still human. There is nothing wrong with admiring an artist's talents, but there is something wrong when an artist is forced to live the life of a prisoner, as Elvis Presley was; or when an artist's attempt to live a normal, above-ground existence is rewarded with death, as in John Lennon's case. One reason fans took Lennon's murder so badly was that everyone knew where he lived, and there was always a small pack of devoted followers waiting for him to come or go from the Dakota, and yet Lennon was the sort of gentleman who always displayed infinite patience with his fans, signing autographs and shaking hands.

Lennon's death made me think hard about what we, who write about music and musicians, are about. John Lennon, to be sure, ushered in a new era when he

> *" Lennon was the sort of gentleman who always displayed infinite patience with his fans, signing autographs and shaking hands. "*

and The Beatles began giving interviews during the '60s; today, it is common practice for a publication like *Rolling Stone* to print every new "star's" outlook on social and political subjects (and the lesson learned from reading some of those interviews is that an artist can make fantastic music and not be qualified in the least to address any issue intelligently!). Certainly, one reason for this is that when reporters asked John Lennon's opinion on virtually any subject, his responses were intelligent, frequently witty, and well-worth hearing. But instead of letting the constant media attention go to his head, Lennon often expressed himself in ways that indicated his concern with the conditions that had elevated four boys from Liverpool to a pedestal from which they swayed a society with even the most insignificant gesture or action. The controversial statement Lennon made about The Beatles being more popular than Christ offended many, but who could deny that the machinery of our communications media put The Beatles under a brighter spotlight than any other figure or group before them?

I'm not sure The Beatles loved the attentive adulation. Many people saw Paul McCartney interviewed the day after Lennon's death, and when he appeared to be detached and off-handed in this comments, they were quick to condemn his "insensitivity" to the tragedy. Few looked beyond what they saw on their television screens, though, to note the insensitivity of the media. Is it terribly humane to subject a human being to a wall of jabbing microphones and impersonal interrogators under any circumstances? Should Paul McCartney be expected to bare his most personal feelings to us, simply because some fans feel their love for an artist gives them the right to pry?

"How did it happen, I hope this suffering was small Tell me every detail, I've got to know it all."

Phil Ochs's line form "Crucifixion" seems particularly appropriate in the wake of Lennon's death.

One of the most unsettling and macabre sidelights of Lennon's murder was that his alleged killer, Mark Chapman, seems by all accounts to have been a fan of The Beatles, and particularly Lennon. It seems that Lennon's assassin found more excitement in Lennon's life than his own; while this may be true of many fans, who look for what they lack in the lives of their idols, it seems that one man's obsession went over the edge of sanity.

John Lennon's death made me look at myself, as big a "fan" of music and artists as can be found. If I didn't love doing it, I certainly would do something other than editing *Goldmine* and writing sporadically for other publications; as all *Goldmine* staff writers know all too well, great fortunes will not be made by most of us in this field. But there is something about music that makes us want to spread the word, share our enthusiasms with others.

For me, there is little I enjoy more than listening to Sam Cooke sing or seeing Bruce Springsteen perform on stage or discovering a hot aircheck of Alan Freed beating the pulp out of a phone book during a Roy Milton record. These are just my individual preferences; everyone reading this had their own, undoubtedly. And for all of us, there are probably a few artists that we've followed and listened to so long as we feel we "know" them... or when we meet them and perhaps shake their hands or get their autographs, it makes us feel great for a week.

But — whether a musician is a former star whose hits stopped coming years ago, or whether he or she is at their peak — no one should forget for a moment that they're just people, doing their job and trying to keep on keepin' on... like all the rest of us. After Lennon's death, I read

"They're just people."

over back issues of *Goldmine*; I guess I was a bit afraid that maybe I'd find that his magazine was just another, albeit smaller than most, insensitive periodical which exploited others' creative skills for profit.

Fortunately, I can objectively say that my considered opinion is that we've successfully aspired to do something more than that. Our interviews and stories cover virtually every kind of popular, rock-related musical style imaginable, but the coverage is bound together by the fact that our writers really have enthusiasm for their subjects. More importantly, I noted that our writers approach their writing with a scholarly attitude oriented towards chronicling pop music history; yet, they have consistently done so with a sense of humor — and more importantly, some compassion

■ *Glenn A. Baker Archives*

for the people interviewed for these stories. And when our writers shove microphones under someone's nose, the line of questioning doesn't extend past music. While we're thorough in our search for accuracy and truth, *Goldmine* has never invaded someone's privacy to give readers a vicarious thrill or two. What's more, I don't think our readership is looking for that.

Over the years, I've met or written people whose main collecting interest, and personal passion, was the music and memorabilia of The Beatles. As a group and as individuals, The Beatles' impact was profound on a whole generation, myself included; but for the serious fans, the tragedy of John Lennon's death has hit much harder and deeper. To those readers, I express my sympathy; more than one person has told me that this event was equivalent to the loss of a close family member, and

when one considers the degree to which some of us grew up with The Beatles providing a sort of "soundtrack," that makes perfect sense.

But I have no sympathies for the off-center individuals who have gained appreciably through the exploitation of John Lennon (or Elvis Presley, or any other artist, for that matter) — when that exploitation take on the ghoulish insensitivity exemplified by the *New York Post* cover photo of John Lennon lying face-up in his coffin. Frankly, I felt nauseous to watch certain parts of the media exploit Lennon in death as they'd done in life, as if to them there were no real difference. I did note that the public was having less tolerance for those who would turn sincere emotions into sheer profit and can only hope the trend continues.

After John Lennon died, many people asked me what *Goldmine* would do in reaction. And aside from this unusually long editorial, I've lived up to my reply: nothing special. We really don't have to; throughout our existence, John Lennon's name cropped up constantly in both the editorial and advertising sections of *Goldmine* — commensurate, I'd say, with his greatness as an artist. And that will certainly continue to be the case, as new listeners become aware of his music as a solo artist and as a Beatle, perhaps for the first time.

For the majority of us, who read and write *Goldmine* each month, John Lennon provided us with many hours of enjoyment in the years he created music. There just doesn't seem to be any point to dwelling on the fact that, because of a senseless act, that creative mind has been silenced. ■

*O*ne night in early March 1974, John Lennon and Harry Nilsson rolled up at the Los Angeles Troubadour, steaming drunk and gratingly abusive. Lennon was particularly out of it, clothes rumpled, hair a mess, and a sanitary napkin stuck on his forehead. He demanded more alcohol, the waitress refused, and the former Beatle, who had doubtless left that famous Lennon wit in the car, instead flashed angrily, "Don't you know who I am?"

"Yeah, I know," the waitress shot back. "You're an asshole with a Kotex on his head."

John Lennon's Lost Weekend, 18 months wildcatting through the bowels of showbiz sleaze, is one of the great tales of rock 'n' roll excess. No matter that the most scintillating retelling is to be found within Albert Goldman's masterpiece of ax-grinding malice, *The Lives Of John Lennon*; neither, as countless subsequent biographies have it, that it has since been reduced to a couple of paragraphs of Hard Love therapy. If the Lost Weekend had never existed, history would have had to invent one — and who better to enjoy it than Beatle John?

He was always a bit of a Jack The Lad. These days, it's fashionable to pin Lennon's most outrageous behavior to the flag of "cutting, acerbic wit" and to blame his victims for any offense they felt — "You just didn't understand John's

> *" 'Yeah, I know,' the waitress shot back. 'You're an asshole with a Kotex on his head.' "*

Five Star Record!

hey marty@ wwnet.net

© MARTY WINTERS 2000

HARRY NILSSON WAS BORN HARRY EDWARD NELSON III IN BROOKLYN, NY IN 1941 AND WILL FOREVER BE KNOWN AS ONE OF AMERICA'S FOREMOST POP SONGWRITERS! IRONICALLY, HIS TWO BIGGEST HITS WERE NOT HIS OWN COMPOSITIONS... "WITHOUT YOU" FROM THIS 1971 RCA LP, WENT TO NUMBER ONE ON THE U·S· CHARTS AND EARNED NILSSON A GRAMMY FOR BEST MALE POP VOCAL OF 1972! IT WAS WRITTEN BY TWO OF THE MEMBERS OF BADFINGER, TOM EVANS & PETER HAM! THE OTHER TUNE MOST CLOSELY ASSOCIATED WITH NILSSON, "EVERYBODY'S TALKIN'" WAS WRITTEN BY FRED NEIL! STILL, HARRY WROTE HIS SHARE OF MEMORABLE SONGS! LONG BEFORE THE SUCCESS OF "NILSSON SCHMILSSON," HARRY WAS WORKING AWAY AT HIS CRAFT, PEDDLING SONGS AND SINGING RADIO JINGLES BY DAY WHILE MAINTAINING A NIGHT JOB AT A BANK! HIS BIG BREAK CAME WHEN PHIL SPECTOR DECIDED TO BUY A FEW OF HIS SONGS—TWO FOR THE RONETTES AND ONE FOR THE MODERN FOLK QUARTET! IN NO TIME HARRY WAS IN DEMAND AND HIS SONGS WERE BEING RECORDED BY EVERYONE ··· FROM THE MONKEES TO THE YARDBIRDS TO DAVID CASSIDY! HIS TUNE "ONE" AS RECORDED BY THREE DOG NIGHT WENT TO NUMBER ONE IN 1969, AND OTTO PREMINGER HIRED HIM TO SCORE HIS 1968 FILM "SKIDOO" (HARRY EVEN APPEARED IN A CAMEO!)! HIS TELEVISION WRITING CREDITS INCLUDE THEME MUSIC FOR "THE COURTSHIP OF EDDIE'S FATHER" (HE SANG OVER THE OPENING CREDITS AS WELL!) AND A GROUP OF SONGS WRITTEN FOR THE 1971 ANIMATED SPECIAL "THE POINT" INCLUDING HIS HIT SINGLE "ME AND MY ARROW"! HIS 1972 RELEASE "SON OF SCHMILSSON" FEATURED "SPACEMAN," HIS LAST REAL HIT, AND HE FOLLOWED THAT WITH TWO THEME LP's ··· A GROUP OF STANDARD POP SONGS ARRANGED AND CONDUCTED BY GORDON JENKINS APPEARED ON "A LITTLE TOUCH OF SCHMILSSON IN THE NIGHT" (1973) WITH NILSSON'S TRIBUTE TO ROCK 'N' ROLL (PRODUCED BY JOHN LENNON) "PUSSY CATS" COMING OUT IN 1974! NILSSON SUFFERED A HEART

MY FRIEND MIKE (AKA MORT) TURNED ME ON TO NILSSON WAY BACK IN THE SEVENTIES AND I'VE HAD THIS LP SINCE THEN! IT'S MY FAVORITE NILSSON LP AND THE SONG LINE-UP IS AN ECCLECTIC TOUR-DE-FORCE OF NILSSON'S TWISTED VOCALIZING! FROM THE LP'S OPENER "GOTTA GET UP" RIGHT THROUGH TO THE END YOU CAN NEVER QUITE GET COMFORTABLE WITH WHAT YOU THINK THIS ALBUM IS ABOUT! YET IT ALL SEEMS TO FIT TOGETHER SO NICELY! NILSSON IS EQUALLY CONVINCING ON THE BALLAD "WITHOUT YOU", THE GOOFY HIT "COCONUT" AND ON THE THROBBING, ALMOST FUNKY "JUMP INTO THE FIRE"*! ASTOUNDING!

ATTACK AND EVENTUALLY DIED OF HEART-RELATED AILMENTS IN 1994.

* MY FAVORITE!!

☆ ☆ ☆ ☆ ☆

humor. He's from Liverpool, you know." But that wasn't always the case. There was a time, while Lennon still lived, when he could be an obnoxious bully, a loudmouth boor, and an ungracefully fading icon who hadn't made a decent record in years. Or, as another Troubadour waitress put it, after Lennon punched her in the ribs one night, "It's not the pain that hurts. It's finding out that one of your idols is a real asshole."

Lennon had arrived in L.A. in September 1973. He traveled light, girlfriend May Pang and a couple of suitcases, and though he wasn't sure what he wanted to do, he knew that this was where he wanted to do it. L.A., thousands of miles from New York and Yoko, was a playground for the rich and famous, and John was certainly both of them. The whole city, or at least that narrow band of Hollywood nightclubs where he'd be spending most of his time, Was a spiritual pick-me-up that never let you down again. There he could reinvent himself; there, he could escape from whatever else he'd become.

Lennon's latest album, *Mind Games* was on the verge of release; his next, a tribute to the rock 'n' roll records he'd loved as a kid, was in the planning stages already. Both were a long way away from the albums he'd made in the past, the cynical politicking of *Sometime In New York City*, the bitter sideswipes of Imagine, the savage purgative of *Plastic Ono Band*. All Lennon needed to do was convince people that he meant it, that he wasn't going to go back to bed or wrap his wife up in a bag anymore.

Tony King, a P.R. man schooled in the furnace of the primal Rolling Stones, was already setting the first set of wheels in motion, convincing the world that this was a kinder, gentler John than they'd seen in a long time; Phil Spector was greasing the axle of the second, hiring a crack studio session band to aid Lennon in his nostalgia-

draped odyssey. And while neither project was to roll as smoothly as Lennon might have wished — *Mind Games* barely scratched the Top 10; Rock 'n' Roll turned into a drama of Dostoevsky-esque proportions — still, they were a cakewalk compared to all he'd been through in the past and to what he'd be undergoing in the immediate future.

Albert Goldman, mastering dramatic hyperbole with a flair that makes lesser scribes blanche, credits Lennon's lost weekend to the fiendish machinations of three evil fairies. Spector was the first; music publisher Morris Levy, somewhat unexcitingly, was the third. And sandwiched in between them, the very earth trembling at the mention of its name, cities crumbling at the sound of its voice, Harry Nilsson was the second. Harry "Theme From Midnight Cowboy" Nilsson. Harry "Without You" Nilsson. "Pahl" as the man himself so memorably snorted. "Nilsson Schmilsson."

Nilsson rolled into Lennon's life like he'd just been dragged in by the cat.

"It was a time when I was really depressed and down," he admitted during interviews for the "Lost Lennon Tapes" radio series. "I was just totally down, I was looking for anyone in the world to talk to, have a drink with, be with, and I went to every bar in the town, called my friends, and there was nobody there. I started studio hopping in case there was somebody around who was alive, and the last stop on the list was A&M and I saw this guy I recognized; I said 'What are you working on?'; he said, 'John and Phil' — Lennon and Spector. So I said 'Where are they?'; he said 'In that room,' and there was every friend I'd ever had in my life in that room. So I just hopped in, did some odds and ends, and I think I was a nice little centerpiece for them both to dance around."

The sessions, of course, eventually ground to a less than harmonious halt, but Nilsson and Lennon remained fast friends. He and May Pang were sharing a duplex suite at the Beverley Wilshire Hotel; they had the top half, Ringo Starr had the lower, and when you put the two together, it was time to hit the town. Nilsson became an inevitable third partner in a fast-expanding drunken knights of the "whose round?" table.

Those were hazy, crazy days for the rock 'n' roll cognoscenti, for those gallant soldiers whose fame offered them access to an excess they couldn't refuse. It was a time when televisions learned to fly and groupies went with fish, when Keith Moon made a solo album and a swimming pool simply wasn't a swimming pool unless it had a Rolls Royce at the bottom. Lennon and Nilsson understood this behavior intuitively, and they understood its purpose as well.

The public, their public, demands entertainment. That's why it creates stars in the first place, to live out the dreams which they themselves are incapable of realizing: Presley's pink Caddy, Jimi's burning guitar, The Who's trashed hotel rooms, Foghat's... well, Foghat's whatever. So long as it went beyond the realms of normal convention, it didn't matter what the stars had or did, it was the fact that they had them and did them which counted.

But how much was too much? Lennon turning up at the Troubadour with a Kotex on his head was one thing; turning up there with a chip on his shoulder was another. On March 13, 1974, Lennon and Nilsson were forcibly ejected from L.A.'s most famous niterie after throwing punches at the staff and hurling abuse at the headliners. Maybe "Hey, Smothers Brothers! Fuck a cow!" does deserve a prize for originality, but beating up waitresses and throwing glasses at walls was going too far.

Reporting on the fracas the following week, the British *New Musical Express* even speculated that the row might wind up in deportation. Lennon was already at loggerheads with the U.S. authorities, remaining in the country with nothing but probation and an expired visa to keep him from a long flight home. NME reporter Chris Van Ness continued, "when legal charges are brought against Lennon, as they almost certainly will be... he will be branded an 'undesirable alien' and deported."

As it happened, no charges were brought, but Lennon and Nilsson didn't seem to care if they had been. A couple of nights after the Troubadour incident, they provoked a near riot on a tram in Palm Springs. And in the midst of the madness, as if to justify the behavior that was now haunting the headlines, they decided to make an album together. It would be called *Pussy Cats*, Lennon determined, because that is how he and Nilsson signed themselves on the apologetic bouquet that they'd sent to The Smothers Brothers the day after the Troubadour fracas.

Lennon explained, "I was just hanging around with Ringo and Harry, we were just... hanging round, it became like a teenage gang only we were all 30, so one day as Harry and I sat there, I looked at him and said, 'What are we doing here? Why don't we go make a record?' Because we're playing pianos in hotel rooms, we're causing riots, we're wasting energy... so I said, 'Look kid, I'm doing nothing, why don't I produce you?' So we went in and we made the record..."

Nilsson admitted that when the idea first surfaced, he did not take it too seriously. "[John] was out of it when he first suggested it, so I didn't pressure him or push him in any way. But a few days later he called and said 'What songs are we going to do?' and I went, 'Jesus Christ, I think he's serious.'"

Lennon was not a recognized producer. His early recordings with Yoko, of course, were by definition self-produced, while he also took a co-credit alongside Spector for his own *Plastic Ono Band*, *Imagine* and *Sometime In New York City* albums. Just two records, however, indicated Lennon's personal studio strengths: *Mind Games*, which really wasn't very good; and David Peel's *The Pope Smokes Dope*, which was great fun to listen to, but was hardly tubular Bells. But of course, the marketing men who approved this new project's recording budget would hardly have worried about something like that. They would simply have studied the sales charts and done a few simple sums before deducing that if Lennon and Nilsson individually were sure-fire million sellers, then the two of them together would be a license to print money.

Of course it didn't work like that. *Pussy Cats — Starring Harry Nilsson, Produced by John Lennon* would become the worst-selling new album to bear Lennon's name on its cover since his and Yoko's *Wedding Album* a full five years before. But the accountants' loss was rock 'n' roll's gain, and *Pussy Cats* remains one of the great albums of the mid-1970s.

Fueled by an all-but-lethal combination of booze, drugs and absurdly high spirits, boasting the services of three wired-up drummers and a barrelful of revelers and pocked with some of the most gorgeously realized cover versions ever committed to wax, it is an album of dynamic extremes, each one more climactic than the last. By the time it reaches its battered finale, rocking around a war-torn clock, the listener is either exalted or exhausted (or more likely, both), and the stereo system is checking itself into Detox. *Pussy Cats* is not an album you should play in the car.

Yet it is also an album of breathtaking majesty, its finest moments matching, even outstripping, the best of either Lennon's or Nilsson's contemporary work, and echoing them as well. Ghosts of the opening, despairing, cover of Jimmy Cliff's "Many Rivers To Cross" feedback through "#9 Dream," the finest cut on John's own next album; "Loop De Loop" and "Rock Around The Clock," on the other hand, prove that the rock 'n' roll session that Lennon had conducted with Spector had not quite exorcised some ghosts of their own. If, as so many critical commentaries insist, *Pussy Cats* was the sound of two mighty talents at the bottom of a pit, they still had one helluva view.

Moving into Marilyn Monroe's old house at 625 Pacific Coast Highway and booking time at Burbank Studios, John and Harry, May Pang and Nilsson's girlfriend Una began piecing together the gang that would double as a band on the projected album: engineer Roy Cicala, Klaus Voorman, Ringo Starr, Jim Keltner, Bobby Keys, Jesse Ed Davis, Danny Kootch, Sneeky Pete, and Ken Ascher. All of them would become shareholders in the party that started in one place when someone woke up, then marched across town to wake up the other; most of them had already been involved in the abortive Spector sessions.

"I like to use the same musicians for a whole album," Lennon said at the time. "Because then they know what I'm talking about if I'm trying to explain myself to them, and I feel more relaxed. And if they've played together before, it's the next best thing to having a permanent group."

On March 28, 1974, the team set up in the studio for the first time, to assault Bob Dylan's "Subterranean Homesick

"Pussy Cats remains

Blues." It was Lennon's intention to create an album that was as spontaneous as the nightclub displays that had by now labeled him a public pariah; tracks would be restricted to no more than a couple of takes, a far cry from the laborious piece-by-piecing into which he'd slipped over his own last few records. Indeed, later in the sessions, when Nilsson announced he wanted to dub a snare onto the Dylan song, Lennon initially refused. There were already enough drums on the song, he said, and besides, as far as he was concerned, it was finished.

As it happened, Nilsson agreed with him entirely — it was just that he'd promised his young cousin, Doug, that he could appear on the record. Lennon finally relented (although he only allowed the youngster one take!); he knew, just as Nilsson knew, that *Pussy Cats* was already awash with percussive chaos. What difference would one more layer of noise make?

The basics of "Subterranean Homesick Blues" were completed in a day, even with two drummers (Keltner and Starr) kicking up an unholy din; even with Nilsson having to contend not only with Dylan's stream-of-something wordiness, but also with the new, savage boogie arrangement that Lennon insisted on grafting to the song.

"I like it because it's sort of mad," Lennon told DJ Tom Donahue once the song was complete, and he was right. He also pointed out "a lot of edits in it that I still hear," then invited the KSAN radio audience to "spot the edits and win an invisible T-shirt." Listen even closer, though, and you can forget the edits; forget Goldman's evil fairies. The four horsemen of the apocalypse are in there as well, uncredited auxiliaries best heard on the headphones.

The mood in the studio was wild and got wilder. Paul and Linda McCartney were in town at the time, and as the

session continued on into the evening and more and more people dropped by to take part, no one was surprised when the McCartneys appeared. Three Beatles in one room — the NME had been laying odds on just that occurrence a mere few days before: 20 to 1, a semipermanent re-formation; 15 to 1, a studio reunion; 2 to 1, a one-off new album; and 4 to 6 against, regular guest spots on each other's records. Nothing, unfortunately, about turning up in the dark of night to run through a bunch of old rock 'n' roll covers and nothing about the whole thing proving ditchwater dull.

When news of the reunion hit the streets, albeit somewhat belatedly, many fans were disappointed that no hint of it was included on the finished *Pussy Cats* album. When a bootleg of the reunion arrived, those same fans were probably glad that it hadn't.

The gathering opens with Lennon introducing a charming little number called "Never Trust A Bugger With Your Mother." Nilsson counters with "Little Bitty Pretty One," before Lennon locks everyone into a rambling attempt at completing "Stand By Me," a song he would return to when he resumed the *Rock n' Roll* sessions. Half rehearsal, half jam, the crowd also ran through a raucous "Lucille," "Midnight Special," "Cupid" and "Take This Hammer." There was a little bit of blues, and only one track that showed any potential or promise a gentle "Sleepwalk" which, with some typically Lennonesque improvisation, swiftly turned into the menacing "Nightmares."

The following evening with normalcy now restored, the gang (minus the McCartneys, of course) reconvened to attempt "Many Rivers To Cross," a song that Nilsson had long been keen to cover. Once again, the arrangement paid no attention whatsoever to the original, the classic

one of the great albums of the mid-1970s."

ska ballad that made a star of Jimmy Cliff: scaling down the beat, slowing down the tempo, it became instead a dark, brooding ballad, hooking itself around a lyric that Cliff's original barely noticed. It falls around a third of the way through the song, as Nilsson's double-tracked vocals rise in real despair... "This loneliness won't leave me alone, it's such a drag..." and where Cliff would have just carried on singing, Nilsson stops; the band stops, and for one heart-stopping moment, it is as though an elevatorful of fat people has just plummeted down from the top floor. Then the song restarts, it drifts beautifully on, and when the same thing happens the next time around, it still grabs your heart in its hand.

Interviewing Lennon a few months later, KSAN DJ Tom Donahue remarked that a lot of people, himself included, were convinced that it was actually Lennon singing lead. Their voices really were similar. Lennon, however, was quick to explain, "He was singing it pretty much as he sang it, but he was holding back. So I just kept asking him for more on it, and it turned out like he did. I liked it; I knew it was going to be 'Oh, it sounds like he's doing John,' but there's a certain point when you get high, on music, whatever, when you're going to go to the same place, and there was nowhere else for him to go but there." Which kind of makes sense if you really pay attention, but it doesn't really matter. The end result still remains one of the most spellbinding performances of Nilsson's entire career.

Like Lennon, Nilsson had been planning a new album of his own in the months before *Pussy Cats* commenced; indeed, a full dozen tracks were already in the can, and Nilsson arrived at Burbank with at least a few of the songs crying out

for reprieve: the plaintive, painful "Don't Forget Me," "All My Life," and the fragmentary "Mt. Elga." On April 3, work began on the first of these, a sparse recording that seated Nilsson alone at the piano, which the comically anonymous Masked Alberts Orchestra soared away behind him. (Joe Cocker would later concoct a fuller version for his 1976 album *I Can Stand A Little Rain*.)

It is a delightful, delicate performance, but the rough edge that catches Nilsson's voice was not simply the choke of vicarious emotion. A few weeks before, the singer had spent a night sleeping on the beach, contracting a throat infection that wouldn't go away. Ordinarily, he would have simply have followed doctor's orders and rested his voice till the problem cleared up. But ordinarily, he would not have John Lennon wanting to make an album with him. Swallowing painkillers, swallowing the pain, Nilsson determined not to give in to a simple sore throat.

> "*Nilsson determined not to give in to a simple sore throat.*"

The roughness, which to the uninitiated sounds more like a legend-confirming drunken wastedness, is the sound of that determination.

The sessions quickly fell into a pattern, and that despite the copious quantities of everything that the participants were imbibing.

"It was a pretty heavy drinking bunch," Nilsson remembered. While Lennon apparently excused himself from many of the late-night parties, preferring to go home with May Pang, the rest of the crew remained hell-bent hell-raisers.

"The roughness is the sound

"Keith Moon and Ringo, and yours truly, and everybody was loaded all the time. We had a couple of limos every night to take us to the studio and back again. But we were pretty organized. We used to get there at 6, finish by 1, then we used to go back home to listen to the tapes and fall on the floor, but the bugaboo was always liquor — a combination of liquor and coke will keep you there indefinitely.

"Anyway, we'd get up and have the strangest breakfasts, pork chops and eggs in grilled something, and we never figured out what the taste or smell was, and some of us would go about our business, some of us would take a little nap, and we'd reconvene about 5 o'clock..."

"All My Life," one of those simple throwaway numbers that Nilsson insisted on including on every album he released, was cut on April 4, and two days later, work began on what would become one of the album's true, defining moments, a massive reworking of The Drifters' "Save The Last Dance For Me."

Already it was evident that Lennon's relative inexperience as a producer was not an obstacle. Nilsson enthused, "He's so fast and easy, 'cos when you say something that's clever or good, he'd just jump on it like it was a candy or something." He also knew when to push for perfection and when to let things slide, and "Save The Last Dance" illustrates both extremes simultaneously.

No longer awaiting the last dance, the old Pomus/Shuman classic now was the last dance, a beautiful spiraling dirge with the Masked Alberts sweeping around Bobby Keys's gently honking sax before the song halts with a funereal drum beat of heart-stopping finality.

Nilsson's voice was wrecked by now, his throat red raw. When he stepped away from the microphone, it was speckled with tiny drops of blood. He refused to call a halt, however; indeed, he refused even to tell Lennon what was going on. One day, John did ask why Nilsson was holding back so much; "I'm saying, 'Where's all that doo-doo-doo stuff?' and he was going 'Kakakaka.'"

Lennon shrugged; it wasn't as if he'd never played games with his voice in the past, and besides, the croak really did seem to work, in a ragged, rough, Tom Waits sort of way. It was only much later, with the very end of the session in sight, that he finally found out what was going on.

"[Harry] was going to doctors, and being injected, and he didn't tell me till later that he was bleeding from the throat, else I'd have stopped the sessions!"

Which was the last thing Nilsson wanted to happen. He knew, as everyone knew, the mercurial nature of Lennon's attention span. If they didn't make the album now, they might never get 'round to doing it.

And so he soldiered on, jamming himself full of painkillers in time for his next date with the microphone, then crooning softly through the medley he and Lennon had designed around "Mt. Elga" and John's own, equally incomplete "Mucho Mungo" — a song, incidentally, that Lennon originally wrote for guitarist Jesse Ed Davis. Recorded on April 8, a faint calypso feel permeates the track, one that Lennon would again use to similar effect on his *Walls And Bridges* album; the song's key, however, was the sax refrain, a naggingly familiar snatch of melody that conjured up the same summer vacation feel as Nilsson's own lyrics were intended to.

Nilsson himself, however, was feeling anything but summery. One of his vocal chords had now ruptured, a condition that could easily have resulted in his losing

"He also knew when to push for perfection and when to let things slide."

# of that determination."

his range, or even his voice, forever. But he would not give up.

All the same, arriving at the studio the following day, his heart sank when he saw what was awaiting him, the massed ranks of rock 'n' roll madness, and a grinning Lennon all ready to create the album's climax. It was party time!

With Keith Moon joining Starr and Keltnet in the drum room, three saxophonists, two guitarists and a dozen backing vocalists, the Masked Alberts Kids Chorale, the menu was as maniacal as it could get: "Loop De Loop" and "Rock Around The Clock," performed to the accompaniment of a bonanza out of bounds. Nilsson, bleeding and hoarse, threw himself into the mood as well as he could, but even the most indulgent listener, familiar with the magnificent tones of "Without You" and so on, would scarcely have recognized the clipped, choking delivery Nilsson etched into the songs... but neither would anyone have realized just how bad the singer's condition now was. Nor how difficult it must have been for him to throw in an impersonation of '50s DJ Dick "Huggy Boy" Hugg at the end.

Rock 'n' roll is made to be bellowed out loud, and Nilsson simply sounds like he's been bellowing all night, a little low in the mix, a little cracked 'round the edges and a little breathless, too, as he sought to keep up with Jesse Ed Davis's lightning guitar licks. Of course it all goes on a bit too long, as most good parties tend to do, and the fast-collapsing coda that brought "Clock" to its battered conclusion registered the musicians' exhaustion. But as finales go, this one was a monster.

Like a Hollywood movie, where they film the conclusion somewhere 'round the middle, the last day of recording must have seemed anti-climactic. But Nilsson had one more song he wanted to record, and the following evening, with his voice in absolute tatters, was the ideal time to do it.

"Old Forgotten Soldier" is one of Nilsson's greatest songs. Opening, at Lennon's suggestion, to a tape of one of Hitler's speeches, it is a simple, weary lament, oozing despair, isolation and pain, a cracked blues that dissolves, as Nilsson's voice finally gave out (around the midway point, with the lyric "fired a round"), into a lonely, fading, whistle. And when the song was over, so were the sessions. Mixing, a traumatic affair as Nilsson grimaced every time he heard the sound of his scarred, scary, voice, was completed as quickly as possible. Then, while Nilsson raced home to bed, Lennon flew to New York.

One final track would be cut before *Pussy Cats* was delivered to RCA, an after-thought as it were, to break up side two's closing barrage of rock 'n' roll numbers. "Black Sails" was recorded more than two months after the original sessions ended, on June 18, although the song itself was even older than that, dating back to an abortive movie about pirates that Nilsson had been asked to write a theme for. The movie never happened, but Nilsson loved the song and didn't want to waste it. It was a smart decision on his part.

"Black Sails" is a masterpiece of lyrical punning. While the orchestra does its damnedest to recapture the desolation of so many other rock 'n' roll sea songs, Procol Harum's "A Salty Dog" their most prominent role model, Nilsson deadpans lines that defy the music's moodiness:

"A cracked blues that dissolves

"black sails in the moonlight, black patch on your eye"; "you shiver your timbers baby, and I'll shiver mine"; and best of all, "you're so veiny, you probably think this map belongs to you." Eat your heart out, Carly Simon.

The album was delivered to RCA with equal panache. According to legend, the first time label head Ken Glancy got to hear it, Nilsson and Lennon were together in his office, cackling about how they'd just completed the greatest album in the history of the world. Then Nilsson pressed the "play" button, and Glancy was assailed by the three-man percussion team that opens "Loup De Loup."

His shock was only echoed by the music press. Condemned as a self-indulgent mess, hammered for its slap-dash chaos, shot through with criminally barely realized moments of vague inspiration, *Pussy Cats* had to contend not only with its makers' own reputations, but also with its makers' old friends as well — 1974 was the year in which Paul McCartney finally stopped making records that he liked and produced one that the critics liked as well, *Band On The Run*. So far as the reviews were concerned, there was no competition, and the charts reflected the mismatch.

Despite being released in both regular stereo format and as a top-end-of the market Quadradisc, *Pussy Cats* itself could reach no higher than a lowly #60 in the U.S.; in Britain, it didn't even make the Top 75. Three singles, "Many Rivers To Cross," "Subterranean Homesick Blues" and "Don't Forget Me," slipped out unnoticed; and as if to add insult to injury, great swathes of the album have since been appended to sundry John Lennon bootlegs, where they masquerade as demos for some unknown Ringo Starr project!

But neither Lennon nor Nilsson ever regretted their efforts, and though *Pussy Cats* remains an overlooked episode in both men's illustrious careers, it was an immensely important one nevertheless.

"Whatever Gets You Through The Night," the song that would return Lennon to the #1 slot in America later in the year, was written during the *Pussy Cats* sessions; indeed, according to Lennon, speaking in a Canadian radio interview that fall, "We wrote the song together, so I put it on my album, and Harry of course wanted to sing it, because he'd been part of it, so he sang the harmonies." The pair also collaborated on "Old Dirt Road," Nilsson dropping in lyrical contributions while Lennon composed on piano, and once Lennon settled in the studio to work on what became *Walls And Bridges*, Nilsson remained ensconced alongside him.

> *" You can hear how much fun everyone was having. "*

Today, of course, both Lennon and Nilsson are dead. So are several of the musicians who worked alongside them through the *Pussy Cats* sessions. Yet of all the records that they made, *Pussy Cats* remains the one that has the most life in it, a raucous, raunchy, remarkable life that has utterly defied the passing of time. Dig it out and crank it up — you can hear how much fun everyone was having leaking out of the grooves; you can feel it in the vibrations that rattle the speakers off the wall.

And when the wind's in the right direction, you can probably smell it as well. Because, just as Nilsson affirmed a few years back, "We were all so blitzed. All of the time."

It shows. ∎

*S*ay that Yoko Ono ranks as one of the most misunderstood recording artists of our time and you'll be opening yourself up to misunderstanding as well. Few performers have generated such hatred in their lifetime, a hatred that appears to stem more from personal, rather than artistic, dislike. Certainly one can understand the confusion critics must have felt in 1970 listening to *Yoko Ono/Plastic Ono Band* without any punk/new wave frame of reference in which to place it. Yet by the 1980 release of *Double Fantasy*, critics were not only praising her music, some found it more in tune with the times than that of her collaborator's, John Lennon.

Whatever the era, Ono's work has provoked extreme opinions, and there were as many positive comments about her music in 1970 as there were critical jibes in 1980. But Ono used music and recording as part of an exploratory artistic process, constantly defining and redefining her artistic vision, creating songs that told stories, painted abstract pictures or just plain screamed.

Ono was born in 1933 and came from wealthy parents, splitting her childhood between America and her native Japan. She left studies at Sarah Lawrence College to live in New York City with her first husband and gradually worked her way into the city's burgeoning avant-garde scene, creating "happenings" out of her "instructional poems" ("Throw a stone into the sky high enough/so it will not come back"). As was to happen with her music, her work met with mixed

" Ono used music and recording as part of an exploratory artistic process, constantly defining and redefining her artistic vision, creating songs that told stories, painted abstract pictures or just plain screamed. "

receptions from the critics. But she continued to create art and in 1966 was invited to participate in a "Destruction In Art" symposium in London. Her appearance generated good reviews (the Financial Times called her performance "uplifting") and she was asked to assemble an exhibit for London's Indica Gallery, whose owners included John Dunbar (then married to Marianne Faithfull) and Peter Asher (one half of Peter & Gordon). It was on the show's preview night, Nov. 9, 1966, that she met Lennon.

Though interested in one another from the start, it wasn't until May 1968 that Lennon and Ono joined forces, both personally and profesionally. During their first night together, they made experimental tapes that would become *Unfinished Music No. 1: Two Virgins*, an album of avant-garde "noise" released in November 1968. The record pined more notoriety for its cover, which featured front and rear shots of Lennon and Ono in the nude. Though pressed on the Beatles' Apple label, EMI refused to distribute the album, leaving that duty to Track Records in the U.K. and Tetragrammaton in the U.S., who shipped the LP in a plain brown wrapper. *Two Virgins* is now one of the rarest Apple records; counterfeits have a stark white cover (the original was off-white) and a green-ish-gold wrapper instead of brown. The album was also reissued in the U.S. in 1985.

By the time of their meeting, Lennon had divorced his wife, Ono had divorced her second husband and the two began an active recording career. The Beatles' *White Album*, released in November 1968, had several contributions from Ono: backing vocals in "The Continuing Story Of Bungalow Bill" and "Birthday," and a Lennon and Ono collaboration on the aural collage "Revolution No. 9." Next, the two appeared on The Beatles' 1968 Christmas flexi-disc (a special gift for Beatles Fan Club members). Their next album was on the short-lived Zapple label, released April 1969 in the U.K., May in the U.S., *Unfinished Music No. 2: Life With The Lions*. Though lacking the controversial cover of *Two Virgins*, the contents still mystified the public, consisting of the heartbeat of Lennon and Ono's child (which Ono later miscarried), Ono reading press clippings about their activities, and their first public performance together at Cambridge University in March 1969.

In July 1969, Lennon released his first solo single, "Give Peace A Chance," with Ono's "Remember Love" on the flip, inaugurating a tradition of Lennon A-side/Ono B-side singles (all future records until 1980 on the Apple label). October 1969 saw the release of Lennon's "Cold Turkey" single with Ono's "Don't Worry Kyoko (Mummy's Only Looking For A Hand In The Snow)" on the flip. The *Wedding Album* fol-lowed, released in October in the U.S., November in the U.K., packaged in a deluxe box that featured photos, posters, a booklet of pictures and clippings and a photo of a slice of wedding cake. This box set was reissued in Japan in the late '70s. The two ended 1969 with two December releases, the 1969 Beatles Christmas flexi-disc and the album *Live Peace In Toronto*, a live LP of their spur-of-the-moment performance at Toronto's "Rock 'n' Roll Revival Show" with Eric Clapton, Klaus Voormann, and Andy White. Original issues of the album also included a 16-page calendar.

> **" It was on the show's preview night, Nov. 9, 1966, that she met Lennon. "**

The next record was Lennon's "Instant Karma!" single backed with Ono's "Who Has Seen the Wind?" released in February 1970. Their next single, released in the U.S. only, did not appear until December 1970; Lennon's "Mother" backed with Ono's "Why" were each taken from *John Lennon/Plastic Ono Band* and *Yoko Ono/Plastic Ono Band*, respectively, both albums also released in December. The screaming and vocal ranting that would provide the starting point for countless punk groups in 1976 was generally slammed by the critics in 1970. Apple also released an album containing all seven of The Beatles' Christmas flexis in December 1970.

In March 1971 Lennon's "Power To The People" single was released, with Ono's "Open Your Box" as the flip in the U.K.; censorship problems forced the two to substitute "Touch Me" (from Yoko Ono/Plastic Ono Band) as the U.S. B-side ("Open Your Box" would resurface on Fly as "Hirake"). The two then cowrote, produced and performed on "God Save Us"/"Do The Oz" along with Bill Elliot as a benefit single for the *Oz* magazine obscenity trial, released on Apple in July 1971. September 1971 saw the U.S. release of Ono's *Fly* LP (released in Britain in December) along with her first solo single, "Mrs. Lennon/Midsummer New York" (released in September in the U.S., October in the U.K.). Another Lennon and Ono 45 was released that December in the U.S., "Happy Christmas (War Is Over)/Listen, The Snow Is Falling" (not released in the U.K. until November 1972). Original issues of the single were pressed on green vinyl and featured a special photo label.

> *"It wasn't until May 1968 that Lennon and Ono joined forces."*

In January 1972, a second single was pulled from *Fly* for U.K. release only, "Mind Train/Listen, The Snow Is Falling." April saw the U.S.-only release of "Woman Is The Nigger Of The World" backed with Ono's "Sisters O Sisters." Both were from the double LP *Some Time* In New York City, released in June in the U.S., September in the U.K. (original copies had a photo label and petition insert). In November 1972, Ono released a third solo single, in the U.S. only, "Now Or Never/Move On Fast." Both songs were from *Approximately Infinite Universe*, released in January 1973 in the U.S., February in the U.K. A second single from the LP, "Death Of Samantha/Yang Yang," was released in February in the U.S., May in the U.K. At this time, Lennon and Ono separated and did not collaborate musically until 1980.

Ono's next single, released in September 1973 in the U.S. only, was "Woman Power/Men, Men, Men," from Feeling The Space, released that November. November also saw the U.K.-only release of "Run, Run, Run/Men, Men, Men." There were also three Japan-only releases in 1973, the LP *Welcome (The Many Sides Of Yoko Only)*, containing previously released material, and the single "Josei Joi Banzai/Josei Joi Banzai (Part 2)." This was followed by another Japan-only release in 1974 (on the Odeon label), "Yume O Motou (Let's Have A Dream)/It Happened."

There were no new Ono releases until 1980, though in October 1975 Apple released *Shaved Fish*, a Lennon "greatest hits" collection, with a snippet of "Give Peace A Chance" and "Happy Christmas" (which had Ono on backing vocals). In 1976, Polydor released The Beatles

Tapes in the U.K. only, a double album of interviews by David Wigg; Lennon and Ono are interviewed on side one. Meanwhile, Lennon and Ono had reunited, Lennon had received his green card allowing him resident status in the U.S., and the two finally gave birth to a child, Sean Ono Lennon. Both then retired from the music world, Lennon concentrating on raising his son and Ono attending to their business affairs.

In the summer of 1980, it was announced that Lennon and Ono had returned to the recording studios. That October, Lennon's "Starting Over" backed with Ono's "Kiss, Kiss, Kiss" was released on Geffen Records, and the album *Double Fantasy* followed in November. The LP had Lennon and Ono alternating tracks, and the critics singled out Ono's "new wave" sound as being especially accessible. Sales of the album soared after Lennon's tragic death in December, and two more singles were released (following the Lennon A-side/Ono B-side pattern), "Woman/Beautiful Boys" (released in January 1981) and "Watching The Wheels/I'm Your Angel" (released in March 1981). Ono also released a solo single in February ,1981, "Walking On Thin Ice/It Happened," released as a 7- and 12-inch single and a special cassette single, with the additional track "Hard Times Are Over" (from *Double Fantasy*) on the latter two. The single was Ono's first solo chart hit, reaching #33 in the *Billboard* charts and #13 in *Billboard's* Disco Club Play chart.

In June 1981 Ono released *Season Of Glass*, which again featured a controversial cover, this time a shot of Lennon's blood-stained spectacles. Ono made no apologies for the photo, stating "If people can't stomach the glasses, I'm

> *"People are offended by the glasses and the blood?..."*

sorry. There was a dead body. There was blood... that's the reality... People are offended by the glasses and the blood? Lennon had to stomach a lot more." Ono's anger permeated the tracks on the LP with a mixture of sadness and hostility, punctuated by gunshots (the opening of "No, No, No") and curses ("You bastards! Hate us, hate me... we had everything!" from "I Don't Know"). The LP reached #49 in the U.S. charts. August saw the U.S.-only release of "No, No, No/Will You Touch Me," released in 7- and 12-inch formats. In September another U.S.-only single was released, "Goodbye Sadness/I Don't Know Why."

There were no new Ono releases until 1982, by which time she'd left Geffen and signed with Polydor. "My Man/Let The Tears Dry" was released in November in the U.S., December in the U.K., from the album It's Alright, released shortly after the single in each country. Geffen also released *The John Lennon Collection* in November 1982, with a full version of "Give Peace A Chance" and "Happy Xmas." "Happy Xmas" was also released as a single backed with "Beautiful Boy" in 7- and 12-inch formats (the latter a promo-only release). In February 1983 a second single was released from It's Alright in the U.S. only, "Never Say Good-bye"/"Loneliness," in 7- and 12-inch formats (the latter with extended versions of each song).

In December 1983, Polydor released *Heart Play*, an interview album from Lennon and Ono's lengthy *Playboy* interviews in late 1980. January 1984 saw the release of *Milk And Honey*, the intended follow-up to *Double Fantasy*, with a similar sequencing of Lennon/Ono alternating tracks, also released as a picture disc. There were three singles from the LP, "Nobody told Me/O' Sanity" (released in

...Lennon had to stomach

January 1984), "I'm Stepping Out/Sleepless Night" released in the U.S. only, and "Borrowed Time/Your Hands," released in the U.S. and U.K. with a special 12-inch release in Britain that included a poster and the additional track, "Never Say Goodbye." In addition, Polydor released *Every Man Has A Woman Who Loves Him* in 1984, a compilation album with artists as varied as Lennon, Elvis Costello, Roberta Flack, and Rosanne Cash covering different Ono songs. A biography, *Yoko Ono: Then & Now* was also released as a video, featuring interviews and clips from her video work.

Ono's "Hell In Paradise" single (backed with an instrumental version of the song) was released in October 1985 in both seven- and 12-inch formats, the 12-inch featuring an extended mix of the song. The 12-inch hit #16 in *Billboard's* Disco Sales chart and #12 in the Club Play chart. The song was from Ono's *Starpeace* album, released in 1985. This was followed in 1986 by the ill-fated Starpeace tour, where poor ticket sales generated the usual mix of positive and negative critical jibes.

1986 also saw the release of *John Lennon Live In New York* City on record (Capitol) and video, a live documentation of Lennon and Ono's One To One benefit performances in 1972. As well as singing backup, Ono performs two numbers on the video, "Sisters O Sisters" and "Born In A Prison." Lennon and Ono's "home movie" *Imagine* was also released in 1986, with two songs from *Fly*, "Don't Count The Waves" and "Mrs. Lennon" (the original Imagine film also included Ono's "Mind Train" and "Midsummer New York"). Ono's last record, released in April 1986 in the U.S. only, was a 12-inch

> *"If it brought John back, I'd rather remain hated."*

single with two remixed of "Cape Clear" (from Starpeace) and a remix of "Walking On Thin Ice."

Since Lennon's death, Ono and her music have gained a grudging respect, though, she says, "Did the world have to lose Lennon for people to change their opinion of me? It's unreal. If it brought John back, I'd rather remain hated."

One can see the roots of the new wave in seminal recordings such as *Yoko Ono/Plastic Ono Band*, and the assimilation of her avant-garde stance into the mainstream Top 40 makes her hit singles "Walking On Thin Ice" and "Hell In Paradise" sound almost conventional. Ono has always mixed her artistic influences into her music, which is why pop music critics have frequently decried her music. But this lack of acceptance is what gives Ono's music its edge, sometimes harsh and grating, sometimes sweeping and mysterious, but always something that elicits a strong reaction from the listener, the true end of any artistic endeavor. ■

■ *The Life With The Lions LP.*

■ *Michael Leshnov photo*

JOHN LENNON AND YOKO ONO WEEK

Love Calls

THE INSIDE STORY   By Gillian G. Gaar

*D*uring most of their time as a couple, John Lennon and Yoko Ono seemed unfamiliar with the concept of "down time." From the moment they joined forces in May 1968, the couple made a wide variety of public appearances, including live performances, art exhibits and interviews with all manner of media, compulsively recording their activities all the time.

1972 would prove to be no exception. Lennon and Ono had moved to New York City the previous September, in an attempt to gain custody of Ono's daughter, Kyoko, from her previous marriage. Within a month they appeared on "The Dick Cavett Show," and during the rest of 1971 they worked on new music, filmed segments for their "home movie" *Imagine*, recorded the single "Happy Christmas (War Is Over)/Listen The Snow Is Falling," appeared in concert in Ann Arbor and at a benefit in Harlem and fraternized with political activists such as Abbie Hoffman and Jerry Rubin.

They began 1972 with another TV appearance, this time "The David Frost Show." During the same period, they began taping a week's worth of appearances for their most high-pro-file TV engagement yet — "The Mike Douglas Show."

> *"It was a fascinating experiment in using the most conventional kind of mass media to put across the idea of John and Yoko and their friends."*

ON "THE MIKE DOUGLAS SHOW"

Not only did Lennon and Ono cohost the show for a week, they also helped select the guests that appeared on the show with them. "It was a fascinating experiment in using the most conventional kind of mass media to put across the idea of John and Yoko and their friends," said Jon Wiener, author of the acclaimed book *Come Together: John Lennon In His Time*. "They weren't just being guests, pitching their own project. They ran the whole week! I don't think that's ever happened before or since. They wanted to try to get their ideas into the mainstream, into middle America, into the middle of the day! So it was an amazing idea."

"The Mike Douglas Show" was one of the top-rated talk/variety shows of the time, airing every weekday and catering to an audience Mike Douglas describes as "Housewives and youngsters coming home from school." The week of Feb. 14-18, 1972, this audience was confronted with an astonishing array of guests on the show not only including Lennon and Ono, but also Chuck Berry, Jerry Rubin, Black Panthers chairman Bobby Seale, consumer activist Ralph Nader, comedian George Carlin, and U.S. Surgeon General Dr. Jesse Steinfeld. The shows have been staples on the Beatles bootleg circuit for years; later, in 1996, they aired in edited versions on VH-1. Now Rhino Video has packaged the entire week's worth of unedited shows in a box set, *The Mike Douglas Show With John Lennon And Yoko Ono*.

In addition to the five tapes, the set also includes a hard-bound booklet with liner notes, including interviews with peo-ple who worked on the show. But in the 26 years since the show originally aired, memories can change,

> " *They wanted to try to get their ideas into the mainstream,...*

and both Douglas and the show's executive producer, Woody Fraser, have a different take on what went on during the production and taping of the shows than the booklet's other interviewees, beginning with how Lennon and Ono came to be on the show in the first place. Though the booklet states the Mike Douglas staff contacted Lennon and Ono, Fraser said it might have been the other way around.

"I think they called Mike," he said. "But I can't remember exactly. I just know that somebody came in to me and said, 'What would you think of John and Yoko being on the show?' And of course we all flipped. But you know, you get a lot of that. Somebody might call up and say, 'Hey, we got Mel Gibson for a week!' And then you call back and you find out no. So I said, 'You've got make sure this is a legitimate situation.'"

The booking turned out to be legitimate, and Douglas' reaction was not surprising: "I was elated. Everybody doing a talk show wanted them!"

Most reviews of the set have focused on the audacity of Lennon and Ono airing their unconventional views in such a mainstream format. Yet "The Mike Douglas Show" was unconventional in its own way. Despite being named after the host, Fraser explains the idea behind the show was spotlighting the guests.

"When I was a kid, I used to watch all these shows, Arthur Godfrey and all these people," he said. "And if you're the guest, they're not interested in you. You're just there as a ploy for them to talk more. And so that was when I got this

...into the middle of the day!"

idea. I wanted a guy or a woman who was a total catalyst, meaning, they're going to make you look good. And it just didn't exist in those days. I wanted the host to be able to do everything: sing, dance, get hit in the face with a pie, ask a serious question. And all within the confines of one show.

"That's how I ended up with Mike, because Mike is that kind of guy," Fraser continued. "It didn't bother him to sit there day in and day out for over 20 years and make the guest the star. And that never changed. He never once said, 'I don't need the cohost, I don't want the cohost.' He never turned to me and said that. I've never been with anybody like that since."

Indeed, one of the most striking aspects of the shows is how much the guests are actually allowed to speak, engaging in bonafide conversations with Douglas, as opposed to the soundbite interview format common on most of today's talk shows.

"I'm one of the few good listeners left in the world."

"I think that's because of the fact that I'm one of the few good listeners left in this world!" said Douglas. "I don't think there are many of them left on television today that listen very well. Some of the best interviews on television, I hear things go by and say, 'Whoa! Why did she let that get away?'"

Having weekly cohosts added freshness to the format, "So each Monday you get to look forward to a brand-new show, essentially," said Fraser, who added that the show was also no stranger to controversy, bringing on guests such as Malcolm X, Jimmy Hoffa, and Martha Mitchell — the latter guest attracting the attention of the White House.

"They called Westinghouse [the show's sponsor] saying, 'Don't put this alcoholic woman on there!' and they were threatening all sorts of stuff," Fraser said. "I can't tell you what I went through with the executives and the legal department at Westinghouse. I ended up putting her on, but I do try to balance it with fun. It's not my intention to do a "Cross-fire." We were criticized by a lot of people who said, 'You're an entertainment show. You have no right to put those kinds of things on.' But it never bothered me. And the way I housed it, billed it and kept a lot of high entertainment and fun in the show, we kept the audience."

"We aimed for the variety," Douglas agreed. "I mean, television, let's face it, it's an entertainment medium. And we didn't try to book controversial things just to titillate the audience, but because we thought people were interested. Because when every time you pick up a newspaper and you're reading about a certain person, obviously people want to see that person on television because it's a whole different world. To see how they'll react to what I would say to them and all. And the fact that I would have them on in the first place; 'Why is he having so and so on the show? He doesn't seem like somebody Mike would want to talk with.'"

Both Fraser and Douglas agree their show's format was probably what enticed Lennon and Ono in the first place, though Ono's previous appearance on the show was undoubtedly another key factor. "I really don't know the genesis of how it happened or what caused them to want to do the show, other than the fact that they were fans of the show," Fraser said. "But I do believe they felt that Mike Douglas would not attack them. They looked at this show,

"W aim d for th vari ty."

and they saw that this is a forum. And what we said we were going to do we always delivered."

"I think they felt they would just be more comfortable with me," Douglas agreed. "They were way ahead of their time. And much of what they said I must admit I was in total agreement with. As an example, the war in Vietnam, which I thought was a terrible, terrible mistake on our part. But you couldn't express those opinions in those days. If you did, you alienated half, or more than half, of your audience. So I couldn't express myself the way I would've liked to have. But it was interesting. And I think a lot of people watched in disbelief, first of all, never thinking that I would ever have them on a show. And secondly, some of the things he said."

Douglas himself couldn't believe some of the things the couple said, starting with their suggestions for potential guests. "When we said, 'Who would you like to have on the show?' I'll never forget it as long as I live, John said, 'The Chicago Seven,'" he said. "And everybody laughed, thinking he was joking. But he wasn't joking! He meant it!" But on Fraser's part, the variety of guests would only help present a more well-rounded view of his cohosts. "My philosophy was, if I'm going to have John and Yoko on for a week, then I want to make it as much their show as I can," he said. "So we sit with them and find out their interests. And I try to get them out of the music area: Are you interested in poetry? What else are you interested in?

"At the same time, I have to bring other things into the show," he added. "If somebody's finished a hot movie, I have to keep that open. So it's not like Lennon and Yoko

> ❝*I think they felt they would just be more comfortable with me.*❞

are getting a full 90 minutes. They were the biggest booking the show ever had, so everybody bent over backwards to get everybody that they wanted. However, we reached a point where the decision was we need a little bit more balance of entertainment stuff in there. And John was fine with that. But Yoko was not fine with that. She had a definite agenda. Matter of fact, I think she was the one that really decided to do this; she was the deciding factor about them doing it. 'Cause if you were around them, you would see very quickly that she runs the show. And John was very much in love with her, and he was very concilliatory toward her. I wouldn't say he was a wimp, at all. Nobody ever said this to me, but it just became apparent that he was really kind of doing this for her."

There was also the attraction of reaching directly into the homes of a new audience (not to mention attracting a new audience to watch the show). "John and Yoko were interested not just in reaching the kids, the hip people, the rock 'n' rollers, they wanted to try to talk to everybody," said Wiener. "And they thought everybody might be interested! Or at least it was worth a try to find out. That's what never happened before. And because Lennon had the celebrity power, he was able to get the hours of TV. I don't think today anyone would get that many hours. They would have their own 12-minute segment or something like that. So it was a unique commitment on their part, breaking out of the rock 'n' roll mold, and the unique situation of Lennon's position that gave him the power to try to do this. And the couple's own interest in experimenting."

A few other concessions were in order before taping could begin. Instead of taping all the shows over the course of a

"They wanted to try to talk to everybody."

week, as was usual, Lennon and Ono's schedule was such that they could only come down one day a week, so that the five shows were taped over the course of five weeks. "I would much prefer to have done it the other way," said Douglas. "It's so much easier. You build kind of a momentum, and then you have to detach yourself from it, and then suddenly here they are again. And you're going, 'Wait a minute, I've gotta get back on that planet, on that level.' You go, 'Whoa, John and Yoko today!'"

Fraser and Douglas have different memories of how the shows were taped. "We just shot on an extra day," Fraser said. "We didn't do another show the day they did theirs." Told that the Rhino booklet, and Douglas, state that a regular show and a Lennon/Ono show would be taped on one day, he conceded, "We may have done it once or twice that way because of their scheduling problems." But whatever the circumstances, Fraser agreed the work amounted to "a long tape day, 'cause there were a lot of stop-downs. Though as far as everybody was concerned, they were used to working very hard. There was no hardship at all. Everybody was so excited. Everybody was walking on air. John Lennon and Yoko, please!"

Fraser explains how a day's taping was put together. "At 9 o'clock in the morning, I meet with the staff," he said. "There's a person assigned to the cohost, and there's a person assigned to the other individual guests — segment producers. Their job is to put together an interview. At 10 o'clock, rehearsal starts. And at the same time, I bring one segment producer in at a time to Mike with the cards. Everything was on cards for Mike, all the questions. And we'd run through the cards. Then Mike would go down to rehearsal about 11 o'clock."

As for rehearsals with Lennon and Ono, Fraser said, "All the problems were musical, pure and simple. We'd go in at 10 and tape at 1; that's three hours, but we really had only two and a half, because at 12:30 you've got to break down, and you've got to get everybody ready to do the show. So we'd try to get all the soundchecks done and try to get Yoko and Lennon's music stuff done. But their framework of what it takes to do a song is totally different than what it takes for us to do on a show, where we're doing a show every day, live.

"All the problems were musical, pure and simple."

"The other thing is, they may have to add musicians, bring in a conductor, add side pieces, extra musicians, then we have to make room for that, and we have to have new micro-phones and we have to have some lighting, and then we have to balance that sound," Fraser continued. "And to be honest, we were woefully lacking in what they would be used to having in a sound studio. So the majority of the time was spent setting up the instruments and doing soundchecks and then getting a sound balance.

"That is really the most difficult part. Especially when they're playing and singing at the same time. They have to hear themselves. Musicians and singers are nuts about hearing themselves. And also, she had to get used to our musicians, and John had to get used to our musicians. He was easy. He was very easy. She was difficult because her music is complicated and different. And she is a composer and so she wants to hear certain things. And if she can't hear the flute, then you've got to stop until you

"Everything's a compromise."

can hear the flute. Then we may hear the flute, but we can't hear the drums. I find some of her music really interesting. I call it metaphysical jazz. Metaphysical jazz-rock. But to be heard over that little television box — you didn't have the big stereo stuff like we do today.

"So we never taped on time, because we had to make sure that the music was right. Once it started, I think it only took about two hours. But we were always late starting. But nobody ever complained, because it was John and Yoko. The audience? They would've waited until midnight! They didn't care."

There were further problems in simply deciding how many songs the couple would perform — and who would perform them. "When the deal was made, the deal was that John would perform three songs every day and she would perform one," Fraser said. "And then when they came in on the first day of taping, she rolled out three songs and he rolled out one. And of course I had to discuss with him, this was not the deal. And she did not take kindly to this. But he finally agreed he would do two and she would do two. Everything's a compromise. But that kind of set her off with an attitude for the week. All she was really interested in was playing her music. That's when I got in trouble. And then I have to go through this summit meeting to get them to change it. And she was not a happy camper. Which I guess anybody wouldn't be — she just wants to play her stuff. It's not that I think her stuff is bad. It's that you've got John Lennon. I mean, come on. You want to get as much of John Lennon as you can."

Actually, over the course of the week, Lennon and Ono performed two songs each. Lennon's performances of "It's So Hard" on Monday, Ono's "Midsummer New York" on Tuesday and Lennon's "Imagine" on Thursday, backed by the New York-based Elephant's Memory Band, were the week's

strongest musical numbers. Ono also performed "Sisters O Sisters" on Wednesday, accompanied by Lennon, and the two performed "Luck Of The Irish" together on Friday. Additional music spots included Lennon and Chuck Berry performing raucous versions of "Memphis" and "Johnny B. Goode" on Wednesday and clips from the Imagine film: "Oh My Love" (Lennon, Tuesday), "Crippled Inside" (Lennon, Wednesday), "Mrs. Lennon" (Ono, Thursday), and "How" (Lennon, Friday).

The shows are a fascinating depiction of the meeting — and sometimes clashing — of two cultures. Ono created a number of conceptual art pieces, taking a broken cup and mending it piece by piece over the week, and starting off an "Unfinished Painting," a bare canvas guests and the audience were invited to draw on, that was supposed to be auctioned off for charity. Jerry Rubin squared off with U.S. Surgeon General Dr. Jesse Steinfeld in the show's most volatile exchange on Tuesday, when Rubin casually denounced Presi-dent Nixon as a "pig," and Douglas and Steinfeld came out strongly in favor of the American mainstream. Bobby Seale, who appeared on Thursday, was much softer spoken.

On Tuesday, Douglas naturally posed the question asked by every journalist of the era who interviewed an ex-Fab; would The Beatles ever reunite? "There's no reason why they never should do it again, but there's no reason why they should," Lennon evenly responded. Douglas also inadvertently revealed his gender/generation gap during a discussion on "women's lib," welcoming attorney Rene Uviller on the show with the comment "Very pretty attorney… I wouldn't be a bit disturbed by your bill!"

Other guests were quick to get into the spirit of things. On Monday, Ono set up her "Love Calls" piece, calling people at random to say "I love you." In the booklet, the show's bandleader, Joe Harnell, said it took an hour to complete this piece alone, as the recipients of the calls inevitably fired off an

"...she was not a happy camper."

expletive and hung up — something neither Fraser or Douglas remember. "I don't recall that happening," said Douglas. "We stopped for commercial breaks. That's it. It was 90 minutes straight ahead. It's very, very difficult to do it the other way. Stopping and starting over. Especially when the show's peaking and it's at a great level. We wanted to do the show as though it were a live show."

But it's clear from the video edit that a "stop tape" of some length occurred, with comedian Louie Nye eventually saving the segment, reaching a woman in Seattle who warmly thanks Nye for his "love call," saying, "And you have a nice day!" Douglas is then inspired to call David Frost, who was unavailable. There's also a clear intimacy between the guests and the audience, due to the studio's small size. "There were only about 150 people in the audience and they were only about 12-14 feet from the guests," said Fraser. "So you're really right there. It's not like you're sitting at "The Tonight Show" where there's a huge gap. You're right on them."

Wiener cites the variety of guests as a reason why the week turned out to be so successful. "Having Chuck Berry and Bobby Seale — those kind of juxtapositions were what really turned me on," he said. "That it wasn't just political rapping, talking. Everything they could think of they put on there. And Yoko's calling people up; when you just explain it, it seems kind of simple and maybe not that interesting. But when she does it, it's completely fascinating."

But Douglas admitted Lennon and Ono's ideas weren't always easy to work with. "I can't say they were easy," he said. "It was a challenge. It really was. It was very challeng-ing, what their reaction would be to certain things that we were doing. And they had to be consulted on everything we planned to do. And then their segments — on some of the things they did, I really didn't know where they were going. I had to figure it out myself while we were doing it! Like break-

ing the cup and putting it together. What was the meaning of this? People trying to piece their lives together or what?"

Neither does he have an answer for a more concrete question: Whatever happened to Ono's "Unfinished Painting," which evidently did not get auctioned for charity? "I really wish I could answer that question!" he laughed. "It's not in my collection of paintings, I'll tell you that!"

Douglas also had concerns about how the guest roster would gel. "You constantly worry about that," he said. "Every day you go in and you think, 'Will the chemistry be right today?' And sometimes you're terribly let down. Sometimes John and Yoko were looking at Louis Nye wondering what planet he was from. And I'm sure he was looking at them and the things they were doing. And then when they started making phone calls and telling people 'I love you,' I thought he was very funny in that segment. He was hysterical. They couldn't figure out whether he was being comedic or doing a straight thing, a straight conversation."

Things didn't always go smoothly behind the scenes either. Some conflicts are detailed in the video set's booklet, though Douglas denied Harnell's contention that the couple smoked marijuana.

"I wasn't aware of any of that," he said. "And usually I can read people when something like that is happening to them. I can see it in their eyes. You forget, I'm a former band singer! And I didn't see any of that on the show. I didn't see it in John, I didn't see it in Yoko."

But he added, "I'll be very, very honest with you, it wasn't easy for the staff. And I heard about it all the time. They were very, she especially, I don't want to say anything to alienate anyone, but she was very rough on the staff. She made demands. And some of the things that they wanted we couldn't come up with. It was very tough. The kids were very young though, and probably fans when they arrived, and probably terribly let down at some of the behavior, but hey, listen, we live with that constantly.

"But it was worth it," he continued. "It was not like one of my normal weeks. It was entirely different. But it's great. It gets you to another level, I think. It was very challenging for me. And I think it was interesting for the viewers."

Fraser, too, agreed that there were conflicts but declines to get specific. "I will tell you that there were some people on the crew that disagreed with them politically," he said. "And [that] would be the extent of what I would want to say. But everybody did their job, and everybody will always remem-ber that week, and everybody on the crew that talks about it, talks about it only the most glowing terms."

Except, perhaps, in Rhino's booklet.

But Fraser also pointed out that even people associated with the show who disagreed with the couple's views weren't immune to their star power. "They were without a doubt the biggest stars we ever had on the show," he said, "and that brought a lot of attention from people that had stopped pay-ing attention to the show within the organization. We suddenly had executives that I hadn't seen in three years hanging around! And people taking interest in the show that never bothered me before, like censors and lawyers. And there were a lot of people, if you're a real conservative and not a music lover, that were not overly fond of John Lennon. But you know what, all those people showed up at the stu-dio. You never saw a studio so filled in your life with people. Lot of security too."

But there was more to the show than backstage heaviness, and Douglas has no hesitation when asked to cite a high point. "The favorite moment for me, because I wasn't a part of it, I

happily got to sit there like the audience, was Chuck Berry," he said. "That turned out to be the best show of the week. 'Cause it was so genuine, John's reaction. Here's the man who was responsible for the kind of music he played. Started it all. That was his idol. He was truly in awe of this man. Imagine a fellow at that level, the level of John Lennon, being in awe of anything! He was like a child with a new toy. It was so infectious just watching it."

Nonetheless, despite the lure of Lennon and Ono and their roster of friends, Douglas said the public response "was kind of mixed. A lot of the people were elated and thrilled that we had them on and thanked us for it. And others were terribly upset about it because of his views and all. I don't have to tell you that that was not the way the world was thinking at the time! But the ratings just went through the roof, because we kept our regular audience and we added to it. I used to get my hair cut in an area called Society Hill, which was a very hip area. And I'd get out of my car and start walking to the shop, and I'd get, 'Yeah, cool Mike, right on!' Suddenly they knew me and called me by my first name."

One segment of the viewing public Douglas did not hear from were agents from the FBI, who took notes on the proceedings, transcribing Jerry Rubin's interview.

"It does seem ridiculous, but it is what the FBI thought their job was," said Wiener. "Jerry Rubin told jokes about Nixon. They wrote it all down. They got mixed up about a lot of things. They didn't really understand the '60s very well."

In fact, U.S. government agencies were already moving against the couple. In a memo dated Feb. 4, Senator Strom Thurmond discussed with Attorney General John Mitchell the possibility of deporting Lennon. And on Feb. 15, FBI director J. Edgar Hoover directed FBI offices around the country to keep tabs on Lennon and Ono's activities.

But at the time of "The Mike Douglas Show" tapings, the two were unaware of the impending trouble looming on horizon. "This was a fairly up time for them," Wiener agreed. "The deportation thing was beginning, but it didn't really get that heavy until later in the spring. So they weren't in legal defense mode, and I think you see that in the exuberance with which they did these shows. The decision had already been made in the Nixon administration that they were going to go after Lennon, but John and Yoko don't know it yet. So that's why they're so cheerful and happy. They're still enjoying life in New York and don't realize how much trouble they're about to be in."

But though Lennon was outspoken in his beliefs, he was hardly a revolutionary; during the "Mike Douglas" shows he repeatedly stressed that any societal change should be nonviolent in nature; he also praised the efforts of people such as Bobby Seale and Nader to organize people to help themselves. Why then was the U.S. government so threatened by his activities?

"One answer is, 'Oh, Nixon was just paranoid,'" said Wiener. "'He worried about everything.' But you have to remember that 1972 was a presidential election year. And this was the first year 18-year-olds had the right to vote, so there were going to be millions of first-time voters. And it was widely believed that young people were the basic anti-war constituency.

"But anyone that knew anything about politics knew that young voters were the least likely to vote of all age groups," Wiener continued. "So the question was, what would it take to get these new voters to go to the polls and vote, presumably against Nixon? Well, Lennon's plan, this is what the Thurmond memo was about, was a national concert tour that would mobilize young people to register to vote and to vote against the war, which meant against Nixon. This was

something that Lennon's celebrity and power might be able to accomplish. And Nixon took it seriously and he was right to do so. So that's why they wanted to get rid of Lennon. Nixon abused the power of the White House against his enemies; that's what Watergate was about. And Lennon was just one of the many targets of this Watergate-style operation."

The U.S. government formally moved against Lennon in March 1972, when they filed a deportation order against him; Lennon appealed. But the escalating immigration problems hardly dampened Lennon and Ono's activities. During the rest of '72 they recorded their joint album *Some Time In New York City* and Ono's *Approximately Infinite Universe*, produced albums by the Elephant's Memory Band and David Peel and made a few concert appearances, notably the "One To One" charity shows held at Madison Square Garden on Aug. 30; an appearance on the Jerry Lewis Telethon followed on Sept. 6. The Imagine film debuted on TV in December. Lennon even found time to appear on "The Dick Cavett Show," insisting the government's harassment included tailing him and tapping his phone, a complaint not believed at the time.

Lennon finally won his immigration battle in October 1975, when the U.S. Court Of Appeals overturned the Immigration And Naturalization Service deportation order. He was granted permanent residency the following July. By then, it was widely known that the FBI had kept track of all of Lennon's activities during the early '70s, including his "Mike Douglas Show" appearances.

"It wasn't that great a surprise, considering what he was up to and the things he was saying," said Douglas, adding, "and that was when Hoover was alive, too."

Douglas had another Beatle on his show when Ringo Starr

appeared on April 17, 1978. He also invited Lennon to make a return appearance in December 1980. "We were doing a week in Honolulu," he said. "And John was booked as a guest. He'd accepted the invitation, and then called again saying, 'I'm sorry, I'm going to have to cancel. I'm busily working on an album, and I can't get away.' He wanted desperately to get over there and do it. And two days later he was murdered. That's absolutely true. So that was terribly unfortunate."

"The Mike Douglas Show" was canceled in 1982, and for years the only way to see the episodes was through bootleg tapes found on the collector's circuit. Douglas himself became aware of bootlegs when a friend's son told him he'd bought tapes of his shows from a dealer in the Los Angeles area. Douglas visited the dealer and bought a tape himself, then contacted Westinghouse.

"I said, 'Are you aware this is going on?' And they of course said no." Douglas had also noted that portions of his show were being aired in foreign markets without appropriate fees being paid, such as footage of an appearance future golf star Tiger Woods made on the show when he was 2 years old.

"Please tell me how Nippon Television got a copy of the tape!" said Douglas. "It played everywhere on earth. And they're so cute. They admit to having played it, but they don't want to say where they got it! All kinds of things like that were happening, which I could do nothing about. The union didn't back anybody up on things like that."

The Rhino set marks the first time the shows have been commercially available in their entirety, something a writer like Wiener would have welcomed at the time he was working on *Come Together*. "Virtually anything any of The Beatles ever did somebody has collected," he said. "But it

was really hard work to track down a full set of these. I ended up just getting them on audio after working for weeks answering ads in fan magazines and talking to collectors. So to have them so easily accessible is just a dream."

Douglas said that the set's importance stands not just as an entertainment package, but as a historical document. "No question about it," he said. "Though I should really say that at the time I wasn't aware it was going to have this kind of an impact. I really wasn't. I thought, 'Well, it'll get good ratings,' but my God, people are still playing these things and people are buying them for their own libraries. So I didn't realize at the time that it would be that strong, quite honestly."

Finally, *The Mike Douglas Show With John Lennon And Yoko Ono* is important in that it chronicles an often downplayed side of Lennon's life, his politics. Since Lennon's death in 1980, the sanctification of what Paul McCartney has called his "Martin Luther Lennon" side has tended to dismiss his political work as a fad. But, as Wiener emphasized, "John and Yoko's involvement in politics was total. They didn't just raise money, it was their life. It was a time when if all you did was raise money for the things you believed in, you'd be a bour-geois sellout. No, the commitment was what made life meaningful, and you wanted your art and your life to be the same thing. That was what made him important."

And as to the specific shows themselves, Wiener said, "I think they're an intense and vivid example of how open he was to experimenting with communicating a political message in forms that rock 'n' rollers had never tried before. And that open experimental attitude, that willingness to try new things, especially things that seemed hopelessly conventional like daytime TV, is part of what made Lennon so interesting and so appealing." ■

■ *This story originally appeared in the Nov. 6, 1998, issue of Goldmine.*

Double Fantasy

THE MAKING OF

AN INTERVIEW WITH PRODUCER JACK DOUGLAS | By Ken Sharp

When you're John Lennon, you can take your pick of who you'd like to produce your first new studio album in five years. It was Jack Douglas who got the call. Entering New York's Record Plant Studios in the summer of 1980, Douglas commanded production chores for John Lennon And Yoko Ono's comeback album Double Fantasy.

A respected producer whose golden track record includes working with the likes of Aerosmith (Douglas manned the controls behind many of the group's most successful '70s albums including *Rocks*, *Get Your Wings* and *Toys In The Attic*), Cheap Trick, and The Knack, Douglas quickly gained Lennon and Ono's trust and confidence, injecting the sessions with a contagious jubilance and laid-back authority. Yet on Dec. 8, 1980, it would all come to a crashing halt. Having just bid goodbye to Lennon and Ono after a hard day's night mixing Ono's single, "Walking On Thin Ice," Douglas was stunned with the news of the assassination of his friend and musical legend. *Goldmine* sat down with Douglas for a fascinating hands-on look at the making of Lennon and Ono's last studio work.

Goldmine: Tell us how Cheap Trick, specifically Bun E. Carlos and Rick Nielsen, became involved with Lennon and Ono on the Double Fantasy *album. Was Lennon aware of Cheap Trick?*

Jack Douglas: No. He had no idea who they were. He thinks he might have heard of them, but here was the thing — it was like, it was they were so

"Who are those guys?"

influenced by The Beatles that it just seemed to make perfect sense to me. Had we continued along those lines, I would have had Robin in there singing backgroundswith them.

That's what I heard; he was scheduled to sing.

Yeah, I mean, it just would have been an absolutely perfect relationship. Those guys....

How did you get them involved? What do you remember about the day?

I remember calling up Ken Adamany [Cheap Trick's manager] first to arrange it, to see if it could be done. I remember Ken giving me the hardest time about the, you know, "Well, will they pay their airfare?" and I'm like, "Hello, I'm asking you to come up and have the guys play with John Lennon," you know? So don't worry about that stuff, please. [He said,] "Well, will we get a piece of the record?" I'm like, "Ken, man, let's get going. Talk to the band and see what they want to do," and they were like, "Of course!" I knew that those guys were big fans, just as big a fan as I was of John, and it was like, two reasons I did it, because I knew it was a perfect marriage for John and I did it 'cause I love the band. I love Cheap Trick. I love those guys.

I've heard the band's track with Ono, "I'm Moving On," and that was quite good as well.

Yeah, "Moving On."

I kind of wish Cheap Trick played on the entire album. Cheap Trick with Lennon on "I'm Losing You" sounds like a hit record.

Yeah.

It's in your face.

It's the lead track.

What do you remember about the day Nielsen and Carlos played with Lennon? Was Lennon charged up?

Yeah... it was so cool. So I let them know that these guys were coming up to cut this track because I felt these were the guys to cut this track, and if we were going to cut more, I wanted to see at least if there was some chemistry and...

Did you send them a tape of the track prior?

No, I don't think so. No, I didn't at all for sure 'cause there's no way I would ever part with those tapes. So the guys came up, they went out in the studio, they started to jam the tune, I played the demo for them there in the studio, Bun E. fell right into it, and John was out there like digging it. Tony Levin, you know, amazing bass player anyway, got into agroove, and Rick came up with ba-ba-da-dada, he came up with the part and then Rick and John were both playing live together and it was just, I mean, it was magic immediately in the room. You could feel it.

He dug 'em?

He absolutely dug 'em. He came in during a break and he said, "Who are those guys?" I said, "Well, they're Cheap Trick, you know, they're a band. They're like your happening." In fact, [The Beatles' producer] George Martin was producing them at that time, which was really funny because I remember having a talk with George about, you know, "You got my act and I got yours," you know.

Do you think Lennon later investigated, to want to hear what they were doing? No. He never did, but he did find out. He did ask. He said to somebody, "You know, I just did some tracks with these guys Cheap Trick" and everybody said, "Yeah, well they're really cool!" He later told me, "Oh yeah, I heard they were a pretty good band." But while it was happening, he just loved it. He said, "Jack, these guys are great," and he loved Rick. He loved him. That's his kind of madman.

Were they a little reserved, do you think?

They were only nervous for a few minutes, but you have to understand it was difficult to be nervous around John because he was the kind of person to put you at ease like immediately. That was part of his magic. So you know, he was a musician, and when he met other musicians, he just got right into it. He just, he spoke that language. He wasn't just like, "John Lennon, Beatle." He was a guy who wanted to play and have fun. More than anything, that was what he lived for, you know, playing.

Those tracks are so exciting and so vital-sound-ing. Why do you think they didn't make the record?

Because Yoko... first she thought, you know, the first part was, "Who are these guys?" She got really mad at me after a while. She said, "Who are these guys and why should they get a free ride on John's coat-tails?" I can remember trying to explain to Yoko, "No, Yoko, it's not like that. If anything, because of where they're at in their career right now, it'll make John seem even hipper that he would know to have these guys come in to work with him. It's like people will know that that was a good choice. I mean, listen to these tracks. They sound great." "Well, no, they're not going to match up with the rest..."

And I said, "But that's not, you know, how we mix these things and stuff. It's how it feels." "No, get rid of them." She got really mad at me about the whole thing. And it was a big issue. And those tracks went away.

And they copied the riff?

Copied it? It was — the way we did "Losing You" was to play — John really loved it, but he was not one to argue with Mother. It just was not worth the — plus he was trying to get laid at that time and he was having a hard time. So John wasn't going to argue with her.

Lennon was trying not to rock the boat?

Yeah, 'cause she was in the office all the time so he wasn't going to start an argument and bring that home and make it even harder, you know, it was like...

Well, I'm glad that came out because the people can see that — I wish Lennon worked with them further on some tracks.

He probably would have. He probably would have... like when we did "Walking On Thin Ice," John said to me, "You know, this is the one that's gonna get Yoko really off the ground. She's gonna get the critics on her side, everybody," he says, "so the next record will be the boys only, if you know what I mean."

So he was thinking that way.

Yeah, yeah. One more thing about how we did "Losing You" with the studio band that I put together. We played the other track, the Cheap Trick track, in their headphones and they played along with it, and that's how I recorded it. Of course, Tony was on both tracks. Tony's amazing anyway, but they just played along. I don't think Andy ever quite got the feel. I mean Andy has his own feel and Bun E. — you just can't copy Bun E.

I didn't realize that you'd worked with Lennon prior to the Double Fantasy *album. Did you work on the* Imagine *album or the song "Imagine"?*

The *Imagine* album.

You engineered some of that?

Yeah. Well, I was second engineer. Roy Cicala was first engineer but that was where I met John.

Where did you do the recording, at Lennon's studio in Tittenhurst Park?

No, no, that was all done at — no, let me explain that. Some of the tracks were recorded at John's house, and they were recorded onto — some of them were on eight-track and some of them were on two-track — only a few, maybe four or five of the tunes. And then they were brought to America and he came to Record Plant, and that's where I was on staff and I was under Roy Cicala who was chief engineer, like Jimmy Iovine. We were all under Roy. He was like, the master. He taught us all.

What was it like working with Lennon during the Imagine *album?*

It was amazing, and it's so weird because we got to be friends. I was working in one studio. I was doing editing while he was tracking in another room and doing vocals. Imean, there was no way I was allowed to do vocals with him. I was way too young. But he came in and I was putting stuff together and editing, and he said to me, "How

ya doing?" You know, I'd met him earlier in the day, but this was the first day, and I said, "OK, OK." I wanted to be nervous, but like I said, he wouldn't let you be. And he lit up a smoke and I said to him, "I've been to Liverpool," and he looked at me and said, "Why the hell would you have been to Liverpool?" And I said, "Well, you want to hear this story?"

Is this the one on the boat?

Yeah. I told him that story. And he like, cracked up. He was like, cracking up 'cause they'd read the papers about these idiots who were held captive on this boat.... After that, he said, "What are you doing?" I said, "Well, after this?" He goes, "Yeah." I said, "Nothing." He goes, "You can come with me." So we went out, you know, and he took me to aparty... see, I told him I was born and raised in New York, and he would say to me, "See that guy over there?" "Yeah," and if I knew him, he'd say, "Well, who is he? What is he?"

I'd say, "That guy's an asshole. Don't even go near him. He'll fuck you and suck your blood." "Thanks, man." It was like, one of those kind of things.

So you continued the friendship through the '70s?

Yeah, all through it. And in fact, I was staying with him out in L.A. during the crazy period while I was producing Alice Cooper.

Oh, OK. Muscle Of Love?

Muscle Of Love, yeah. And so I was hanging,

I was hanging with him and I was doing Yoko records. All those crazy records with Yoko which John was most of the time not allowed in the studio.

Really?

Yeah. You know, I never let those two — very rarely when I did *Double Fantasy* did I ever have them in the room at the same time.

Really? Why?

It just didn't work. John always wanted to get into Yoko's stuff, and she could not bear it. It was already — there was already too much competition between those two.

There was competition between them then?

Yeah. Absolutely. And so it was, it just was — when John came in and heard what she did after it was done, it was like, "Yeah!"

He'd get really excited. But if he was there....

Would she be excited, conversely, with what he did?

Nah. "That's good, John," you know. But, yeah, he was always good, you know, for her.

Getting her part done was the biggest challenge, you know. And... I mean, for me, he was the ultimate guy to produce because he was such a true professional. He always left his ego outside the door when he came into work.

What was Lennon like as a guitar player?

He was a great rhythm player. He could not play lead to save his life. Very small hands, so he had no reach at all.

But man, rhythm....

He played some good piano, too.

Yeah. He was OK. He was more than OK, and I'll tell you why — because of his feel. And he just had the most amazing feel and rhythm. And that's, you know, he was like, a rhythm guitarist. I mean, that was, that used to be important. It meant something in the '60s, you know.

It's true.

It was, you know, [The Rolling Stones'] Brian Jones, you know, rhythm guitar player, you know, which is, you know, one of the magic components of both Rick Nielsen and Joe Perry, another rhythm lead player. He bases everything on, on his Portuguese heritage, you know. There's something in there that makes for that funk.

Joe Perry of Aerosmith?

Yeah. And Rick. And there are other guys out there doing it, but John had it in every — in his vocals, in everything.

How did you get enlisted to produce Double Fantasy? Wasn't it a secret for a while?

Yeah. How did I get — I think I ran into John about six months before we did that record, maybe almost a year. I was in a health food store over on the East Side and in comes John and Sean, who was maybe three, and the nanny. They were just coming from the YMCA over on the East Side where they'd been swimming. And John comes up and goes, "Hey, Jack," and I hadn't seen him in years. "Jack, how ya doing? What's happening? Oh, you're a big producer now."

"He always left his ego outside the door"

He was always kidding me or goofing with me. And yeah, and I was goofing back with him. He told me, "Why don't you call me?" gave me his number and he said, "Come on over to The Dakota and hang out." I just took the number and I stuck it in my pocket

By Lennon?

Yeah. So I erased that tape because it was a real painful tape.

Tell us more about the "Walking On Thin Ice" sessions that Lennon oversaw the night he was killed.

Those whole sessions were so strange because he was supposed to have gone to Bermuda after we finished *Double Fantasy*. It was in the can, all done, so I booked another album.

I was doing an album for RCA called Karen Lawrence And The Pins, kind of a punk thing, and John called me up and he said, "Let's go back in now." He was just so full of energy. It was like he was nuts. He had sketches of the live show that they were gonna do, he was writing tunes for Ringo's album, we were gonna do a Ringo album. We were gonna do that after the beginning of the year.

"Life Begins At 40" was for Starr?

Yeah. And so he had all these tunes, had all these plans, and he was not gonna go down to Bermuda and just hang. He was too excited. He felt great. He said, "Let's go do that 'Walking On Thin Ice' thing. It was only a, we made a loop of it and we played on it, John and I. At this point now, it was only John and I and Yoko, and there were no engineers.

Lennon played a lot of guitar feedback, is that correct?

Yeah. There were no engineers, and it was a loop. We made up a loop and we were just doing everything ourselves and having a riot. And I mean, it was a great time. And Yoko was like, everybody was up, so up. David Geffen was coming by, and he was excited. The BBC interviews happened during that point.

Can you recall the last words Lennon said to you or you to him?

The last thing I said to him and he said to me was, "I'll see you in the morning at 9 a.m." The usual. We were going to meet and then we were mastering that next morning. We were going to master "Walking On Thin Ice." It was done.

We'd finished the mix so I mean, I said good-bye to him. I saw him with this huge, with this big smile on his face and his new leather jacket that he'd gotten at The Gap a few weeks earlier which he loved, and there's just this big smile on his face, "I'll see you in the morning."

How long after did you hear Lennon was killed?

About 45 minutes later.

How did you hear about it?

My wife came in and told me. We lived only a few blocks away.

You must have thought you were hallucinating when you heard that.

I absolutely did that. I thought I was hallucinating for a good six months. It was like, gone. It wasn't a good six

"I thought I was hallucinating

months, a bad six months. I mean, I just flipped out.

You were involved in a lawsuit with Ono at one point because you weren't paid royalties. You straightened that out and you finally got paid?

Yeah, yeah. Boy, what a trip that was, 'cause I waited like, I waited like, two years, three years. I had a contract. I waited like three years then I finally said to Yoko, "You know, it's like, really like a lot of royalties probably accruing here. You know, I think it's time like, we maybe have lawyers like, not lawyers, but accountants, have somebody, you know — you don't have to deal with it. Let's just sort it out, let our people sort it out."

And I got like, a nasty letter. Almost like, "Fuck you. You're not getting anything." And it was like, "What? I don't get this." And uh, I mean, all kinds of nasty business went down after that you know, being followed and having people offered money to say bad things about me. None of which, even if they had succeeded, I mean, Cheap Trick was approached....

To say bad things about you?

Yeah, yeah.

By her? By someone in...

Yeah, someone in her camp, ex-FBI guys, Elliot Mintz.

What do you think of Mintz?

Ugh. All I can tell you about Elliot is he came to...

Is it OK to tape this?

Yeah, I'm not an Elliot fan. You know, he doesn't like me. I don't like him...

So you had problems with Mintz?

It was so weird because John, you know, never had a good word for Elliot. Sorry, Elliot. In the studio, like if Elliot was coming, John was like, "Ugh."

He was more of Ono's friend.

Yeah. I can remember Elliot coming by my place, you know. Someone brought him there, not knowing that it was not a good idea, but he came up and it was a house I had in the Hollywood Hills so I was doing some records out there. And I so treasured these great pictures that I had of John and I that I would take them with me when I was traveling. I was going to spend six months in a house in Los Angeles, so in my little office I had pictures of John and I. Amazing picture of John and I listening to "Starting Over" for the first time while we were doing *Double Fantasy*, because we released it as a single. Somebody from maintenance said, "Hey, they're playing 'Starting Over' on the radio." John and I went running into the maintenance shop and we're both standing like, dumbfounded with these stupid smiles, like kids, listening to "Starting Over" and there's a little radio, me and John leaning over it, unposed just like kids, and somebody took a snap of it. So I had all these pictures and someone brought Elliot by and Elliot saw these pictures around my place, and the next day my place was burglarized and you know what they stole? Pictures. That's all.

Oh, my God.

All the pictures were gone. Every picture I had. There must have been a dozen, really beautiful.

for a good six months."

we never — we always wanted to do something like, but it never got done exactly the way we wanted to do it.

Do you remember how Lennon wanted to redo those songs?

He played them on guitar.

And how were they different?

They were either — maybe the tempo was a little differ-ent, but it was more like ideas he had for what the rest of the band was gonna do. But that was gonna be in the show.

He was going to do some Beatles songs?

Oh, yeah, absolutely.

So he had reconciled himself to that?

Yeah.

This may be apocryphal, but I heard that Paul McCartney or George Harrison called the studio during the sessions and Ono didn't allow the call to be placed through, the message.

No, it was McCartney.

McCartney called?

Yeah.

What happened?

Well, from what I heard and from what I heard from

John as well, he was looking to get like, hooked up with Paul before Paul went to Japan to do some writing. They were going to write together? Yeah. And after the sessions, John never left immediately. He'd always sit in the control room and usually took a little grass. He had this old opium pipe — it was probably 500 years old — and he'd say to me, "Is it all over?" 'cause he would never do anything if we were working. And I'd say, "It's over, John," and he'd sit back and put his feet up on the console and he'd load up the pipe and sit back and light up and a few of us — I'd ride home with him because I only lived two blocks from him — and he'd start talking, you know, reminiscing about things. We'd listen to the radio and if a Beatles song came on, he'd talk about it. But the one thing, the overwhelming feeling about the things that he was saying was that he loved the guys in that band more than anybody else, you know. He was pissed off at George because George's book had come out and didn't mention John. You know, like, "How can he write a book about his life and not mention me? I'm the most important...."

Yeah. But he loved the guys in The Beatles.

He loved them. And he loved that band. And, you know, it was like, his band. And I mean, the way he went on about it.

And he was going to write with McCartney?

He was looking to get hooked up with Paul, yeah. But yeah, that call came through and that didn't happen. And Paul went off and got in trouble. And when he got in trouble....

He didn't get the message from anyone?

No.

Who kept him away? Who do you think it was?

I think Yoko probably thought — I can't speak for Yoko. Maybe she thought it'd be a distraction. I don't think it would have been. Who knows what would have happened? But when Paul got busted for pot in Japan, we were in the studio when that call came in that he was in trouble, man, you oughta see John flippin' out.

Was he upset?

Oh, he went crazy. He was going, "All right," I mean, he got right down to business. "Who do we know in Japan? Yoko, what influences do we have there? Let's get on the phone right away. This has to be done."

I always heard the opposite — they were laughing about it.

No.

Good. So Lennon was concerned?

He was flipped out.

You think he made any calls to help out?

I think so. I think Ono did.

Yoko? Good, that's nice.

Yeah, I mean, well, she knows some people over there. But yeah, he made some comments outside of the studio, like, "Paul, what an idiot. How could you do that?" All that kind of stuff. But the real business of this going down was like, when that call came in, it was like panic. I mean, like you don't know what's going to happen in Japan. You got serious shit.

You worked with Harrison, too, didn't you?

Yeah, on Bangladesh.

What was that like?

It was just George and I. It was the film mix of Bangladesh. It had to be done in 48 hours. So we worked 40 of 48 hours and he just, he hung right in there, and Patti would come by with tea every four hours — I mean every four hours and little sandwiches and stuff.

He had a Fender Rhodes on one side of his bed, and behind him, hanging on the wall, was this thing called the Sardonicus guitar, which looked like a Flying V. It was just a guitar that he'd hung on the wall and he could reach back — he didn't even look. He could just reach back and pull this guitar down — it was short-necked, short-scale neck — pull it down off the wall and then play it and then just stick it right back behind him. It hung there all the time.

So he played that?

That's what he played. He also had a Hummingbird for acoustic.

A Gibson Hummingbird?

Yeah, and an Everly Brothers guitar.

Oh, a J-200?

"If word got out that these things

J-200, yeah.

He didn't use an Ovation? Because I've seen pictures where he was playing an Ovation.

Yeah, he did, he did use an Ovation on a number of tunes because we wanted the direct off of it.

Let's talk about the Double Fantasy *sessions.*

Let me just go back a little bit. Now the band didn't know, had no idea who they were. Tony DeVileo and I did all the charts for all the songs except for "Starting Over," which did not exist at that time, just didn't exist. So I'm singing all of the songs to the band at rehearsal an octave lower than he would sing 'em. And they're like, "Wow, great songs, Jack, but really, the vocals, I mean, who's singing these things?" Apparently, a couple of the guys had guessed but didn't say anything because I told them, you know, this is a secret session. They all loved it. The pay was good. They're all getting double.

Double scale?

Yeah. The same with the studio. I booked the time, but they didn't know who for.

The Hit Factory, right?

Way West — Hit Factory was long gone — 'cause it was out of the way. No one would know. We could go in and out of there without ever being seen.

So what was it like when Lennon first walked into the studio?

Well, there was one more rehearsal, the last, the night before the sessions. The last rehearsal was at The Dakota. So I just told the band to meet me on the corner of 72nd and Central Park West. The guys in the band just meet there and so everybody showed up, and I could see from their faces when they looked over at The Dakota, they knew exactly who we were gonna make a record for. We went up into The Dakota, and John answered the door, "Oh, howya doing" — everybody big smiles — "OK, come on in." So we rehearsed, dry rehearsed, I mean. John had tons of equipment, so we just set up a couple of little amps, the piano in the living room — we played around and as we were leaving, John says, he grabs me, he goes, "I got one more I want you to hear," he says, and I think maybe Tony Levin was the only guy who hadn't left at that point or maybe Tony and Hughie. And he sits down at the Fender Rhodes and he plays "Starting Over," and I said, "Where'd that come from?" He said, "Oh, I dunno, it just kinda came." He said, "You think it'll make it onto this record?" I said, "Make it?" I said, "It's gonna be the first single." I said, "It's gotta be the first song on the record. You know, come on, it's perfect." So we recorded that. We went in and rehearsed that in the studio and even charted it.

"Starting Over" is the first track you recorded?

The first track we recorded. And it just went down. Now, all this time now, we're in there, we were in there a month before there was any acknowledgment that these sessions were going on. Here was the deal: If you, if word got out that these things were happening, it was over. It was gonna end. So, I mean, I'd tell that to the musicians....

Why were the sessions so secretive?

were happening, it was over."

Because he wasn't sure if he could do it. You know, he was very, very insecure about this stuff. He didn't think he had it any more, you know. He thought he was too old, he just couldn't write, he couldn't sing, he couldn't play, nothing.

Do you think once he started playing again with the band....

It took a while, it took a while. There were some moments there where yeah, he was like, "I don't know..." I used to have breakfast with him every morning, he insisted, at 9 a.m. I'd come to The Dakota, and he was always so punctual. 9 a.m., he came out his door and we would walk from The Dakota to La Fortuna on 71st Street, a little cafe.

We'd sit in the back, in the garden, and have chocolate-iced cappuccinos and talk over what happened last night, what was gonna happen, what was going on with Yoko, everything.

> " *He was very very insecure about this stuff.* "

And then he'd go back and he'd like, take a nap and by 11 o'clock I'd be working with Yoko. But we'd sit there for a couple of hours and talk through everything. There were moments at La Fortuna where I had to say, "John, really, I swear, it's good, you know. It's good, I'm telling ya. Even the live vocals, everything. You sound great."

I heard that some of the Double Fantasy *sessions were videotaped. There's even a bootleg out with audio from the video.*

Oh, man, there was an amazing shoot. Some day those things, you know, John told me — now the guy that shot it was, I don't know if you remember these commercials

called, they were Crazy Eddie. "Come on down to Crazy Eddie,"

It was an ad, right? For a record store or electronics.

Yeah, electronics. I got the guy who did those commercials to come in and do this video.

Do you remember what songs, or was it just a session?

He was there for a week. There's a bootleg out where someone says, "Look at the camera, Johnny," and he says, "I know what I look like. I look like a fucking bird."

Who has the footage?

Now here's what — I asked John where it was. I've heard two things: I tore it up in the bathtub, I sunk it in the pool... but I heard that it exists somewhere and that he was so thin at the time that he didn't like, you know. It was so weird because he was always, he told me he was always John The Fat Beatle and that he finally felt great to be John The Skinny Guy, you know, but, he felt that he looked too thin and he had his hair — we used to call him Skinny Head. He'd tie his hair back in a ponytail and his face looked like about, like it was this narrow. It looked great, actually, but he didn't like it.

But I'm telling you, these things were fantastic. I saw the footage. I wish I could remember the guy's name. It's like, on the tip of my tongue, the guy who shot them.

You'd think that if Ono had it, she'd release something.

"John, really, I swear,

I know. I know. I wonder if it really got destroyed. I hope it didn't. It was such a professional job.

But how could it have gotten destroyed if there's audio on a bootleg?

Why? The audio's from my hidden mike tapes.

That's it then.

There's audio of everything, every breath that existed from day one to the last day.

Ono has it?

No, the [tape of the] last day got tossed. I tossed the last day. Doesn't exist.

What happened during the "Walking On Thin Ice" session, the night Lennon was killed?

It was the end of "Walking On Thin Ice." It was the last day of mixing, but there were things, there were some strange things said in the control room.

Like what?

I don't want to talk about it. I erased the tape. "...as we were leaving, John says, he grabs me, he goes, 'I got one more I want you to hear,' he says, and I think maybe Tony Levin was the only guy who hadn't left at that point or maybe Tony and Hughie [McCracken]. And he sits down at the Fender Rhodes and he plays 'Starting Over,' and I said, 'Where'd that come from?'

He said, 'Oh, I dunno, it just kinda came.' He said, 'You think it'll make it onto this record?'" ∎

DOUBLE FANTASY U.S. DISCOGRAPHY
by Tim Neely

The vinyl LPs

Label/# A-side/B-side Year NM $

Geffen GHS 2001 Double Fantasy (original; off-white label; titles on back are listed out of order) 1980 $ 10

Geffen GHS 2001 Double Fantasy (second pressing; off-white label, titles on back are in the correct order) 1981 12

Geffen GHS 2001 Double Fantasy (Columbia House edition, back cover titles in order, "CH" is on label) 1981 75

Geffen GHS 2001 Double Fantasy (Columbia House edition, back cover titles in order, no "CH" on label) 1981 12

Geffen R 104689 Double Fantasy (RCA Music Service edition) 1981 40

Nautilus NR-47 Double Fantasy (SuperDisc reissue, same cover design as Geffen editions) 1982 80

Nautilus NR-47 Double Fantasy (SuperDisc reissue, experimental cover with yellow background and red heart over John and Yoko) 1982 2000

Geffen GHS 2001 Double Fantasy (third pressing, black label) 1986 50

Capitol C1-91425 Double Fantasy (reissue) 1989 20

Capitol C1-591425 Double Fantasy (Columbia House edition of reissue) 1989 60

The compact discs

Geffen 2001-2 Double Fantasy 1985 50

Geffen 2001-2 Double Fantasy (longbox only) 1985 50

Geffen M2G-2001 Double Fantasy (Columbia House edition) 1986 20

Capitol C2-91425 Double Fantasy (reissue) 1989 8

Capitol D 100333 Double Fantasy (BMG Direct Marketing edition of reissue) 1989 10

Capitol CDP-591425 Double Fantasy (Columbia House edition of reissue) 1991 10

Mobile Fidelity UDCD-600 Double Fantasy (gold-plated edition) 1994 15

Capitol 28739 Double Fantasy (remastered reissue, three bonus tracks) 2000 8

The 45s

Geffen 49604 (Just Like) Starting Over/Kiss Kiss Kiss 1980 4

Geffen 49604 (Just Like) Starting Over/Kiss Kiss Kiss (picture sleeve) 1980 4

Geffen 49644 Woman/Beautiful Boys 1980 4

Geffen 49644 Woman/Beautiful Boys (picture sleeve) 1980 4

Geffen 49695 Watching the Wheels/Yes, I'm Your Angel 1981 4

Geffen 49695 Watching the Wheels/Yes, I'm Your Angel (picture sleeve) 1981 4

Geffen GGEF 0408 (Just Like) Starting Over/Woman ("Back To Back Hits" reissue, cream label) 1981 4

Geffen GGEF 0415 Watching The Wheels/Beautiful Boy (Darling Boy) ("Back To Back Hits" reissue, cream label) 1981 4

Geffen 29855 Happy Xmas (War Is Over)/Beautiful Boy (Darling Boy) (only the B-side is from Double Fantasy) 1982 5

Geffen 29855 Happy Xmas (War Is Over)/Beautiful Boy (Darling Boy) (picture sleeve) 1982 5

Geffen GGEF 0408 (Just Like) Starting Over/Woman ("Back To Back Hits" reissue, black label) 1986 10

Geffen GGEF 0415 Watching The Wheels/Beautiful Boy (Darling Boy) ("Back To Back Hits" reissue, black label) 1986 10

Capitol 58894 (Just Like) Starting Over/Watching The Wheels ("For Jukeboxes Only!" series, blue vinyl) 2000 5

Capitol 58895 Woman/Walking On Thin Ice (B-side is a bonus track on the new Double Fantasy; 2000 5

"For Jukeboxes Only!" series, clear vinyl)

The 12-inch singles (promos)

Geffen PRO-A-919 (Just Like) Starting Over/Kiss Kiss Kiss ("Starting Over" is 4:17, longer than anywhere else) 1980 80

Geffen PRO-A-1079 Happy Xmas (War Is Over)/Beautiful Boy (Darling Boy) (only the B-side is from Double Fantasy) 1982 30 ∎

It's good, I'm telling ya."

John Lennon Remembered

On Dec. 8, 1980, I spent much of the evening doing some early (for me) Christmas shopping. I was in a great mood. I had just had a great time shopping with some good friends, it was the holiday season, and of course John Lennon had just released *Double Fantasy*, his first new album in five years.

The Beatles, both as a group and as individuals, had been a big part of my life ever since that fateful night nearly 17 years earlier when my life was changed by a certain telecast of "The Ed Sullivan Show" on Feb. 9, 1964. I had all the records, read most of the books and magazine articles and spent much time think-ing about and discussing those four lads from Liverpool.

When I got home that night, I listened to the first side of Jackson Browne's *Hold Out* album, which was one of my favorites at the time. At the end of side one, I flipped my amplifier's selection switch from "Phone" to "Tuner." It was at that moment that I got one of the great shocks of my life. The announcer on one of my favorite rock stations said, "John Lennon has been shot. We don't know much more about it than that, but John Lennon has been shot and is apparently dead."

I froze. I remember exactly where I was standing in my bedroom and what went through my mind at that moment. John Lennon DEAD? It was impossible. And from a gunshot? That didn't make sense either. Rock stars died from drug

Goldmine readers share their memories of the late Beatle.

"Who would want to shoot a Beatle?"

overdoses or alcohol problems. They didn't get shot. And on top of that, this was one of the BEATLES: Who would want to shoot a Beatle? None of this made any sense. But as the evening wore on and my radio supplied the horrible details as they became available, the sad reality set in. John Lennon was dead. It was a night I'll never forget.

It's been nearly 17 years since that tragic night. It seems strange, but as much time has passed since John's death as had passed between that first time I saw him on "The Ed Sullivan Show" and the night he died. It doesn't seem like it.

The last 17 years have seen many changes in the world. One of the most amazing is the surviving three Beatles putting aside their differences to give us the fantastic wealth of audio and video material known as *The Anthology*. There were even two new songs that Paul, George, and Ringo helped John to posthumously fin-ish, giving the world the first new Beatles songs in more than 25 years. Sad to say, the life of John Lennon was prematurely cut short on that December night in 1980. But he lives on through the legacy of his music, a great gift to be enjoyed forever.

— Michael Rinella; Peoria, Ill.

I remember how I learned about John Lennon's death, a very unpleasant memory. Since I started work very early, I would go to bed by 10 p.m. The next morning I did what I always did, turn the radio on as I was getting ready for work. In hushed tones I heard two announcers talking (it was WMCA-AM in New York), one of whom said something like, "Did he come to New York to kill him?" to

which the reply was, "We don't know yet."

It sounded bad. My first thought was that something terrible had happened to Mayor Koch. But about a minute later I found out. Driving into work I was stunned with disbelief. It was one of the most difficult days I've ever had.

— Gary Wilbur; New Hyde Park, N.Y.

I heard about John Lennon's death at 1 in the morning on my car radio. Having gone to bed early on the night of Dec. 8, I hadn't heard any news. As I began my nightly routine as a carrier for the Arkansas Democrat, I switched on the radio to get a little night music, only to hear the shocking news that former Beatle John Lennon was shot to death in New York City.

> " *It was one of the most difficult days I've ever had.* "

I couldn't think; I couldn't breathe. I had to talk to someone. The nearest pay phone was in the tiny town of Thornton. I woke my wife, Pam, from a sound sleep, although she didn't complain. She too was a Beatles fan and couldn't believe the news.

After a while, I knew I had to regain my composure and finish my route. My '75 Comet had only AM radio, and I spent the rest of the night feverishly spinning the dial as I drove, trying to get every scrap of information I could. John's Imagine album had helped me get through a lonely time as a college freshman in 1972, and every time I heard the song "Imagine" that night, I felt as if an important part of my past had withered and died.

At home the next morning, I continued my scramble for knowledge of what had happened, switching from "Good

"I couldn't think; I couldn't breathe."

Morning America" to "Today" and back again, trying to understand it all. I had John's single, "(Just Like) Starting Over," but "hadn't gotten around" to buying *Double Fantasy*. I asked Pam to get it for me. She found it at the local Wal-Mart. It was the last copy. I suppose the after-death buying frenzy had begun.

Perhaps death is not necessarily all-conquering. I think John, wherever he is, appreciates that his former bandmates paid tribute to him with two new Beatles songs. The four of them are still together, in a sense, and always will be. In that same mode, John Winston Lennon will be with the rest of us forever.

— Dale Waldrop; Fordyce, Ark.

I first heard about the shooting of a man "identified as former Beatle John Lennon" on a sports update program airing at the time on a local television station in New York. This short, two-minute or so program aired nightly at 11:30 p.m. right after syndicated reruns of "M*A*S*H." "The sportscaster had no further information.

I immediately turned to Monday Night Football and heard Howard Cosell report the horrifying news that it was indeed John Lennon who was shot and that he was "dead on arrival." So what? you might say. Millions of people found out about the tragedy via the dramatic mouth of Mr. Cosell. Well, let me introduce two interesting wrinkles into the picture. At the time I was writing for, and editing, a local entertainment magazine. And as a music critic, I was sent many records by the record companies to review. In mid to late November I received the "(Just Like) Starting Over"/"Kiss Kiss Kiss" 12-inch plus the *Double Fantasy* LP.

I had immediately listened to the 12-inch, but I kept putting off John and Yoko's new album in lieu of stuff I had in my

possession longer — an unfortunate habit that has grown out of control over the years since my wife and I started to have kids. In a sense, I was "saving" *Double Fantasy* — John's recorded comeback after five long years — for the "perfect time."

Thus, I never listened to the album until after John was killed. And I've never forgiven myself for this and am extremely jealous of people who had the foresight (?) to put the damn thing on the turntable as soon as it came out.

What this all means is I never had the opportunity to hear these new songs in the context they were originally meant to be heard, e.g., "Beautiful Boy (Darling Boy)" ("I can hardly wait to see you come of age" and "Life is what happens to you while you're busy making other plans"); "I'm Losing You" ("So what the hell am I supposed to do?, just put a Band-Aid on it?, and stop the bleeding now"); "Cleanup Time" ("The gods are in the heavens, the angels treat us well, the oracle has spoken, we cast the perfect spell"); "Hard Times Are Over" ("It's been very rough, but it's getting easier now, hard times are over, over for a while"); etc. etc. etc.

The other ironic thing about this whole mess was that I was, at the time, in the midst of writing a long monthly series for the magazine on the music of The Beatles and the solo Beatles. After doing a nine-part series on The Beatles as a group, I then dove into a multi-part series on the music of John, Paul, George, & Ringo. After dealing with first Ringo, then George, then Paul, I saved John for last since I had always felt his solo material was the most impressive. After dealing with his early experimental work with Yoko as well as the *Live Peace In Toronto* 1969 LP in a chapter or two, my segment on *The Plastic Ono Band* album hit the streets on Dec. 3, 1980.

"I'm not kidding you man. They say he's dead!"

The sad thing about all this was that I wrote each part of the entire Beatles/solo Beatles series month to month, like a serial, so after Dec. 8 I now had to write the rest of the John Lennon portion — eight or nine more parts — knowing John had died. It certainly affected my point of view, though I tried not to let it alter my critical thinking.

— Martin E. Horn; South Plainfield, N.J.

I was a 25-year-old apprentice electrician working the midnight shift at the old Pontiac Motor Division complex in Pontiac, Mich., on December 8, 1980. This is the place that made GTOs during The Beatles' tenure from 1964 through 1970.

My shift in the trade school started at 10:30 p.m. and was totally uneventful for the first two hours. Sometime after midnight my friend Gary came walking in and said, "Did you hear John Lennon has been shot?" Knowing that Gary was a practical joker, I blurted out, "bullshit!!!" Gary stared at me without a smile and replied: "I'm not kidding you, man. They say he's dead!"

I ran to the nearest radio and the instant I turned it on, the announcement of John's death was heard. I had a lot of quiet nights working the midnight shift back then, but that night was the quietest of them all. We were all in our 20s and it hit us like a ton of bricks because we had grown up with The Beatles.

When Keith Moon died in '78 and John Bonham died in early '80, I would morbidly joke that drummers have to die in threes, meaning that Ringo or Charlie Watts would be the next to die. I had no idea that by the end of 1980, one of The Beatles would actually leave us.

— Carl Johnson; Lake Orion, Mich. ∎

∎ *This story originally appeared in the Nov. 8, 1997, issue of Goldmine.*

Producer Walter Shenson chats with John Lennon on the set A Hard Day's Night.

George Harrison

(1943-2001)

GUITARISTS BATTLE WITH CANCER EVENTUALLY TAKES ITS TOLL   By Dave Thompson

A t the end, the question wasn't "how long," but "how soon"; not if, but when. George Harrison died in Los Angeles at 1:30 p.m. Nov. 29, 2001, and the only shaft of consolation was that those who knew and loved him — family, friends and fans alike — had already had time to prepare for the end. Now all they were left to cope with was the sickening inevitability of it all; that, and another reminder that it doesn't matter how rich you are, how good you are, how courageous you are. Your guitar will still be left gently weeping.

Harrison was all of those things, and the first obituaries off the block could not help but remind us of that. One quarter of the single most successful and influential musical group in history, Harrison's credentials as a songwriter, a musician and a performer are indeed equaled by only three other men — bandmates Paul McCartney, Ringo Starr, and John Lennon, whose own death, in 1980, would be remembered just nine days after Harrison's.

As a guitarist, Harrison was as influential as any of his generation — more so, in fact, as he dispensed with the flash and pizzazz of the "heroes" of the age in favor of gentle licks and riffs that anyone imagined they could play, including the young Lennon, who himself learned the instrument from Harrison.

Like his bandmates, then, Harrison had nothing to prove. But when they went solo in 1970, they unveiled their little records and demanded that they be regarded as "statements." Harrison delivered a statement, then behaved as though it was

> *" He left this world as he lived in it, conscious of God, fearless of death, and at peace, surrounded by family and friends "*

nothing of the sort. Today, the triple album *All Things Must Pass* is regarded as the quintessential recording by any of the former Fabs. It was certainly the first to prove that there could be more to life than the Moptops.

Harrison was also the first true superstar of the rock 'n' roll era to try and turn his fame into something more than dollars in the bank and posters on the wall. Having already spearheaded the pop pilgrimage to Rishikesh, India, in 1967, after he and his first wife, Patti, became enamored with the teachings of the Maharishi Mahesh Yogi, Harrison's 1971 single "Bangla-Desh," and the mammoth Aug. 1, 1971, benefit in New York City for that same infant nation, foreshadowed everything from Live Aid to the recent Concert For New York City. Both the "Bangla Desh" single and concert proved — at a time when such things still needed to be proved — that even art had a heart, and rock 'n' roll wasn't simply a squalling monster bent on tearing down the walls of the establishment.

Or, rather, it was, but it had very firm ideas of the kind of spirituality it wanted to erect in their place.

That Harrison's private interests lay somewhat deeper than the bacchanalian pits into which life as a Beatle routinely plunged him became evident very early on. No sooner had the world's media figured out that there really were separate personalities lurking beneath the manes of unkempt hair that provided the quartet's initial passage into the spotlight, than Harrison was being dubbed "The Quiet One." This was a tribute to both the stoic silence with which he regarded the madness that surrounded him and, just as pervasively (if, thanks to Lennon/McCartney, less frequently), to the pensive, thoughtful lyricism that hallmarked his songwriting. "Don't Bother Me," from The Beatles' second album, might not be Harrison's most accomplished composition, but it would certainly remain among the most self-defining.

In later years, Harrison concurred with Lennon's view that the group's true potential was always going to come a poor second to the insanity that surrounded them. "Even the best thrill soon got tiring," he remarked in his 1980 autobiography *I Me Mine*. "Your own space, man, it's so important. That's why we were doomed, because we didn't have any. We were like monkeys in a zoo."

He even delighted in demolishing at least a portion of the mythological edifices that time had constructed around the band — including the infamous "smoking pot at the palace" tale. Indeed, while he later told the *British Daily Telegraph* that "we had the time of our lives, we laughed for years," he rarely let on what they were laughing about. This same wry reticence, and an almost self-negating aversion to exaggeration, flavored what remain two of his finest later compositions, 1987's darkly nostalgic (and distinctly walrus-flavored) "When We Was Fab" and the Lennon memorial "All Those Years Ago."

As a solo artist, Harrison remained uncomfortable with his stature. He was the youngest of the four young men (he was born at 11:42 p.m. on Feb. 24, 1943, and not, as is frequently stated, early the following day), a status that certainly conferred a degree of insecurity. But it was also true that, when confronted with his continued fame, Harrison simply didn't care enough to pursue it.

His hobbies included Formula 1 racing and the cinema and, in 1984, he came close to leaving the music industry altogether to concentrate on movie production. He eventually recanted, but his HandMade Films company nevertheless consumed more of his attention than his music. (He ultimately sold the company, for $8.5 million, in 1994.) His disdain for stardom remained, however, and, in 1989, Harrison was a motivating force behind possibly the most recalcitrant supergroup of all time, The Traveling

Wilburys' union of Jeff Lynne, Bob Dylan, Tom Petty, and Roy Orbison.

His reputation for restraint, however, was sometimes deceptive. At The Beatles' first recording session with producer George Martin, it was Harrison who disrupted the serious demeanor of the day by answering the question, "Is there anything you don't like?" with a withering, "Yes, your tie." And it was Harrison who composed "Taxman," the first and, still, one of the most acerbically personal political attacks in mainstream pop history. Other artists, assaulting the policies of the government, aimed at figureheads and generalities. Harrison came right out and named his foes — British Prime Minister Harold Wilson and Opposition leader Edward Heath.

■ *Glenn A. Baker Archives*

It is nevertheless ironic that this most peaceful of men was also often at the center of the most turbulent disruptions. He lost his first wife, Patti, to his best friend, Eric Clapton; and, in 1971, Harrison became the first high-profile victim of what is, today, a sadly all-too-common state of affairs, when former manager Allen Klein successfully sued him for plagiarism, citing the similarities between Harrison's "My Sweet Lord" and The Chiffons' "He's So Fine." Five years later, Harrison's own Dark Horse label was the subject of protracted litigation with its then-distributor A&M.

In 1979, Harrison's financing of the Monty Python movie *Life Of Brian* incurred the wrath of the religious right, leading to a wave of indignation unseen since John Lennon made his "bigger than Jesus" crack 14 years before; and, in December 1999, Harrison was seriously injured when an intruder broke into his home and attempted to kill him, under the impression that he'd been commissioned by God to do so.

Harrison survived, but he had already been diagnosed with the cancer that would eventually kill him. Much of the last two years of his life — interrupted though they were by the phenomenal success of The Beatles' #1s collection, *1* — were spent seeking treatment for the illness, with periodic news bulletins either raising or lowering the hopes of his fans. Harrison himself, however, was already at least partially resigned to his looming demise, a fatalism evidenced by the last recording he is reported to have made. "Horse To The Water" is credited it to the pseudonymous RIP Ltd 2001.

Harrison was cremated shortly after his death. His ashes were taken to India by Olivia, his second wife, and the couple's son, Dhani, 24, along with two Hare Krishna devotees from London. Harrison was a longtime follower of India's Hindu faith. His ashes were immersed in the holy Ganges River in the northern city of Varanasi. The ashes were also be sprinkled off Allahabad, where the Hindu faith's three holiest rivers converge: the Ganges, Yamuna and the ancient Saraswati.

A family statement confirmed his final dignity. "He left this world as he lived in it, conscious of God, fearless of death, and at peace, surrounded by family and friends."

And then there were two. ■

The Music of George Harrison

AN ALBUM-BY-ALBUM GUIDE   By Dave Thompson

In November 1976, George Harrison became the third former Beatle to release a greatest hits collection but the first to be forced to admit he had been a Beatle in the first place. Whereas John Lennon (*Shaved Fish*) and Ringo Starr (*Blast From Your Past*) padded their smash singles with key album tracks and favorites, Capitol/EMI neatly sliced Harrison's best-of set down the almost-middle, drawing just six songs from his solo career and seven from the '60s.

The decision infuriated Harrison. It was bad enough that the album was spitefully timed to coincide with the release of his own latest release, Thirty-Three & 1/3, but the album's layout ensured that he wasn't simply competing with himself in the marketplace. He was up against the biggest band in the world as well. "What they've done is take a lot of songs which happen to be me singing lead on my songs but which were Beatles songs," he snapped. "There was really a lot of good songs they could have used of me separately. Solo songs. I don't see why they didn't do that." That was not the end of his woes. In peaking at #31, *The Best Of George Harrison* struggled to the lowest chart placing endured by any ex-Beatle since Lennon's so-misguided Some Time In New York City four years previous.

But, one could also argue that *The Best Of George Harrison* actually did him a favor. For eight years of Beatledom, after all, Harrison had suffered silently in the shadows of the Lennon/McCartney songwriting team,

> " *What they've done is take a lot of songs which happen to be me singing lead on my songs but which were Beatles songs.* "

watching while, album after album, his songwriting contributions were squashed into the corner by sheer weight of numbers. This new release proved to the world what only the label-lookers had hitherto known. Even in his youth, Harrison could compete with the best in the world.

In fact, Harrison's songwriting career got off to a very promising start, long before Lennon/McCartney ignited their own special chemistry. In 1958, as a member of The Quarry Men, Harrison joined with McCartney to write "In Spite Of All The Danger," a tasty little original that The Quarry Men promptly preserved on a demonstration disc. Four years later, it was Lennon who looked to Harrison for a partner, and the ensuing "Cry For A Shadow" became the sole band original to be recorded during The Beatles' Hamburg sojourn.

Across the remainder of the decade that he helped to define, however, Harrison had just 22 songs included on a Beatles record, with three more emerging via the *Anthology* series. Cobbled

■ *Pictorial Press U.K.*

together on a single disc (all 25 clock in at just under 79 minutes), one has a compilation that could stand alongside any collection of Lennon and McCartney compositions. But *The Best Of George Harrison* was the first time anyone had even dreamed of such a compilation, and that was the problem. No matter that Harrison was responsible for some of the best songs in the band's entire catalog — think of The Beatles and one automatically thinks of John and Paul. *The Best Of George Harrison* was Capitol's way of giving people a whole new way of looking at The Beatles. Unfortunately, in the process, it stopped them looking at George.

Between 1970-2001, Harrison placed 13 solo singles on the *Billboard* Top 40, including three #1s, a total that established him as second only to Paul in the Most Successful Solo Beatle stakes — John (at least during his own lifetime) and Ringo tie on 10 apiece, with two chart-toppers each. In terms of albums, too, Harrison holds his ground. Nine Top 40 albums, two more with the Traveling Wilburys and the *Concert For Bangla Desh* set readily eclipses John's eight and Ringo's five.

Such statistics look and, indeed, are impressive. But ask anyone, bar a committed Harifan, to name more than half of them — or better still, to sing a few songs from each one — and you've got a long search ahead. (No, the follow-up to *Traveling Wilburys Volume One* was not *Traveling Wilburys Volume Two*.) In fact, you'd be better off staying at home for the weekend and playing them all for yourself. You might well be surprised at what you find.

1963-70: HARRISONGS and their appearance on CD

"Don't Bother Me" (*With The Beatles*); "You Know What To Do" (*Anthology 1*); "You Like Me Too Much," "I Need You" (*Help*); "If I Needed Someone," "Think For Yourself" (*Rubber Soul*); "Taxman," "Love You To," "I Want To Tell You" (*Revolver*); "Within You Without You" (*Sgt. Pepper*); "Only A Northern Song," "It's All Too Much" (*Yellow Submarine*); "Blue Jay Way" (*Magical Mystery Tour*); "The Inner Light," "Old Brown Shoe" (*Past Masters 2*); "Piggies," "Long Long Long," "Savoy Truffle," "While My Guitar Gently Weeps" (*The Beatles*); "Not Guilty," "All Things Must Pass" (*Anthology 3*); "Something," "Here Comes The Sun" (*Abbey Road*); "For You Blue," "I Me Mine" (*Let It Be*).

To even contemplate assessing Harrison's contributions to The Beatles on the basis of his songwriting contributions is an asinine quest. It was his ability as a guitarist and his presence as a bandmate — not his periodic appearances as band leader — that assured his integral role within both band and studio, and it was his resistance to the latter that arguably prevented The Beatles from completely vanishing up their own behinds.

Discussing *Sgt. Pepper* for *The Beatles' Anthology* project, Harrison admitted, "it was becoming difficult for me, because I wasn't really into it. Up to that time, we had recorded... like a band; we would learn the songs and then play them. *Sgt. Pepper* was the one album where things were done a bit differently... and for me it became a bit tiring and a bit boring. Generally I didn't really like making the album very much."

With Lennon, McCartney and producer George Martin, however, having the time of their lives on that record, one could argue that The Beatles as a functioning unit ended there, killed by the LP that, probably more than any other, confirmed their immortality. Irony seldom comes any sweeter.

Of course, it was this collapse that opened the door for Harrison the songwriter to step out from behind the already acknowledged presence of Harrison the lead guitarist. His earliest songs for the band, after all, were little more than Beatlemanic shadowplay, no better/no worse than any of the myriad other Merseybeaters in the Lennon/McCartney wake. Moreover, while it was certainly Harrison's absorption of sub-continental Indian influences that initially directed the band toward the vast, open pastures of their future, from a musical point of view, they were an absolute dead end.

Revolver's "Love You To," with its integral and more or less innovative use of sitar and tabla (by Anil Bhagwat) opened creative doors through which Harrison's bandmates may not — and Martin certainly would not — have ever dreamed of passing. But the similarly themed "Within You Without You" and "The Inner Light" added nothing to that original breakthrough, and it was not until Harrison himself made the sharp swerve into the miasmic psychedelia of "Blue Jay Way" on the one hand and the mental mettle of "It's All Too Much" and "Savoy Truffle" on the other that he was truly functioning as his bandmates' songwriting equal. Indeed, songs the caliber of "While My Guitar Gently Weeps," "Old Brown Shoe," "Here Comes The Sun," "Sour Milk Sea" (gifted to Jackie Lomax for an early Apple 45) and "Badge" (the Eric Clapton cowrite that brought Cream their farewell hit) rank among the finest Beatles compositions of the group's final years, and the only regret is that neither of the latter two ever made it into a Beatles recording session.

In their stead, however, the winsome "Long Long Long" and "Something," the rootsy "I Me Mine" and "For You Blue," and the whimsically foreboding "Piggies" certainly pointed the way toward Harrison's first solo triumphs. The gritty "Not Guilty" might have lain unreleased until *Anthology*, but it nevertheless found a distinct echo in, of all things, Wings' "Medicine Jar" — a song composed by guitarist Jimmy McCulloch but surely influenced by bossman Paul's own stash of Fabs outtakes.

Further gems may or may not abound. Among Anthology's other discoveries were the Hard Day's Night–era "You Know What To Do" and a rough solo demo of "All Things Must Pass," recorded by George on his 26th birthday and inexplicably passed over by his bandmates. However, among the best-known of

Harrison's other Beatlesongs, "Not Unknown" and "Pink Litmus Paper Shirt," have long since been discredited, while "Circles" officially exists only in the remake rendition featured on 1982's Gone Troppo album.

So let "Harrisongs," its title taken from George's own post-Beatles' publishing empire, stand as the so-far definitive take on Harrison as a pen-wielding Beatle and, until the day Apple gets 'round to finishing the job that began with that Best Of — CD burners at the ready!

WONDERWALL MUSIC
Released: November 1968 (U.S. #49)

ELECTRONIC SOUND
Released: May 1969 (U.S. #191)

Less a listening experience, *Wonderwall Music* and *Electronic Sounds* are more a pair of aural bookends to stop the rest of your musical mindscape from falling out of your ears. Demonstrating Harrison's mastery (or otherwise) of a Moog synthesizer, his first two "solo" records are, respectively, the soundtrack to a long-forgotten psychedelic movie and the second release on Apple's shortlived avant-garde Zapple subsidiary.

Neither truly sits comfortably within Harrison's canon — indeed, with no songs, no lyrics and not many tunes, they are best regarded as period-piece artifacts that bleep and burble to their hearts' content. Nevertheless, anybody itching to sample such wares is directed toward Rhino's DVD reissue of Wonderwall, accompanied as it is by a 120-page "making of" book and a limited-edition box set packed with a host of additional goodies.

ALL THINGS MUST PASS
Released: November 1970 (U.S. #1, U.K. #4)

Throughout 1970, all post-Beatle eyes were on Lennon and McCartney, with Harrison and Starr widely regarded as mere sideshows alongside the main attraction. How, after all, could they even hope to compete with the proven masters — Starr was simply a singing drummer, while Harrison had barely contributed more than a couple of songs to any Fabs album you could name. The announcement, in mid-year, that his solo debut was to be spread across six full sides of vinyl led a scarcely credulous media to just two conclusions. Either he'd devoted his entire career-to-date to stockpiling songs for some future rainy day, or he'd spent a lot longer jamming with his heavyweight friends than anyone could have guessed. The result, November's *All Things Must Pass*, did not contradict either prediction.

Some of the music on the first two discs did date back to The Beatles, although only as far as the Let It Be sessions, during which the band tried out "Isn't It A Pity," "All Things Must Pass," "Let It Down," "Wah Wah" and the Bob Dylan cowrite "I'd Have You Anytime." "Apple Scruffs," dedicated to the die-hard fans who still gathered at the band's decaying Saville Row offices, was clearly inspired by life as a Fab, while the chart-topping "My Sweet Lord," written when Harrison was aboard Delaney & Bonnie's star-studded 1969 U.S. tour, also falls chronologically within The Beatles' remit.

The superstar party, too, was given full rein, with one entire disc surrendered to five lengthy jams. Ringo Starr, Eric Clapton, Ginger Baker, Jim Price, Jim Gordon, Carl Radle, Dave Mason, Pete Drake, Bobby Whitlock, Billy Preston, Klaus Voormann, Gary Wright, Gary Brooker, Alan White, and the members of Badfinger all trouped through the Phil Spector–produced sessions, together with a revolving door of friends and passers-by, many of whom were roped into one song or another. Phil Collins, drummer with little-known London prog merchants Flaming Youth, now dines out on tales of his uncredited conga playing on "The Art Of Dying," and he is surely not alone in claiming such a distinction.

But, at its heart, *All Things Must Pass* was an album of songs — and absolutely marvelous songs at that, possessed by an honesty, a simplicity and, above all, a resonance that neither McCartney nor Lennon's Plastic Ono Band even hinted toward. Those albums, classics though they certainly are, were more concerned with establishing their sires as songwriters in their own right, the irrevocable sundering of the best-known double act in music history. *All Things Must Pass*, on the other hand, gave the impression that it simply didn't care what people thought. That was its magic.

"Beware Of Darkness" and "The Art Of Dying," respectively opening and closing the album's second platter, rate among the finest compositions of Harrison's entire career, while the utterly buoyant and heroically guitar-laden "What Is Life" not only brought its maker a U.S. Top 10 hit in February 1971, it returned to chart duty the following year, when Olivia Newton-John sent a truly lovely cover into the U.K. Top 20. She had, of course, already scored with a similarly superb version of another All Things highlight, Dylan's "If Not For You," and she made it no secret that her take was wholly modeled on Harrison's arrangement. (Dylan himself never truly got to grips with what remains one of his most affecting love songs.)

Dylan resurfaces, spiritually at least, on the country-ish "Behind That Locked Door" — indeed, this tribute to Dylan's famous reticence sounds so close to a lost Zim

original that His Bobness' own "Baby, Stop Crying" (from 1978's Street Legal) is all but reduced to tributary status itself in comparison.

Neither did the 17 songs, five jams and one reprise that comprise *All Things Must Pass* exhaust Harrison's stockpile of songs. Outtakes, famously available on a slew of bootlegs, include "Everybody Nobody," "Window Window," "Nowhere To Go," "Cosmic Empire" and "Mother Divine," plus three songs to which Harrison would return later in his career. "Beautiful Girl" became a highlight of *Thirty-Three & 1/3*; "I Live For You" was the sole unissued song included on the parent album's 2001 remaster, and another Dylan song, "I Don't Want To Do It" was re-recorded for the *Porky's Revenge* soundtrack, of all things.

LIVING IN THE MATERIAL WORLD
Released: June 1973 (U.S. #1, U.K. #2)

Three years elapsed between All Things Must Pass and its similarly chart-topping successor, a span during which Harrison's profile remained high. He produced Starr's maiden hits "It Don't Come Easy" and "Back Off Boogaloo," while 1971 also brought Harrison's own "Bangla-Desh" single and a star-studded concert to raise funds for and awareness of the famine striking that same country. Early 1972 then delivered a second triple album, this time capturing the event's highlights — it went to #1 in Britain, #2 in America.

A new single, the plaintive "Give Me Love (Give Me Peace On Earth)," arrived in May 1973; it, too, topped the chart, and its parent album followed in its footsteps, commercially and stylistically. While history insists that *Living In The Material World* could not help but be eclipsed by its gargantuan forebear, with the two albums in the CD player and the

"It's difficult to play favorites."

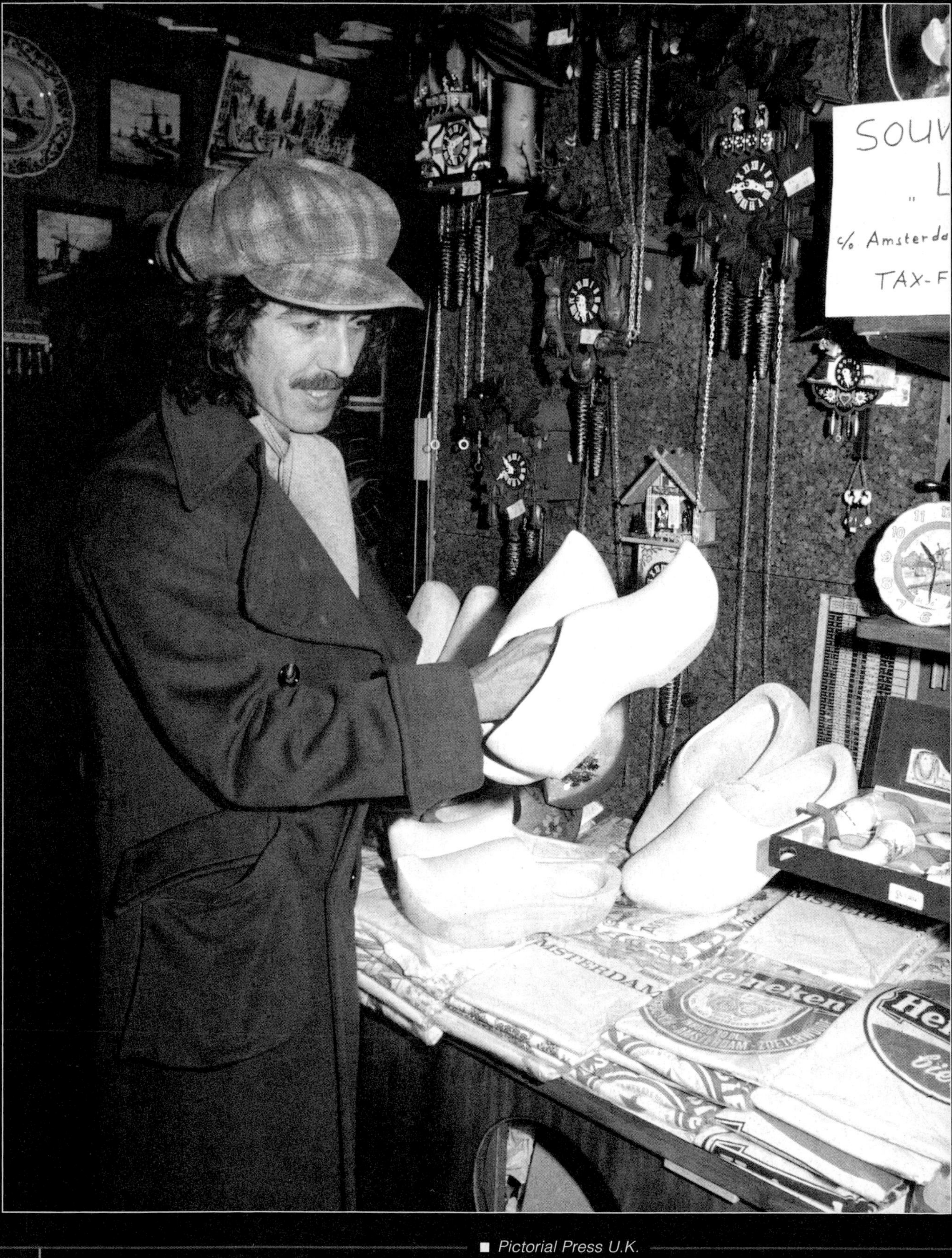

■ Pictorial Press U.K.

"shuffle" function mixing them up, it's difficult to play favorites.

Again, the mood was distinctly homespun roots, with at least a handful of songs drawing straight from the same wellspring that fired its predecessor. Unquestioned highlights include "The Light That Has Lighted The World," a song hallmarked by distinct echoes of Lennon's Imagine, the Harry Nilsson–esque "Who Can See It" and the deliciously downbeat "Be Here Now," written during Harrison's stay in L.A. in 1971, working on a new Ravi Shankar album.

Less eternal but equally enjoyable, "Sue Me, Sue You Blues" took a wry look at the legal shenanigans that surrounded the dissolution of The Beatles; "The Day The World Gets 'Round" was written in his New York hotel room the morning after the Bangla Desh concerts, and "Try Some Buy Some" was culled from sessions for a Ronnie Spector album, which Harrison and Phil Spector launched in early February 1971 (Ronnie's own version of "Try Some Buy Some" was issued as an Apple single in April 1971).

The album outtakes, meanwhile, include "Miss O'Dell," composed in L.A. for Apple employee Chris O'Dell and issued as the B-side of "Give Me Love"; "You've Gotta Stay With Me" (featuring old Mersey pal Cilla Black on vocals and Clapton on guitar; and "When Every Song Is Sung," an early version of the number better-known to Starr fans as "I'll Still Love You" (from his Rotogravure album).

DARK HORSE
Released: December 1974 (U.S. #4)

This was the album that suggested that, whatever magic Harrison had sprinkled over his solo career thus far, it was finally running dry — Dark Horse is best-remembered today first, for sharing its title with Harrison's own then-recently formed record label; second, for prompting his first major solo tour, a 43-date undertaking heralded by the LP's opening instrumental, "Hari's On Tour (Express)"; and finally (ignobly) as the first major Beatle album not to even scrape the U.K. chart. Neither did George's problems end there. Both tour and album were so marred by a persistent bout of laryngitis that critics were soon referring to the tour as "dark hoarse" — and not really discussing the album at all.

Recorded in just four weeks in September at Harrison's Friar Park, Henley, home, then rushed to release little more than a month later, Dark Horse includes little that could be compared to past triumphs. "So Sad" and the title track alone can be considered classic Harrison, but both go on way too long. However, the sweetly simplistic "Ding Dong, Ding Dong" was a sterling stab at a Christmas anthem and one that deserved far better than its low Top 40 chart placings in the U.S. and Britain. A superbly stylized cover of The Everly Brothers' "Bye Bye Love" — featuring contributions from estranged wife Patti and her new beau, Clapton — must surely rate among the most wryly pointed songs in any ex-Beatle's repertoire. "I Don't Care Anymore," an outtake issued as the B-side to the U.K. "Ding Dong" single, is also pleasant enough, while the devotional "It Is He (Jai Sri Krishna)" at least has a hauntingly mantric quality that stays stuck in one's head long after the song is over.

Otherwise, though, Dark Horse is more or less disposable, and one cannot shake the suspicion that it was issued simply so George could have something new in the stores in time for the tour. This suspicion is compounded by the fact that just three songs from the album ("Hari's On Tour," "Dark Horse" and the workaday "Maya Love") made it into the set, and one cannot help but feel Harrison would've been better served if he'd simply toured for the fun of it, then issued a live album for Christmas. 28 years later, people are still talking about the subtly rewritten version of Lennon's "In My Life" ("I love God more") that was a highlight of the show. Has anybody even listened to *Dark Horse* in that time?

EXTRA TEXTURE (READ ALL ABOUT IT)
Released: October 1975 (U.S. #8, U.K. #16)

Extra Texture is another patchy album, a state of affairs only partly explained by the patchwork of material that went into it. Many of the songs were relatively new — "This Guitar (Can't Keep From Crying)," for example, was written over Christmas, while Harrison was on holiday in Hawaii with new girlfriend Olivia Arias. Others, however, dated back several years — the backing track for "You" was taken from the same 1971 Ronnie Spector album session as "Try Some Buy Some"; "Tired Of Midnight Blue" harked back to Harrison's trip to L.A. that same year and documents a visit to a local nightspot; and "A Bit More Of You" was based on recordings he made at Abbey Road in February 1971. Armed with that knowledge, how predictable it is that these three — the magnificent "You" in particular — should be the finest songs in sight.

Do not, however, overlook the Dylan-esque "The Answer's At The End," the contemplative (if somewhat Wings-ish) "Ooh Baby" and the whacked "His Name Is Legs (Ladies & Gentlemen)," a six-minute semi-jam built around the presence in the studio ("I only came here to mend the central heating") of Legs Larry Smith, a former member of the Bonzo Dog Doo Dah Band and now one of Harrison's closest friends.

THE BEST OF GEORGE HARRISON
Released: October 1976 (U.S. #31)

Worthwhile for the non-album "Bangla-Desh," otherwise a predictable gathering of recent hits and, oh yeah, seven Beatles songs.

THIRTY-THREE & 1/3
Released: November 1976 (U.S. #11, U.K. #35)

Early in the year, Harrison predicted his next album would be out by spring. In fact, recording did not even begin until May and stretched into September, a prolonged (by his standards) gestation that resulted in his finest release since *Material World.* Titled for Harrison's own age at the time of the album's release, his own first LP for his Dark Horse label swung from the fruity upbeat "Woman Don't You Cry For Me," with its subtly farting synthesizer rhythm, to the All Things Must Pass–era "Beautiful Girl," exquisitely re-recorded for the occasion. There were also a splendid cover of Cole Porter's "True Love" and the Top 20 hit "Crackerbox Palace" (titled for Lord Buckley's former home).

The most-discussed number, however, was "This Song," the first single from the album and a brilliantly constructed commentary on Harrison's most recent travails, defending himself against a charge of "subconscious plagiarism," regarding similarities between "My Sweet Lord" and The Chiffons' "He's So Fine." In his defense, Harrison confessed that he'd actually been trying to capture the feel of Edwin Hawkins' "Oh Happy Day," but September 1976 saw the court find against him regardless. Incidentally, the popular notion that the lawsuit was brought by former Beatles associate Allen Klein is not true — his ABKCO organization did not purchase the song's publishing until 1980. A decade after that, in a New York court, Harrison was himself granted the rights to The Chiffons' song for the U.K., U.S. and Canada.

GEORGE HARRISON
Released: February 1979 (U.S. #14, U.K. #39)

When one remembers the fuss that surrounded the resumption of Lennon's recording career after a four-year absence, it seems remarkable that Harrison's return after almost as long did not raise more than an eyebrow. Like Lennon, he had spent much of the hiatus out of the limelight; like Lennon, he'd had a child (Dhani) in the midst of his seclusion. Indeed, he later admitted that he did not write a single song during 1977, preferring to spend his time watching Formula 1 racing and working on his autobiography, I Me Mine, for publication as a high-priced limited edition in 1980.

Whatever Harrison's motives for keeping his songwriting securely locked away, clearly he could not wait to pick up his pen again, once "the year I took off from music" was over. New Year's Day itself saw him begin work on two new songs, "If You Believe" and "Blow Away" — the latter was then completed during a winter storm, when he feared the entire house was indeed about to blow away. He poured his devotion to motor racing out in "Faster," a song that has since become an anthem of sorts for auto events in the U.K.; a visit to his local pub saw him start work on "Soft Hearted Hana"; and, by mid-1978, not only was much of George Harrison already written, but he'd also begun accumulating songs for the future as well —

including the still-unreleased "Sooty Goes To Hawaii," concerning the adventures of a popular English television puppet bear.

Recording at Friar Park, Harrison spent some time listening back to All Things Must Pass, and certainly the experience did him good. George Harrison would emerge his most natural-sounding album since that time and, if a few of the tracks do seem slight, the Top 20 hit "Blow Away" is exquisite.

SOMEWHERE IN ENGLAND
Released: June 1981 (U.S. #11, U.K. #13)

The most troubled of Harrison's solo albums, Somewhere In England, was taped with producer Ray Cooper over the course of a full year, October 1979-October 1980, only to be rejected by Warner Brothers, who decided the whole thing was too gloomy and needed to be brightened up. Reluctantly heeding his masters' voice, Harrison remixed the entire album, replaced four of the songs with more upbeat concoctions and then wrote the caustic "Blood From A Clone" to let Warner's know precisely how he felt about it all.

It was a criminal decision on the label's part, utterly shattering an album that, as bootleg pressings of the original tape prove, could easily have taken its place among the elite of solo Beatledom. However, one gem did emerge from the carnage, a number Harrison originally worked up with Starr during the latter's Can't Fight Lightning album sessions in November 1980 and then completed in the dazed aftermath of John Lennon's murder weeks later. The magnificent "All Those Years Ago," the most significant of all the many tributes to the slain Lennon to be issued in early 1981, featured contributions from both Starr and a visiting McCartney, and it flew to #2 in the U.S. in May 1981. (Kim Carnes' "Bette Davis Eyes" held it off the top.)

(Of the excisions, "Flying Hour," recorded at Friar Park in April 1978, during the *George Harrison* album sessions; "Sat Singing" and "Lay His Head" ["Got My Mind Set On You"'s B-side] appeared on a limited edition CD/EP issued with 1988's *Songs By George Harrison* songbook; "Tears Of The World" made it onto the subsequent *Songs By... Volume Two*.)

GONE TROPPO
Released: November 1982 (U.S. #108)

Since first venturing into movie production as backer of *Monty Python's Life Of Brian* in 1979, Harrison had found cinema a far more fascinating outlet than rock music. However, although his Handmade Films production company was now consuming more and more of his time, he still wrote one more album before effectively retiring from the music industry for five years. Of course the weight of that decision must have been lightened by *Gone Troppo's* absolute non-performance chart-wise, although to accuse the album itself of hastening that demise is grossly unfair.

Not a vital Harrison album by any means, it is nevertheless no worse than much of McCartney's period output; indeed, a couple of tracks at least stand alongside any number of Harrison's minor classics — a remix of "Dream Away," the closing number in the Handmade Films production *Time Bandits*, and a remake of the Beatles-era "Circles," cut at Friar Park in April 1978 during the George Harrison album sessions.

Recorded over a three-month period, beginning in May, Gone Troppo took its title from Harrison's recent decision to withdraw to sunnier climes (Hawaii) and its failure from his refusal to embark on even minimal promotion for the record. In terms of its commercial impact, then, the sole statistical evidence for the album's very existence was an appearance at #53 for the single "Wake Up My Love."

CLOUD NINE
Released: September 1987 (U.S. #8, U.K. #10)

In the five years since his last album, Harrison made only a handful of recorded appearances. He cut "Save The World" for 1985's Greenpeace charity album and re-recorded the All Things Must Pass–era Dylan cover, "I Don't Want To Do It," for the Porky's Revenge soundtrack. He also was involved with various Handmade Films movie soundtracks, but work on a new album did not get underway until early 1987.

Recorded over a three-month span with producer Jeff Lynne, an album littered with highlights included a quirkily compulsive cover of James Ray's 1962 hit "Got My Mind Set On You," which promptly became Harrison's first U.S. chart-topper (and biggest British hit — it reached #2) since 1973. The pretty "This Is Love" is also a jewel, but best of all is "When We Was Fab," an affectionate look back at his Beatles years, with Lynne wringing every last Beatles-esque effect out of his box of sonic tricks. For months before the album's release, rumor insisted that Harrison had reunited with Starr and McCartney for one song on the set — he hadn't, but "When We Was Fab" is almost as good. The accompanying video, directed by Kevin Godley, is similarly superlative.

TRAVELING WILBURYS VOLUME ONE

Released: October 1988 (U.S. #3, U.K. #16)

The musical union of Wilbury clansmen Nelson (Harrison), Lucky (Dylan), Otis (Lynne), Lefty (Roy Orbison) and Charles T. Jr. (Tom Petty) had its roots in friendships and associations that dated back many years. Even in the months before it was publicly unveiled, Harrison appeared on stage with Dylan in London and on air with Lynne in Los Angeles, while the full Wilburys lineup debuted in the studio in April to record "Handle With Care," eventually selected as the group's first single.

Rough, rootsy and utterly good-natured but definitely a case of its parts being far greater than its whole, the Wilburys' debut is nevertheless one of the most cherished of recent decades, with its continued CD non-availability a bone of contention with collectors of all persuasions. Few of the songs rank among their makers' best, however, and it's ironic that the most impressive performances on the first album were by Orbison — who passed away before work began on the second.

Harrison's contributions include lead vocals on "Heading For The Light," shared lead on "Handle With Care" and "End Of The Line" and backing vocals elsewhere.

THE BEST OF DARK HORSE 1976-89

Released: October 1989 (U.S. #132)

Two new songs recorded earlier in the year, "Cockamamie Business" and "Poor Little Girl," pad out an otherwise unnecessary collection of material dating back to Thirty- Three & 1/3. Also included is "Cheer Down," a song originally written for Clapton but since recorded by Harrison himself (with Lynne) for the Lethal Weapon 2 movie soundtrack.

TRAVELING WILBURYS VOLUME THREE

Released: November 1990 (U.S. #11, U.K. #14)

The tragic loss of Lefty Wilbury (Orbison) did more than derail his Traveling brethren; it also prompted them to rename themselves. Reconvening after a two-year absence, they now lined up as Spike (Harrison), Boo (Dylan), Clayton (Lynne), and Muddy (Petty), although cruel critics pointed out that, this time around, the names were about as creative as things got.

Titled Volume Three out of ironic deference to the Volume Two bootleg collection of outtakes and alternates, the album features no solo Harrison tracks whatsoever; his one contribution, "Maxine," was rejected by his bandmates. However, a ghost from The Beatles' Hamburg repertoire got on board, with a spirited version of "Nobody's Child."

LIVE IN JAPAN

Released: July 1992 (U.S. #126)

In December 1991, Harrison launched a six-venue/12-show tour of Japan, accompanied by Clapton and his band. It was his first concert outing since 1974 and his first trip to Japan since 1966.

The set comprised nine Beatles songs (including an extended "Piggies," featuring a Lennon-penned verse that was dropped for the studio version), together with a career-spanning selection of solo material, while Clapton's own four-song interlude added "Badge" to the show. It was all rather jolly, and the accompanying live album is genuinely enjoyable, especially if one doesn't pay too much attention. Listen closely, however, and it does lack spark. The energy levels so rarely get above sea level that, while the album itself ends with a spirited "Roll Over Beethoven," it might as well wrap up with McCartney's "Lonely Old People" "...passing the time of day..."

Live In Japan was Harrison's final album, although he remained active through the 1990s. April 1992 saw Harrison and Clapton resume their double act with a concert at London's Royal Albert Hall in aid of the spiritually inclined Natural Law Party. The show, which was Harrison's first-ever solo British concert — hinged around the Japanese live set and featured guest appearances from Starr, his son Zak, and Harrison's son Dhani.

Over the next eight years, he made a number of recorded appearances, including contributions to Bob Dylan's 30th Anniversary tribute concert in 1992; he donated a track to a six-CD promo box set produced to mark Warner Bros.' chief executive Mo Ostin's retirement in 1994, and, of course, he recorded a couple of songs with former bandmates McCartney and Starr. Indeed, though a new solo album was mooted as early as 1993, the sheer enormity of The Beatles Anthology project conspired to delay it so long that, by 1996, Harrison had all but given up on ever finishing it. Litigation surrounding the sale of Handmade Films and, more pleasurably, work on a new Shankar album also proved time-consuming, while his health, too, was causing him concern.

In July 1997, Harrison discovered a lump on his throat and, the following month, was treated for suspected throat cancer at the Princess Margaret hospital in Windsor, England. Ironically, Harrison was still undergoing radiation therapy when the news broke that Derek Taylor, one of The Beatles' most loyal associates, had died of the same ailment. George was the only Beatle to attend the funeral, on Sept. 12.

> " *I'm saving them up for when I kick the bucket.* "

In January 1998, the Mayo Clinic in Rochester, Minn., gave him the all-clear. Just months later, however, and barely two weeks after Linda McCartney's death, MTV was reporting Harrison had been diagnosed with advanced lung cancer — a rumor that Harrison himself was quick to scotch. It would be close to two years more before his true state of health was officially acknowledged.

In the meantime, plans for Harrison's return to action continued to fly. Another new solo album was rumored — among the songs prepared for it was a Jim Capaldi composition, "You Got A Hold On Me." Petty contemplated reconvening The Traveling Wilburys; Harrison worked at a box set of solo outtakes and demos, designed along similar lines to The Beatles' and Lennon's own *Anthology* projects. He was also realigning his own catalog for reissue, with the first stage in this process, a sensational 30th anniversary remastering of *All Things Must Pass,* appearing last year. It would be his final release. Having battled his cancer for as long as he could, Harrison passed away Nov. 29, 2001.

The immediate future of the remainder of Harrison's catalog is now shrouded in uncertainty, although it is unlikely that his death actually threatens more than a slight delay. After all, Harrison himself has long been aware of mortality's affect on the marketplace, as he told the *Melbourne Herald Sun* newspaper in March 1999, when they asked him when we could expect to see his next release.

"I don't know," he replied. "Maybe next month, maybe not. Maybe sometime, maybe not. Actually, I'm saving them up for when I kick the bucket. Some people will really want it then, and I will sell more copies." ■

Wings~ First Flights

PAUL AND LINDA MCCARTNEY | By Dave Thompson

O n April 6th, 1993, Paul McCartney headlined a massive "Early Earth Day" concert in Los Angeles. He was the star of the show and it was his music the audience came to hear. The former Beatles' latest album, Hope of Deliverance, was universally regarded as his finest in years and the new songs slipped effortlessly, even seamlessly, in alongside the classics of his past.

But the Earth Day triumph was not Paul's alone. Beside him on stage, as she has been at almost every concert Paul has played since the end of the Beatles, was Linda, his wife and constant companion for the past 25 years. It was Linda who awakened Paul to the ecological perils that confront man today and who has, throughout the couple's marriage, maintained a constant interest in the well-being not only of the planet, but also of its inhabitants.

It was Linda who persuaded Paul to become a vegetarian one Sunday afternoon when they sat down for dinner and saw "our young lambs racing happily in the fields. Glancing down at our plates we suddenly realized we were eating the leg of an animal that had until recently been gamboling in a field itself."

It was Linda who involved Paul in recording a series of "radical" messages for the animal welfare orgainzation, PETA, and it was Linda who was called to the phone

" The sounds of Paul McCartney's post-Beatles career were as much Linda's as Paul's. "

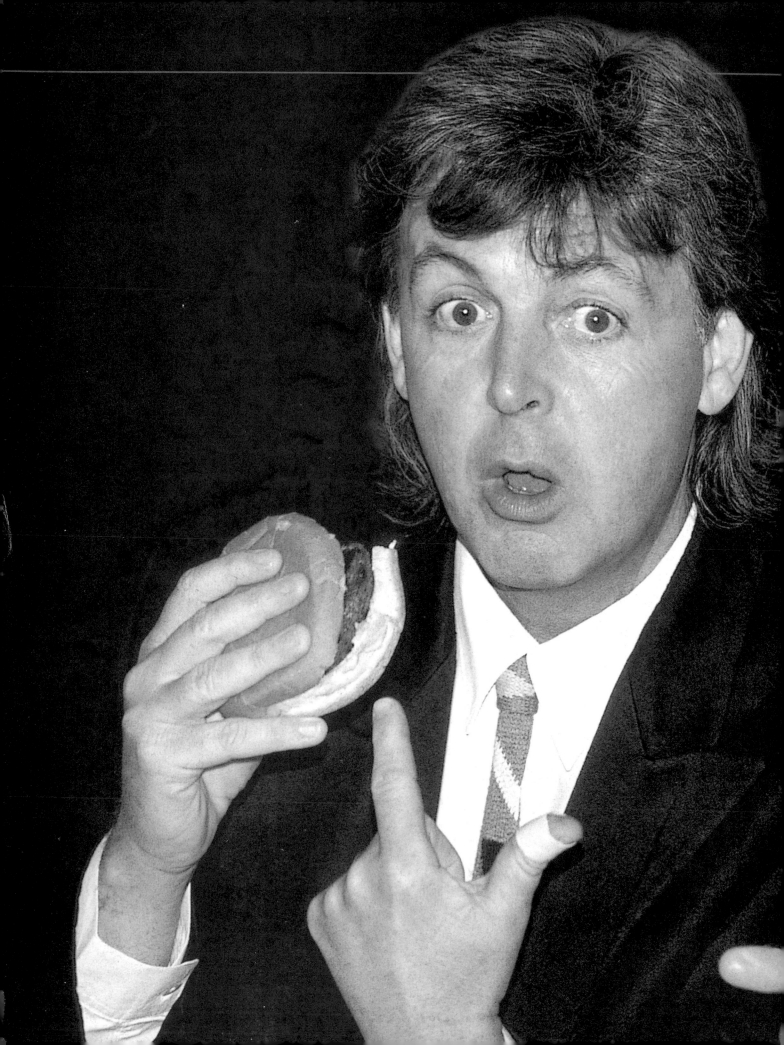

at all hours of the of the night when the local branch of Britain's RSPCA (Royal Society for the Prevention of Cruelty to Animals) needs an emergency home for an injured animal. According to Linda's closest friends, her love of animals is no less powerful than her love of Paul and their children. After all the shit that has landed her in over the past 25 years, you couldn't demand further proof of her commitment.

Perhaps more than any of the millions of words written about Linda in the quarter-century since she rose out of nowhere to marry Paul McCartney, that single sentence truly sums her up. She suffered not only the barbs of jealous fans, but also the malice of critics who simply cannot understand how Paul could trade the Beatles for a photographer. Linda McCartney has never once flinched from her husband's side and he has paid her back with a passionate loyalty. In a business where infidelity is the passport to tabloid publicity, there has never once been the suggestion that either Paul or Linda has strayed. Attempts to insinuate otherwise, as one author did in 1990, have been laughed out of sight. Even if one did have eyes for another, it is joked, they're never apart long enough to do anything about it!

In a career which writes off its heroes on a regular basis, and has never truly accorded Linda that status, Paul has retained his faith in his wife's abilities. He continued to insist on her taking her place on stage, even when critics and crowd alike are against her. Linda has responded with the same grace she has exhibited in every other aspect of her life, answering her critics with the slightly crooked smile which won Paul's heart in the first place, Her patience and forbearance, one friend marveled, is almost Biblical in its strength.

But silence does not necessarily denote inaction. For the first five or six years at least, Paul's post-Beatles career followed a course which Linda, by her very omnipresence, helped him map out. The sounds of that career were as much Linda's as Paul's and though she herself claims that she cannot sing, her vocal harmonies are as integral to Paul's music as Paul himself.

Privately Linda's beliefs and convictions have become inseparable from Paul's, at the same time as retaining their own distinct integrity. While she and Paul have, on occasion, committed themselves to projects which fall beyond the confines of their partnership, Linda's have proven the most successful. Her books, displaying a selection of the thousands of photographs she took of rock groups during the '60s, have been universally acclaimed and the line of Beauty Without Cruelty make-up products she launched in the mid-1980s established her as a businesswoman as well.

The popularly held notions that she is "nothing" without Paul, that she was, as one of Paul's many biographers cruelly alleged, simply "a silver spoon groupie" who lucked along at the right time, are shattered by these successes. As if the enduring success of Paul and Linda marriage itself did not finally torpedo such malice. The fact remains that Linda McCartney is a grossly misunderstood and maligned, woman; one who, had she accomplished the same achievements from beyond the shadow of a famous husband, would already have been the subject of a dozen questing biographies.

As it is, even the most in-depth books about Paul accord Linda little more than a poor second billing, portraying her at best as a creative afterthought; at worst, as an over-bearing bitch who literally battered Paul into submission. In reality, the "hold" which Linda allegedly has on Paul is not only reciprocal, it is the very foundation of their relationship. An examination of Linda McCartney's career is more than the biography of a pop star's wife. It is the story which turns the tables on history. Paul and Linda's musical career is too vast to fully examine in one article. Neither would it be accurate to credit Linda with the same influence today as she exercised at the outset of Paul's solo career, though the couple still maintains the appearance of togetherness.

For all musical intents and purposes (and certainly for the purposes of this article), Linda's input can be said to have ended the first time she got to sing an entire song solo, "Cook of the House" on 1976's *Wings at the Speed of Sound*. But it began with the Beatles, although there aren't too many people around who can claim to have made their recorded debut on one of their recordings. Linda sang backing vocals on "Let It Be," and has admitted, "it was supposed to be me and Mary Hopkin, but she had to go home."

> *"Me and some of the girls used to sing doo-wop together for fun"*

Linda Louise Eastman was born on September 24, 1941. Her mother, Louise Eastman, was heir to the Cleveland Linders department store chain; her father, Lee Epstein (he adopted his wife's maiden name before Linda was born), was a Harvard graduate and show-business copyright lawyer, whose affluence was manifested in his art collection.

The family divided its time between homes in Scarsdale, East Hampton and an apartment in Park Avenue. Dinner parties — entertaining Lee's showbiz clientele — were sumptuous affairs. Visitors to the Eastman home included songwriters Hoagy Carmichael and Tommy Dorsey, actor

William "Hopalong Cassidy" Boyd and another writer, Jack Lawrence. It was he who gave Linda her first taste of fame, late in 1947. In return for some legal work, Lee Eastman requested Lawrence write a song about the 6-year-old Linda. He came up with "Linda," later to be recorded by Jan and Dean.

Linda was, she says, "the black sheep of the family," even before she discovered rock 'n'roll music — and musicians. Childhood piano lessons were abandoned in the face of the headstrong child's objections. By her late teens, Linda was regularly playing truant from school in Scarsdale to attend the all-day rock 'n' roll shows emceed by disc jockey Alan Freed at the Brooklyn Paramount in New York. (She attended Scarsdale High School and the exclusive Sarah Lawrence School in nearby Bronxville, which was also Yoko Ono's former alma mater.)

Freed, she enthuses, "never played a bad record. The Dells, the Doves, the Moonglows, I was into them all," For a girl who grew up "with an ear to the radio," her first sight of Chuck Berry, Bobby Darin and Fabian were her first taste of true freedom. Though she was never in a band, "me and some, of the girls used to sing doo-wop together for fun, up in our school's music Tower."

In 1960, at age 18, Linda started Princeton University, where she studied art and history. She was dating a geophysics student, Melvin See, at the time. He became Linda's first husband when she began desperately trying to reconstitute her life following the death of her mother in an air crash.

"When I met (Lennon) ...

The marriage was doomed. See dreamed of continuing his studies in Africa, following graduation. Linda would travel no further afield than Tucson, Arizona, where the couple's first and only child, daughter Heather, was born on December 31, 1963. Linda initiated divorce proceedings shortly after. It was in Tucson that Linda first decided what she wanted to do with her life. Arizona, she said, "opened up my eyes to the wonder of light and color," and having taken a course in Art History at the University of Arizona, Linda moved on to a course in photography presented by Hazel Archer at Tucson Art Center. She also spent a lot of time traveling through the desert and, she says, "for the first time... going round with artists, actors and writers, discovering who I am. It changed my life, meeting so many interesting, intelligent people."

In 1964, Linda — now in the process of getting a divorce — returned to New York with baby Heather. She was working as a receptionist at *Town and Country* magazine, when one morning's mail delivery brought an open invitation to photograph the visiting Rolling Stones aboard a boat on the Hudson River.

Linda took the invitation for herself. She arrived at the reception and discovered she was the only photographer on board. Rock 'n' roll photography, as opposed to the straightforward showbiz shots of the past, was still a growing child at this time, but Linda understood it intuitively.

But it was not her abilities which first brought her notice, it was the exclusivity of her photographs. As the only photographer at the reception, she found her work was in enormous demand among the magazines which had not been represented. "That got my name around... that was a great piece of luck."

Resigning from her receptionist's desk, Linda set herself up as a freelance photographer. It was a precarious role, but one to which she seemed ideally suited. Combining the rebelliousness which, even as a child, had so often helped her get her own way, with a genuine love for meeting people ("particularly successful people," complained one rival), Linda learned that if she couldn't bully her way into a commission, she could cajole instead.

The following year, 1965, she was traveling as far afield as California to work with the Beach Boys (the first band she ever met back in Arizona when they played the University) and Austria, photographing the Beatles during the making of their second movie, "Help!" Later, when Bill Graham opened the Fillmore East in New York, Linda became house photographer, an unpaid but nevertheless prestigious position.

John Lennon was the first Beatle to catch Linda's eye, and when she was introduced to the group at Shea Stadium in August, 1966, it was to his side that she gravitated. Unfortunately, "when I met him the fascination faded fast." The dour Lennon wit and the working class abrasiveness which he wore as protective clothing, were scarcely calculated to make a good impression on the pretty little rich girl from the Hamptons. His songwriting partner, Paul McCartney, was another matter entirely.

In May, 1967, Linda arrived in London to photograph one of the newly-rising, talents of British pop, Steve Winwood's Traffic, for a now very collectible paperback, *Rock and Other Four Letter Words: Music of the Electric Generation*. Written and designed by Marks, this exhilarating collection of words, pictures and diagrams would be published by Bantam Books the following year, with Linda described as "rapidly becoming known as one of the major rock photographers." By the time the book hit the racks, however, she was better known for something else entirely.

...the fascination faded fast."

On the evening of May 15, 1967, Jimi Hendrix's manager, ex-Animals bassist Chas Chandler, took Linda to the Bag o'Nails, a nightclub on Kingley Street, to see Georgie Fame and the Blue Flames. Paul was sitting at the table next to them.

"It was one of those things," Linda later remarked. "We just fancied each other." Afterwards, she joined Paul at the Speakeasy club. Four nights later, she and Paul met again at Brian Epstein's home on Chapel Street. Pete Brown, Epstein's aide, had given Linda one of the handful of exclusive invitations for the Beatles' *Sgt. Pepper* launch party (she was one of just 15 photographers present).

Maybe one could never argue, as has been successfully said of Yoko Ono, that marrying a Beatle was the worst career move Linda Eastman ever made. But there is no doubt that shifting herself from one side of the lens to the other was certainly not to her professional advantage.

In later years, Beatles fans (and more specifically, Linda's critics) were to regard this and those other meetings with Paul, as examples of her "pushiness." In reality, it was a tribute to her abilities and renown as a photographer. No less than Mankowitz in the U.K. and Hoffman and Ochs in the United States, Linda Eastman belonged to that increasingly select, increasingly rarified circle of "superstar photographers," welcome in the most tightly controlled dressing room. It wasn't for who or what she was (and being an attractive female with a documented taste for musicians, had become a constant barb), but for what she could do with her camera.

> *" It was one of those things. We just fancied each other "*

Some of the most enduring images of the mid-late 1960s were taken by Linda and *Rock and Other Four Letter Words* is stuffed with them. While she was certainly fortunate to be working at a time when musicians themselves were operating under a heightened sense of visual orchestration, enough bad photographs exist of her own favorite subjects, Hendrix, Traffic, the Airplane and the Dead, to prove there was more than an inkling of genuine photographic talent at large.

Into the Void

In May, 1968, almost a year after she last saw him, Linda learned that Paul, with John, was giving a press conference in New York as part of their drive to launch Apple Records. She attended, and as the event wound down, passed Paul her telephone number and then went home and waited. Paul did not let her down. The couple met that evening at the New York apartment of Beatles' attorney, Nat Weiss and for the next few days seemed inseparable. Indeed, Heather, now age 6, made such an impression on Paul that when Linda had to take off to photograph a show at the Fillmore, Paul remained behind babysitting.

The Beatle returned to London at the end of the month, but just a few weeks later was in Los Angeles. Immediately, he telephoned Linda, asking her to join him. She did and the pair stayed together for a week. Throughout most of the Beatles' most successful years, Paul had been dating actress Jane Asher, who was four years Linda's junior. Her influence on Paul was prodigious. It was Jane who persuaded him to the

"**Paul remained behind babysitting.**"

purchase the High Park Farm in Scotland where he still lives today and she was the one who found the Cavendish Avenue, St. John's Wood, house where Paul now lived while in London.

The talk of an imminent marriage between Paul and Jane was little more than that — simple talk. Although Jane admitted, as early as 1964, that she "would be most surprised if I married anyone else but Paul," her beau constantly denied even an engagement. It was Christmas, 1967, before he finally proposed and seven months later, Jane announced on BBC television that the engagement was off.

Paul returned to his role as "the world's most eligible bachelor," but his status was not to remain secure. By November, just four months after his break-up with Asher was confirmed, Paul was spotted moving a new lady into his life, as Linda and Heather moved into Cavendish Avenue with him. Four months later, with Linda four months pregnant, they were married on March 12, 1969, at Marylebone Register Office.

Linda arrived in Paul's life at both a fortuitous, and a fraught time the former, because if ever he needed someone beside him, it was now; the latter, because with the break-up of his relationship with Jane Asher to be followed, with precipitous haste, by the onset of the break-up of the Beatles, the world was desperate to find a scapegoat. Yoko Ono's presence alongside John and the increasingly bizarre activities the pair was now publicly indulging in, provided too easy a target. Linda a divorcee like Yoko, but unlike Yoko, a well-known face on the New York rock scene, was a more suitable target.

Her familiarity from a thousand backstage parties fired the inevitable rumors that she was little more than a well-shod groupie. The fact that she had leaped so swiftly into the void left by Jane Asher suggested she was also a gold-digger. The haste with which the pair married and Linda's already visible pregnancy, opened the door to allegations of bullying, as though Paul only married the girl out of a sense of old-fashioned decency. Now, with, the Beatles publicly (if not openly) crumbling, a fourth crime could be added to her indictment. Not only was Linda Eastman the girl who stole a Beatle, she was also the woman who broke them. Matters worsened when it became public that one of the greatest divisions in the group related to the member's legal representation. Late in 1968, Linda introduced Paul to her father, show-business lawyer Lee Eastman, and brother John, a partner in the family firm. Although Paul had joked "I've been had," when it was revealed that contrary to rumor, Linda was not heir to the Eastman-Kodak photography fortune, the Eastmans' own wealth was nothing to turn his nose up at. Seeing John and Lee at work in their 5th Avenue chambers elegant, efficient, and indescribably upper class — Paul was convinced that Eastman and Eastman Inc. was the answer to Apple's prayers.

The rest of the band, however, preferred the vociferous Allen Klein. While it is obvious that much of Eastman's appeal to McCartney was sentimental, the studied elegance of the family firm and the civilized manner in which the elder Eastman executed even the dirtiest tasks were also undeniable influences. Although Lennon frequently berated Paul for. What he, (John). perceived as the bassist's incipient snobbery, McCartney was in fact, a natural overachiever, forever looking to lift himself from one milieu to another, whatever the cost. Allying himself to the Eastmans, whether through marriage or business, was not a calculated move. It was his destiny.

Domestic Bliss

Mary McCartney was born on August 29, 1969, just six months after Paul and Linda wed (official announcements insisted she was not expected until December); with Paul having already adopted Heather, the McCartney family was ready-made. It took the place of one which was now undergoing its final death throes. Although the Beatles would continue to release records for another year, they would record little more than one album's worth of material. On August 20, 1969, John, Paul, George and Ringo attended a session together for the last time. By the end of the year, the Beatles were no more and by early 1970, they didn't care who knew.

Paul was the first Beatle to acknowledge the end of the group. Although John and George had both released low-key extracurricular albums, with John even enjoying a couple of hit singles with his and Yoko's Plastic Ono Band, it was the release of Paul's self-titled debut album in; March, 1970, which placed the lid on the coffin.

Although Linda's musical contributions to McCartney were restricted to some harmonies and perhaps, some of the background sounds (slamming doors, clinking cutlery, etc) which give the album the sparse' homemade feel its maker had, so evidently yearned for, her presence hangs heavy over the record. indeed, the opening track. "The Lovely Linda," was written just days after the couple's marriage, while other songs "Momma Miss America," "That Would Be Something" and the classic "Maybe I'm Amazed," echo that initial statement

> " *Paul was the first Beatle to acknowledge the end of the group.* "

of love. In later years, Paul would snipingly admit that the songs which comprise McCartney "weren't quite throwaways." He is doing himself, and Linda, a serious disservice.

Paul continued to revel in domesticity within the album's gatefold sleeve. Of the 21 photographs scattered across the two faces (all, of course, taken by Linda), only one reflected Paul's profession. The remainder showed baby Mary, step-daughter Heather, sundry pets, Paul at play and Linda herself. The overall impression of McCartney, both visually and aurally, is of a family photograph album.

This sense of domestic bliss was to dominate McCartney's work over the next four years, until 1974's *Band on the Run* album finally catapulted Wings — the group Paul and Linda formed in 1971 — into the superstar league from which they had hitherto been hiding. Unfortunately, albums like *Ram, Wildlife and Red Rose Speedway*, while arguably containing some of the best and, in the case of *Wildlife*, rawest work of McCartney's entire career, were to suffer at the hands of fans and critics alike. They described them as "weak," "syrupy," "uninspired" and worse. The root of the problem was Linda.

It was with the release of *Rain*, in 1971, that the anti-Linda lobby truly took the bit between its teeth. Hitherto, Linda's influence upon Paul, encouraged by a burgeoning belief that John had been the aggressive heart of the Beatles, had been likened to the application of heat to a record album. She softened him up and made him even more pliable than he already was.

In fact, Paul and Linda had already answered those criticisms. "Another Day," Paul's first solo single, was a ballad in melody alone. Lyrically, it reveals a darkness and desperation which would not have been out of place on Lennon's own solo album; while musically, Linda's soaring harmonies continue to defy the prevalent belief that she couldn't carry a tune if you give her a bucket to put it in. As if that wasn't enough, flip the single over, and things get even wilder as "Oh Woman Oh Why" reveals itself to be one of the hardest rockers of McCartney's entire career. But *Ram*, credited jointly to Paul and Linda McCartney (with Denny Seiwell on drums), still owed little to Paul's shining past and scarcely anything more to the stark (and in sudden retrospect. respectable) acoustics of McCartney. Rather, it was a collection of inconsequential ditties with infantile lyrics and titles which could scarcely be mentioned in the same breath as the Beatles' classics: "Uncle Albert" (a U.S. hit that same year; no single was released from the album in Britain), "Monkberry Moon Delight," "Smile Away," and the seemingly obligitory ode to Linda, "Long Haired Lady."

That was what the reviews said, anyway. Actually, *Ram* remains McCartney's most overtly enjoyable and most obviously innocent record. Like the sonic minimalists who turned up at the fringes of the alternative rock scene during the late 1980s, the McCartneys were experimenting with the basest limitations of themselves and their audience. They offered up a bill of musical fire which was light years removed from the increasingly pompous and procrastinating sounds of their peers — John and George included.

Quite simply, Ram was the sound of a Good Time Being Had By All, with Thrillington, the recently reissued "orchestral Ram" that Paul unleashed in 1977, was the sound of that same Good Time being shared even further. Unfortunately, Paul's fans and his publishers didn't see it like

that. To Lew Grade, the owner of Northern Songs, the album's songwriting credits, every number claimed jointly by Paul and Linda, was a not-so-subtle attempt by Paul to cheat Grade out of his share of the songwriting royalties.

A lawsuit was initiated, maintaining — incredibly, but at the time, quite acceptably — that Linda was not capable of writing any song. The case was eventually dropped (and Linda would continue to replace John Lennon across Paul's next album), but the hostility shown by Grade did not go away.

Had Linda had her way, she would have faded into the background immediately following the debacle over Ram. Paul, however, was having none of it. Reawakening in his wife the vague curiosities which had prompted her to take piano lessons during her childhood, but standing for none of the tantrums which finally dissuaded Mr. and Mrs. Eastman, McCartney began teaching Linda to play keyboards, a move which was to dramatically affect his own career, and not only in terms of the music.

Paul's reviews, both for records and live performances, were to be tainted by Linda's presence. It says a lot for both Paul and Linda that their love for one another could remain undaunted... let alone their continued work together. "Obviously I was never in the band because Paul thought I was the world's greatest musician," Linda later admitted. "It's about us being together. When I started, I only knew a few chords." Today, "well, I could play in a punk band at least."

Rumors that Paul was, in fact, grooming Linda for her own solo album around this time, of course, came to naught. It would be another two years before she finally ventured out alone, under the Suzy and the Redstripes pseudonym, with the mock reggae "Seaside Woman" single. It was five years after that before the record was finally released, with an instrumental version on the flip, "B-Side to Seaside." Incidentally, Jimmy McCullough, formerly of Thunderclap Newman and Stone The Crows, and a future member of Wings, plays guitar on the song.

One other solo Linda track, "Oriental Nightfish," has surfaced. Like "Seaside Woman," this very bizarre (Linda sings mock-cockney) song is best-known from the mid-1980s "Rupert and the Frog Chorus" video, where it is accompanied by a suitably spacey video, itself dating from 1978. "Oriental Nightfish" was recorded several years earlier, possibly during the *Venus and Mars* sessions.

Taking Wings

Paul and Linda's second child, Stella Nina, was born on September 12, 1971. She arrived midway through the sessions for Paul's next album *Wildlife*. This was the record which would debut Wings — Paul, Linda, drummer Seiwel and guitarist Kenny Laine. Today Wildlife stands among the most enduring of the McCartney's early albums But it earned its promotion the hardest way possible. Universally hammered by the press it has since been savage by its makers as well, with Linda con fessing, "we could have done it better."

But she was also aware that the pared down simplicity of the record, the bare-bones at arrangements which give the record its unique flavor, could not have been recaptured had they "done it better." *Wildlife's* weaknesses are the very same factors that ensure its strengths. And besides that, comparisons between Wildlife and the early (pre-Spector) mixes of the Beatles' *Let It Be* album prove that everything

McCartney was now accomplishing with Wings, he had first envisioned during those last, fraught years of Beatledom.

Nevertheless, plans to release a single from the album, pairing "Love is Strange" with the emphatically tongue-in-cheek (on Linda's behalf at least!) "I Am Your Singer," were scrapped. Paul wasted no time in making amends.

In February 1972, he struck back at his newly acquired (and Lennon-sponsored) image for "sappiness" with the hard-hitting "Give Ireland Back to the Irish" single. Inspired by the Bloody Sunday riots of the previous month, "Give Ireland Back to the Irish" was promptly banned by the BBC. While it still rose to a respectable #16 in the U.K. (and #1 in Spain), it remains a difficult single to find. Find it you should, though. Even with Paul's entire solo catalog having been released on CD, "Ireland's" own lilting instrumental flip, "Give Ireland back to the Irish (Version)" remains infuriatingly unavailable. And like "B-Side To Seaside," it is generally considered so insignificant that this situation is unlikely ever to change.

If this latest release was unexpected, Paul's next move was even more surprising. Early that same month, he packed the family and band up in a van and Wings (now augmented by another guitarist, Henry McCulloch) embarked on an impromptu tour of Britain's university circuit. Unannounced and unheralded, the van arrived at its first stop, Nottingham University, on February 8.

"Hi, we're Wings," Paul told the bemused Student Union organizers. "Can we play here tomorrow night?" Tapes dating from the earliest Wings' tours (just one song from which, the live-in-Holland "The Mess," has seen an official release) reveal that Wings has lost none of their studio

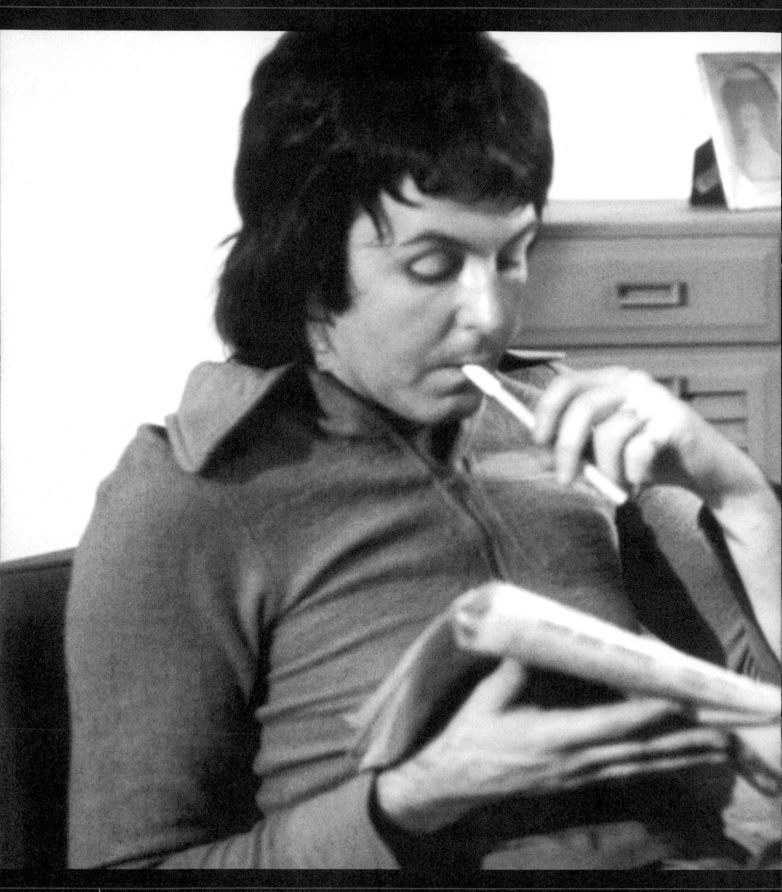

naivete. High volume and lengthy jams often represent the kind of rehearsing an artist of Paul's status was expected to have indulged in, and the critics swooped accordingly.

The headlines these earliest spreading of the Wings garnered, were not for the unquestionable magic being generated on stage, they were for the pickets and demonstrators who were bitter about McCartney's apparent support for Irish terrorism. They were for the McCartneys' increasingly' eccentric activities; for the drug busts (the first came in Sweden on August 10, 1972), unscheduled tours, and now, for following "Give Ireland Back to the Irish" with what must be the most bizarre single ever released by a Beatle. (Pete Best included!)

Discussing his most recent work, Paul had already admitted that Linda and the children were now the supreme barometer of his musical moods. But nobody could ever have anticipated "Mary Had a Little Lamb," an adaptation of the children's nursery rhyme which Paul released during the spring of 1972. It was recorded for daughter Mary, "because she likes hearing her name on the radio." The B side, "Little Woman Love," continued to evince McCartney's flair for simple, but so memorable, love songs. The sight of the rustic McCartneys performing "Mary" on "Top of the Pops," on a stage stuffed with sheep, continues to haunt many witnesses.

"It wasn't a great record," Paul conceded later that year. "But the funny thing about it is, we've got a whole new audience of 8-year-olds. Like Pete Townshend's daughter." It was, perhaps, to restore their grown-up credibility that Paul and Linda next chose to lend backing vocals to a track by that doyen of angst-ridden adults, Carly Simon. They can be heard on "Night Owl," from Simon's No Secrets album. (A former Apple recording artist, Simon's husband and the song's composer, James Taylor, would himself enjoy Paul and Linda's musical accompaniment on his Walking Man album in 1974. The duo appear on "Let It All Fall Down" and "Rock and Roll Is Music Now.")

Another drug bust, for growing cannabis on their farm, was still to come to court when Wings released their next single, a Paul and Linda composition which did indeed reflect upon these problems. Hardly surprising, the raucous "Hi Hi Hi" made it two out of three for the group, as the BBC promptly ranked it alongside "Give Ireland Back to the Irish" and banned it. It wasn't only for the drug references in the chorus either, but also for the implied sexuality of the verses. "Get you ready for my body-gun" indeed! The McCartneys had already foreseen these difficulties, however; "Hi Hi Hi" was released as a double A side, and "C Moon," a semi-nonsensical rocker which has been construed as everything from another drug anthem to a lesbian love song (and which later donated one of its lyrics to the all-girl group L7!), went on to become Wings' biggest hit yet. It reached #5 in the U.K.

Red Rose Speedway, Wings' second album, was released in April, 1973, preceded by another hit single, "My Love" (backed with the aforementioned live "The Mess"). A remarkable record in that it was the first to present a truly united band front. Speedway is particularly notable for one track, "Loup (First Indian On the Moon)," which not only revels in its own goofiness, it also proved that Paul, at least, had enjoyed a sneak preview of Pink Floyd's epochal (and still unreleased) Dark Side of the Moon album. A more perfect parody of "space rock," in all its permutations, has never been released!

Elsewhere, a medley of four semi-songs indicated that even when Paul couldn't be bothered to finish a song, the end result was still superior to most peoples' opuses. The one *Red Rose Speedway* outtake to have officially surfaced, "I Would Only Smile" (from Denny Laine's *Japanese Tears* album), at least suggested that if Linda's pen ever dried up, Paul had another potentially great collaborator in his guitarist.

On May 11, Wings returned to the road, for the first scheduled British tour by an ex-Beatle since 1966. A month later, "Live and Let Die," composed by Paul for the latest James Bond movie, gave Wings their fourth consecutive U.K. Top 10.

But despite the sense, of genuine camaraderie which Wings, on and off-stage, evinced, it was not a happy family. Henry McCulloch, in particular, disliked Linda's involvement in the band, arguing volubly that without her on keyboards, Wings could develop into as great a group as the Beatles. Yet when McCulloch quit in September, 1973, it was not Linda who hastened his departure. Indeed, she almost sympathized with him in sentiment if not in deed. It was Paul, his insistence that Linda remain by his side, who executed McCulloch just as, over the years, he was to pronounce similar unforgiving sentences on others who mocked or maligned Linda's contributions in his life.

His actions held a great sign up to the world — "if you don't like Linda, fine. But if you don't like Linda, then you don't like me either... so don't try and pretend otherwise." Denny Seiwell followed McCullough out the door. Watching such comings and goings (and these were not the only ones during Wings' tempestuous history) with increasing bewilderment was Linda herself. Finally she confided to Steve Holley, one of several drummers to pass through Wings, "I didn't want to do this. It's him. He wants me here all the time."

"I didn't mind Linda being there," Denny Laine would later concede. "She didn't have the ability to play freely, (but) she was alright picking things up. If we'd had her and another keyboard player as well, we would have been fine. But Linda was given too much to do.

"She was a professional, though — she got paid like the rest of us." Laine's manager, the late Tony Secunda, seconded Denny's sentiments, although he would also admit there was little love lost between him and Mrs. McCartney. On one occasion, he once recalled, Linda described him as looking like a rat. Secunda returned home, called a pet shop, and had them deliver one big, ugly rat to the studio. Secunda was, for a time, widely expected to take over the management of Wings as a whole. He turned down the offer in the end, but still made an appearance on the group's next album; he is the "Sailor Sam" who came "from Birmingham" in the title track, "Band on the Run."

Recorded in September and released just two months later, in December, 1973, *Band on the Run* was Paul's fifth album since the Beatles' split. it was also his first to be greeted unreservedly as a legitimate successor to that band's work. Bookended by a brace of meaty singles — "Helen Wheels" (absent from European pressings of the LP) prefaced the album's release; "Junior's Farm" followed it; and both the title track and "Jet" were culled from the disc itself. *Band on the Run* was regarded by many as the album upon which Paul finally found his own two (two, not four) feet. A number one on both sides of the Atlantic, it also topped the charts in Australia, Norway and Sweden,

The singles also did extremely well, with "Band on the Run" itself establishing a new U.K. chart high of #3, aided, no doubt, by the presence of the instrumental "Zoo Gang" on the B side. The track was the custom-written theme to

151

a then-popular British television series, starring John Mills. (U. S. pressings of the single replaced "Zoo Gang" with another cut culled from the album, "1985.")

It was ironic that in terms of personnel, Wings was now it its most constricted — guitarist Denny Laine alone joined Paul and Linda it the Nigerian recording studios where the album was created. With Wings now rightly feted among the year's most vital bands (and with former favorite Lennon) now suffering a reversal in his critical fortunes), Paul further emphasized his rehabilitation by producing brother Mike (McGear)'s self-titled solo debut.

A stunning collection of mostly McCartney-McGear compositions, McGear saw that duo joined in the studio by Linda (moog and backing vocals), Laine, the latest Wings guitarist, Jimmy McCullough, and 10cc's Godley and Creme, (McGear was recorded at that band's Strawberry Studios.) McGear is currently available on CD through Rykodisc. This same sibling relationship was further bolstered when Paul and Linda donated one of their now increasingly sporadic joint compositions, "Ten Years After Strawberry lain" to the Scaffold, the novelty trio in which Mike McGear enjoyed his greatest musical successes. The song appears on the flip of the Scaffold's mid-74 "Liverpool Lou" single. A second otherwise unrecorded Paul and Linda composition, "July 4," was released around this same time by John Christie. The pair also appeared, this same year, on comeback albums by Adam Faith (*I Survive*) and Peggy Lee (*Let's Love*).

The McCartney's initial plan was to follow *Band on the Run* with a new album recorded in Nashville, which would include a succession of invited local superstars. Paul had already hinted at his affection for country

music with two recent B sides — "I Lie Around," on the flip of "Live and Let Die" and "Country Dreamer," found backing "Helen Wheels."

In June, 1974, Wings, now augmented by drummer Geoff Britton, descended upon that city to record Nashville Diary, comprising the clutch of songs which have subsequently leaked out over a string of disparate releases, and those which remain in the vaults, awaiting the day Paul finally comes good on his now 23 year old pledge to compile a collection of his *Hot Hits and Cold Cuts*. The storming "Junior's Farm," its B side "Sally G" (a showcase for guests Pete Drake and Chet Atkins), and the pseudonymous Country Hams' instrumental coupling of "Walking in the Park With Eloise" (written by Paul's father)/"Bridge Over the River Kwai uite," were the first Nashville fruits to see the light of day, in October, 1974. "Send Me the Heart," written by Paul and Denny Laine, which appeared on Laine's *Japanese Tears* album in 1980, rounds out the readily available Nashville recordings.

Bootlegs fill in the gaps, offering up "The Heart That You Broke," "Penny O'Dell" (no relation to George Harrison's "Miss O'Dell") and "Soily," a stormy rocker which had been in and out of Wings' live set since 1972 (and would return there the following year) and had still to be recorded. There was also another instrumental, "One Hand Clapping," which Paul intended as the theme for a documentary of the Nashville sessions; directed by David Litchfield, the film sadly went the same way as the recordings — into the McCartney vault. Of these tracks, the best are typically Nashville in their execution, at the same time as being unmistakably McCartney, but the sessions were never completed.

Back in England, and with several months to kill before resuming work on their next album, Paul and Linda enjoyed a period of quite intense visibility. The "Junior's Farm" single was climbing the charts, and on November 21, 1974, they appeared on "Top of the Pops" performing their own song, and then joining David Essex on stage to add backing vocals to his "Gonna-Make You a Star". Three days earlier, they had appeared in a similar capacity alongside Rod Stewart and the Faces, in concert at Lewisham Odeon — Stewart's latest solo album, *Sailor*, included Paul's stirring "Mine For Me."

Paul's heart was now set on recording in another of the cities from which he drew the greatest inspiration. Immediately after Christmas, Wings whose ranks had been unexpectedly sundered when drummer Britton was replaced by Joe English after recording just five songs- and no gigs — decamped for New Orleans, where that city's flavor (not to mention memories of that excellent James Bond, movie!) was instead absorbed.

Venus and Mars, an album of comparable stature to its illustrious predecessor (and recorded with a newly acquired full complement of musicians). Nevertheless remains a schizophrenic release. Unlikely, though it seems, it was the first,album, Paul had recorded from the position of a solo superstar; the first to be made since he had finally escaped. the shadow of the Beatles. That was the pressure which disabled the Nashville sessions and that is the specter' which continues to haunt *Venus and Mars*.

At its best — and the majestic "Letting Go" certainly rates alongside any other McCartney composition *Venus and Mars* is phenomenal. But it also suffers from a certain self-consciousness; the cringe-worthy namedropping of "Rock Show," the mockdrama of "Magneto and Titanium Man," and the overdone, cajun-

isms of "Listen to What the Man Said," makes it all the more ironic that perhaps the most honest moment on the entire record should be the one which the critics were quickest to crucify.

"Lonely Old People," an almost bitter (and certainly more world-weary) riposte to "When I'm 64," bleeds into the instrumental "Crossroads," a meaningless gesture in America, but to English audiences, a moment of supreme embarrassment. Until its cancellation in the early 1980s, "Crossroads" was indisputably Britain's most-mocked television soap, and McCartney's defense, that he recorded the theme because what else was there for lonely old people to do but watch the show, should have been taken at face value. Instead, it opened him up for more mirth — particularly after he gave "Crossroads'" producers permission to use his rendition over the closing credits of the occasional cliffhanger ending!

Venus and Mars proved as successful as *Band on the Run*, yet even at the height of the group's powers, the specter of Linda, or at least of Linda's "reputation" was never far away. *Wings at the Speed of Sound* (March, 1976) was not likely to receive anyone's vote as their favorite McCartney album, although it did introduce a new democratic Wings, with the songwriting and vocal credits divided between the individual bind members. Still Linda's detractors pounced. In truth, the rubbery "Silly Love Songs" and an otherwise unavailable French 12" disco mix of "Beware My Love" were the only truly classy performances throughout this squib of a disc.

"Let 'Em In" was originally written by Paul for Ringo Starr, and really should have been given to him; Joe English's "Must Do Something About It" was aptly titled, but that was about all that could be said for it; and Jimmy

eight■ *Robert Matheu photo*

McCullough's "Wino Junko" was both sad and sadly prophetic. Yet it was Linda's "Cook of the House" alone which was singled out for the most approbation. Again prophetic, at least in the light of Linda's recent business enterprises, "Cook of the House" was a harmless enough song, but that, of course, was its crime. Paul McCartney's supporters insisted, should not associate himself with "harmless enough" songs. An interesting glimpse into the doublestandardizing minds of those people was provided when Linda's work was compared unfavorably with Yoko Ono's!

Linda landed in even deeper trouble when she was busted for pot while driving in Los Angeles. Although the stash was, technically, communal property, Linda pleaded that it was her's alone, well aware that with two busts already behind him, the American immigration authorities might not be so understanding over a third, the next time Paul applied for a visa. There are two ways of looking at this self-sacrificial episode — the loving wife looking out for her superstar husband, which is the angle most observers chose to adopt; or, Linda's last chance of getting out of the band. Even after five years, she was still uncomfortable on stage; still uncomprehending of the hatred her very presence behind a microphone could cause. Paul had two busts behind him, but so did she. Whatever fate Linda imagined the authorities might have in mind for Paul would therefore be her's by default.

Matters became considerably more serious when a second charge of contributing to the delinquency of minors was thrown at her. Heather, Mary and Stella were all traveling in the car at the time of the bust. That charge was eventually dropped; the bust also turned out to be less serious than had originally been envisioned. The judge merely sentenced her to six sessions with a drug counselor. Perhaps he had also considered the possibility of Linda being barred from the United States and realized that the alternative, standing on stage every night while an audience alternately booed or ignored her, was a far greater punishment than any he could devise, as Wings fans will gladly testify. "When Paul introduced the band, he would always leave Linda until last. That was because even he knew that when he called her name, there would be so much booing that the next introduction would be lost. It was easier for him to just drown out the noise with another song."

Those feelings were put to the test later that same year, when Wings touched down for their most extensive U.S. tour yet. In an age of mammoth tours, Wings Over America left even the greatest in the shadows, as did the live album which was culled from the shows. Double live albums were still only just coming into vogue in the wake of Peter Frampton and Kiss live albums; Wings was offering their fans a lavishly packaged triple.

Unlike subsequent McCartney live albums, *Wings Over America* is truly representative of an artist at ease with both his past and present. Beatles songs are at a premium (as are selections from *Speed of Sound*, with just five clustered around the center of the set and rubbing shoulders with now-established Wings classics (and a remarkable version of Paul Simon's "Richard Cory"). Denny Laine takes the spotlight for his trademark "Go Now" and the whole thing rounds off in quite ferocious fashion with an extended version of "Hi Hi Hi" and the otherwise unavailable rocker, "Soily." (Hands up everyone who remembers when an otherwise unavailable McCartney track, tacked onto the end of a live album, was considered a monumental event!)

Fans who could not afford the triple album were instead tempted with "Soily's" reappearance on the B side of the "Maybe I'm Amazed" single. *Wings Over America* is a great record, but even better than the live experience is a bootleg collection known (among other titles) as *Working Holiday*. It is comprised primarily of rehearsal tapes for this same tour, recorded in Nashville. Aching renditions of "Maybe I'm Amazed" and "My Love" are joined by highlights of both the recorded and unrecorded concerts: "1985," "Junior's Farm," and a phenomenal and phenomenally loose medley of "Little Woman Love" and "C Moon."

Wings Over America all but marks the end of an era. Although Wings would continue operating until the end of the 1970s, from hereon out, the increased regimentation of their live and studio counterparts saw the group become less a grinning, goofy free-for-all and more a vehicle for Paul, and Paul alone.

The Wings which ushered in the second half of the '70s was a much slicker, sleeker, glossier creation than any which had previously been recorded; much more anonymous, too. By the time the group finally shattered, in the wake of Paul's Tokyo drug bust, it was difficult to reconcile even their loosest recordings with the gloriously dishevelled sounding bunch which made albums of such irrepressible joy as *Ram, Wildlife, Red Rose Speedway*, or singles like "Mary Had a Little Lamb," "C Moon" and "Junior's Farm." Maybe Paul had finally regained the confidence and control he had let slip during the first half of the decade; maybe he had simply tired of having his best work written off as filler and decided it was time to take all the credit (and, therefore, blame) for himself. Or maybe Linda simply, finally put her foot down and told Paul to stop spreading his spotlight around.

Just one further release can truly be said to match that original magic, Denny Laine's cruelly underrated *Holly Days*. Paul's 1976 acquisition of the Buddy Holly publishing catalog remains one of the greatest coups of the era (second only to Michael Jackson's acquisition of Paul's own!).

DISCOGRAPHY OF ORIGINAL RELEASES, 1970-76 SINGLES

PAUL McCARTNEY
Apple 1829 Another Day/Oh Woman, Oh Why 1971

PAUL & LINDA McCARTNEY
Apple 1839 Admiral Halsey - Uncle Albert/Too Many People 1971

WINGS

Apple	1847	Give Ireland Back to the Irish/version 1972
Apple	1851	Mary Had a Little Lamb/Little Woman Love 1972
Apple	1857	C Moon/Hi Hi Hi 1972
Apple	1861	My Love/The Mess (live) 1973
Apple	1863	Live and Let Die/I Lie Around 1973
Apple	1869	Helen Wheels/Country Dreamer 1973
Apple	1871	Jet/Mamunia 1974
Apple	1871	Jet/Let Me Roll It 1974
Apple	1873	Band on the Run/1985 1974
Apple	1875	Junior's Farm/Sally G 1974
Capitol	4091	Listen to What the Man Said/Love In Song 1975
Capitol	4145	Letting Go/You Gave Me the Answer 1975
Capitol	4175	Venus & Mars - Rock Show/Magneto & Titanium Man 1975
Capitol	4256	Silly Love Songs/Cook of the House 1976
Capitol	4293	Let 'Em In/Beware My Love 1976
Capitol	4385	Maybe I'm Amazed (live)/Soily (live) 1977

COUNTRY HAMS
EMI 3977 Walking In the Park With Eloise/Bridge Over the River Kwai Suite 1974

SUZY & THE RED STRIPES
Epic 50403 Seaside Woman/B-Side To Seaside 1977 (released in 7" and 12" formats)

DENNYLAINE
Capitol 4340 Looking, For Someone to Love/It's So Easy - Listen to Me 1 976
Capitol 4425 Heartbeat/Moon Dreams 1977

ALBUMS

PAUL McCARTNEY
Apple 3363 McCartney 1970

PAUL AND LINDA McCARTNEY
Apple-3375 Ram 1971

WINGS
Apple 3386 Wildlife 1971
Apple 3409 Red Rose Speedway 1972
Apple 3415 Band on the Run 1973
Capitol 11410 Venus and Mars 1975
Capitol 11524 Wings at the Speed of Sound 1976
Capitol 11593 Wings Over America (live) 1977
Capitol 11905 Wings Greatest (compilation) 1978

DENNY LAINE
Capitol 11588 Holly Days 1977 ■

Flight Plan: Wings '10-year Journey

By Gillian G. Gaar

When Paul McCartney toured with his post-Beatles band, Wings, in the '70s, audiences wished he would perform more Beatles songs. But in his '89, '90 and '93 world tours, the situation was reversed — audiences wished he'd perform more Wings songs. Clearly, McCartney had achieved what he'd wanted in the '70s; he had established Wings as a band in their own right.

McCartney has been more ambivalent about the group, telling Musician in 1986, "I was never very happy with the whole thing." But Wingspan, the TV documentary and two-CD set, which reached #2 (U.K. #5), have ushered in a Wings renaissance.

Wings' roots go back to the recording of McCartney's second solo album, *Ram*, (credited to him and wife Linda) which began in New York City in November 1970. The couple planned to draw on New York's network of studio musicians, and veteran studio drummer Denny Seiwell was among those who turned up to audition, not knowing who it was for.

"I go to this burned-out building on 43rd St., and it had no electricity," he remembered. "I said, 'Jesus, I'm gonna get mugged here!' There's a guy sitting at a desk. 'You're here for the demo?' 'Yeah.' 'Downstairs.' I walk down in the basement, and I think, 'Jesus, I should have a gun or something,' and there's Paul and Linda sitting there! He said, 'Do you mind playing for us?' 'I'd be glad to! What

> *" Wings' roots go back to the recording of McCartney's second solo album, Ram (credited to him and wife Linda) which began in New York City in November 1970. "*

would you like to hear?' 'Just play some rock 'n' roll.' I had some tom-toms with me. I set 'em up, and I just went to it. A few days later I got the call, and I just about dropped the phone!"

In addition to Seiwell, McCartney also used guitarists Hugh McCracken and David Spinozza and members of the New York Philharmonic. Though McCartney directed the sessions, the musicians were able to create their own parts.

"Paul didn't have to tell us much what to do," Seiwell explained. "We'd make a part that would go with the song, and as soon as it sounded right we'd start recording it. We started at 9:30 in the morning, and we usually had the track by two or three o'clock at the end of the day."

After a move to Los Angeles, the album was finished in April '71, though the first single from the sessions, the unassuming "Another Day"/"Oh Woman, Oh Why," had been released in February, reaching #5 (#2 U.K.). Neither track appeared on the eclectic *Ram,* which followed in May, peaking at #2 (#1 U.K.). Two more singles were released in August, the catchy "Uncle Albert/Admiral Halsey" in the U.S., which reached #1, in sharp contrast to the U.K. single, the road-movie themed "Back Seat Of My Car," which only reached #39.

As would prove typical with McCartney, additional tracks were recorded during the sessions. "Little Woman Love" became the B side of "Mary Had A Little Lamb"; "Get On The Right Thing" and "Little Lamb Dragonfly" appeared on *Red Rose Speedway*; "Sunshine, Sometime," "Rode All Night," "A Love For You" and "Hey Diddle" remain unreleased.

The critics were not kind to *Ram*; *Rolling Stone* slammed it as "the nadir in the decomposition of Sixties rock thus far." Undaunted, McCartney decided it was time to form a new

band, and he extended an invitation to Seiwell and McCracken. McCracken declined ("Who couldn't say yes to Paul McCartney, except Hugh?!" said Seiwell), but Seiwell agreed. "I was tired of working so damn hard!" he joked. "No, the real reason was I just fell in love with the music. And knowing I was going to leave my mark in history with probably one of the most talented people on the planet."

McCartney then tapped Denny Laine, whom he had met during Laine's days with The Moody Blues in the '60s, to be Wings' guitarist, and added Linda on keyboards. It was a move that would provoke much derision but came from McCartney's need to have his wife share in his career completely (Linda repeatedly stated in interviews she would have been happy being the band's photographer).

"I thought, 'Well, that's a novel idea,'" said Seiwell of his reaction to Linda's joining. "But they were in love. And she was a safety blanket. Linda was always, always there. And that's the way he wanted it — that was his choice." The as-yet unnamed band headed into the studio in August '71 to record their first album, *Wild Life*. Recording was quick in an effort to capture spontaneity; most of the tracks were first takes. "Paul wanted to give the world a real honest, true look at a new band," Seiwell explained. "And there was some really neat stuff on the record. 'Love Is Strange' was the first reggae track done by a white pop group, ever. And 'Mumbo,' that starts off, 'Take it, Tony!' which was Paul screaming at the engineer to turn the record button on. 'Cause we were making this song up at the studio, and it was getting good. [Tony] was just sitting up there drinking his cup of tea!"

The band was christened Wings after the birth of the McCartneys' daughter Stella in September; the birth had been difficult, and the couple felt she'd arrived "on the wings of an angel." A lavish launch party was held at London's Empire Ballroom Nov. 8, and Wild Life was

released the next month — to even more damning reviews, and fair sales, peaking at #10 (U.K. #11).

The hurried nature of the recording hadn't served the project well. Even McCartney agreed, later saying, "I must say you have to like me to like the record." But Seiwell has another take. "I think Paul was trying to shake that whole Beatle thing, 'OK, I'm gonna give you something you can't compare to The Beatles' records. This is a new band,'" he said. "And when I look back on it, for what it was, it was pretty darn good."

"Love Is Strange" was to be the first single. Then, in January '72, British troops killed 13 people at a protest in Northern Ireland. The event, dubbed "Bloody Sunday," prompted McCartney to make a rare political statement with the rousing "Give Ireland Back To The Irish." Accounts differ as to whether "Love Is Strange" was canceled because of *Wild Life's* slow sales or to make way for "Irish," but "Irish" became Wings' debut single, released in February b/w an instrumental version of the song (only available on the original single). Though banned in England, the single still reached #16 (#1 in Ireland and #21 in the U.S.).

The single also marked the debut of Henry McCollough, from Joe Cocker's Grease Band, as Wings' new lead guitarist. Less than a month after McCollough's arrival, the new lineup hit the road, using a tactic McCartney once suggested to The Beatles; performing unannounced at small venues. The first show, at Nottingham University Feb. 9, was followed by 10 more gigs, primarily at universities. The set list included *Wild*

Life tracks, "Irish" and, the only nod t[...] Beatles past, "Long Tall Sally." The perfo[...] rough, but audiences were thrilled at se[...] Beatle up close. The tour also helped th[...] camaraderie. "It was really a bonding time," [...] "We stayed in some really funky little places[...] all in the room, playing and singing and hang[...] couldn't close the door they were that small! [...] so much fun."

The following month, the band recorded their n[...] which, to the public's disbelief, turned out to [...] Had A Little Lamb," released in M[...] was kind of an embarrassmen[...] were a rock 'n' roller!" [...] admitted. "I thought, 'What th[...] this? I thought we were tr[...] make some rockers here.'" [...] so, the pleasant tune peaked [...] in the U.K., faring less [...] stateside, reaching only #28.

With the band warmed up, a European [...] was planned for summer, traveling in a ga[...] painted double-decker bus. High production cos[...] (including two projectors that screened film clips) mea[...] little revenue was generated, but the band's fan bas[...] continued to grow; the tour was marred only when the [...] McCartneys and Seiwell were arrested for marijuana posession in Sweden.

Footage was also shot for the uncompleted film Bruce McMouse, about a family of mice traveling with the band.

"That was one of the most embarrassing moments I ever had," remembered Seiwell. "They asked me to stand in front of this room full of people and speak to an imaginary

> " *When I look back on it, it was pretty darn good.* "

house. And they kept saying, over and over, 'Keep going!' I started getting embarrassed. I'm not doing a good job. I'm not an actor, and talking to an imaginary mouse in your hand is kind of tough. That was one of the hardest things I had to do in Wings, I'm sure."

Wings' reputation was further enhanced with "Hi, Hi, Hi"/"C Moon," recorded in November and released the following month. The A side is an out-and-out rocker, McCartney's strongest single since "Uncle Albert," the B side another reggae-flavored tune with McCartney on piano, McCullough on drums, and Seiwell on bass.

"Paul needed some tunes that weren't 'Bip Bop' and 'I Am Your Singer' and all these cute little ditties he was writing," said Seiwell of the band's new direction. "He had to go to work and build some stuff that would work live."

The public responded in kind; the single reached #10 in the U.S., and, in the U.K., where the A side was banned for alleged references to drugs and sex, #5.

Wings had been recording throughout '72, working in five different studios on a proposed double album, but *Red Rose Speedway* was eventually slimmed to a single album. Numerous outtakes have appeared over the years: "I Lie

■ *courtesy of Columbia*

Around," B-side of "Live And Let Die"; "Country Dreamer," B-side of "Helen Wheels"; "Bridge On The River Suite," B-side of "Walking In The Park With Eloise"; "Mama's Little Girl," on "Put It There"; and "I Would Only Smile" on Laine's 1980 album *Japanese Tears*. "Night Out," "The Mess," "Thank You Darling," "Jazz Street" and "Tragedy" remain unreleased.

Though uneven, *Speedway,* on release in April '73, was the first of five Wings albums to top the U.S. charts (U.K.: May, #5). The album is also the first to be credited to "Paul McCartney & Wings." "My Love" (released in April b/w "The Mess" from the Aug. 21, 1972 show) also hit #1 (U.K.: March, #9). The romantic ballad became an instant standard.

"You could tell when you were doing it, 'This is going to be a classic,'" said Seiwell. "Henry was asked to play this guitar solo that took him probably longer than any record we'd ever made! He spent a couple of days working it out until he got it right. And it was such a beautiful melodic line. I still get goosebumps thinking about recording some of these things."

Now firmly on track, Wings scored again with their next single, the title song from the James Bond film *Live And Let Die,* recorded in October '72.

"I watched him write the song in 10 minutes," remembered Seiwell. "It was like he was thinking, 'James Bond, chase scenes,' so he started doing the da-da-da, da-da-da, da-da part, and pretty soon he knocked it out. Then he wrote the classic Paul McCartney melody line, he wrote a little lyric and the song was done! And we were in and out of the studio in three hours."

The song, which became a live favorite, was released in June '73 and reached #2 U.S. and #9 U.K. Yet another

"I watched him write the song

session followed in November '72, recording Linda's reggae romp "Seaside Woman," not released until 1977.

Wings flew to Morocco in February '73, ostensibly to work on an upcoming TV special, though Seiwell said little was actually done ("We laid around the pool and took little side trips into the village"). Serious work on James Paul McCartney began on Feb. 19 and continued through March 18, when the group performed before a live audience (followed by a surprise appearance at a charity event at London's Hard Rock Cafe). The special aired April 16 in the U.S., May 10 in the U.K., and received mixed reviews for its uneven nature — particularly an elaborate dance sequence with McCartney in a pink tux, surrounded by dancers dressed as half men/half women.

Wings' first proper U.K. tour began the day after James Paul McCartney aired in Britain. With a roster of their own hits to perform, the band was finally coming together as a unit.

"We had the band just cookin'," Seiwell said. However, at this critical juncture, Wings' lineup was about to go through the first of many disruptions. Following the tour, the band was at McCartney's Scottish home and studio, rehearsing for *Band On The Run*, with recording set to begin in August in Lagos, Nigeria. "We really had that material sounding great," Seiwell said. "Paul didn't change much of what we played when he recorded that album. I thought the two-track demo we made was better than the record, to tell you the truth."

Conflict first erupted when McCartney and McCullough came to loggerheads over playing a certain guitar part. "It was one of those days where Paul was really trying to get Henry to just go along with the program," said Seiwell. "And Henry was a little belligerent and said, 'Screw this!' and left."

While McCartney didn't see McCullough's departure as a

problem, Seiwell disagreed. "We'd worked so hard at becoming a band," he said. "I asked Paul to put the trip off for a month and break in another guitar player. But he wouldn't hear of that. 'No we'll just go down and overdub like we did Ram.' That's when I got a little bugged. After all of this work, we're gonna go back to a bunch of overdubs on a record rather than that true live sound that we accomplished."

Seiwell's dissatisfaction, coupled with financial woes ("I was working for a very, very small retainer that wasn't really enough to live on at the time") led to his leaving Wings as well — on the eve of the band's departure for Lagos. While admitting it was "a shitty thing to do," he added, "I was starting to miss my old studio world where I got to do a different thing with a lot of people. It just seemed like time."

The loss of two band members was only one problem McCartney faced during the recording; while in Nigeria, McCartney suffered a bronchial spasm, a mugging, a sub-par recording studio and, instead of the African sun, found he'd arrived during monsoon season. Perhaps the difficulties strengthened his resolve, for Band On The Run would become his most acclaimed post-Beatles work, topping the U.S. and U.K. charts when released in December '73, winning a Grammy for Best Pop Vocal Performance By A Group. Instead of half-completed numbers or improvisational jams, *Band On The Run* features uniformly first-rate songs and excellent production.

The album's singles also performed well. The bouncy "Helen Wheels," released in November, reached #10 in the U.S.; the song also appeared on the U.S. album (U.K.: October, #12). "Jet" followed in January, reaching #7 (U.K.: February, #7), and the title track, released in April, topped the charts (U.K., June, #3; the single has the unique B side, "Zoo Gang").

in 10 minutes."

Another Linda track, "Oriental Nightfish," was recorded during the *Band On The Run* sessions (an animated short set to the music was released in May '78), and two more of her songs were recorded in Paris in November '73 — "I Got Up," and the title song of her posthumously released 1998 album, *Wild Prairie*. The sessions also marked the arrival of Jimmy McCulloch, Wings' next lead guitarist. The McCartneys, Laine, and McCulloch spent early '74 recording McGear, the second solo album by McCartney's brother Michael, who had adopted the surname "McGear" (though "Leave It" was recorded in '73 with Seiwell on drums). The album was released in October '74 (September in the U.K.), and despite its inventive, off-the-wall nature, it failed to chart.

Auditions added drummer Geoff Britton, and the band traveled to Nashville in July '74. The sessions resulted in Wings' next single, the rocker "Junior's Farm" b/w the countrified "Sally G," released in November and reaching #2; on switching the A and B sides in January '75, "Sally G" reached #17 (U.K.: October, #16). The band also recorded the instrumental "Walking In The Park With Eloise," written by McCartney's father, but since the single, released in December (U.K., October), was under the name "The Country Hams," it didn't chart. Another track, "Send Me The Heart," appeared on Japanese Tears.

This shortest-lived of the Wings lineups can be seen in the unreleased *One Hand Clapping*, shot in August '74 at Abbey Road; among other songs, the film included a performance of the unreleased "Suicide." In January '75, Wings arrived in New Orleans for more sessions. Arguments within the band led to Britton leaving, with American Joe English brought in to replace him.

After overdubs and mixing in L.A., *Venus And Mars* was released in May '75, and with the band's identity firmly established, was solely credited to Wings (and released on Capitol, not Apple). This confident slice of rock topped the U.S. and U.K. charts; the singles charted more erratically. The effervescent "Listen To What The Man Said," also released in May, reached #1 (#6 U.K.), but the soulful "Letting Go," released in September, reached only #39 (#41 U.K.), and "Venus And Mars Rock Show," released in October, reached #12 (U.K.: November, didn't chart). The album also features McColloch's "Medicine Jar." Outtakes include "Lunch Box Odd Sox," B side of "Coming Up"; "My Carnival," B-side of "Spies Like Us"; and "New Orleans," on *Wide Prairie*.

Having assembled what McCartney later called the band's best lineup, Wings set out on a world tour that began in Southampton, England, Sept. 9, 1975. An Australian tour followed in November, a short European tour in March '76, and the 31-show Wings Over America tour in May and June. The band's harder-edged live sound won over critics and audiences, who hailed the sold-out tour as a triumph — Wings' high-water mark.

In between tour legs, Wings managed to record a new album, *Wings At The Speed Of Sound*, another U.S. #1 when released in March (U.K.: April, #2). The album moved away from the rock terrain of the last two albums and gave everyone a lead vocal; Laine wrote "Time To Hide" and McCulloch cowrote "Wino Junko." But the singles were McCartney's — "Silly Love Songs," released in April (#1 U.S., #2 U.K.) and "Let 'Em In" (U.S.: June, #3; U.K.: July, #2). Between the end of the U.S. tour and a final European/British leg in the fall, McCartney produced and performed (with Linda on backing vocals) on Laine's album of Buddy Holly covers, *Holly Days* (released in May '77, the album didn't chart).

Capping off 1976 was another U.S. #1 album, the triple album Wings Over America, released in December (U.K. #8). The accompanying single, "Maybe I'm Amazed," was released in January '77, peaking at #10 (U.K.: February, #28). The tour is further documented in the TV special *Wings Over The World* (released in 1979) and the film, Rockshow (released in 1980, ostensibly the June 10 Seattle show but featuring New York City and L.A. footage as well); the TV special, broken up by interview clips, is more engaging.

Wings began recording again in February '77, working until early '78 in two London studios, McCartney's Scottish home and the yacht Fair Carol in the U.S. Virgin Islands. Laine cowrote five songs with McCartney, giving the album a decided folk influence; "Waterspout" and Laine's "Find A Way Somehow" remain unreleased. A June '77 session in Jamaica produced two more Linda songs, "Sugartime," and The Chordettes' "Mr. Sandman," which appeared on *Wild Prairie*. Linda's "Seaside Woman" was also released as a single, b/w a newly recorded instrumental version of the song, in May, under the name "Suzi & The Red Stripes." Despite the pseudonym, the single still reached #59 — at least better than The Country Hams.

In September '77, Wings' lineup changed again, with McCulloch leaving after one too many altercations; he died of a drug overdose in September '79. English hung on for the August "Mull Of Kintyre" session, then also left, pleading homesickness. "Mull Of Kintyre," a majestic ode to McCartney's Scottish home, was released in November and became Britain's then–best-selling single, topping two million (and topping the charts). But in the U.S., the flip side, the tongue-in-cheek rock treat "Girls' School," got the push — and stalled at #33.

London Town, released in May '78, broke Wings' string of five #1 albums, peaking at #2 (U.K. #4). The singles had mixed success; "With A Little Luck," released in March, was another #1 (U.K. #5), but the tougher "I've Had Enough," released in June, reached #25 (U.K. #42) and the title track, released in August, reached #39 (U.K. #60). *Wings Greatest*, released in November (U.K. December), also had varied success; #5 U.K., but only #29 U.S.

The first new Wings member, drummer Steve Holly, turned up in the "Little Luck" video, having met Laine through sessions for the latter's *Japanese Tears*. Laine also brought guitarist Laurence Juber into the group, having played with him on a David Essex TV show. Juber met the band during a mixing session for "Oriental Nightfish," later auditioned and was asked to join. Like Holly, Juber was a successful session musician, "but I really couldn't imagine turning down the opportunity to work with Paul McCartney," Juber told Goldmine. "Even though there was a nanosecond where I weighed the options as far as what I was giving up in order to do the gig."

Juber's first session was in May '78, recording "Same Time, Next Year," a proposed song for the film of the same name. Ultimately rejected, it appeared on the "Put It There" single. Another soundtrack song, "Did We Meet Somewhere Before?" was recorded for the film Heaven Can Wait; it too was rejected but later appeared in the 1979 Ramones film Rock 'N' Roll High School.

A film starring the new Wings lineup was also considered, with a script by Willy Russell, who'd written the play John, Paul, George, Ringo... And Bert, but it remained uncompleted. Yet another film venture that Wings worked on was centered around the adventures of Rupert The Bear, a character in British children's comics. The band recorded a demo tape of 11 songs, none of which were used in the charming *Rupert And The Frog Song* animated short released in 1984.

Work began in June '78 on what would be Wings' final album. Chris Thomas, an assistant engineer from McCartney's Beatles days who'd recently worked with the Sex Pistols, was brought on as co-producer "to help rough things up!" Juber said. "It was a back-to-basics, garage-band kind of feel. That was probably why Steven and I had a great deal of freedom — they really wanted us to bring some kind of edge to things. I think Paul was deliberately wanting to be a little punky in his attitude.

"There weren't too many times when Paul gave me specific things to play," Juber continued. "There's a little guitar lick on 'Daytime Nighttime Suffering' that he had me do because he wrote the song with that lick. But most of the time I was free to do my own thing."

Recording remained in Britain but still offered variety — the Scottish farm, Kent's Lympne Castle, Abbey Road and a facsimile of Abbey Road's Studio Two in the basement of the McCartney Production Ltd.'s offices, dubbed "Replica Studio."

"I don't know that it really made a huge difference to the music itself," said Juber. "But the castle was a cool environment to work in. Paul recorded 'How Many Million Miles' sitting on a balcony that overlooked the English Channel; I'm sure that influenced his performance a little bit. On 'We're Open Tonight,' I played a 12-string guitar part in the stairwell, and the sound of the stairwell made a difference to the sound of the guitar."

The album's most noteworthy session was undoubtedly for "Rockestra Theme" and "So Glad To See You Here," featuring a Who's Who of British rock, including Hank

Marvin, John Paul Jones, and John Bonham, among others. The session was Oct. 3 at Abbey Road.

"It was one of the most memorable sessions I've done," Juber said. "I looked down the guitar section, and there was Pete Townsend at one end and Dave Gilmour the other!" A film made of the session remains unreleased.

Back To The Egg, released in May '79 (on Columbia in the U.S.), peaked at #8, not the smash hit the band wanted (U.K.: June, #6). Hopes had been high, as the non-album single "Goodnight Tonight"/"Daytime Nighttime Suffering," released in March, had reached #5 in the U.S. and U.K. But Egg's musical variety was slammed as "just about the sorriest grab bag of dreck in recent memory" by Rolling Stone, and the singles suffered. The lively album opener, "Getting Closer," released in June, reached #20; the cool "Arrow Through Me," released in August, #29. The U.K. singles did worse. The screamer "Old Siam Sir," released in June, reached #35; "Getting Closer," released in August, managed to get to #60. Given the recent rise of punk and new wave, Juber's verdict makes sense: "There was no way that it could ever be punky enough for what was going on in the music scene at that time."

Perhaps sensing the band might have run its course, McCartney began working on another solo album. His holiday single, "Wonderful Christmastime"/"Rudolph The Red-Nosed Ringo," released in November, was credited solely to him. The *Egg* sessions had produced a few outtakes (the unreleased "Cage" and Juber's "Maisie," which appeared on his 1982 album *Standard Time*), and a summer '79 session at Lympne Castle a few more (the unreleased "Robber's Ball" and "Weep For Love," which appeared on Japanese Tears). In November, Wings returned to performing with a U.K. tour, the first step in another eventual world tour.

Juber remembered the group's Glasgow shows as a highlight. "You listen to 'Every Night,' and Paul's playing just amazing bass and is singing great, and the band sounded very tight," he said. "Kampuchea [a charity concert and Wings' last-ever show] was a little frustrating because it's a very long night. And we'd had Christmas [break], so we all got up there a little bit cold. But my favorite moment was when we did 'Let It Be.' I realized that nobody else was going to take the solo, so I just jumped forward and did it. And Pete Townsend was kind of looming over my shoulder!"

Wings planned to start 1980 with a Japanese tour, followed by a U.S. summer tour. Instead, McCartney was arrested on arrival in Japan on Jan. 16, when marijuana was discovered in his luggage. He was deported Jan. 25 and laid low for some weeks. But Wings was still a going concern.

"[Wingspan] made it seem like everything fell apart after Japan," said Juber, "and it really didn't. I mean, we won a Grammy for Rockestra [for Best Rock Instrumental Performance], we had a [U.S.] #1 record with 'Coming Up' — there was still life in it. And we worked pretty consistently throughout 1980."

"Coming Up" was indeed a hit, also reaching #2 in the U.K., but in different versions; a live version from Glasgow (Dec. 17, 1979) in the U.S., and McCartney's solo studio version in the U.K. (though both songs were on the single). The band also rehearsed for the upcoming *Tug Of War* album and worked on the long-delayed *Cold Cuts* album, a collection of McCartney/Wings outtakes. During the summer Juber and the McCartneys also recorded five tracks for Ringo Starr's *Stop And Smell The Roses* album.

But that fall, Juber and Holly received calls saying that *Tug Of War* would be a McCartney solo album, not a Wings record.

"Even though it wasn't the end of Wings, it might as well have been," said Juber. "Although the history book says the band officially broke up in April '81, I moved to New York at the end of January '81. If I'd been aggressive about it, I probably could've ingratiated myself in on some of the Tug Of War sessions. But I just didn't see the point."

As Juber sees it, McCartney may have outgrown his own creation. "I think as the band progressed, the dichotomy between his own creativity and the momentum the band generated was starting to show," he said.

"Wings was a real band to a lot of people, and it was a real band to us while we were doing it. I think in the end it became a bit too much of a real band for where Paul wanted to go with his own career. The reality was that he wanted to work within a band situation but still have creative control and still be able to go off and be Paul McCartney where it was appropriate."

McCartney's own comments at the time seemed to concur. "I got bored with the whole idea," he said in 1982, "and I thought 'Christ! I'm coming up to 40 now. I don't really have to stay in a group.'"

But McCartney may have needed a band more than he realized. Since 1982 he hasn't had another Top 10 album — until 1997's *Flaming Pie* (#2) followed by *Wingspan,* (#2). McCartney has come to look upon his work with Wings with

> **" *Wings was a real band to a lot of people.* "**

"I got bored with the whole idea."

■ *Glenn A. Baker Archives*

REMEMBERING A PHOTOGRAPHER, AN ACTIVIST,

Linda McCartney

(1942-1998)

By Dave Thompson

I n December 1995, Linda McCartney revealed that she was undergoing treatment for breast cancer. It was a stunning revelation. Linda had always preached that positive thinking and a vegetarian diet would lead to good health and a long life, but rumors concerning Linda's health had been flying for months. Now, as she dropped completely out of public view, they flew even faster. It would be nine long months before husband Paul was finally able to quell public fears when he announced that his wife had made a full recovery, a revelation that was quickly heralded among the most inspiring medical stories of the age.

No longer simply the plucky fighter whose ability to withstand the slings and bows of critical and public distaste had at least earned her the world's admiration, Linda was now a survivor as well, someone who could combat the most horrific odds and make it through. Her battle with cancer alone was one of colossal bravery. Added to the long campaign of other battles she had fought and won, it became one of absolute inspiration, the courage to keep going, whatever the odds. But this apparent happy ending was not to be. In March, the cancer was found to have spread to Linda's liver. Less than a month later, she died on the McCartneys' ranch near Tucson, Arizona.

Linda Louise Eastman was born on Sept. 24, 1942. Her mother, Louise, was heir to the Cleveland Linders depart-ment store chain; her father Lee was a Harvard graduate and show business copyright lawyer; and the family divided

> *" Linda was someone who could combat the most horrific odds and make it through. "*

its time between homes in Scarsdale, East Hampton and an apartment on Park Avenue. Visitors to the Eastman home included actor Hopalong Cassidy and songwriters Hoagy Car-michael, Tommy Dorsey, and Jack Lawrence — who composed "Linda" (later recorded by Jan And Dean) for the 6-year old-girl in return for legal work by Lee.

Linda was, she admitted, "the black sheep of the family." Childhood piano lessons were abandoned in the face of the headstrong child's objections, and by her late teens, Linda was regularly playing truant from school in Scarsdale. Neither would her attendance record improve when she enrolled at exclusive Sarah Lawrence College in nearby Bronxville (coincidentally, Yoko Ono's alma mater). She took off from there as well, to attend Alan Freed's all-day rock 'n' roll shows in New York.

In 1960, Linda enrolled at Princeton, studying art and history. She was dating a geophysics student, Melvin See, soon to become her husband, but the marriage was doomed. See dreamed of continuing his studies in Africa; Linda would travel no further afield than Tucson, where the couple's daughter Heather was born on Dec. 31, 1963. Linda initiated divorce proceedings shortly after.

It was in Tucson, however, that Linda first realized what she wanted to do with her life. Arizona, she said, "opened up my eyes to the wonder of light and color," and having taken a course in art history at the University Of Arizona, Linda moved on to a course in photography, presented by Hazel Archer at Tucson Art Center.

She returned to New York in 1964, landing a job as recep-tionist at *Town And Country* magazine. It was there that one morning's mail delivery brought an open invitation to photograph The Rolling Stones aboard a boat on the Hudson River. Linda took it for herself, arrived at the reception and discovered she was the only photographer there.

"That got my name around," she later said. "That was a great piece of luck."

Resigning from her receptionists' desk, Linda set herself up as a freelance photographer, a precarious role but one to which she seemed ideally suited. Combining the rebelliousness that had so often helped her get her own way with a genuine love for meeting people, Linda learned that if she couldn't bully her way into a commission, she could cajole instead. Soon she was traveling as far afield as California, to work with The Beach Boys, and Austria, photographing The Beatles during the making of *Help!* She cowrote one of the first serious books of the rock generation, 1967's *Rock And Other Four Letter Words*, and when Bill Graham opened the Fillmore East in New York, Linda became house photographer.

In May 1967, Linda arrived in London to photograph Traffic, and on May 15, Jimi Hendrix's manager, Chas Chandler, took her out to the Bag O'Nails nightclub to see Georgie Fame And The Blue Flames. Paul McCartney was seated at the next table.

Thus began one of the most remarkable courtships and love stories in rock history, a 30-year partnership during which the couple were apart just once, the nine days that Paul spent in a Japanese jail cell.

It was not always a bed of roses. Alongside Ono, Linda found herself the media scapegoat for The Beatles' demise, a role that her subsequent involvement in McCartney's solo career did not diminish. Almost unanimously, the world's press mercilessly scorned the music that the couple would make together, the string of albums that ran from 1971's Ram through to 1976's *Wings At The Speed Of Sound* (with *Band On The Run* an honorable exception). Linda's onstage contribu-tions to Wings were cast as intolerable aberrations within what could have been a great rock 'n' roll band.

Yet Linda weathered the storm, just as she had weathered so many in the past, and by the 1980s, with Wings disbanded and Paul himself an increasingly unpredictable talent, Linda's involvement in his music was not only accepted, it was often even praised. Maybe the world was not yet ready for the Linda McCartney solo album that astute listeners to Paul's "Oobu Joobu" radio series compiled from broadcast outtakes, but it wasn't calling for her head either. In the minds of his critics as well as his fans, the only partnership in the ex-Beatle's life that mattered now was the one that the world had spent so long trying to sunder.

No longer the scheming groupie who stole away the heart-throb of millions or the musical incompetent who bewitched and bedraggled a genius, Linda was now accorded unre-served respect by Paul's fans, love by his peers. And if that was the least of her accomplishments, she would already have been a remarkable woman. Of course it wasn't. As a mother, she ensured that the couple's four children grew up com-pletely untouched by the oppressive heat of superstardom. As a wife, Paul himself admitted, Linda kept his feet firmly on the ground. And as an ecological campaigner, she raised the profile of that debate higher than it had ever been before.

> *" The others were girls—she was a woman. "*

It was Linda who involved Paul in recording a series of "radical" messages for the animal welfare organization PETA (People For The Ethical Treatment Of Animals); it was Linda who was called to the phone whenever local animal welfare groups needed an emergency home for an injured animal. And of course, it was Linda who persuaded Paul — and a great many other people too — to give up eating meat. Indeed, speaking in the aftermath of Linda's death, Paul insisted that the best tribute anyone could pay his wife's memory would be to turn vegetarian.

Photographer and author, songwriter and musician, ecological campaigner and animal rights activist, Linda McCartney was one of the most remarkable women of her generation, one who deliberately pitted herself against the harshest odds and came out on top every time. As a teenager struggling to make her name in the world of rock photography, as the onstage partner of one of the most famous musicians in the world, as a vegetarian voice in a carnivorous society, Linda was irrepressible and continued to be so until her death. Just weeks before she died, she announced to the world, "I'm back"; just days before the end, she was horseback riding with her family.

"She was just different," Paul said of the first time he met the brash American blonde. "The others were girls — she was a woman. I just went for her in a big way, and that was it. We've never looked back."

In the wake of Linda's death, looking back is all that Paul, and the couple's countless fans and admirers can do — look back on a life that may have ended tragically early but that was crammed with living nonetheless. ■

■ *This story originally appeared in the May 22, 1998 issue of Goldmine.*

They were my boys, the greatest in the world

A CHAT WITH PRODUCER GEORGE MARTIN ABOUT THE FAB FOUR   By Bill De Young

*A*t age 67, George Martin is one of the longest-lived architects of rock 'n' roll. Born in London, he was an oboe player and composer of classical melodies who found steady work as a staff producer and conductor at EMI's recording studios at No. 3 Abbey Road. In the '50s and early '60s, Martin's pop successes included hits by singer Matt Monro and comedy discs by the likes of Peter Sellers, Rolf Harris, and Beyond The Fringe.

He was 36 and bored with his job when Brian Epstein presented him with The Beatles' demo recordings. Every other label in England had turned Epstein down, but Martin — with his keen ear for melody and complex harmony and an affection for warmth and humor — heard something that no one else had.

The middle part of this story is blood-familiar to every Beatles person worth his salt (or, should we say, his pepper). Martin shaped, developed, encouraged, discouraged and forged The Beatles' sound over their nearly eight-year relationship. He arranged almost every song they ever recorded, wrote all the orchestral scores (with a few exceptions) and — save the *Let It Be* debacle — is listed as producer on every single Beatles record.

Martin has written and recorded numerous instrumental works over the years (most of them Beatles-related) and, in those heady days of 1963-64 produced many, many charttoppers for British artists (the great majority of them managed by Epstein).

> *" Martin — with his keen ear for melody and complex harmony and an affection for warmth and humor — heard something that no one else had. "*

The Beatles with Muhammad Ali on their first U.S. Tour in February 1964.

After the Fabs' breakup, he went on to man the boards for America, Jeff Beck and others, and he produced a triumvirate of Paul McCartney solo albums in the '80s. Most recently, he handled production chores for the original cast album of Tommy, at the behest of Pete Townshend.

That's all well and good, but if Martin had never crossed paths with The Beatles (and they with him), his work with other artists would be little more than a footnote in the book of rock 'n' roll. His credits are a mile long, but one stands head, shoulders, knees and toes above the rest. He was truly the Fifth Beatle, one of the most important figures in popular music history. His contributions may never be fully absorbed.

Although AIR Studios, which he began in 1966 (contracting out to The Beatles and EMI until 1970) is still operational in London, its branch on the Caribbean island of Montserrat was destroyed by 1989's Hurricane Hugo.

Martin supervised the digital remastering of the anthology albums, The Beatles 1962-66 and The Beatles 1967-70 at EMI. His Beatles work, as you'll read in this interview, is far from over.

Goldmine: John Lennon used to say that when he heard a Beatles song, it automatically brought him back to the recording session, what he was playing, how he was feeling that day.

George Martin: Not really. Looking back at all the songs, it's a long time ago, and I purposely over the years hadn't

> **" His contributions may never be fully absorbed. "**

looked back at the songs. My life has been so busy, I've tended to go on and look at tomorrow rather than today or even yesterday. And I find that you can get too obsessive about the past. I did find, however, that when I did that television program on The Making Of Sgt. Pepper a couple of years ago, that of course forced me to look back and see what was going on. And it was the first time, to be honest, in all those years I'd really looked back and started thinking deeply about the past.

When I think of a song — if you play me "Paperback Writer" or "Norwegian Wood" — sometimes I will think about things. In the case of "Norwegian Wood," it immediately brings it back to a hotel in St. Moritz, where John and I had a skiing holiday together. And he wrote the song during the time there, so that's obviously very evocative. But if you take a song that doesn't have that particular kind of nostalgia, it's a kind of blur. "Fool On The Hill," I can remember how we did that... but there were so many, and there are so much of them, that it's all one sort of melting, shimmering haze.

You played piano on a lot of songs during the early years; it's particularly evident on the *Hard Day's Night*–era tracks. Was that literally because no one else could do it?

To begin with, of course, none of them knew what a keyboard was like. They were guitar players. When I first met them, I was aware that they were guitar men and I was a keyboard man. And if you're running through a new song for the first time, a guitar player will look at another guy's fingers and see the shapes. You can see what the guy's doing on the fret, and you know what chord he's playing.

If you then take that guitar player, and he doesn't know anything about keyboards, what you play on the piano will be completely meaningless to him. He won't understand the chords at all. And a keyboard player, if he knows a bit about guitar, won't understand what the chords are by looking at his hands. There's a hidden language there.

So I actually said to myself, "Hey, I'm going to have to learn the guitar, because I'll need to communicate with these guys on their level." And Paul, at the same time, said the same thing to himself. He said, "I think I'll have to learn piano, to see what George is up to." Because what I used to do, whenever Paul or John sang me a song, I'd sit on a high stool and they'd play it in front of me. And I'd learn it, and I'd then go to the keyboard and I'd say, "Is it this?" and I'd play through the chords and hum the tune. And they'd say, "Yeah, that's fine, OK," and I'd know the song.

That piano sound was very distinctive.

Piano's a very useful instrument. And, of course, Paul was the one who actually took it up and learned it more quickly and more adaptably than anybody else. I mean, he's such a fine, versatile musician, he could play almost any instrument if he set his mind to it. So that by the time he got to "Lady Madonna," he was doing a bloody good solo. He couldn't possibly have done that in 1962.

And John never really mastered the keyboard. His idea of playing the piano was having a group of triads — you know, three notes that formed a chord — and just go up and down the scale with them. He could play rhythm all right on keyboard, but he wasn't very clever at doing single notes or lines.

It's been theorized that your classical music background and your work on comedy records were big factors in making the unprecedented new pop sound that you made.

I tried to turn them on to it. We did get counterpoint into their work. I remember during "Eleanor Rigby," which was quite a breakthrough in a way, when we were actually recording it I realized that one of the phrases could work against another phrase, that they hadn't designed it that way.

In other words, "Ah, look at all the lonely people" actually could come at the end of the piece. Which it does. I put it in, got them to sing it... they were knocked out by that. "Hey, yeah, those two things go together! It's great, innit? It works well." It had never occurred to them, never occurred to Paul. But that was a lesson for him. Because I'm sure that when he came to write "She's Leaving Home," that was, definitely, two lines working against each other. It was one broad melody, and another one kind of answering underneath it. He learned how to use that weaving of lines.

They were like sponges, in a way, weren't they?

They learned so quickly. But when I first met them, I had absolutely no idea at all they could write decent material. They wrote songs that were pretty awful — "One After 909" and "P.S. I Love You" and "Love Me Do" was the best of them. It was pretty rough stuff.

I didn't really blame the guy who turned them down so much. In fact, everybody turned them down, more or less,

> *"I didn't really blame the guy who turned them down."*

■ *Glenn A. Baker Archives*

on the grounds that their material wasn't very good, I imagine.

Do you remember exactly when they stopped being your students in the studio and started pretty much calling their own shots, coming to you simply for advice?

There was no one moment. It was a gradual drift. By the time we got to a song like "Walrus" or any of John or Paul's later songs, they would have very definite ideas on what they wanted to do, which they hadn't to begin with. It was a gradual drift so that they became the teachers, almost, at the end, and I was the pupil.

What I do remember, though, was that having rejected all the stuff that they had and accepting only "Love Me Do," I had actually rejected "Please Please Me," in those very early days of 1962, saying "This is no good, this song, it's very dreary. If you're going to make anything of it at all, you need to double the speed and really put some pep into it. Make something really worthwhile. Maybe use some harmonica on it." Because when they played it first to me, it was Paul singing a very kind of winsome, Roy Orbison slow ballad. Which was very dreary.

Well, they learned from that, because when I gave them "How Do You Do It" and we made a record of that, they still wanted to have their material. They said, "We've been working on 'Please Please Me.' We'd like you to listen to it." And the result was good. And that gave them an incentive, then, to do better things from that moment onward.

Had you tried that in 1968, say around "Hey Jude" time, would they have said, "Don't tell us what to do, George"?

I don't think so. I don't think they ever rejected anything I said. All of us in the studio, including Ringo, had equal voices. And the five of us would look at things and try to make things better. They were much more fruitful by this time, so that if I did have something that I didn't like... in the case of "Hey Jude" I said, "Do you think we're being a bit unwise, going on for seven minutes?" And Paul said, "No, it's there. Can you get it on a record?" I said, "I can get it on, but it's not exactly a single. DJs will fade it, won't they?" He said, "Well, let them fade it." I was being practical, and I was wrong, because he was right, because it was right that it should be seven minutes. And it always has been, ever since.

Curiously enough, Paul and I have always been good friends, and we've often had dinner with our wives and so on. And about eight years later, '78 or '79 I'd say, we were having dinner one night and Paul, at the end of it said, "By the way, I'd like you to produce my next record."

I fell apart and I said, "I'm not sure that's a good idea."

He said, "Come on! Don't be so silly! Why not?"

I said, "Because things have changed now. You're a good producer in your own right, and I don't want to spoil a beautiful friendship, thank you very much."

He laughed and said, "Why, don't you think it'll work?"

> " *They became teachers, almost, at the end, and I was the pupil.* "

"Well, let them fade it."

I said, "Because I don't think you will accept the direction that I have to give you as a producer."

He said, "Of course I will. We know each other too well for that. How could it not work?"

I said, "Well there's selection of songs, for a start."

"Do you want me to audition for you?!" he said, jokingly.

I said, "Not quite, Paul." But, I said, "I've got to be able to choose your songs and tell you what's good and what's bad."

And he swallowed. That had never occurred to him. By this time, all of them had got to the stage where everyone revered them so much that they hadn't quite thought anyone would dare to suggest that anything they did wasn't terribly good.

He said, "You're quite right. I've got 14 songs."

I said, "Give them to me, and I'll listen to them over the weekend. I'll tell you about them on Monday."

He rung me on Monday and said, "What about it, then?"

I said, "Well, I've listened to every one of them."

He said, "Good."

I said, "Four are great."

He said, "Four?!"

I said, "Six need a lot of work on them, and the other four you can throw away."

There was a kind of distant silence. But Paul is a sensible and honorable fellow, and he said, "All right, you and I had better talk about it, and we'd better sort them out." And we did, and we made a very happy album.

I think that people, when they become superstars, they have to have someone to tell them … they're surrounded so many times by people who tell them they're the greatest thing in the world, they need to have an honest opinion. It's the emperor and his new clothes, isn't it?

Near the end of the Beatles years, did you consider yourself friends? Or was the relationship like that of an employee to an employer? This was White Album/Abbey Road time.

The *White Album* was a funny one, because at the time they came back from abroad and they all had a huge collection of songs they wanted to record. And they wanted them done all at the same time. By this time, they were four individuals with their individual songs, wanting to record them with the assistance of the other people, rather than being a group. I couldn't cope with it all at once. We were actually recording in a couple of the studios at the same time, identically. John would be in one studio, and Paul would be in another. And I was running from one place to another. I had a very able assistant by this time, a guy called Chris Thomas, who's now a first-class producer. We shared the work, so I would come in and see what he'd been doing and supervise and so on.

But it was such a frantic time, I never really worried about any sort of splits there. The real cracks appeared during Let It Be. That was the worst time.

With regard to The White Album, you've said that you tried to get them to cut it down to a single-disc, 14-track

"Six need a lot of work."

album. What would you have cut out?

That's a good question, because it's now such an accepted album. Everyone thinks it's terrific. A lot of people say it's their favorite album. Don't forget, I was looking at it from the point of view of the songs when I heard them, rather than the songs when they were finished. I said to myself, "Let's pick the best and most commercial songs, and let's work on those. Let's forget the other ones for the moment."

I'm not saying we wouldn't have recorded those other songs, but I would like to have made a really great album out of the best of the stuff there and concentrate and work very hard on them. But they wanted everything done at once. That was my concern. There are one or two items of dross on The White Album.

Such as?

I haven't got the list in front of me. You'll have to read them off. Was "Bungalow Bill" on that? "Honey Pie"?

Yes, and "Revolution 9." "Birthday."

"Birthday." Well, there you go. You're picking them for me! There are songs that are not at the front rank, put it that way. From other groups they probably would be front rank, but these are my boys, they're the greatest in the world, and that's the way I saw it.

The songs that remain unreleased today: "Leave My Kitten Alone." "If You've Got Troubles," "That Means A Lot."

Was there a sense while you were cutting them that they were hopeless? Or were they just culled at the end of the sessions?

There were many instances when they would come in and not get very good results. I don't remember the specific circumstances; quite often, they would be done at the tail end of sessions, or sometimes they would be done because they came into the studio and they didn't have anything else.

The bootleg CDs that are out now, some of the stuff is pretty phenomenal.

> "There are one or two items of dross on The White Album."

So I understand! And where the material came from in the first place is most interesting. I'd love to know. I've heard some of it, and some of the quality is remarkably good.

You don't think anyone knows how they got out?

I think all these things will probably be incorporated in what I'm talking about. It doesn't make sense for them to go out on bootlegs, does it?

In his 1970 Rolling Stone interview, John made several disparaging remarks about Beatles recordings, what he called the "Dead Beatles sound." Did that hurt your feelings at the time?

Very much! John went through a really crazy period. I was very incensed about that interview. I think everybody was. I think he stagged off everybody, including the Queen Of England. I don't think anyone escaped his attention.

When I saw him back in L.A. some years later and we spent an evening together, I said "You know, you were pretty rough in that interview, John." He said, "Oh, Christ, I was stoned out of my fucking mind." He said, "You didn't take any notice of that, did you?" I said, "Well I did, and it hurt."

He went through a very, very bad period of heavy drugs, and *Rolling Stone* got him during one of those periods. He was completely out of it. John had a very sweet side to him. He was a very tender person at heart. He could also be very brutal and very cruel. But he went through a very crazy time. The tragedy of John was that he'd been through all that and he'd got out the other side. And he really was becoming the person that I knew in the early days again.

I spent an evening with him at the Dakota not long before he died, and we had a long evening rapping about old times, which was marvelous. That's now my happiest memory of him, because he really was back to his own self.

> " *He really was becoming the person that I knew in the early days again.* "

You were recording Tug Of War with Paul the day John died. Just for the record, where were you when you heard about it?

I lived 80 miles west of London, and he [Paul] lived 70 miles south. We were both in our respective homes. It was six o'clock in the morning, and somebody rang me from America and told me the news, which was not a good way to start the day. I immediately picked up the phone and I rang Paul, and I asked if he'd heard it. He had heard it.

And after a few moments together I said, "Paul, you obviously don't want to come in today, do you?" He said, "God,

I couldn't possibly not come in. I must come in. I can't stay here with what's happened. Do you mind?" I said, "No, I'm fine. I'll meet you."

So we went into AIR Studios in London. We were supposed to record that day. Of course, we didn't put down a single note, because we got there and we fell on each other's shoulders and we poured ourselves tea and whiskey and sat 'round and drank and talked. And we grieved for John all day, and it helped. At the end of the day we went back to our homes.

Now, one of the ironies and one of the bitter bits about life is that Paul, when he came out of the studio, of course was surrounded by reporters and journalists. He still was in a deep state of shock. They photographed him, and they flashed him, and they said to him the usual sort of zany and stupid reporter questions. The question was, "How do you feel about John dying then, Paul?" I don't know what you're supposed to say to that. And he looked and he shrugged and he said, "Yeah, it's a drag, isn't it?" and went off into the night.

And he was slated for that. He was mercilessly attacked, saying, "How callous can you be?" And I felt every inch for him. He was unwise, but he was off his guard. It was tough.

You recently scored Paul's song "C'Mon People." You must have a pretty good working relationship with him.

I don't produce because I'm too old and he's a good producer anyway. I don't want to produce. In fact, he's asked me if I would. But life's too short. But he had this song and

artwork by Klaus Voormann.

he said, "Would you mind doing a bit of scoring for me?" So I listened to it and I said, "OK, why not?" and it was fun. It's nice occasionally working together. I wouldn't want to make a habit of it.

You've done a lot of remastering and CD transfer for EMT on these Beatles projects. When you get to the Phil Spector songs, "The Long And Winding Road" and that, are you ever tempted to twiddle the knobs and just wipe out those strings and choirs?

[Laughing] You bet I am! It's a silly thing, really, because that was a wounding thing. And I don't honestly think those tracks are as good as we should have made them. But hell, they were there, and they're history now. If you're a sensible bloke, you just say, "That's it." And obviously, when you're transferring to CD, it's got to be as it was when it was issued, and that's the end of it.

On the American LPs, they added all that echo and awful stuff. Did you used to hear that and throw your hands in the air?

Of course I did, but I was powerless to do anything about it. Capitol ran the roost. And they used to take the credit for it, too.

Do you know why they did those things?

Ego? I don't know! I mean, there's a guy who actually put his name on the records, saying he produced them. So you tell me. Eventually, when we do this anthology thing, then we'll go back over all those albums and make sure they're in the right order and in the original versions as well as other stuff. It'll be quite a big job, but it'll be fascinating to do. The last thing I'll ever do with The Beatles.

You think so?

I guess so. The final thing. The final solution.

So you're content with being known as The Beatles guy now?

Well, you can't escape these epithets. You get pigeon-holed. Some people think I've never done anything else. ∎

> **" Some people think I have never done anything else. "**

∎ *This story originally appeared in the Nov. 12, 1993, issue of Goldmine.*

England. He was very enthusiastic. They've all known what I've been doing.

You produced the Jeff Beck album *Blow By Blow* and you had him cover "A Day In The Life."

Jeff and I have been mates for a long time although we haven't worked together for a long time. But we've talked about working together and never got around to it. And Jeff came to see me when I was working on the *Anthology* at Abbey Road. And it so happens that the day he came in Paul was already there listening to stuff that I'd selected for him to hear. It was then, in front of Paul, where we talked about him doing a track for the album. And Jeff said to me, "Can I choose the track?" And I said, "Sure, if you want to." And he picked "A Day In The Life."

He covered The Beatles' "She's A Woman" on the *Blow By Blow* album.

That's right. It was good track, wasn't it? He used "the bag" on that. Anyhow, you could have knocked me sideways when he chose to do "A Day In The Life." I thought he would have chose to do something like "Yer Blues." When he did it, I was very pleased to hear what he'd done.

Goldie Hawn's version of "A Hard Days Night" is interesting, as she croons the song.

■ *MCA photo*

hear someone whistling 'I Am The Walrus.'"

I've always adored Goldie Hawn, ever since she was in her 20s. I remembered she could sing, and she'd been one of my idols. I wasn't sure if she would go for this. I hadn't met her. And we contacted her and met up and got on like a house on fire. She said she would come over to England to record it, which was lovely, but she didn't because she was offered a film to direct and she had to do that. I had to come to Texas, in fact, to record her. To do it, I explained to her I wanted a nightclub version of it, slow, sexy, moody. I said, "Think of Peggy Lee, think of Marilyn Monroe and think of yourself as well." And so I booked a jazz trio — piano, bass and drums — in a little studio in Austin, Texas. We spent an afternoon together and that was it. I was delighted by what she did. We had a nice dinner in the evening, and she flew off in one direction and I flew off in another. I brought the tapes back to England and overdubbed a better backing. She had a very good sense of what I was looking for. She put in quite a lot of her own style.

I wanted to speak about your two compositions that appear on the record.

Right. Well, the first one is the "Pepperland" one. The reason I put that in is "Yellow Submarine" was a pretty important piece of film for me. I'd already done some film work, but it was the first major film that I'd done and it was a very difficult thing to do and very rewarding. We made that animated feature in a year from start to finish, which is incredibly quick. Disney takes two years for most of them. In order to do this I had to work very close with the director writing music as he was animating. I would exchange my music with him and he would exchange his animation as we went along. I'd work on reel four and reel seven and so on. All pickle-dee, pickle-dee, I'd obviously had the whole script and sometimes the reels would be empty with just storyboards. And I would write descriptive music that would fit, really like free writing. He said, "I trust

■ *MCA photo*

you. Just do what you can. We have not time for anything else." I wrote over an hour of music to go with the film.

Wasn't "The Pepperland Suite" a hit?

Yes, in Brazil, it was a big hit and high in the charts. So I thought, getting back to the record, let's bring back "The Pepperland Suite." I put together a very small selection of items from that. I thought that was very worthwhile doing. The second one was a theme that I thought of quite a few years ago just after John died. I was in Montserrat, my island — it's a beautiful place, and I thought of this tune and thought of the way it should be done and orchestrated it. Then I put it aside and forgot about it. It's one of things that you can't use, you can't put it on an album out of the blue. I thought if I get asked to do a picture and it needs a good, moody, slow theme, that'd be useful. Then when I wanted to do the last track which was rather a serious track with Sean Connery ("In My Life"), a very dangerous track to do. I thought, "Let me link these two things up because my piece can act as an introduction, a prelude if you like, into 'In My Life.'" "In My Life" is such a personal song for me because part of it is me anyway, part of it is my writing with the solo in the middle which happened originally, and the words are so evocative of what my life is all about. I've been lucky all my life working with the greatest of people, and I've had great fun. I've really had a marvelous time. And I'm very grateful to all those people, a lot of them aren't with us anymore, "some are dead some are living, in my life, I've loved them all." And those words meant so much to me that I wanted them to be spoken, not sung. I couldn't have them sung because no one could sing them better than John. By speaking it, it brings out the meaning of the words. It is dangerous territory, but I wanted to have a very memorable voice and Sean Connery has one of the most identifiable voices in the world.

Previously, in 1964 you worked with Peter Sellers doing some spoken-word versions of Beatles songs.

Doing spoken-word that is humorous is no problem. It's when you start getting serious. I did a lot of stuff with Sellers of course. We did "Hard Day's Night." Have you heard all the other ones like "She Loves You"?

Yes, it's hilarious. Were there any heroes that you did not approach? Brian Wilson comes to mind.

Brian? Well indeed, he's not really a performer as such. He's a great writer and a great thinker. I was with Brian last year because I have a television series that hasn't come out here called *The Rhythm Of Life*, three one-hour shows, a series where I'm talking about music which aired on BBC One. I've been going around the world talking to people. I've had people in the classical world as well as people like Paul McCartney, Billy Joel, Elton John, Celine Dion, and also Brian Wilson. I went down to his house and chatted to him about his work. It's so nice to see him coming back to life again. He's got two babies now and he's very happy. And he's creating again, which is great. We've managed to get permission to get a copy of his old masters, and we went into a studio and opened them up. Like I did with "Pepper." I dissected them, listened to all the tracks and put them back together again. He was so excited by this. I asked him, "Haven't you done this?" And he said, "I haven't heard this stuff since we recorded it," "God Only Knows" and "Good Vibrations." And I tore them apart and said, "Brian, tell me what this track is?" And he said, "Oh, that's an instrument called a theremin." And it was extraordinary how he came to life with that.

Tell us about your musical beginnings at Guildhall School Of Music and how that background influenced your later work.

"I was a jobbing oboe player."

Well, I was very similar to both John and Paul in a way where I wasn't taught music to begin with. I just grew up feeling music and naturally making music. I can't remember a time where I wasn't making music on the piano. I was running a band by the time I was 15.

What was the name of the band?

[laughs] Very corny but I thought it was fantastic. The first one was a four-piece and then it became a five-piece. When it was a four-piece I called it "The Four Tune Tellers." [laughs] And then it became "George Martin And The Four Tune Tellers." Very clever. And I had T T's on the stands in front. We made quite a little bit of money as well. And then the war intervened, and by the time I was 17 I was in the Fleet Air Arm, which is part of the Royal Navy. We flew off carriers and we were fliers in the Navy. That was the tail end of the war. I was four years in the service. I was 21 when I came out. Having managed to evade Japan, I was all right. And I had no career. A professor of music who befriended me, he'd received from me during the war various compositions that I'd painfully put together. I went to see him and he said, "You must take up music." I said, "How can I? I'm not educated. I've never had any training." He said, "Well, get taught. I'll arrange it for you." He arranged an audition for me to play some of my work to the principal of the Guildhall School Of Music And Drama, which is a college in London. And he said, "We'll take you on as a composition student." And I got a government grant for three years to study. I started composition, conducting and orchestration, and I took up the oboe. I took up the oboe so I could make a living playing some instrument. You can't make a living playing the piano. I just played piano naturally. I wasn't taught. I didn't take piano as a subject, because I didn't see any future in it. I didn't rate myself as being a great pianist. I could never see myself making a living at it. I wanted to be

a film writer. So that's what happened. I was trained and I came out and I would work playing the oboe in different orchestras in the evenings and sometimes afternoons in the park, that kind of thing. I was a jobbing oboe player.

Do you still play?

No. [laughs] I don't think I could now. I took a job during the day to make some extra money, that was in the music department at the BBC. Then out of the blue I got a letter from someone asking me to go for an interview at a place called Abbey Road. So I cycled along there and the guy said, "I'm looking for someone to help me make some classical recordings, and I gather you can do this." Because I was a woodwind player and educated by now, I got the job of producing the classical baroque recordings of the Parlophone label. And I got hooked. Gradually this guy who was running the label gave me more and more work to do. I started doing jazz records, orchestral, pop of the period — it wasn't rock. Over a period of five years I worked as his assistant gradually doing more and more. By the time the five years was up I was virtually doing everything. And five years later in 1955, he retired. He was 65 years old and he left. I thought somebody was going to be brought in over me because I was in my 20s still. But to my astonishment I was given the job of running the label. I was the youngest person ever to be given that job.

I'm surprised you didn't try to sign The Four Tune Tellers.

[Hearty laughs] Exactly. And that was the beginning of my work with Parlophone.

Prior to your work with The Beatles, you worked in many different musical idioms. How did that impact your production skills? It seemed you were very willing to be experimental in your work with The Beatles.

Oh absolutely. But I always was experimental even before The Beatles came along. One of the records I made was an electronic record called "Ray Cathode," which was collaborating with the BBC radiophonics people. I made a lot of what I call "sound pictures" with actors and comedians because it was fun to do. I'm a person who gets bored quite easily, and I don't like doing the same thing over and over again. Once I was running the label I didn't earn much money, but I did have freedom to do what I wanted to do.

Discuss your approach toward string arrangements. Your work on Beatles songs such as "Strawberry Fields Forever," "Eleanor Rigby" and "Glass Onion" is extraordinary.

The writing of the parts is me and the requirements is them. It varied between John and Paul. Paul was generally quite articulate with what he wanted. Mostly we would sit down at the piano together and play it through and work out how it would sound. Paul still doesn't know how to orchestrate, but he knew what he wanted and would give me ideas and I would say, "You can't do that," or "You can do this." We'd talk about it, talk it through. John would never take that kind of attention. John was less articulate and much more full of imagery. He would have ideas which were difficult to express. It was quite difficult for me to interpret. One of the problems was getting inside his brain and find what he really wanted. Quite often he would say, "You know me. You know what I want." In the case of "I Am The Walrus," when I first heard that he just stood in front of me with a guitar and sang it through. But it was weird. I said to him, "What the hell am I going to do with this, John?" And he said, "I'd like for you to do a score and use some brass and some strings and some weird noises. You know the kind of thing I want." But I didn't, but I mean I just went away and did that.

Didn't you hire The Mike Sammes Singers for that?

Yes, that was a surprise for him. He didn't know that. I thought, "Well, let's do this because it adds to it." I had a group of singers called The Michael Sammes Singers who were pretty corny people. They were very good at reading what you wrote. If you wrote something, they could pretty much sing it instantaneously. They were very good. In the score you've got the directions for them where they have to shout or all the glasses, the up and downs and the ha ha ha's and hee hee hee's and so on. And when we ran it through and John heard it, he fell about laughing and thought it was so funny. So that's why "Walrus" was such an important song to put on the album.

What is the orchestral arrangement that you did for The Beatles of which you're most proud?

"Strawberry Fields Forever" is a wild score.

The Beatles wanted something unusual. Although at the core of it is orchestration that I liked to do. I liked to have clean orchestration. I've got various theories about orchestration. I don't think the human brain can take it too many notes at once. For example, when you're listening to a fugue of Bach or someone and you hear the first statement and the second one joins it, you can catch hold of that all right and then the third one comes in and it starts to get more complicated. Any more than that and then it becomes a jumble of sound. You can't really sort out what is what.

Tell us about the time you tried to turn John Lennon onto a piece of classical music.

He went back to my flat one night. We had dinner and were rapping away. We were talking about different kinds of music. I wanted to play him one of my favorite pieces of classical music. It was the Deathless and Fairy Suite Number Two by Ravel, which is a gorgeous piece of music. It lasts about nine minutes, and he sat through it patiently. I mean, it's one of the best examples of orchestration you can get, because it's a swelling of sound that is just breathtaking. And he listened very patiently and said, "Yeah, it's great. The trouble is by the time you get to the end of the tune you can't remember what the beginning's like." And I realized it was too stretched out for him to appreciate in one go. He couldn't assimilate it. He was so used to little sound bites. A lot of people are nowadays. It's the curse of advertising and television that we are now tuned to little jingles that we can connect to and recognize right away. And we can't listen to anything longer than that, so consequently the way people write sometimes is to connect together a lot of little jingles, which is not maybe the best way of doing things.

For a long time when asked about unreleased Beatles material you would state that it was all "rubbish" and there was nothing worth issuing. Working on Anthology 1, 2 *and 3 disproved that.*

I was convinced that there was nothing in the vaults that people hadn't heard that was worthwhile. But I was thinking like singles. Is there a great song that people hadn't heard? No, there's not a great song that people hadn't heard, there's little bits of rubbish. But what did emerge is I was given a brief by EMI, who asked me to put together stuff that would reflect the visual *Anthology* that wouldn't be a soundtrack but like an accompaniment or a companion. I thought the only way to do that is to see what there is. And I started listening and I found that there were different versions of songs that people would be interested in. The more I listened, the more I was convinced that people would want to have an analysis of

what's gone. In order, admittedly, to give me more material, I would then put in things like "Eleanor Rigby" without the voices to show you the construction of it. Conversely, "Because" without the accompaniment to show you the beauty of the voices, that kind of thing. And I thought, "OK, I'm spinning things out a bit here," but I think it's valid.

The unreleased George Harrison song "You Know What To Do" was quite a treat. You listen to that an then something like "I Need You" and "Savoy Truffle" and George kind of blossomed all at once.

He did blossom, didn't he? To begin with, most of the songs he did were rubbish.

What was the first song George wrote where your ears perked up and you thought, "He's gotten much better as a writer"?

I like "I Need You." [sings chorus of "I Need You"] Nice little song. I remember the song I hated most of all, "Only A Northern Song." "Taxman" wasn't bad, typical George bitching about the world. Really, the one that I thought was better than any of those was "Here Comes The Sun." I mean that was the first time he showed real cleverness in a song. From "Here Comes The Sun" onwards everything he did was pretty good.

On Anthology *you showed not only the musical side of the band but the zany side such as "And Your Bird Can Sing," where John and Paul are cracking up doing the vocal.*

Isn't that super? [laughs] They were stoned out of their minds, of course, but it was also very funny. When I played it to Paul when I discovered it, I'd forgotten about it. We actually fell around laughing listening to it, too. We had marvelous times. We had such fun in the studio. I have such happy memories. John was very funny. John would do impersonations and send-ups of people, sometimes quite cruel but always very very funny.

In the '70s, John vacillated between loving and hating his days with The Beatles.

John went through some very bad times, like the Let It Be sessions. Later on he got pretty into drugs. During his time with May Pang, he admits it was a year and a half lost weekend.

Hypothetically, if John were still alive would he have gotten involved with Anthology and recorded with Paul, George, and Ringo?

I think he would have taken part in it. I think he would have been very active in putting it together 'cause John actually was an obsessive collector anyway. He would keep almost anything. I think he would have done it. John actually regained himself at the end, which was lovely. It was just too tragic having got back to himself that he was killed.

When you met up with John in the '70s he would tell you if he had the chance he would re-record every Beatles song. Could you understand where he was coming from?

It's a funny thing. When John said this to me originally was when we were spending an evening together, and it shook me to the core when we were talking about old things and he said, "I'd love to do everything again." To me that was just a horror. And I said, "John, you can't really mean it. Even 'Strawberry Fields'?" And he said, "Especially

> **"I don't think I could do anything better than what we did."**

'Strawberry Fields!'" I thought, "Oh shit, all the effort that went into that." We worked very hard on that trying to capture something that was nebulous. But I realized that John was a dreamer. In John's mind everything was so beautiful and much better than it was in real life. He was never a person of nuts and bolts. The bitter truth is music is nuts and bolts. You've got to bring it down to horse hair going over a bit of wood, people blowing into brass tubes. You've got to get down to practicalities.

How about you, George, is there one Beatles song you wish you could redo?

Would I like to do something again? No, I wouldn't want to do anything again. I'm not a person to look back, although having said that on this album I'm doing that. But I'm not trying to do anything better than what we did. I don't honestly think I could do anything better than what we did. I think what we did was right. It becomes solidified with time. You can't imagine any other way of doing it. You get surprised if you hear someone doing something that does work. When Joe Cocker came out with "With A Little Help From My Friends," I thought that was great, but that wouldn't have worked with Ringo. So the answer is I'd rather leave it to history, thanks.

When Paul, George, and Ringo recorded the two new Beatles songs, "Free As A Bird" and "Real Love," did they ask you to be involved?

I kind of told them I wasn't too happy with putting them together with the dead John. I've got nothing wrong with dead John, but the idea of having dead John with live Paul and Ringo and George to form a group, it didn't appeal to me too much. In the same way that I think it's OK to find an old record of Nat King Cole's and bring it back to life and issue it, but to have him singing with his daughter is another thing. So I don't know, I'm not fussy about it, but it didn't appeal to me very much. I think I might have done it if they asked me, but they didn't ask me.

Did you enjoy Jeff Lynne's production of "Free As A Bird" and "Real Love"?

I thought what they did was terrific. It was very, very good indeed. I don't think I would have done it like that if I had produced it.

What would you have done differently?

Well you see, the way they did it, you must remember, the material they had to deal with was very difficult. It was a cassette that John had placed on top of his piano, played and sang. The piano was louder than the voice and the voice wasn't very clear, and the rhythm was all over the place. So the way they tackled it was first of all they tried to separate the voice and the piano, not very successfully. Then they tried to put it into a rigid time beat so they could overdub easily other instruments. So they stretched it and compressed it and put it around until it got to a regular waltz control click, and then they were done. The result was, in order to conceal the bad bits, they had to plaster it fairly heavily, so what you ended up with was quite a thick homogenous sound that hardly stops. There's not much dynamics in it. The way I would have tackled it if I had the opportunity would have been the reverse of that. I would have looked at the song as a song and got The Beatles together and say, "What can we do with this song?" bearing in mind we have got John around as well somewhere. I would have actually have started to record a song and I would have dropped John into it. I wouldn't have made John the basis of it. So where

possible I would have used instruments probably and we would then try and get his voice more separate and use him for the occasional voice so it would become a true partnership of voices. Whether that would be practical or not I don't know. This is just theoretically the way I would tackle it.

You did some beautiful scoring for Paul on his recent album, Flaming Pie, especially your orchestral work on "Somedays" and "Beautiful Night."

Oh thank you. I worked on "Great Day" and "Calico Skies" too. On Ringo's new album I did a score for him too ("I'm Yours"). Paul I know very well. When he came along doing Flaming Pie, the stuff he was demonstrating for me was pretty good. I think it's the best album he's done in a long time. He asked me if I would collaborate with him. I said, "Choose something you think I can be helpful on." He actually gave me the numbers and said, "Would you like to do this?" It's always a challenge with Paul because you're on your mettle to try and do something that he won't be disappointed in. He was very pleased with "Beautiful Night" and the others too. On "Calico Skies" it was just a question of production. There was no real arrangement, really, very, very simple. I enjoyed working with him very much as I always do.

After The Beatles broke up there were quite a score of "power pop" bands who mined a Beatles-esque sound, such as Badfinger and The Raspberries. Were you aware of this power pop movement?

I worked with Badfinger [orchestral score for "Money"/"Flying"], but I didn't actually produce them. Geoff Emerick worked with them. I was aware of all this. It was inevitable that The Beatles would spawn imitators and emulators. People wanted to be like The Beatles. So there's nothing wrong with that.

Still do.

Still do. How are you Liam? [laughs]. In an oblique way I worked with another group who had much more individuality but they weren't dissimilar with The Beatles, and they were America. America were like an American version of The Beatles, but they had their own homespun kind of songs. They were all good guitar players and all good singers and harmony singers. So there was that kind of illusion there. But I don't find anything wrong with people, providing they don't imitate. I think that Oasis have made a mistake in being so close to The Beatles and admitting. Noel actually said to me if he'd been born 20 years earlier he would have been Paul McCartney. Noel is a good songwriter — you can't knock him in that respect. I think he would have made it anyway regardless.

You worked with the power pop band Cheap Trick and produced their All Shook Up *album. Why did you get involved with them?*

I liked them. [laughs] I like Cheap Trick. It was a different thing. It's part of the business of liking to do different things and not get stuck in one groove. So I would try everything. I had one little assay into heavy rock, which was a terrible mistake, UFO. Cheap Trick I enjoyed very much.

What's your take on Badfinger? It seemed being on Apple Records got them tagged as Beatles wannabees when they had much more to offer.

I thought they were very good. It was a terrible tragic thing, all of that, the suicides and the ripping-offs that went on. It was terrible. It was all the seamy side of our business. They were a good group and they should have survived and they should have come through and been brilliant. But they didn't and they were one of the victims, I'm afraid. I don't remember working with them, although I did. It's difficult to remember everything after 48 years. [laughs] What did you have for breakfast on Tuesday the 19th of June, 1945? [laughs]

Can you assess the instrumental talents of The Beatles?

Paul's the most talented instrumentally in that he could play very good guitar. He was probably the best guitar player in the group. Of course he played bass guitar — he could tackle almost anything. He played very good drums too. His bass playing is wonderful. He was irritatingly good to other people. Sometimes he would put up the backs of the other guys 'cause he would get on the drums and tell Ringo what to do, and Ringo would get a bit irked by it. John was good, but he was careless. John was a gut man, and if it happened it happened and if it didn't he would fling the guitar across the room and say, "Get me a better one." John hated tuning his guitar, for example, such a mundane thing. He would get good sounds, good ideas. Some of his riff ideas were terrific. George was the painstaking one. He would be brilliant after 45 years. He would assemble his work. I used to think he used to assemble his recordings like a guy in Turkey making a carpet. He would work away in every room and every little inch would be detailed and beautiful. But it would take time and he would overdub and he'd track and correct and so on. He's a very good guitar player, of course.

We can't forget Ringo.

Ringo is a sweet guy. As you know he's given up booze and cigarettes. He's too clean for words. He and his wife Barbara are such sweet people. And as a drummer he is unique. He's not a great technical drummer if you measure him against someone like Steve Gadd or Jeff Porcaro — he wouldn't be able to play like that. But he has a unique sound. When you hear Ringo, you know it's Ringo. There's no one else. He contributed an enormous amount to The Beatles' sound with his distinctive-sounding drums. Enormously supportive, he was always there. Apart from his drumming he would be the catalyst. His opinions counted. If John was doing something a bit dubious and Ringo would say, "That's crap, John," John would take it out. He wouldn't get angry, he would accept it.

In the '60s, did any of the other major British bands such as The Who, The Kinks, The Small Faces, or The Rolling Stones attempt to have you produce them?

They didn't approach me, mainly because I was so damn busy. I really couldn't have worked any harder than I did. All of the people from Brian's [Epstein] stable came along. I was just about able to cope with those and very little more. I had a tremendous roster of artists. But going back to Ringo again, one of the essential things about his drumming is he took infinite pains on getting the tone of his drums right. He tuned assiduously and got them exactly right. He was intently interested in the way that we recorded, so he would come and listen and say, "I'd like to hear more space on this one."

The drum sound changed on Revolver.

He had a lot of influence on that. He would put his input in. He would come up to the control room and talk to Geoff Emerick and try to get it to sound better. He was very keen on their sound.

You did work later in your career with another major '60s band, The Bee Gees. How would you characterize their talents?

Terrific songwriters. I remember going to meet with them in The Bahamas when we were talking about doing the Sgt. Pepper film, and they played me the tracks that they just recorded for a new film that nobody had ever heard about called Saturday Night Fever. I couldn't quite connect what I was hearing with the guys that I knew because it was so hip. I was looking at Barry and Maurice and Robin and I was saying it was a great dance sound. It could have been Motown, it was so good. I asked, "Have you done this? It's fantastic. You've got big hits here." I was enormously

impressed. What was good about them was they weren't just writing good songs, but they were writing good production ideas into the songs the way that they were putting it together and the guitar work. Barry is very, very talented, and the others also contribute quite a bit too.

Lastly, it's been more than 15 years since Paul McCartney's Tug Of War *album was released. What are your memories of working with Paul on that record, acclaimed by many as one of Paul's best solo records?*

With *Tug Of War* the way it started was funny because we'd always been good friends and had dinner from time to time. One night we all went out to dinner. Paul and Linda were staying at their flat in town. I dropped them off and we said our good-byes. Just as I was about to drive off, Linda nudged Paul and then Paul ran through and knocked on the window. I thought we'd left something behind. He said, "I forgot something." And I said, "What is it?" He said, "Would you like to produce my next album?" I said, "Paul, we've been together all night and you give me a sledgehammer like that. We'd better talk about it." I said, "I'll ring you. We've got to talk about this, Paul, because I'm not sure how it's going to work." And he said, "Why?" I said, "Because for eight years or more you've been making very, very good records. You're a very good record producer. What do you need me for?" He said, "I think it would be a good idea." I said, "You may not like it." He said, "Well, why not?" I said, "Because I don't think you'll like being told what to do." He said, "We know each other so well it won't be a problem." So I said, "OK, all right, if you want to try it. What about the songs?" And he said, "What do you mean, what about the songs?" I said, "Well, I'll need to have a look at them and judge them first of all." And he said, "Well, you mean I'll have to audition for you?" And I said, "Well, the material is pretty important." So he said OK and gave me about 14 songs he had on tape. I listened to them over the weekend and we met up on Monday. He said, "What do you think of them?" I said, "Four are great." He said, "Four?" And I said, "Of the other 10, six need a lot of work and the other four you should just throw away." He kind of gulped and said OK. He was a bit miffed, but you see it was necessary. It was vital. It's no good working with someone and being a yes man. You've got to be honest about it. He knows I'm always honest, so that was it. Working with Paul from that moment on, once we established the ballpark area, was a delight, an absolute delight. He did revise all the six songs that needed working on. "Ebony & Ivory" was one of them. We got Stevie [Wonder] up. He agreed to come to Montserrat. We had a great time there. We'd generally work from two in the afternoon 'til about seven, we'd have a break for dinner and then we'd work until about midnight. He would spend the following morning on the beach with the kids. Ringo came out, Stevie Wonder came out. He looked through the glass of our control room and said, "Isn't that a beautiful sunset?" [laughs] He also brought out the very first Linn drum machine, and it went wrong. He said to get the engineer to open the box and that he could fix it. I said, "Are you sure?" So he opened up the lid and he said, "Now switch it on." And I said, "Stevie, there are 440 volts running through there." And he said, "I know, but I can't fix it unless it's on." And there he was in the live chassis, and I expected to have a fried Stevie Wonder at any minute and he fixed it. He's an amazing man. And dear Carl Perkins. He's never been to the West Indies in his entire life. I put him in a bungalow down by the beach. I rang him the next morning to see if he slept OK. And he said, "Man, I thought I'd died and gone to heaven." He was a lovely man. When he did our Montserrat show in September for the victims of Montserrat, I purposely didn't ask anyone from America because I didn't want to pay expenses for anybody. I only asked people from England because I wanted every penny to go to those victims. And Carl rang up and said, "I want

to come and do this for you." I said, "Carl, honey, I'd love you to but we can't pay expenses." And he said, "I'll come anyway." And so did Jimmy Buffett. They paid their own way to come over. And Carl turned up in his winkle-picker blue suede shoes. He really did have them.

"We got Stevie [Wonder] up. He agreed to come to Montserrat. We had a great time there.... He looked through the glass of our control room and said, 'Isn't that a beautiful sunset?' He also brought out the very first Linn drum machine, and it went wrong. He said to get the engineer to open the box and that he could fix it. I said, 'Are you sure?' So he opened up the lid and he said, 'Now switch it on.' And I said, 'Stevie, there are 440 volts running through there.' And he said, 'I know, but I can't fix it unless it's on.' And there he was in the live chasis, and I expected to have a fried Stevie Wonder at any minute and he fixed it. He's an amazing man."

— George Martin

"We embarked on making an album that would be fun to do, fun for myself and for the performers and hopefully fun for the people who listen to it. And certainly it's done that. I was just going to have a few friends on and then I extended that by saying, 'Well, let it be friends and heroes.'"

— George Martin

"It's always a challenge with Paul because you're on your mettle to try and do something that he won't be disappointed in. He was very pleased with 'Beautiful Night' and the others too. On 'Calico Skies' it was just a question of production. There was no real arrangement really, very, very simple. I enjoyed working with him very much as I always do."

— George Martin ∎

■ *Abbey Road Studios, photo by Gillian G. Gaar*

Together When We're Apart

THE BEATLES' COLLABORATIONS AFTER THEIR SPLIT

By Casey Piotrowski

ertainly, it is the most unforgettable breakup in the history of rock 'n' roll. With the possible exception of the split between Dean Martin and Jerry Lewis, no breakup in the history of show business has received as much attention.

April 10, 1970 — It's a day that will live in rock infamy, an event so big that each of the principals felt the need to address it in his work (John Lennon's "How Do You Sleep," Paul McCartney's "Dear Friend," George Harrison's "Sue Me, Sue You Blues" and Ringo Starr's "Early 1970," among a number of other titles). It is an event so large in rock's history that it merits being written about, as this article demonstrates, more than 30 years after the fact.

The dream was over. The Beatles had broken up.

Or had they? After Martin and Lewis split, they never appeared in each other's movies or TV shows or on each other's records. The Police have been apart for more than a decade, yet Sting, Andy Summers, and Stewart Copeland have given each other precious little help in their respective solo efforts.

The Eagles, the preeminent band of the '70s, have each enjoyed some degree of solo success before their mid-90s reunion, but almost none of it has come with the assistance of their fellow bandmates.

> *"April 10, 1970 — It's a day that will live in rock infamy"*

Fleetwood Mac is another band where its members (most notably Stevie Nicks, Lindsay Buckingham, and Christine McVie) would move in and out of the band, record as solo artists and do quite well for themselves. But each did it largely on their own without contributions from the band they were ultimately still a part of.

But The Beatles had broken up, and their split was bitter, vicious. They dragged each other through the mud in the courts, in the press, even on their own solo records. (According to their partnership, McCartney shared equally with Lennon in the profits of Lennon's *Imagine* LP — even as McCartney was continually skewered musically by his former partner.)

The Beatles didn't just break up the band. They took sledgehammers to it, ran over it with a tank, then threw it into an atom smasher just for good measure. If members of any band had reason to go their separate ways and never, absolutely never look back, it was The Beatles.

Of course, that never happened.

The last three decades are filled with examples of The Beatles in twos, threes and yes, sometimes even all four of them, working with each other and with George Martin. We include Martin here because he was more than just their producer, their arranger or the ignitor of their imaginations. More than any other person, Martin has earned the right to be called their collaborator. He has been the architect of their sound, their growth, their creative legend. He has been the fifth side of the square. And any look at the collaborations of the ex-Beatles has to include their work with him.

But, getting back to that breakup. If The Beatles really hated each other so much, why did Lennon plug McCartney's "Coming Up" when he was in the midst of his own comeback? Why did Harrison help Starr write "It Don't Come Easy" yet not accept co-writers credit? Why did Harrison agree to play a slide guitar solo on McCartney's "Wanderlust"? Why indeed.

Perhaps each of The Beatles were using professional reasons to express their personal feelings, practicing while apart what they so consistently preached while they were together — love, in this case, for one another.

Maybe it was like Harrison said in "When We Was Fab" — "The microscopes that magnified the tears." As vicious as it may have seemed at the time, perhaps the worst of their split really lasted only a few embarrassingly public moments. With the perspective of time, it's clear that the rift among the four was nowhere as deep as it appeared. Time has also showed us that as much as each needed to go out and prove his own mettle, each still ultimately realized that he needed the other three around.

With that in mind, we thought it would be interesting to see, in light of all the acrimony — real and imagined — just how frequently these four guys wound up working together after that fateful day in April more than three decades ago.

We turned to three marvelously well-researched books — *Eight Arms To Hold You* by Chip Madinger and Mark Easter, *Beatles Undercover* by Kristofer Engelhardt and *The Beatles After The Break-Up* by Keith Badman — as primary reference sources and put together a fairly complete list of John, Paul, George, and Ringo's work together after The Beatles.

We think you'll be surprised and, if you're a Beatles fan, quite pleasantly so, as we look at the post-separation work of a band that never quite broke up.

First, we'll look at their work together — apart from the group — long before their split.

1960

Ringo (at that time still the drummer for Rory Storm & The Hurricanes) join John, Paul, and George in the studio to play on Lu Walters' recording of "Summertime." (Oct. 15, 1960)

1963

All four Beatles play on a (recently discovered) demo for "I'll Be On My Way," intended for Billy J. Kramer & The Dakotas.

1964

Lennon and McCartney do the arrangement, McCartney plays piano and Martin produces "It's For You," a song McCartney wrote for Cilla Black. (July 2, 1964)

1965

Lennon and Harrison do background vocals on a broadcast version of Adam Faith's "I Need Your Lovin'." (April 16, 1965)

Lennon produces, McCartney plays guitar and Harrison plays tambourine on The Silkie's version of "You've Got To Hide Your Love Away." (Aug. 9, 1965)

1966

McCartney writes the soundtrack for The Family Way. Martin produces. (Sept. 10, 1966)

1967

Lennon and McCartney add backing vocals to The Rolling Stones' "We Love You." (May 18, 1967)

Lennon and Harrison appear on British TV's David Frost Show. (Oct. 4, 1967)

1968

Lennon and McCartney help produce The Grapefruit's single "Dear Delilah." (Jan. 19, 1968)

Martin produces McCartney's "Step Inside Love" for Cilla Black. (Feb. 28, 1968)

Lennon and McCartney appear on "The Tonight Show. "(May 15, 1968)

Harrison and Starr attend the premiere of Wonderwall, for which Harrison wrote the soundtrack. (May 15, 1968)

McCartney and Starr are interviewed for the BBC television documentary *All My Loving*. (May 23, 1968)

Harrison produces, plays and writes and McCartney and Starr play on Jackie Lomax's *Is This What You Want*? LP. (June 24, 1968)

McCartney produces, Martin plays piano on Mary Hopkin's *Postcard* LP.

McCartney writes the liner notes for Lennon and Yoko Ono's *Two Virgins* LP.

McCartney plays bass and Harrison sings background vocals on James Taylor's "Carolina On My Mind."

1969

Lennon, McCartney, and Starr appear playing an untitled jam in Yoko's film *Then & Now*. (Jan. 10, 1969; film released December 1984)

All four Beatles back up Billy Preston as he records demos for two of his own songs. (Jan. 28, 1969).

Lennon and McCartney play on Ono's "Lennon, Lennon (Let's Hope for Peace)." (Jan. 23, 1969) (This version remains unreleased.)

Harrison plays and Martin produces an early version of "It Don't Come Easy." (This version remains unreleased.)

McCartney produces and Harrison plays on Jackie Lomax's "Thumbin' A Ride" and "Going Back To Liverpool." (March 1969)

Starr appears on Martin's YTV special *With A Little Help from My Friends*. (Aug. 14, 1969)

McCartney and Starr play on "Qué Será, Será" and "The Fields Of St. Etienne." (August 1969)

Starr plays on Lennon's "Cold Turkey." (Sept. 25, 1969)

Harrison and Starr play on Leon Russell's self-titled LP. (September 1969)

Harrison plays with Lennon's Plastic Ono Band (and a cast of 1,000s) at the Benefit For UNICEF. (Dec. 15, 1969)

Lennon makes a cameo appearance and McCartney contributes "Come & Get It" for Starr's film *The Magic Christian*.

McCartney arranges "Stardust" for Starr's *Sentimental Journey* LP.

Martin produces Starr's *Sentimental Journey* LP. (Sessions continue into 1970)

Harrison produces, writes and plays and Starr plays on Doris Troy's self-titled LP. (Sessions continue into 1970)

1970

Harrison plays lead guitar on Lennon's "Instant Karma." (Jan. 28, 1970)

Harrison produces and plays lead guitar on Starr's "It Don't Come Easy." (March 1970)

Harrison produces, writes and plays and Starr plays on Preston's *Encouraging Words* LP. (April 6, 1970)

Lennon produces and plays and Starr plays on Ono's *Plastic Ono Band* LP. (Sept. 10, 1970)

Harrison plays lead guitar on Starr's "Early 1970." (October 1970)

Lennon, Harrison, and Starr play on Ono's "Greenfield Morning, I Pushed An Empty Baby Carriage All Over The City." (October 1970)

Starr plays on Lennon's *Plastic Ono Band* LP. (Oct. 11, 1970)

Starr plays on Harrison's *All Things Must Pass* LP. (May 10, 1970)

According to drummer Alan White, Lennon plays on

Harrison's "My Sweet Lord."

Harrison and Starr play on "In Praise Of Lord," an unreleased track by Aashish Khan.

Lennon, McCartney, Harrison and Starr appear on BBC Radio One's special *Let It Be*.

1971

Lennon contributes background vocals to Ronnie Spector's "Tandoori Chicken," which Harrison produced. (Feb. 1, 1971)

Lennon produces and Starr plays on the Elastic Oz Band's "God Save Oz," which Lennon wrote. (May 1, 1971) (A version with Lennon's lead vocal is subsequently released on The John Lennon Anthology.)

Harrison plays on Lennon's Imagine LP. (May 1971)

Harrison and Starr play at The Concert For Bangla Desh. (Aug. 1, 1971)

Martin arranges orchestration for the New York Philharmonic on McCartney's "Uncle Albert/Admiral Halsey."

Harrison and Starr play on an unreleased recording by British actor Nicol Williamson.

All four Beatles and Martin give new interviews for the BBC radio series *The Beatles Story*. (The series is broadcast from May to August 1972.)

1972

Harrison and Starr play on Harry Nilsson's *Son Of Schmilsson* LP. (March 3, 1972)

Harrison produces and writes and Starr plays on "You've Got To Stay With Me" and "I'll Still Love You" for Black. (August 1972)

Harrison and Starr play on Nilsson's "Daybreak" single. (September 1972)

Martin produces McCartney's "Live & Let Die." (October 1972)

Starr plays on Harrison's *Living In The Material World* LP. (Oct. 10-11, 1972) (Sessions continue in 1973.)

Harrison produces and plays lead guitar on Starr's "Back Off Boogaloo." (Starr later admits that, though uncredited, Harrison also helped him write the song.)

1973

Lennon, McCartney, and Harrison write, sing and play on the *Starr* LP. (March 4, 1973)

Harrison produces and plays and Starr plays on the *Shankar Family & Friends* LP. (April 1973)

Starr plays on Harrison's "Ding Dong, Ding Dong" single. (November 1973)

1974

Lennon produces, writes and sings and Starr drums on Nilsson's *Pussy Cats* LP. (April 6, 1974)

Lennon writes, plays and sings on Starr's *Goodnight Vienna* LP. (Aug. 11, 1974) (Versions of Lennon singing lead on "Only You" and "Goodnight Vienna" are subsequently released on The John Lennon Anthology.)

Lennon does the voice-over for TV and radio commercials for Starr's *Goodnight Vienna*. (Nov. 14, 1974)

Starr does the voice-over for TV and radio commercials for Lennon's *Walls & Bridges*. (Nov. 14, 1974)

Lennon and Harrison appear (though not together) from Harrison's hotel room in a radio interview following Harrison's last stop on his 1974 American tour. (Dec. 20, 1974)

1975

Martin is interviewed for the ABC TV special *David Frost Salutes The Beatles*. (May 21, 1974)

1976

Lennon and McCartney write and play and Harrison writes for Starr's *Rotogravure* LP (April 6, 1976)

Starr joins McCartney on stage during his L.A. Forum concert appearance. (June 21, 1976) (Their backstage meeting appears on McCartney's *Wings Over The World* TV special, which aired in 1979.)

Martin remixes tracks for The Beatles' *Rock & Roll Music* repackage.

1977

All four Beatles give their consent to the release of *The Beatles At The Hollywood Bowl.*

McCartney and Martin are interviewed for The Beatles' episode of ITV's *All You Need Is Love* series.

1978

Harrison appears on the Starr TV special.

Harrison and Martin are interviewed for a Capitol Radio feature on The Beatles.

Lennon records several demos for Starr's (then-titled) *Can't Fight Lightning* LP (later to be called Stop And Smell The Roses).

1980

McCartney appears on the episode of This Is Your Life honoring Martin. (Jan. 30, 1980)

McCartney writes, plays and sings on Starr's *Can't Fight Lightning* LP. (July 1980)

Martin begins sifting through McCartney's demos to choose material for the next Wings LP (which will become McCartney's solo *Tug Of War*.) (August 1980)

Martin produces McCartney's "We All Stand Together" single (Oct. 11, 1980)

Harrison produces, writes, sings and plays on Starr's *Can't Fight Lightning/Stop And Smell The Roses* LP. (Nov. 19-25, 1980)

Martin produces McCartney's *Tug Of War* LP. (Sessions continue into 1981.)

1981

Starr drums on Harrison's *Somewhere In England* LP. (February 1981)

Starr drums for McCartney's *Tug Of War*. (Feb. 15-19, 1981)

Starr and Martin appear in a video for McCartney's "Take It Away." (June 18-23, 1981)

McCartney sings, Starr plays, and Martin assists in the production of Harrison's "All Those Years Ago."

McCartney produces and appears with Starr in T*he Cooler*, an 11-minute video featuring music from Starr's *Stop And Smell The Roses*.

1982

Martin presents a check to the recipient of the first John Lennon Scholarship. (Nov. 13, 1982)

Martin produces tracks for McCartney's *Pipes Of Peace*. (Sessions continue into 1983)

Starr plays on McCartney's "Average Person."

Martin does interviews for United Artists' *The Compleat Beatles* video.

1983

Starr costars in McCartney's film *Give My Regards To Broad Street*. (Feb. 5, 1983)

Starr plays and Martin produces McCartney's *Give My*

Regards To Broad Street LP. (Sessions continue into 1984)

McCartney and Martin are taped for LWT's *South Bank Show*. (Nov. 12, 1983)

McCartney and Martin appear on the BBC TV program *Hardy*. (Dec. 14, 1983)

1984

Martin collects McCartney's Ivor Novello Award for "We All Stand Together." (March 13, 1984)

Starr appears in McCartney's *So Sad* video.

Harrison and Starr appear (playing in a concert segment) in the film *Water* (which was released by Harrison's Handmade Films).

Harrison writes and plays and Starr plays on the soundtrack of *Water*.

1985

Harrison and Starr play and sing on the Carl Perkins' *Blue Suede Shoes* special. (Oct. 21, 1985)

1986

McCartney and Starr contribute tracks to *The Anti-Heroin Project: It's A Live-In World* benefit LP. (Released Nov. 24, 1986)

Martin begins remixes of The Beatles recordings for release on CD. (This continues into 1987.)

1987

Starr plays drums on Harrison's *Cloud Nine* LP. (Jan. 8, 1987)

McCartney and Harrison play (separately) on Duane Eddy's self-titled LP. (February 1987)

McCartney and Harrison appear in the Granada TV documentary *It Was 20 Years Ago Today*. (Broadcast June 1, 1987)

Harrison and Starr appear at the Prince's Trust Benefit Concert at Wembley Arena. (June 5-8, 1970)

Martin orchestrates and mixes McCartney's "Once Upon A Long Ago" and produces overdubs on two other McCartney songs. (July 1, 1987)

Martin produces McCartney's music for his *Rupert The Bear* animated film. (Dec. 1, 1987)

Harrison and Starr shoot a video for Harrison's "When We Was Fab" video. (Dec. 18, 1987)

Martin produces the soundtrack for McCartney's unreleased animated film *Tropical Island Hum*.

1988

Harrison and Starr attend The Beatles' induction into The Rock And Roll Hall Of Fame. (Jan. 20, 1988)

Harrison and Starr appear together on TV's *Aspel & Company* talk show. (March 3, 1988)

Martin does the string arrangements for McCartney's "Put It There."

Martin prepares Beatles music for use in the *John Lennon: Imagine* movie.

1989

McCartney and Martin appear on French TV's Sacree Soiree (May 31, 1989).

Harrison and Starr appear in Tom Petty's "I Won't Back Down" music video.

1990

Starr records "I Call Your Name" to be used for the John Lennon Scholarship Concert. (March 1990)

McCartney's taped performance of is played at the John Lennon Scholarship Concert in Liverpool. (May 5, 1990)

McCartney is interviewed for BBC Radio 1's series *In My Life: Lennon Remembered*. (Broadcast 10/6/90)

Harrison and Starr contribute tracks to the *Nobody's Child — Romanian Angel Appeal* charity CD. (All four Beatles wives co-chair the effort.)

1991

McCartney writes and demos "Angel In Disguise" for Starr's *Time Takes Time* LP. (The track remains unreleased.)

1992

Harrison and Starr play together at the Natural Law Party benefit concert. (April 6, 1992)

Martin produces McCartney's "Calico Skies" and "Great Day." (September 1992) (These songs would not be released until McCartney's 1997 *Flaming Pie* LP.)

McCartney, Harrison, and Starr appear on Martin's ITV and Disney Channel special *The Making Of Sgt. Pepper*. (Broadcast in the U.S. in September 1992)

Martin arranges orchestral overdubs for McCartney's "C'mon People."

1993

Starr joins McCartney on stage at The Hollywood Bowl for the chorus of "Hey Jude." (April 16, 1993)

Harrison joins Martin for a press conference to launch the CD release of *The Beatles '62-'66* and *'67-'70*. (Sept. 9, 1993)

McCartney and Starr make separate guest appearances on the ITV special Cilla — A Celebration. (September 1993)

McCartney and Harrison tape interviews for MTV Europe's Beatle Day. (Nov. 1, 1993)

1994

McCartney inducts Lennon into The Rock And Roll Hall Of Fame. (Jan. 19, 1994)

McCartney, Harrison and Starr begin their "reunion" sessions, which will ultimately yield "Free As A Bird." (Feb. 11, 1994)

Martin prepares *Beatles Live At The BBC*.

McCartney and Starr appear in the "Drive My Car" promotional message for Recording Artists, Actors And Athletes Against Drunk Driving. (RADD).

McCartney, Harrison, and Starr tape interviews for *The Beatles Anthology* video.

1995

McCartney, Harrison and Starr complete "Real Love" from Lennon's demo. (Jan. 2, 1995)

1996

Starr sings and plays on McCartney's *Flaming Pie*. (May 1996)

All four Beatles contribute music to Perkins' *Go Cat Go* LP.

McCartney, Harrison, and Starr do new interviews to promote the *Anthology 3* CD.

1997

Martin arranges the orchestra for McCartney's "Beautiful Night." (Feb. 14, 1997)

Starr and Martin are interviewed for McCartney's *Flaming Pie* radio special. (April 1997)

McCartney plays at the Music For Monserrat concert organized by Martin. Martin conducts the orchestra for McCartney's performance of the medley from *Abbey Road*. (Sept. 15, 1997)

Starr appears in McCartney's "Beautiful Night" video. (October 1997)

Starr and Martin contribute interviews for the Black episode of the Granada TV series *Brit Girls*. (Broadcast Nov. 22, 1997)

McCartney tapes a segment for George Martin's Rhythm Of Life TV series. (Dec. 28, 1997)

Starr and Harrison appear in McCartney's *In The World Tonight* documentary.

McCartney plays and sings, Harrison plays, and Martin arranges on Starr's Vertical Man LP. (Sessions continue into 1998)

1998

McCartney and Martin are interviewed for ITV's documentary *The Story Of Abbey Road*. (Broadcast Jan. 4, 1998)

McCartney, Harrison, and Starr all send video congratulations as Martin is presented with an Outstanding Achievement award at the Music Industry Trust's Dinner in London. (Oct. 23, 1998)

Martin appears on the Lennon episode of VH-1's Legends series. (Dec. 8, 1998)

Martin produces The Lennon Anthology version of Lennon's "Grow Old With Me."

1999

Martin conducts the Tribute To The Beatles concert to reopen The Hollywood Bowl. (June 25, 1999)

McCartney, Harrison, and Starr all take a "strong interest" in and are interviewed for the re-release of the *Yellow Submarine* movie.

2000

McCartney, Harrison, and Starr work on *The Beatles Anthology* DVD release.

McCartney, Harrison, and Starr are interviewed for *The Beatles Anthology* book.

2001

Harrison and Starr perform (on separate tracks) for the Larry "Legs" Smith album.

Harrison and Starr perform (on separate tracks) for the new Electric Light Orchestra album, *Zoom*.

McCartney does the introduction for Starr's All Starr Band DVD and TV special.

All in all, it's pretty amazing. Every year since their breakup — more than three decades now — there's been at least one project, usually many more, in which two or more of The Beatles have participated. In the last several years, since their rapprochment, those projects have, again, centered around the group.

Knowing how loathe all four of them have been through the years to talk of a reunion, there's probably a good chance that there has been other work between two or three or even all four of them over the years that we'll never know about. But that is speculation.

This much is fact — the days of divisiveness among The Beatles are far outnumbered by the years of cooperation, support and love on both sides of their "breakup."

One of the most appealing qualities of The Beatles has been their willingness to support one another, whether it related directly to the band or not. We saw it when Harrison and Starr hawked Lennon's book, *In His Own Write*, on an early '60s BBC radio appearance; when the other three stood by Lennon during the "bigger than Jesus" controversy; when they stood by McCartney after Linda's death; and when McCartney told fans to "boycott that book" after the release of Albert Goldman's scandalous *The Life And Times Of John Lennon*, and countless times in between. After 40 years, this kind of unity has become as much a part of The Beatles' persona as shaggy hair and "yeah, yeah, yeah."

Maybe the same can be said for members of all bands, but with The Beatles' level of fame and the individual recognition for each that has come with it, this particular example of male bonding seems unique.

For that kind of loyalty to exist for this long a time seems remarkable, particularly among men who've reached the station in life these four have. If anything, each has proven time and again that he doesn't need the other three to achieve either commercial or artistic success. Ultimately, they have chosen to remain in each other's lives.

In his last words on The Beatles, Derek Taylor called their story "the 20th century's greatest romance" and, as we work our way through the beginnings of a new millenium, that love story — between The Beatles and the world and among The Beatles themselves — goes on. ∎

■ *Glenn A. Baker Archives*

"the 20th century's greatest romance"

*I*t was an amazing time. The Beatles were constantly at the top of the charts. Seemingly, every time you turned on the radio, you heard a new Beatles record. They were always in the press or on TV. Who can forget those incredible days of 1974? That's right, 1974... really, mid-1973 through mid-1975.

Because of the way they controlled pop music as a group in 1964, almost overlooked was the way they nearly duplicated (and in some ways surpassed) the feat as solo artists a decade later.

Certainly, immediately after the breakup, The Beatles' enormous popularity gave momentum to the fledgling solo careers of John, Paul, George, and Ringo. In fact, each had a #1 single million seller within 18 months of the group's breakup. But, by 1972, much of that early goodwill had dried up.

John Lennon was coming off his *Some Time In New York City* disaster, an album that peaked no higher than #33 nationally, along with the even-then politically incorrectly titled single "Woman Is The Nigger Of The World," which peaked no higher than #57 nationally (in *Billboard*) and couldn't break the top 85 in either Cashbox or Record World.

Paul McCartney was ravaged by the press for his first *Wings* LP, *Wildlife*, which peaked at #8 (after his first two LPs each topped the charts). And neither of his first two Wings singles could crack the American Top 20. The first, "Give Ireland Back To The Irish," was

> *" Immediately after the breakup, The Beatles' enormous popularity gave momentum to the fledgling solo careers of John, Paul, George, and Ringo. "*

panned for being too political. The second, "Mary Had A Little Lamb," was knocked for not being political enough. George Harrison had gone two and a half years since his last studio album and 18 months since his last single, and that ("Bangla Desh") failed to make the national Top 15. And Ringo Starr had only two pop singles (though both Top 10 hits) and two specialized albums, neither of which had Beatles-esque chart numbers (the album of standards, *Sentimental Journey*, peaked at #20, and the country album, *Beaucoups Of Blues* peaked at #31) in the more than three years since the group broke up. Fans of the group had to wonder just how much each needed the others professionally, if not personally.

A modest return to form began with McCartney's "Hi, Hi, Hi" single, which peaked at #6 in Cashbox in February 1973. But the comeback began in earnest, ironically enough, with the first post-breakup releases from the group, the '62-'66 and the '67-'70 greatest hits packages. Each hit #1, though, oddly enough, not in the same national publications. ('67-'70 reached #1 in *Billboard*, '62-'66 in both Cashbox and Record World). This was in late May '73 but, before either album could get comfortable in the top spot, it had competition from within the family. That started a run on the charts that had only been seen once before.

In late May, '67-'70 was knocked out of the top spot by McCartney's *Red Rose Speedway*, which was, in turn, knocked out of the top spot by Harrison's *Living In The Material World*. Continuously, from mid-May to the end of July, a Beatles album, either from one of the group or the group as a whole, was in #1. It was something that hadn't been seen since it was done 10 years earlier by... guess who? And, in an achievement that rivaled their having the nation's top five singles in April 1964, these four albums were all in the top five of Cashbox's album chart for the week ending June 23, 1973. This was something that never happened even during the halcyon days of 1964.

Meanwhile, McCartney's ballad from *Speedway*, "My Love," was

racing up the singles chart, hitting the #1 spot on June 2 (becoming, surprisingly, the first time a Beatle had hit the top spot in more than 18 months). It stayed there for four weeks until McCartney was again knocked out of #1 by Harrison with his "Give Me Love" single.

By the time Harrison was falling from the Top 10, he was replaced by McCartney with his "Live And Let Die" single, which would also hit #1 (in Cashbox and Record World). When the James Bond theme finally left the Top 10 near the end of September, it ended a string of four months when at least one ex-Beatle had a single in the Top 10. And before "Live And Let Die" dropped off the chart completely, the other ex-members of the group were about to be heard from.

Starr was then climbing the charts with "Photograph." As it reached the Top 10 (in *Billboard* on Nov. 10, 1973), Lennon was climbing the charts with his "Mind Games" single, which would hit the Top 10 in both Cashbox and Record World. By the time "Photograph" reached #1 (Nov. 23, 1973), McCartney was back on the charts with "Helen Wheels." Within three weeks, the (solo) Beatles would have three records in the Top 20. In fact, with the exception of two weeks, from Oct. 27, 1973 to June 29, 1974... more than eight months, there was always at least one record from some member of the group in the Top 10, something that the group never achieved while together. During that time, besides "Photograph," "Band On The Run" and "You're Sixteen" both hit #1. "Oh My My," "Jet" and "Helen Wheels" all hit the Top 5 nationally.

The action on the album charts was no different. The *Ringo* album was in the Top 10 by its third week on the chart (Nov. 23, 1973) and was joined there by Lennon's *Mind Games* LP, followed closely by McCartney's *Band On The Run* album. By the first week in January 1974, all three solo albums were in the national Top 20. Never before (or since) had three solo projects from members of the same group charted that high simultaneously. Both *Ringo* and *Band On The Run* would peak at #1. *Mind Games* would top out at #6.

The charts had a chance to cool down a bit. (There were no singles on the charts from any of the four from Aug. 24, 1974 to Sept. 21, 1974.) But it was only the calm before another storm.

Lennon was first out of the box with "Whatever Gets You Through The Night," which debuted on the charts on Sept. 28, 1974. It would reach #1 eight weeks later, as McCartney's single, "Junior's Farm" and Starr's first release from *Goodnight Vienna,* "Only You," and Harrison's "Dark Horse" were also on the way to becoming major hits. On Nov. 30, 1974, all of The Beatles would have a single in the Top 40. In fact, from mid-November 1974 to mid-February 1975, a period of 13 weeks, each of The Beatles had at least one single continuously on the charts at the same time. And, during one week (Jan. 25, 1975), the four of them collectively had seven of the Top 100 singles in the country, a feat not matched since... well, you know.

It was no different on the album charts. While *Band On The Run* was concluding its phenomenal run on the charts, Lennon's Walls And Bridges was headed for #1, which it would reach on Nov. 16, 1974. Two weeks after Lennon's album fell from the Top 10 (Dec. 21), Starr's *Goodnight Vienna* LP took its place, eventually peaking at #5 (in Record World). Harrison's Dark Horse album, which would climb as high as #4, would join it in the Top 10 for the last two weeks of January 1975... the last time two members of the same band would have Top 10 albums at the same time. Within two weeks of Dark Horse dropping from the Top 20 (Feb. 22, 1975), Lennon's *Rock 'N' Roll* climbed to that level on the charts on its way to #4 (in Record World). During the period from Dec. 21, 1974 to April 19, 1975, all four members of the group had albums continuously on the chart.

As Lennon's album left the Top 10 at the end of April, this incredible run by The Beatles, separately this time, would end. Lennon would give us nothing new for more than five years until his tragically brief comeback. Harrison's "This Guitar" single, released in December 1975, would fail to chart in any of the national trades. Starr would never see the sunny side of the Top 20, either album or single charts again. Even McCartney, who would have three more #1 albums in a row, couldn't get his "Letting Go" single any higher than #39 in October 1975.

But there's no taking away from what the four of them had achieved during the previous 24 months. Each member of the group had at least one #1 single and one #1 album... seven #1 albums in all. Eight #1 singles in two years. Five gold singles. Eleven gold albums (again, something they couldn't match during their years together). Four more albums reaching the Top 6 nationally. Five more singles hitting the Top 5. Three more hitting the Top 10. One more hitting the Top 15. Collectively, 35 weeks in the singles Top 10 in 1973, 33 weeks in 1974. 48 weeks in the album Top 10 in 1973 (with the first album not getting there until the end of April). 42 weeks there in 1974.

All this came during a time when radio station formats were getting fragmented and playlists getting smaller. Also, unlike 1964, each of those releases gave competition, not synergy, to the others. Each solo release would be looked upon as a new "Beatles" record, and stations would hesitate adding, for example, a new Lennon record if they were already playing something from McCartney, Harrison, and Starr.

It was a tribute not only to immense popularity of these four men, but also to their immense talent. No one can make this kind of a sustained chart run on personality alone. Looking back, much of the music that these four men produced individually during this time still ranks with the most creative and entertaining work of the era, as was the case of their work as a group 10 years before.

Just as no group has since dominated the charts as John, Paul, George, and Ringo did in 1964, no group of individuals has since dominated the charts as John, Paul, George, and Ringo did 10 years later. ■

■ *The Beatles with producer Walter Shenson while filming Help! (photo courtesy of Walter Shenson).*

Conspicuous By Their Absence

HOW THE BEATLES DOMINATED THE MUSIC CHARTS — AFTER THEY BROKE UP   By Casey Piotrowski

The Beatles' predominance in American rock 'n' roll in the '60s? Oh, yeah, I heard something about that. The 23 #1 singles? Not bad. The 16 #1 albums? Worth a mention. Had all Top 5 singles in America in April 1964. Probably beginner's luck.

Obviously, what The Beatles did during those magnificent seven years before their breakup was remarkable. But don't forget, during all that time, The Beatles were there, selling their music as well as making it. They toured, made movies, had TV and radio appearances and, eventually, produced music videos. Seemingly, they always had time for an interview or a photo op. (Try finding a music magazine from that time that didn't feature a piece on The Beatles.) There was always a steady stream of great new product being released.

But how their success as a group continued after their breakup may be an even greater achievement. Remember, after 1970, all "new" Beatles product consisted of either repackages (Beatles fans who bought *Reel Music* enjoyed the privilege of getting "And I Love Her" for the seventh time) or the group's own second choices.

Frequently, those packages would have to compete with usually good, often great, new solo releases from the group's members. Instead of John, Paul, George, and Ringo celebrating their past, the four of them have spent the

> **"** *After 1970, all "new" Beatles product consisted of either repackages or the group's own second choices.* **"**

best part of the last 30 years throwing rocks at the group's legacy and at each other. That's hardly the best way to promote your catalog. Still, the public knew much better. It is the fans' loyalty and the quality of the group's work that has made The Beatles the most successful music act not only from 1964 to 1970 but, arguably, from 1970 to today as well. Without question, they have enjoyed more success after their breakup than any other act.

Consider the following: Since the invention of the longplay record, only 11 acts (besides The Beatles) have had as many as five #1 albums. The Beatles have had that many #1 albums since they broke up ('62-66, '67-70 and all three volumes of *Anthology*). Along with that, three other Beatles packages (*Hollywood Bowl*, *Live At The BBC* and *Rock 'N' Roll Music*) peaked at #2. Using that as the yardstick, over the last 30 years, only Paul McCartney (in all the permutations of his solo career), with 10, and The Rolling Stones, with nine, have charted more albums as high as the disbanded Beatles. (And we're not counting two more #1 albums — *Let It Be*, new recordings released after the group's breakup and *The Beatles Again* (Hey Jude), which held #2 the week the group split.) In fact, discounting the new reunion recordings from the Eagles and Fleetwood Mac, no band has had even one archival release hit #1 — much less five of them. If we stretch that point to include solo artists, only two of them have had albums reach #1 after their deaths — Janis Joplin (Pearl) and, predictably enough, John Lennon (*Double Fantasy*).

> ❝ *Only 11 acts have had as many as five#1 albums.* ❞

In their native England, it was more of the same. Both *Hollywood Bowl* and *Live At The BBC* hit #1, as did the five other titles that reached #1 in America, giving The Beatles seven #1 albums in their homeland after their split. (Three more albums, *Love Songs*, *20 Greatest Hits* and *Rock 'N' Roll Music* also hit the Top 10.) In the past three decades, only four other artists (McCartney, Queen, ABBA, and David Bowie) hit #1 more frequently than The Beatles did after they broke up!

A couple more quick notes about their post-breakup albums. The Beatles hit #1 three times in one year with the release of *Anthology 1, 2* and *3*. Only Elvis Presley, who did it in 1960, and The Beatles themselves, who had four #1 albums in 1964 and three #1's in 1965, 1966 and 1970, hit the top spot on the album chart that many times in one year. (They would have done it in 1969, too, but Yellow Submarine was blocked from #1 by *Abbey Road*.) No other band has had three albums debut at #1 (which all three volumes of *Anthology* did).

As for singles, The Beatles have had four major hit singles since their breakup. (We're not counting "The Long And Winding Road," which was already in pre-release when McCartney announced his intention to leave the group.) In order of their release, they include "Got To Get You Into My Life" which peaked at #3, "The Beatles Movie Medley" (#12), "Free As A Bird" (#6) and "Real Love" (#10). No other band has hit the Top 10 even once after their breakup.

Even reunion efforts from other bands failed to do much. The Eagles' terrific "Get Over It" could do no better than #15. Fleetwood Mac, with a tour and a #1 album to support them, couldn't chart either of the wonderful singles from The Dance ("Silver Springs" and "Landslide").

Only three solo artists had major hits after their passing — Janis Joplin ("Me And Bobby McGee," hitting #1), Jim Croce ("Time In A Bottle" hitting #1, "I've Got A Name" hitting #10 and "I'll Have To Say I Love You In A Song" peaking at #12) and, of course, John Lennon ("Woman" hitting #1, "Nobody Told Me" hitting #5 and "Watching The Wheels" hitting #10). But the chart success of those artists pretty much stopped not long after their deaths. The Beatles have had at least one major hit in every decade since their breakup.

(In Britain, "Movie Medley" hit the Top 10. So did "Yesterday," finally released as a single there in 1976. "Love Me Do" finally became a Top 5 there with its 20th anniversary release in 1982. "Baby It's You," from *Live At The BBC*, hit #7 in 1993. Both "Free As A Bird" and "Real Love" hit the Top 5 in 1996. That gave The Beatles six Top 10 singles in the U.K. after they split.)

As for gold singles, the recent certification of "Got To Get You Into My Life" gave The Beatles three singles released after their breakup to go gold. No other disbanded group has even one. As for departed solo artists, Elvis Presley (with "Way Down" and "My Way") has two. Lennon, Joplin, and Croce have one each.

Speaking of 24-carat hardware, while together The Beatles earned 19 gold albums. They've earned 20

> " *One gold album every 15 months for 30 years after they've broken up.* "

more gold albums with packages released after their breakup. In fact, every package Capitol has issued since the group's split has gone at least gold; most have gone platinum. The '62-66 and '67-70 packages have earned the RIAA's new diamond certification with sales of more than 10 million units each. *Rock 'N' Roll Music* has gone gold three different ways — as a double album and as two single albums.

In the last 30 years, as record sales have exploded, more than 20 artists have earned at least 21 gold albums. It's a list wide enough to include The Rolling Stones, Elton John, Barbra Streisand, George Strait, and Kiss.

Still, for The Beatles — who spent much of the last three decades not speaking to one another, much less working together — to average one gold album every 15 months for 30 years after they've broken up is staggering!

All in all, they haven't done badly. While the artists who followed in the '70s, '80s and '90s worked intently to perfect their art and then feverishly to sell it, The Beatles just about matched them stride for stride while pretty much doing nothing.

This part of The Beatles' history — where they threw away their crowns but remained kings nonetheless — is overlooked. Though it doesn't contribute to the body of their work, it does add to the legacy of their popularity. It offers more proof that The Beatles didn't just fill our ears, they also filled our hearts. ■

■ *(Thanks to Ed Ford and Gil Perez for contributing to this article.)*

Background images from Glenn A. Baker Archives

Eight Days a Week, 366 Days a Year

EVERY DAY IN THE BEATLES' LIFE ON THE CHARTS   By Casey Piotrowski

There's probably been a Beatles' fan or two over the years that's made the casual statement, "I'll bet there wasn't a day that's gone by that The Beatles didn't have a record on the charts." They probably never realized that they were almost right — literally!

A thought became an idea became a project — sifting through nearly 40 years of *Billboard* charts, then adding in Cashbox and Record World charts to fill in any gaps. What we came up with was a list of every Beatles record — group and solo — that was on the charts for every day of the year — yes, even Feb. 29.

Mostly, as I mentioned, we're using *Billboard* as our source for the numbers, but, if a record didn't chart there, but charted in Cashbox or Record World, or charted earlier or later or, in some cases, charted higher, we turned to the numbers from those magazines. We've noted references from Cashbox with "CB" and from Record World with "RW."

So, sit back, strap yourself in and think of your birthday, the day you met the person you love, even the day you totaled your car and check to see what Beatles' records were on the charts that day.

> *" A thought became an idea became a project. "*

January   POSITION

1   We Can Work It Out (1966) 2
    The Girl Is Mine (1983) (PMc) 3
    Day Tripper (1966) 18
    Happy X-Mas (1972) (JL) 36
    This Song (1977) (GH) ....38 (RW)
    Hey Baby (1977) (RS) 83
    Obladi Oblada (1976) ....94 (RW)

2   I Feel Fine (1965) 1
    My Sweet Lord (1971) (GH) 1
    Shes A Woman (1965) 4
    Got My Mind Set On You (1988) (GH) 4

3   Starting Over (1981) (JL) 1
    Something/Come Together (1970) 12
    Cold Turkey (1971) (JL) 33

4   Junior's Farm (1975) (PMc) 4
    Only You (1975) (RS) 7
    Dark Horse (1975) (GH) 16
    Hey Jude (1969)................................23
    Spies Like Us (1986) (PMc) 24
    Whatever Gets You
    Thru The Night (1975) (JL) 79

5   No More Lonely Nights (1985) (PMc) 5
    Helen Wheels (1974) (PMc) 12
    You're Sixteen (1974) (RS) 16
    Mind Games (1974) (JL) ....22 (CB)
    Photograph (1974) (RS) 32

6   Hello Goodbye (1967) 1
    Free As A Bird (1996) 6
    Hi Hi Hi (1973) (PMc) 22
    I Am The Walrus (1967) ....46 (CB)
    Wonderful Christmastime (1985) (PMc) ....87 (CB)

7   Say Say Say (1984) (PMc) 1
    So Bad (1984) (PMc) 34
    Girls' School (1978) (PMc) 34
    Handle With Care (1989) (GH) 63

8   We Can Work It Out (1966) 1
    The Girl Is Mine (1983) (PMc) 2
    Day Tripper (1966) 10
    This Song (1977) (GH) 25
    Hey Baby (1977) (RS) 79

9   I Feel Fine (1965) 1
    My Sweet Lord (1971) (GH) 1
    Got My Mind Set On You (1988) (GH) 2
    She's A Woman (1965) ....8 (CB)
    Wrack My Brain (1982) (RS) 63
    Mother (1971) (JL) 87

10 Starting Over (1981) (JL) 1
    Something/Come Together (1970) 16
    Cold Turkey (1970) (JL) 33

11 Junior's Farm (1975) (PMc) 3
    Only You (1975) (RS) 6
    Dark Horse (1975) (GH) 15
    Spies Like Us (1986) (PMc) 19
    Hey Jude (1969) 30
    #9 Dream (1975) (JL) 35
    I Want To Hold Your Hand (1964) 80
    Ding Dong, Ding Dong 81

12 You're Sixteen (1974) (RS) 6
    Helen Wheels (1974) (PMc) 10
    No More Lonely Nights (1985) (PMc) 23
    Mind Games (1974) (JL) 29
    Photograph (1974) (RS) 45

13 Hello Goodbye (1968) 1
    Free As A Bird (1996) 15
    Hi Hi Hi (1973) (PMc) 18
    I Am The Walrus (1968) ....76 (CB)
    Wonderful Christmastime (1985) (PMc) ....83 (CB)
    Figure of Eight (1990) (PMc) 92

14 Say Say Say (1984) (PMc) 1
    So Bad (1984) (PMc) 31
    Girls' School (1978) (PMc) 33
    Handle With Care (1989) (GH) 72

15 We Can Work It Out (1966) 1
    The Girl Is Mine (1983) (PMc) 2
    Day Tripper (1966) 6
    This Song (1977) (GH) 25
    Hey Baby (1977) (RS) 77

16 I Feel Fine (1965) 1
    My Sweet Lord (1971) (GH) 1
    Got My Mind Set On You (1988) (GH) 1
    She's A Woman (1965) ....8 (CB)
    Mother (1971) (JL) 60
    Wrack My Brain (1982) (RS) 97

17 Starting Over (1981) (JL) 1
    Something/Come Together (1970) 20

    Cold Turkey (1971) (JL) 30
    Woman (1981) (JL) 36

18 Junior's Farm (1975) (PMc) 7
    Only You (1975) (RS) 12
    Spies Like Us (1986) (PMc) 13
    #9 Dream (1975) (JL) 29
    Dark Horse (1975) (GH) 33
    Hey Jude (1969) 38

I Want To Hold Your Hand (1964) 45
Ding Dong, Ding Dong (1975) (GH) 59

19 You're Sixteen (1974) (RS) 5
Helen Wheels (1974) (PMc) 12
Mind Games (1974) (JL) 34
No More Lonely Nights (1985) (PMc) 35
Photograph (1974) (RS) 74

20 Hello Goodbye (1968) 3
Hi Hi Hi (1973) (PMc) 12
Free As A Bird (1996) 32
Figure of Eight (1990) (PMc) 95

21 Say Say Say (1984) (PMc) 2
So Bad (1984) (PMc) 28
Nobody Told Me (1984) (JL) 36
Girls' School (1978) (PMc) 59
Handle With Care (1989) (GH) 83

22 We Can Work It Out (1966) 2
The Girl Is Mine (1983) (PMc) 2
Day Tripper (1966) 5
This Song (1977) (GH) 32
Hey Baby (1977) (RS) 76

23 My Sweet Lord (1971) (GH) 2
I Feel Fine (1965) 4
Got My Mind Set On You (1988) (GH) 4
She's A Woman (1965) 14
Mother (1971) (JL) 45

24 Starting Over (1981) (JL) 1
Something/Come Together (1970) 22
Woman (1981) (JL) 27
Cold Turkey (1970) (JL) 32

25 I Want To Hold Your Hand (1964) 3
Spies Like Us (1986) (PMc) 10
Junior's Farm (1975) (PMc) 17
#9 Dream (1975) (JL) 21
Only You (1975) (RS) 27

Ding Dong, Ding Dong (1975) (GH) 46
Dark Horse (1975) (GH) 49
She Loves You (1964) 69

26 You're Sixteen (1974) (RS) 1
Helen Wheels (1974) (PMc) 17
Mind Games (1974) (JL) 44
No More Lonely Nights (1985) (PMc) 66

27 Hello Goodbye (1968) 6
Hi Hi Hi (1973) (PMc) 11
Free As A Bird (1996) 57
Figure of Eight (1990) 95

28 Say Say Say (1984) (PMc) 7
So Bad (1984) (PMc) 25
Nobody Told Me (1984) (JL) 27
Girls' School (1978) (PMc) 95
Handle With Care (1989) (GH) 100

29 We Can Work It Out (1966) 1
The Girl Is Mine (1983) (PMc) 5
Day Tripper (1966) ....10 (CB)
This Song (1977) (GH) 64
Hey Baby (1977) (RS) 64
Crackerbox Palace (1977) 66

30 My Sweet Lord (1971) 2
Got My Mind Set On You (1988) (GH) 7
I Feel Fine (1965) 11
She's A Woman (1965) 37
Mother (1971) (JL) 43

31 Starting Over (1981) (JL) 2
Woman (1981) (JL) 17
Something/Come Together (1971) 29
Cold Turkey (1971) 46

February

1 I Want To Hold Your Hand (1964) 1
Spies Like Us (1986) (PMc) 8
#9 Dream (1975) (JL) 17
She Loves You (1964) 21
Only You (1975) (RS) 35
Ding Dong, Ding Dong (1975) (GH) 38
Sally G (1975) (PMc) 66
Please Please Me (1964) 68
No More Lonely Nights (1985) (PMc) 86
I Saw Her Standing There (1964) 117

2 You're Sixteen (1974) (RS) 2
Helen Wheels (1974) (PMc) 20
Mind Games (1974) (JL) 60
Jet (1974) (PMc) 71

3 Hello Goodbye (1968) 3
Hi Hi Hi (1973) (PMc) 10
Free As A Bird (1996) 63
Figure of Eight (1990) (PMc) 96

4 Say Say Say (1984) (PMc) 13
Nobody Told Me (1984) (JL) 22
So Bad (1984) (PMc) 24

5 We Can Work It Out (1966) 4
The Girl Is Mine (1983) (PMc) 16
Day Tripper (1966) 22
Crackerbox Palace (1977) (GH) 49
Hey Baby (1977) (RS) 62

No No Song (1975) (RS) 40
My Bonnie (1964) 54
From Me To You (1964) ....89 (CB)

23 You're Sixteen (1974) (RS) 9
    Jet (1974) (PMc) 27

24 Hi Hi Hi (1973) (PMc) 38
    Blow Away (1979) (GH) ....88 (CB)

25 Nobody Told Me (1984) (JL) 7
    So Bad (1984) (PMc) 37
    Say Say Say (1984) (PMc) 56
    End of the Line (1989) (GH) 63
    Penny Lane (1967) 83
    Strawberry Fields Forever (1967) 85

26 We Can Work It Out (1966) 26
    Maybe I'm Amazed (1977) (PMc) 26
    Crackerbox Palace (1977) (GH) 30
    This Song (1977) (GH) ....61 (CB)
    Hey Baby (1977) (RS) ....73 (CB)
    The Girl Is Mine (1983) (PMc) 91

27 Eight Days A Week (1965) 19
    When We Was Fab (1988) (GH) 34
    My Sweet Lord (1971) (GH) 36
    Got My Mind Set On You (1988) (GH) 51
    I Don't Want To Spoil The Party (1965) ...59
    What Is Life (1971) (GH) 66
    Hope of Deliverance (1993) (PMc) 84

28 Woman (1981) (JL) 3
    Starting Over (1981) (JL) 16
    Instant Karma (1970) (JL) 85

29 I Want to Hold Your Hand (1964) 1
    She Loves You (1964) 2
    Please Please Me (1964) 6
    I Saw Her Standing There (1964) 28
    My Bonnie (1964) 42
    From Me To You (1964) ....77 (CB)

March

1   #9 Dream (1975) (JL) 13
    Ding Dong, Ding Dong (1975) (GH) 31
    Sally G (1975) (PMc) 64
    Spies Like Us (1986) (PMc) 42

2   You're Sixteen (1974) (RS) 11
    Jet (1974) (PMc) 20
    Oh My My (1974) (RS) ....66 (CB)

3   Nobody Told Me (1984) (JL) 5
    So Bad (1984) (PMc) 51

Say Say Say (1984) (PMc) 76
Blow Away (1979) (GH) 79

4   Penny Lane (1967) ....15 (CB)
    Strawberry Fields Forever (1967) 45
    End of the Line (1989) (GH) 63

5   Maybe I'm Amazed (1977) (PMc) 20
    Nowhere Man (1966) ....23 (CB)
    Crackerbox Palace (1977) (GH) 26
    When We Was Fab (1989) (GH) 31
    We Can Work It Out (1966) 48
    Got My Mind Set On You (1989) (GH) 65
    This Song (1977) (GH) 68
    The Girl Is Mine (1983) (PMc) 97
    What Goes On (1966) 118

6   Eight Days A Week (1965) ....1 (CB)
    What Is Life (1971) (GH) 27
    I Don't Want To Spoil The Party (1965) ...47
    Another Day (1971) (PMc) 55
    Mother (1971) (JL) ....56 (CB)
    Oh Woman Oh Why (1971) (PMc) ....58 (CB)
    Hope of Deliverance (1993) (PMc) 87

7   I Want To Hold Your Hand (1964) 1
    Woman (1981) (JL) ....1 (CB)
    She Loves You (1964) 2
    Please Please Me (1964) 4
    I Saw Her Standing There (1964) 18
    My Bonnie 31
    Starting Over (1981) (JL) 38
    From Me To You (1964) ....57 (CB)
    Twist and Shout (1964) ....68 (CB)

8   No No Song (1975) (RS) 25
    #9 Dream (1975) (JL) 47
    Spies Like Us (1986) (PMc) 58

9   Jet (1974) (PMc) 14
    You're Sixteen (1974) (RS) 20
    Oh My My (1974) (RS) 65

10 Nobody Told Me (1984) (JL) 6
    So Bad (1984) (PMc) 61
    Blow Away (1979) (GH) 69
    Say Say Say (1984) (PMc) 99

11 Penny Lane (1967) ....3 (CB)
    Strawberry Fields Forever (1967) 16
    End of the Line (1989) (GH) 66
    Give Ireland Back To The Irish (1972) (PMc) ....73 (CB)

12 Nowhere Man (1966) ....5 (CB)
    Maybe I'm Amazed (1977) (PMc) 15
    Crackerbox Palace (1977) (GH) 24

Silly Love Songs (1976) (PMc) ....52 (CB)	
I'm Down (1965) 105	

22 A Hard Day's Night (1964) 3
And I Love Her (1964) 17
Ain't She Sweet (1964) 19
I'll Cry Instead (1964) 29
If I Fell (1964) 57
All Those Years Ago (1981) (GH) 81
Teardrops (1981) (GH) ....93 (CB)
I'm Happy Just To Dance With You (1964) 118

23 Give Peace A Chance (1969) (JL) 15
Coming Up (1980) (PMc) 34
Press (1986) (PMc) 39
Listen To What The Man Said (1975) (PMc) 44
Twist & Shout (1986) 55

24 No charted records

25 Live & Let Die (1973) (PMc) 2
Getting Closer (1979) (PMc) ....77 (CB)
Arrow Through Me (1979) (PMc) ....73 (RW)

26 All You Need Is Love (1967) 2
I've Had Enough (1978) 90

27 Yellow Submarine (1966) 8
Eleanor Rigby (1966) 65

28 Let Em In (1976) (PMc) ....1 (CB)
Help! (1965) 2
Take It Away (1982) (PMc) 10
Got To Get You Into My Life (1976) ....11 (CB)
Uncle Albert/Admiral Halsey (1971) (PMc) 12
Bangla Desh (1971) (GH) 31
Silly Love Songs (1976) (PMc) ....59 (CB)
I'm Down (1965) 102

29 A Hard Day's Night (1964) 4
And I Love Her (1964) 13
Ain't She Sweet (1964) 24
I'll Cry Instead (1964) 25
If I Fell (1964) 54
All Those Years Ago (1981) (GH) 87
Teardrops (1981) (GH) ....98 (CB)
I'm Happy Just To Dance With You (1964) 116

30 Give Peace A Chance (1969) (JL) 15
Press (1986) (PMc) 28
Twist & Shout (1986) 39
Coming Up (1980) (PMc) 47
Listen To What The Man Said (1975) (PMc) 57
Waterfalls (1980) (PMc) 106

31 No charted records

September

1 Live & Let Die (1973) (PMc) 5
Arrow Through Me (1979) (PMc) 73
Getting Closer (1979) (PMc) ....100 (CB)

2 All You Need Is Love (1967) 2
I've Had Enough (1978) ....97 (CB)

3 Yellow Submarine (1966) 5
Eleanor Rigby (1966) 47

4 Help! (1965) 1
Uncle Albert/Admiral Halsey (1971) (PMc) 1
Let Em In (1976) (PMc) 3
Take It Away (1982) (PMc) 10
Bangla Desh (1971) (GH) 24
Got To Get You Into My Life (1976) 53
I'm Down (1965) 102

5 A Hard Day's Night (1964) 8
And I Love Her (1964) 12
Ain't She Sweet (1964) 30
I'll Cry Instead (1964) 34
If I Fell (1964) 53
Matchbox (1964) 81
All Those Years Ago (1981) (GH) 95
Slow Down (1964) 99
I'm Happy Just To Dance With You (1964) 112

6 Give Peace A Chance (1969) (JL) 14
Press (1986) (PMc) 26
Twist & Shout (1986) 32
Coming Up (1980) (PMc) 82

7 No charted records

8 Live & Let Die (1973) (PMc) 7
Arrow Through Me (1979) (PMc) 63

9 All You Need Is Love (1967) 6
London Town (1978) (PMc) 75
This One (1989) (PMc) 95
Sgt Pepper/Help From My Friends (1978) ....98 (CB)

10 Yellow Submarine (1966) 3
Eleanor Rigby (1966) 26

11 Help! (1965) 1
Uncle Albert/Admiral Halsey (1971) (PMc) 5
Let Em In (1976) (PMc) 8
Take It Away (1982) (PMc) 10
Bangla Desh (1971) (GH) 24
Got To Get You Into My Life (1976) 60
I'm Down (1965) 101

4   Twist & Shout (1986) 26
       You (1975) (GH) 41
       Press (1986) (PMc) 50
       Letting Go (1975) (PMc) 74

5   Hey Jude (1968) 1
       Revolution (1968) 12
       Whatever Gets You Thru The Night (1974) (JL) 33

6   Arrow Through Me (1979) (PMc) 30
       Live & Let Die (1973) (PMc) 36
       Let Em In (1976) (PMc) 56
       Photograph (1973) (RS) ....68 (CB)

7   London Town (1978) (PMc) 42
       Sgt Pepper/Help From My Friends (1978) 71

8   Yellow Submarine (1966) ....11 (CB)
       Eleanor Rigby (1966) 21
       Wings (1977) (RS) ....119 (RW)

9   Yesterday 1
       Help! (1965) ....7 (CB)
       Uncle Albert/Admiral Halsey (1971) (PMc) 7
       Act Naturally (1965) ....30 (CB)
       A Dose Of Rock & Roll (1976) (RS) 44
       Tug Of War (1982) (PMc) 64
       Take It Away (1982) (PMc) 88

10   Matchbox (1964) 18
       Slow Down (1964) 25
       A Hard Day's Night (1964) 50

11   You (1975) (GH) 33
       Twist & Shout (1986) 36
       Letting Go (1975) (PMc) 54
       Press (1986) (PMc) 72

12   Hey Jude (1968) 1
       Revolution (1968) ....12 (CB)
       Whatever Gets You Thru The Night (1974) (JL) 24

13   Arrow Through Me (1979) (PMc) 29
       No More Lonely Nights (1984) (PMc) 48
       Photograph (1973) (RS) ....44 (CB)
       Live & Let Die (1973) (PMc) ....66 (RW)

14   London Town (1978) (PMc) 39
       Sgt Pepper/Help From My Friends (1978) 75

15   Yellow Submarine (1966) ....24 (CB)
       Say Say Say (1983) (PMc) 26
       Eleanor Rigby (1966) 37
       Jealous Guy (1988) (JL) 84
       Wings (1977) ....119 (RW)

16   Yesterday (1965) 1
       Uncle Albert/Admiral Halsey (1971) (PMc) 7
       Help! (1965) ....12 (CB)
       Act Naturally (1965) ....28 (CB)
       A Dose Of Rock & Roll (1976) (RS) 35
       Tug Of War (1982) (PMc) 58
       Imagine (1971) (JL) ....66 (CB)
       Let Em In (1976) (PMc) 94
       Take It Away (1982) (PMc) 98

17   Matchbox (1964) ....17 (CB)
       Slow Down (1964) 39

18   Something (1969) 20
       Come Together (1969) 23
       You (1975) (GH) 25
       Letting Go (1975) (GH) 42
       Twist & Shout (1986) 47

19   Hey Jude (1968) 1
       Whatever Gets You Thru The Night (1974) (JL) ....9 (CB)
       Revolution (1968) 17

20   Photograph (1973) (RS) ....20 (RW)
       No More Lonely Nights (1984) (PMc) 38
       Arrow Through Me (1979) (PMc) 46

21   London Town (1978) (PMc) 39

22   Say Say Say (1983) (PMc) 19
       Yellow Submarine (1966) ....40 (CB)
       Jealous Guy (1988) (JL) 80
       Wings (1977) (RS) ....120 (RW)

23   Yesterday (1965) 1
       Uncle Albert/Admiral Halsey (1971) (PMc) 13
       Imagine (1971) (JL) 20
       Help! (1965) ....21 (CB)
       A Dose Of Rock & Roll (1976) (RS) 31
       Act Naturally (1965) ....36 (CB)
       Tug Of War (1982) (PMc) 53
       Let Em In (1976) (PMc) ....66 (CB)
       Boys (1965) ....75 (CB)
       Kansas City (1965) ....81 (CB)
       Take It Away (1982) (PMc) 98

24   Matchbox (1964) 24
       Got My Mind Set On You (1987) (GH) 66
       Beaucoups of Blues (1970) (RS) 126

25   Something (1969) 11
       Come Together (1969) 13
       You (1975) (GH) 25
       Letting Go (1975) (PMc) 39
       Twist & Shout (1986) 56

26   Hey Jude (1968) 1
      Whatever Gets You Thru The Night (1974) (JL) .....4 (CB)
      Revolution (1968) 17

27   Photograph (1973) (RS) ....8 (CB)
      No More Lonely Nights (1984) (PMc) 30
      Arrow Through Me (1979) (PMc) 93

28   London Town (1978) (PMc) 89

29   Say Say Say (1983) (PMc) 11
      Jealous Guy (1988) (JL) 81
      Handle With Care (1988) (GH) 83
      Wings (1977) ....131 (RW)

30   Yesterday (1965) 1
      Imagine (1971) (JL) 6
      Uncle Albert/Admiral Halsey (1971) (PMc) 18
      A Dose Of Rock & Roll (1976) (RS) 28
      Help! (1965) 32
      Let Em In (1976) (PMc) 36
      Act Naturally (1965) 47
      Tug Of War (1982) (PMc) 53
      Got To Get You Into My Life (1976) ....63 (RW)
      Boys (1965) 73
      Kansas City (1965) 75

31   Got My Mind Set On You (1987) (GH) 54
      Beaucoups of Blues (1970) (RS) 121

November

1   Something ....2 (CB)
      Come Together (1969) 10
      You (1975) (GH) 20
      Starting Over (1980) (JL) 38
      Letting Go (1975) (PMc) 39
      Twist & Shout (1986) 71
      Venus & Mars/Rock Show (1975) (PMc) 82

2   Hey Jude (1968) 1
      Whatever Gets You Thru The Night (1974) (JL) 2
      Revolution (1968) ....19 (CB)

3   Photograph (1973) (RS) ....5 (RS)
      No More Lonely Nights (1984) (PMc) 25

4   London Town (1978) (PMc) ....99 (CB)

5   Say Say Say (1983) (PMc) 6
      Handle With Care (1988) (GH) 66
      Jealous Guy (1988) (JL) 91
      Wings (1977) (RS) ....150 (RW)

6   Yesterday (1965) 3
      Imagine (1971) (JL) 4
      Uncle Albert/Admiral Halsey (1971) (PMc) 26
      A Dose Of Rock & Roll (1976) (RS) 28

      Help! (1965) ....35 (CB)
      Let Em In (1976) (PMc) ....40 (RW)
      The Girl Is Mine (1982) (PMc) 45
      Act Naturally (1965) 54
      Got To Get You Into My Life (1976) ....68 (RW)
      Boys (1965) ....77 (CB)

7   Got My Mind Set On You (1987) (GH) 44
      Wrack My Brain (1981) (RS) 79
      Beaucoups Of Blues (1970) (RS) 100

8   Something (1969) ....2 (CB)
      Come Together (1969) 3
      You (1975) (GH) 20
      Starting Over (1980) (JL) 32
      Venus & Mars/Rock Show (1975) (PMc) ....51 (CB)
      Letting Go (1975) 61
      Twist & Shout (1986) 75

9   Hey Jude (1968) 1
      Whatever Gets You Thru The Night (1974) (JL) ....2 (CB)
      Revolution (1968) 19
      Junior's Farm (1974) (PMc) 59

10   Photograph (1973) (RS) ....3 (CB)
      No More Lonely Nights (1984) (PMc) 19
      Mind Games (1973) (JL) ....67 (CB)

11   No charted records

12   Say Say Say (1973) (PMc) 4
      Handle With Care (1988) (GH) 62

13   Imagine (1971) (JL) 3
      Yesterday (1965) ....5 (CB)
      A Dose Of Rock & Roll (1976) (RS) 26
      The Girl Is Mine (1982) (PMc) 36
      Let Em In (1976) (PMc) ....42 (RW)
      Got To Get You Into My Life (1976) ....69 (RW)
      Obladi Oblada (1976) ....82 (CB)
      Tug Of War (1982) (PMc) 94

14   Got My Mind Set On You (1987) (GH) 38
      Wrack My Brain (1981) (RS) 65
      Beaucoups of Blues (1970) (RS) ....73 (CB)

15   Come Together (1969) 2
      Something (1969) 3
      Starting Over (1980) (JL) 10
      Venus & Mars/Rock Show (1975) (PMc) ....29 (CB)
      You (1975) (PMc) 39
      Cold Turkey (1969) (JL) ....81 (CB)
      Stranglehold (1986) (PMc) 97
      Twist & Shout (1986) 99

16 Hey Jude (1968) 1
Whatever Gets You Thru The Night (1974) (JL) 1
Revolution (1968) 20
Junior's Farm (1974) (PMc) 43
Only You (1974) (RS) 63

17 Photograph (1973) (RS) ....2 (RW)
No More Lonely Nights (1984) (PMc) 14
Mind Games (1973) (JL) ....37 (CB)
Helen Wheels (1973) (PMc) ....69 (CB)

18 No charted records

19 Say Say Say (1983) (PMc) 2
Handle With Care (1988) (GH) 56
Girls' School (1977) (PMc) 83

20 Imagine (1971) (JL) ....2 (CB)
Yesterday (1965) ....8 (CB)
The Girl Is Mine (1982) (PMc) 14
A Dose Of Rock & Roll (1976) (RS) 38
Let Em In (1976) (PMc) ....50 (RW)
Obladi Oblada (1976) ....57 (CB)
Wake Up My Love (1982) (GH) 68
This Song (1976) (GH) ....77 (RW)
Tug Of War (1982) (PMc) 95

21 Got My Mind Set On You (1987) (GH) 26
Wrack My Brain (1981) (RS) 53
Beaucoups of Blues (1970) (RS) ....73 (CB)

22 Come Together (1969) ....1 (CB)
Something (1969) ....3 (CB)
Starting Over (1980) (JL) 9
Venus & Mars/Rock Show (1975) (PMc) 27
Cold Turkey (1969) (JL) 74
Stranglehold (1986) (PMc) 84
You (1975) (GH) 91

23 Hey Jude (1968) 1
Whatever Gets You Thru The Night (1974) (JL) .....7 (CB)
Junior's Farm (1974) (PMc) ....25 (CB)
Revolution (1968) 29
Only You (1974) (RS) 53
Spies Like Us (1985) (PMc) 59
Dark Horse (1974) (GH) 69

24 Photograph (1973) (RS) 1
No More Lonely Nights (1984) (PMc) 11
Mind Games (1973) (JL) ....28 (CB)
Helen Wheels (1973) (PMc) 66

25 No charted records

26 Say Say Say (1983) (PMc) 2
Handle With Care (1988) (GH) 48
Girls' School (1977) (PMc) 71

27 Imagine (1971) (JL) ....3 (CB)
The Girl Is Mine (1982) (PMc) 9
Yesterday (1965) ....13 (CB)
Obladi Oblada (1976) ....53 (CB)
Wake Up My Love (1982) (GH) 60
This Song (1976) (GH) 63
A Dose Of Rock & Roll (1976) (RS) ....52 (RW)

28 Got My Mind Set On You (1987) (GH) 19
My Sweet Lord (1970) (GH) ....37 (CB)
Wrack My Brain (1981) (RS) 43
Isn't It A Pity (1970) (GH) 62
Beaucoups of Blues (1970) (RS) ....71 (CB)

29 Something/Come Together (1969) 1
Starting Over (1980) (JL) 8
Venus & Mars/Rock Show (1975) (PMc) 17
Cold Turkey (1969) (JL) 47
Stranglehold (1986) (PMc) 81

30 Hey Jude (1968) 2
Junior's Farm (1974) (PMc) 12
Whatever Gets You Thru The Night (1974) (JL) 21
Only You (1974) (RS) ....20 (CB)
Spies Like Us (1985) (PMc) 47
Dark Horse (1974) (GH) ....40 (CB)

December

1 Photograph (1973) (RS) ....1 (RW)
No More Lonely Nights (1984) (PMc) 10
Mind Games (1973) (JL) ....21 (CB)
Helen Wheels (1973) (PMc) ....27 (RW)

2 Hello Goodbye (1967) 45
I Am The Walrus (1967) 102

3 Say Say Say (1983) (PMc) 2
Handle With Care (1988) (GH) 47
Girls' School (1977) (PMc) 60

4 Imagine (1971) (JL) ....7 (CB)
The Girl Is Mine (1982) (PMc) 8
Yesterday (1965) 34
A Dose Of Rock & Roll (1976) (RS) 42
Obladi Oblada (1976) 49
This Song (1976) (GH) ....48 (RW)
Wake Up My Love (1982) (GH) 53

5 My Sweet Lord (1970) (GH) ....11 (CB)
Got My Mind Set On You (1987) (GH) 11
I Feel Fine (1965) 22
Wrack My Brain (1981) (RS) 39

	She's A Woman (1965) 46	
	Isn't It A Pity (1970) 50	
	Beaucoups Of Blues (1970) ....69 (CB)	

6   Come Together (1969) ....1 (CB)
       Starting Over (1981) (JL) 6
       Something (1969) ....10 (CB)
       Venus & Mars/Rock Show (1975) (PMc) 14
       Cold Turkey (1969) (JL) ....42 (CB)
       Stranglehold (1986) (PMc) 81

7   Hey Jude (1968) 2
       Junior's Farm (1974) (PMc) ....11 (CB)
       Only You (1974) (RS) ....15 (CB)
       Dark Horse (1974) (GH) ....33 (CB)
       Whatever Gets You Thru The Night (1974) (JL) .....40 (CB)
       Spies Like Us (1985) (PMc) 41

8   Photograph (1973) (RS) ....2 (RW)
       No More Lonely Nights (1984) (PMc) 6
       Mind Games (1973) (JL) ....14 (RW)
       Helen Wheels (1973) (PMc) ....18 (RW)
       You're Sixteen (1973) ....70 (CB)

9   Hello Goodbye (1967) ....7 (CB)
       I Am The Walrus (1967) ....61 (CB)

10   Say Say Say (1983) (PMc) 1
       Handle With Care (1988) (GH) 45
       Girls' School (1977) (PMc) 46

11   The Girl Is Mine (1982) (PMc) 5
       Imagine (1971) (JL) 13
       This Song (1976) (GH) 38
       Obladi Oblada (1976) 47
       Wake Up My Love (1982) (GH) 53
       A Dose Of Rock & Roll (1976) (RS) ....55 (CB)
       Yesterday (1965) ....74 (CB)
       We Can Work It Out (1966) 101
       Day Tripper (1966) 103

12   My Sweet Lord (1970) (RS) ....3 (CB)
       Got My Mind Set On You (1987) (GH) 10
       I Feel Fine (1965) 12
       She's A Woman (1965) 29
       Wrack My Brain (1981) (RS) 38
       Isn't It A Pity (1970) (GH) 46

13   Something/Come Together (1970) 4
       Starting Over (1981) (JL) 4
       Venus & Mars/Rock Show (1975) (PMc) 12
       Cold Turkey (1969) (JL) 39

14   Hey Jude (1968) 6
       Junior's Farm (1974) (PMc) ....8 (CB)

Only You (1974) (RS) ....14 (CB)
Whatever Gets You Thru The Night (1974) (JL) .....28 (CB)
Dark Horse (1974) (GH) ....29 (CB)
Spies Like Us (1985) (PMc) 31

15   No More Lonely Nights (1984) (PMc) 6
       Photograph (1973) (RS) ....7 (RW)
       Mind Games (1973) (JL) ....11 (RW)
       Helen Wheels (1973) (PMc) ....13 (RW)
       You're Sixteen (1973) (RS) ....36 (RW)

16   Hello Goodbye (1967) ....2 (CB)
       I Am The Walrus (1967) ....56 (CB)
       Hi Hi Hi (1973) (PMc) ....167 (CB)

17   Say Say Say (1983) (PMc) 10
       Girls' School (1977) (PMc) 41
       Handle With Care (1988) (GH) 46

18   The Girl Is Mine (1982) (PMc) 4
       We Can Work It Out (1965) ....18 (CB)
       Imagine (1971) (JL) 23
       This Song (1976) (GH) 33
       Obladi Oblada (1976) ....49 (CB)
       Day Tripper (1965) 56
       Happy X-Mas (1971) (JL) ....63 (CB)
       Hey Baby (1976) (RS) ....95 (CB)
       Wake Up My Love (1982) (GH) 100

19   I Feel Fine (1964) ....1 (CB)
       My Sweet Lord (1970) (GH) ....1 (CB)
       Got My Mind Set On You (1987) (GH) 5
       She's A Woman (1964) 14
       Wrack My Brain (1981) (RS) 43
       Isn't It A Pity (1970) (GH) ....46 (CB)

20   Starting Over (1980) (JL) 3
       Something/Come Together (1969) ....5 (CB)
       Venus & Mars/Rock Show (1975) (PMc) ....33 (CB)
       Cold Turkey (1969) (JL) 35

21   Junior's Farm ....5 (CB)
       Only You (1974) (RS) ....8 (CB)
       Hey Jude (1968) 11
       Dark Horse (1974) (GH) 24
       Spies Like Us (1985) (PMc) 28
       Whatever Gets You Thru The Night (1974) (JL) .....45 (CB)
       #9 Dream (1974) (JL) 68

22   Helen Wheels (1973) (PMc) ....8 (RW)
       No More Lonely Nights (1984) (PMc) 8
       Mind Games (1973) (JL) ....10 (RW)
       Photograph (1973) (RS) ....11 (RW)
       You're Sixteen (1973) (RS) ....19 (CB)

23	Hello Goodbye (1967)	2 (CB)
	Hi Hi Hi (1972) (PMc)	42
	I Am The Walrus (1967)	48 (CB)
24	Say Say Say (1983) (PMc)	1
	Girls' School (1977) (PMc)	37
	So Bad (1983) (PMc)	49
	Handle With Care (1988) (GH)	59
25	The Girl Is Mine (1982) (PMc)	3
	We Can Work It Out (1965)	3 (CB)
	This Song (1976) (GH)	27
	Day Tripper (1965)	28
	Happy X-Mas (1971) (JL)	42 (CB)
	Imagine (1971) (JL)	45 (CB)
	Obladi Oblada (1976)	57 (CB)
	Hey Baby (1976) (RS)	86 (CB)
26	I Feel Fine (1965)	1
	My Sweet Lord (1970) (GH)	1
	She's A Woman (1965)	4
	Got My Mind Set On You (1987) (GH)	4
	Wrack My Brain (1981) (RS)	52
27	Starting Over (1981) (JL)	1
	Something/Come Together (1969)	7
	Cold Turkey (1969) (JL)	33
	Venus & Mars/Rock Show (1975) (PMc)	97
28	Junior's Farm (1974) (PMc)	5 (CB)
	Only You (1974) (RS)	7 (CB)
	Hey Jude (1968)	15
	Dark Horse (1974) (GH)	20
	Whatever Gets You Thru The Night (1974) (JL)	47 (CB)
	Spies Like Us (1985) (PMc)	24
	#9 Dream (1974) (JL)	58
29	Helen Wheels (1973) (PMc)	6 (RW)
	No More Lonely Nights (1984) (PMc)	8
	Mind Games (1973) (JL)	10 (CB)
	You're Sixteen (1973) (RS)	12 (CB)
	Photograph (1973) (RS)	26 (RW)
	Wonderful Christmastime (1984) (PMc)	87 (CB)
30	Hello Goodbye (1967)	1
	Free As A Bird (1995)	10
	Hi Hi Hi (1973) (PMc)	27
	I Am The Walrus (1967)	46 (CB)
31	Say Say Say (1983) (PMc)	1
	Girls' School (1977) (PMc)	31
	So Bad (1983) (PMc)	49
	Handle With Care (1988) (GH)	59

So, just in case you weren't keeping a running count, The Beatles had a record on the charts for 360 out of 366 possible days. They had #1 records for 122 days out of the year... or more than 2 number one's every 7 days. They had at least one top ten record for 277 days... or about 5 top tens every 7 days. Not "eight days a week", but still pretty amazing.

Overall, if you look at The Beatles entire life on the singles chart...almost exactly 34 years, by the way, from the first, pre-Beatlemania appearance of "From Me To You" in the first week of August, 1963 to the last charting of McCartney's "The World Tonight" single in the last week of July, 1997, the group, individually and collectively had more than 1800 chart appearances on the national singles charts. That averages out to more than one single on the charts each week for all of those 34 years!

It includes more than 175 charted titles. That's more than Presley. More than the Stones. More than the Beach Boys. And, almost, more than all of them combined!

And, if you want to consider Madonna or Mariah Carey or N Sync or anyone else having the ability to eclipse that success, trust me, all those artists will ultimately do is what anyone who loves rock and roll would do when they see those numbers... stand with their jaws open in amazement.

Yep, The Beatles, indeed, have turned out to be a 100 megaton blast. And the world is still feeling the shockwaves 40 years on. ■

And the Grammy goes to... The Beatles!

By J.G. Schuberk

What do Anita Kerr, The Carpenters, Glen Campbell, New Vaudeville Band, Roger Miller, Bobby Russell, and The Statler Brothers all have in common? They all have the distinction of beating The Beatles out of a Grammy Award!

Over the course of its history, the Grammy Award presentations have often been exciting and unpredictable, yet strangely inconsistent. They are responsible for elevating the careers of artists such as The Police and Bette Midler. Singers Tina Turner, Bonnie Raitt, and Natalie Cole have experienced an amazing renaissance in their respective careers after Grammy victories. On the other hand, artists such as Milli Vanilli and Rick Springfield have disappeared into musical obscurity subsequent to receiving their awards. Worse yet, classic rockers such as Jimi Hendrix, The Rolling Stones, Bob Dylan, and Elvis Presley have been practically ignored by the Recording Academy.

In the 1960s, no artists achieved more sustained critical and commercial success than The Beatles. From 1964 through 1970, the Fab Four dominated the radio charts whenever they released new records. They were showered with more entertainment awards than most of their fellow colleagues in the music world. By example, The Beatles were recipients of England's Show Business Personalities of 1963; New Musical Express Poll Winners in 1963 and 1964; and they scored numerous Ivor Novello Awards (presented by the British Music Industry) between 1963 and 1970. They also were the beneficiaries of countless recording industry

In the 1960s, no artists achieved more sustained critical and commercial success than The Beatles.

Silver and Gold Record Awards for the sale of their records worldwide.

However, though John Lennon, Paul McCartney, George Harrison, and Ringo Starr were nominated for more than 35 Grammy Awards between 1964 and 1970, they would only win seven gramophone statuettes during that time.

The Grammy Award is the American music industry's highest honor. Presented annually since 1958, the Grammy Award is, according to the National Academy of Recording Arts & Sciences (NARAS), "awarded for artistic or technical achievement, not sales figures or chart positions, and the winners are determined by the votes of their peers." The chief aim of the Recording Academy is to recognize excellence and foster a greater public awareness of cultural diversity and contributions of the recording industry.

Given the artistic and technical achievements scored by The Beatles and their producer George Martin, most people might assume that the group would have routinely swept the Grammy Awards during the '60s. Instead, The Beatles found themselves nowhere man when most of the awards were handed out.

Several theories have been posed as to why The Beatles did not win more Grammy Awards during their tenure as a group. Some contend the Fab Four were too radical for the times. Perhaps the long hair, admitted drug use, controversial comments and meditation with the Maharishi were just too much for the "old guard" that dominated the 1960s Academy membership. Their musical category, rock 'n' roll, was not well recognized by the Academy in the '60s. In fact, throughout the Grammy Award's history, critics often accused the Academy of failing to properly recognize rock 'n' rollers. It was not until 1979 that rock music was given several of its own special categories.

Politics is perhaps the best explanation for The Beatles' failure to take home more golden gramophones. At its inception, NARAS was created by the more conservative forces within the music industry to resist the new rambunctious, degenerate rock 'n' roll music. To this day, the struggle between conservative and progressive elements within the music industry continues.

In the 1960s, the older, conservative membership had a strong foothold on voting. There were perhaps only a handful of members under the age of 30. Block voting by geographical region determined Grammy Award outcomes significantly, with Nashville and Los Angeles battling for their own artists. Safe ballads and love songs, over loud rock 'n' roll, was the norm in the '60s. They still are.

Nomination categories were also politicized in the 1960s. Frequent dropping, adding and changing of nomination categories caused artists to lose opportunities for nomination. In other instances, award category politics crowded certain nomination fields with nominees whose music did not properly belong.

To its credit, the Recording Academy did acknowledge the efforts of The Beatles by bestowing upon them a substantial number of nominations. Fortunately for The Beatles, who were selling records eight days a week in the '60s, winning these awards was not particularly crucial to their continued commercial success.

This article presents a year-by-year overview of The Beatles' wins, losses and nominations at the Grammy Awards. It also includes a "Grammyography," listing Beatles and post-Beatles solo awards. So sit back and enjoy The Beatles at the Grammy Awards, commercial free. May I have the envelope, please...

1964

The 1964 awards were presented April 13, 1965. The Beatles were nominated in the following categories: Record Of The Year ("I Want To Hold Your Hand"); Song Of The Year ("A Hard Day's Night," Lennon/McCartney songwriters); Best New Artist; Best Performance By A Vocal Group (A Hard Day's Night); Best Rock 'n' Roll Recording ("A Hard Day's Night") and Best Original Score Written For A Motion Picture Or TV Show (A Hard Day's Night).

The group walked away with only two awards that night, namely, Best New Artist and Best Performance By A Vocal Group. The popular mainstream hit, "The Girl From Ipanema," was deemed to be superior to "I Want To Hold Your Hand" for Record Of The Year. "Hello Dolly" took Song of The Year honors, and good old Mary Poppins trounced A Hard Day's Night in the Best Original Score category.

The ceremony was aired a month later on NBC's The Best On Record, May 18, 1965. Although The Beatles did not appear live on the broadcast, a tape of their presentation was shown. The tape was filmed during a break in the making of the "pub scene" in Help! Comedian and friend Peter Sellers presented the four with their Grammy Award. Led by John Lennon, The Beatles and Sellers (never ones to let a serious ceremony spoil the party) happily spoke French-sounding gibberish into the camera and broke into the song "It's A Long Way To Tipperary."

1965

The 1965 awards were presented in March 1966. This was perhaps the Academy's most controversial awards year in terms of its treatment toward The Beatles. The Fabs were nominated in the following categories: Album Of The Year (Help!); Record Of The Year ("Yesterday," Lennon/McCartney

songwriters); Song Of The Year ("Yesterday"); Best Vocal Performance ("Yesterday," McCartney); Best Performance By A Vocal Group ("Help!"); Best Contemporary (Rock 'n' Roll) Single ("Yesterday"); Best Contemporary (Rock 'n' Roll) Performance By A Group ("Help!"). The Beatles' producer George Martin was also nominated for Best Arrangement Accompanying A Vocalist Or Instrument ("Yesterday").

The theme song for this ceremony should have been titled "I'm A Loser" because that aptly describes The Beatles and producer Martin in 1965. Although nominated for nine categories, alleged ballot stuffing by the Academy's new Nashville chapter completely shut out The Beatles on this night!

Perhaps the biggest mistake in Grammy Awards history occurred in 1965 when country and western's Anita Kerr Quartet took honors for Best Performance By A Vocal Group over The Beatles. The Quartet's winning album (for all the trivia enthusiasts out there) was the unforgettable We Dig Mancini. Would it be a surprise to learn that Kerr was a very popular friend of the Academy's voting membership at the time? As recounted in Thomas O'Neil's book, The Grammys — For The Record (Penguin Books USA, Inc., 1993) Kerr was vice president of the Nashville chapter of NARAS and regularly involved herself in the affairs of the New York and Los Angeles chapters. Thus, her victory over The Beatles, though surprising to the public and news media, was probably expected by Nashville insiders of that era.

The surprises in store for The Beatles at the 1965 Awards ceremony did not stop with Kerr's victory. Another series of Nashville upsets over the Fab Four included non-rock singers Roger Miller and The Statler Brothers. Miller's "King Of The Road" topped The Beatles' "Yesterday" in both the Best Contemporary (Rock 'n' Roll) Single and Best Male Vocal Performance categories. And perhaps the most bizzare coup of the Nashville "mafia" was country's Statler Brothers. They were victorious over The Beatles for Best Contemporary (Rock 'n' Roll) Performance By A Group. The Statlers' winning entry was "Flowers On The Wall." Besides besting The Beatles, the Statlers finished ahead of Herman's Hermits ("Mrs. Brown"), Sam The Sham And The Pharaohs ("Wooly Bully") and The Supremes ("Stop In The Name Of Love").

Only politics and strong Nashville chapter voting could explain the placement of these country twangers into rock 'n' roll categories in the first place, especially when country and western music already had six categories designated to its own genre. As a result, Nashville's domination of the 1965 Grammy Awards struck a dissonant chord. Beatles supporters were not the only ones disappointed. Many of the other Academy members viewed the awards that year as disproportionately balanced in favor of the Nashville clan.

1966

Awards for 1966 were handed out on March 2, 1967. The Beatles were again acknowledged through several nominations, this time successfully winning some Grammy hardware. The group and some of its collegues were up for the following categories: Album Of The Year (Revolver); Song Of The Year ("Michelle," Lennon/McCartney songwriters); Best Vocal performance, Male ("Eleanor Rigby," McCartney); Best Contemporary (Rock 'n' Roll) Recording ("Eleanor Rigby"); Best Contemporary (Rock 'n' Roll) Solo Vocal Performance, Male Or Female ("Eleanor Rigby," McCartney); Best Arrangement Accompanying Vocalist On Instrument (George Martin, "Eleanor Rigby"); and Best Album Cover (Revolver, Klaus Voormann, artist).

A Grammy was awarded to Lennon and McCartney (for "Michelle") in the prestigious category Song Of The Year, perhaps to make up for the criticism received by the Academy

for snubbing The Beatles in 1965. McCartney's vocal performance on "Eleanor Rigby" also took top honors. It is interesting to note that both awards clearly reflected the voting Academy's long-standing preference for ballads and love songs over hard rock. Voormann, longtime friend of the Fabs, took the Grammy Award for his wonderful collage on the cover of Revolver.

Perhaps more than one music critic winced when the New Vaudeville Band ("Winchester Cathedral") took the trophy for Best Contemporary (Rock 'n' Roll) Recording. Not only did these one-hit wonders surpass The Beatles ("Eleanor Rigby") in this category, but they also trounced four other classic recordings as well. The four other artists overlooked by the Academy included The Association ("Cherish"), The Beach Boys ("Good Vibrations"), The Monkees ("Last Train To Clarksville") and The Mamas And The Papas ("Monday, Monday")!

Other major categories of 1966 were dominated by the "old guard" of Frank Sinatra, Ray Charles, Duke Ellington and, yes, once again, The Anita Kerr Quartet. Kerr's group took the crown for Best Performance By A Vocal Group. Unbelievable as it may seem, this was a category in which The Beatles were not even nominated in 1966!

1967

The Beatles and friends fared well at the 1967 Grammy Awards, which were presented in February 1968. Sgt. Pepper's Lonely Hearts Club Band won the coveted Album Of The Year and Best Contemporary Album awards. However, once again, middle-of-the-road academy voting prevented a Beatles sweep by choosing the safe 5th Dimension ("Up, Up And Away') for Best Performance By A Vocal Group and Best Contemporary Group Performance, Vocal Or Instrumental. Martin lost a bid for Best Arrangement Accompanying A Vocalist ("A Day In The

Life") to Jimmie Haskell ("Ode To Billie Joe"), but his engineer Geoff Emerick did win a Grammy Award for Best Engineered Recording Non-Classical (Sgt. Pepper). Peter Blake and Jann Haworth took the award for their art direction on the Sgt. Pepper album cover. Also that year, Beatles buddy Ravi Shankar won the Best Chamber Music Performance award.

All in all, the 1967 Grammy Awards were remarkable in that members of the Academy were bold enough to reward The Beatles for their groundbreaking album that featured creative experimentation in concept, songwriting, music, engineering technology and its cover art. However, this nod to the cutting edge would not become a trend as the years rolled on; neither would innovation be the key to more trophies for The Beatles.

1968

The 1968 awards, given away on March 12, 1969, were marked by a return to safe, pleasant pop. The Beatles garnered four nominations, for Album Of The Year (Magical Mystery Tour); Record Of The Year ("Hey Jude"); Song Of The Year ("Hey Jude," Lennon/McCartney songwriters) and Best Contemporary Pop Vocal Performance, Duo Or Group ("Hey Jude"). However, once again they were shut out.

The gentle Glen Campbell (By The Time I Get To Phoenix) took Album Of The Year honors. The sweet sounds of Simon & Garfunkel ("Mrs. Robinson") walked off with Record Of The Year and Best Contemporary Pop Vocal Performance. The corny Bobby Russell ("Little Green Apples") was deemed best songwriter, for Song Of The Year.

A comparison between the Grammy Award years of 1967 and 1968 reveals that changes in category designations may have cost The Beatles an award or two. Two categories where The Beatles would likely have been favored were removed in 1968. Absent were awards for Best Contemporary Single

(how about "Hey Jude"?) and Best Contemporary Album (perhaps Magical Mystery Tour?). Of course, we will never know the outcome for the two dropped categories. But then, there was always a possibility for the return of the amazing Anita Kerr Quartet to sweep away The Beatles' chances.

1969

The ceremony was held on March 11, 1970, just one month before McCartney would announce to the world that The Beatles had broken up forever. This time around, The Beatles and company were nominated for four awards, namely, Album Of The Year (Abbey Road), Best Contemporary Vocal Performance, Group (Abbey Road), Best Original Score Written For A Picture Or TV Special (Yellow Submarine, composers Lennon, McCartney, Harrison, and George Martin); and Best Engineered Recording, Non Classical (Geoff Emerick, Phillip McDonald, Abbey Road).

Once again, Academy voting generally embraced traditional values and more conservative music, which meant The Beatles would come up empty-handed. Blood, Sweat & Tears took Album Of The Year honors over not only Abbey Road, but the debut of Crosby, Stills & Nash. In an encore performance, The 5th Dimension aced The Beatles in the Vocal Performance category with the now dated "Aquarius"/"Let The Sunshine In," from the Hair musical. Only Geoff Emerick and Phil McDonald received an award for their engineering on Abbey Road.

1970

Presented on March 16, 1971, this was the first-ever live telecast of the Grammy Awards. The now-defunct Beatles pulled in five nominations for their commercial swan song album (but not the last recorded), Let It Be. The nominations included Record Of The Year ("Let It Be"); Song Of The Year ("Let It Be," Lennon/McCartney,

"Thank you."

songwriters); Best Contemporary Vocal Performance By A Duo, Group or Chorus ("Let It Be"); and Best Original Score Written For A Motion Picture Or TV Special (Let It Be, Lennon, McCartney, Harrison, Starr, composers).

The Beatles' last chance to sweep the Grammy Awards came up short again, as they were practically shut out by the safe, soft sounds of Simon & Garfunkel and The Carpenters. The group's last Grammy award would be for Best Original Film Score. Paul McCartney surprised the audience by showing up to personally receive the award on behalf of his former bandmates. McCartney's acceptance speech consisted of a simple two words, "Thank you."

1992

By 1993, the former Beatles had been pursuing individual endeavors for some 23 years. And as everyone knows, the prospect of a Beatles reunion became moot on Dec. 8, 1980, with John Lennon's passing. Yet this fact did not stop the Academy from resurrecting The Beatles' album Sgt. Pepper's Lonely Hearts Club Band for its 1992 Hall Of Fame Award. The Hall Of Fame Award honors recordings of "lasting historical or qualitative significance" that were released more than 25 years ago.

While the Grammy Awards remain today the most prestigious of the music industry, they were not always so generous to The Beatles. The awards are supposedly presented based upon artistic or technical achievement. Yet, given their inconsistent track record with The Beatles and other rockers, many critics might aptly present NARAS with its own Grammy Award for the category, Most Political Home Town Middle Of The Road, Ballad Lovers.

In recent years the Academy has begun to appreciate The Beatles in its own retroactive fashion by awarding the afore-

mentioned Hall Of Fame Award as well as Lifetime Achievement Awards to Lennon (posthumously) and McCartney. It is anyone's guess if and when the Academy will bestow similar awards to Harrison and Starr.

The fact that the Fab Four were able to achieve such popular, commercial and critical success during their reign in the '60s (without winning more Grammy Awards) is to their credit. However, one still has to wonder how The Beatles would have fared if Anita Kerr (and her Quartet) had never been born. ■

Beatles Grammyography

1 9 6 4 - 1 9 7 0 & 1 9 9 2

- Best New Artist N/A
  The Beatles

- Best Performance By a Vocal Group
  The Beatles - A Hard Day's Night

- Song Of The Year (Songwriter)
  John Lennon/Paul McCartney - "Michelle"

- Best Contemporary (R & R)
  Solo Vocal Performance, Male or Female
  Paul McCartney - "Eleanor Rigby"

- Album Of The Year
  Beatles - Sgt. Pepper's Lonely Hearts Club Band

- The Beatles Best Contemporary Album
  Sgt. Pepper's Lonely Hearts Club Band

- The Beatles Best Original Score Written for a Motion Picture or TV Special (Composer)
  Let It Be

- Beatles Hall Of Fame Award
  Sgt. Pepper's Lonely Hearts Club Band

- *Help! and its title track were both nominated for Grammys in 1965.*

- *Klaus Voormann won a Grammy Award in 1966 for his album cover artwork on Revolver.*

This article originally appeared in Goldmine issue #347, Nov. 12, 1993.

■ The author gratefully acknowledges assistance he received from Mrs. H.L. Schuberk in the preparation of this article.

■ Astrid Kirchherr/K&K/Star File

■ *The Beatles with Pete Best (left) and Stuart Sutcliffe (right).*

261

45s

Apple Records numerical listing

GM/OYB-1 [DJ] Ono, Yoko
Greenfield Morning/Open Your Box ....1971........800.00
—*Exactly six copies made for the personal use of Yoko Ono.*

1800   Foster, John, and Sons Black Dyke Mills Band
Thingumybob/Yellow Submarine ....1968........100.00
—*With "Thingumybob" on uncut apple side*

1800   Foster, John, and Sons Black Dyke Mills Band
Thingumybob/Yellow Submarine ....1968........100.00
—*With "Yellow Submarine" on uncut apple side*

1800   Foster, John, and Sons Black Dyke Mills Band
Thingumybob/Yellow Submarine ....1968........120.00
—*With black star on uncut apple side*

1801   Hopkin, Mary Those Were the Days/Turn, Turn, Turn.1968.............10.00

1802   Lomax, Jackie ....Sour Milk Sea/
The Eagle Laughs at You...........................1968..........20.00
—*With B-side author listed as "(George Harrison)"*

1802   Lomax, Jackie ....Sour Milk Sea/
The Eagle Laughs at You...........................1968..........20.00
—*With B-side author listed as "(Jackie Lomax)"*

1803   Badfinger ....Maybe Tomorrow/
And Her Daddy's a Millionaire.........................1969..........30.00
—*By "The Iveys"; with star on label*

1803   Badfinger ....Maybe Tomorrow/
And Her Daddy's a Millionaire.........................1969..........20.00
—*By "The Iveys"; without star on label*

1804   Trash   Road to Nowhere/Illusions ....1969........100.00
—*With star on A-side label*

1804   Trash   Road to Nowhere/Illusions..................1969..........50.00
—*Without star on A-side label*

1805   Taylor, James Carolina in My Mind/Taking It In ..1969 ....300.00

1805   Taylor, James Carolina in My Mind/
Something's Wrong ....1970..........10.00
—*With star on A-side label*

1805   Taylor, James Carolina in My Mind/
Something's Wrong ....1970............8.00
—*Without star on A-side label*

1805 [DJ] Taylor, James Carolina on My Mind/
Something's Wrong ....1970..........30.00
—*Promo with error in title on A-side*

1806   Hopkin, Mary Goodbye/Sparrow....................1969............8.00

1806 [PS] Hopkin, Mary Goodbye/Sparrow....................1969..........12.00

1807   Lomax, Jackie New Day/Thumbin' a Ride........1969..........75.00
—*With star on A-side label*

1807   Lomax, JackieNew Day/Thumbin' a Ride ....1969..........60.00
—*Without star on A-side label*

1808   Preston, BillyThat's the Way God Planned It/
What About You ....1969............8.00

1808 [PS] Preston, Billy That's the Way God Planned It/
What About You ....1969..........10.00

P-1808/PRO
6555 [DJ]   Preston, Billy ....That's the Way
God Planned It (Parts 1 & 2) (mono/stereo).....1969..........60.00

1808   Preston, Billy ....That's the Way God Planned It/
What About You ....1972............8.00
—*With "Mono" on both sides of record and reference to LP*

1809   Lennon, John Give Peace a Chance/
Remember Love..1969............5.00
—*As "Plastic Ono Band"*

1809 [PS] Lennon, John Give Peace a Chance/
Remember Love..1969..........15.00
—*As "Plastic Ono Band"*

1809   Ono, Yoko Give Peace a Chance/Remember Love1969............5.00
—*As "Plastic Ono Band"; Yoko sings backup on A-side, lead on B-side*

1809 [PS] Ono, Yoko Give Peace a Chance/Remember Love1969 ....12.00
—*As "Plastic Ono Band"*

1810   Radha Krishna Temple Hare Krishna Mantra/
Prayer to the Spiritual Masters ....1969............8.00

1810 [PS] Radha Krishna Temple Hare Krishna Mantra/
Prayer to the Spiritual Masters ....1969........400.00
—*Only one copy is known to exist. The price is highly speculative.*

1811   Trash Golden Slumbers-Carry That Weight/
Trash Can1969..15.00
—*A-side listed as "Golden Slumbers/Carry That Weight"*

1811   Trash Golden Slumbers-Carry That Weight/
Trash Can1969..20.00
—*A-side listed as "Golden Slumbers and Carry That Weight"*

1811   Trash Golden Slumbers-Carry That Weight/
Trash Can1969..20.00
—*A-side listed as "Golden Slumbers Carry That Weight"*

1812   Hot Chocolate Give Peace a Chance/
Living Without Tomorrow ....1969..........10.00
—*As "Hot Chocolate Band"*

1813   Lennon, John Cold Turkey/Don't Worry Kyoko
(Mummy's Only Looking for a Hand in the Snow).1969.............5.00
—*As "Plastic Ono Band"; most copies skip on A-side on the . third chorus because of a pressing defect*

1813   Lennon, John Cold Turkey/Don't Worry Kyoko
(Mummy's Only Looking for a Hand in the Snow).1969 ....10.00
—*As "Plastic Ono Band"; some copies don't skip on A-side. . They tend to have wider, bolder print than those that do.*

1813 [PS] Lennon, John Cold Turkey/Don't Worry Kyoko
(Mummy's Only Looking for a Hand in the Snow).1969 ....40.00
—*As "Plastic Ono Band"*

1814   Preston, Billy Everything's All Right/
I Want to Thank You ....1969............8.00

1815   Badfinger Come and Get It/Rock of All Ages ...1969............6.00

1815   Badfinger Come and Get It/Rock of All Ages ...1969............8.00
—*With Capitol logo on B-side bottom*

1816   Hopkin, MaryTemma Harbour/Lantano Dagli Occhi1970 ......8.00

1816 [PS] Hopkin, MaryTemma Harbour/Lantano Dagli Occhi1970 ....12.00

1817   Preston, BillyAll That I've Got (I'm Gonna Give It to You)/
As I Get Older ....1970............8.00

1817 [PS] Preston, BillyAll That I've Got (I'm Gonna Give It to You)/
As I Get Older ....1970..........15.00

1818   Lennon, John Instant Karma! (We All Shine On)/
Who Has Seen the Wind? ....1970............4.00
—*As "John Ono Lennon"; B-side by "Yoko Ono Lennon"*

1818 [DJ] Lennon, John Instant Karma! (We All Shine On)1970........200.00
—*As "John Ono Lennon"; one-sided promo*

1818 [PS] Lennon, John Instant Karma! (We All Shine On)/
Who Has Seen the Wind? ....1970..........15.00
—*As "John Ono Lennon"; B-side by "Yoko Ono Lennon"*

1819   Lomax, Jackie How the Web Was Woven/
I Fall Inside Your Eyes......................................1970............8.00

1819 [PS] Lomax, JackieHow the Web Was Woven/
I Fall Inside Your Eyes......................................1970..........10.00

1820   Troy, Doris Ain't That Cute/Vaya Con Dios.......1970............8.00

1821   Radha Krishna Temple Govinda/Govinda Jai Jai..1970............8.00

1821   Radha Krishna Temple Govinda/Govinda Jai Jai..1970..........10.00
—*With Capitol logo on B-side label bottom*

1821 [PS] Radha Krishna Temple Govinda/Govinda Jai Jai..1970..........10.00

1822   Badfinger No Matter What/
Carry On Till Tomorrow......................................1970............6.00

1822   Badfinger No Matter What/Carry On Till Tomorrow1970 ....20.00
—*With star on A-side label*

1823   Hopkin, Mary Que Sera, Sera (Whatever Will Be, Will Be)/
Fields of St. Etienne ....1970............8.00

1824   Troy, Doris Jacob's Ladder/Get Back ....1970............8.00

1825   Hopkin, Mary Think About Your Children/Heritage1970............8.00

1825   Hopkin, Mary Think About Your Children/Heritage1970..........12.00
—*With star on A-side label*

1825 [PS] Hopkin, MaryThink About Your Children/Heritage 1970 ....12.00

1826   Preston, Billy My Sweet Lord/Little Girl ....1970............8.00

1826   Preston, Billy My Sweet Lord/Little Girl ....1970..........12.00
—*With star on A-side label*

1826 [PS] Starr, Ringo Beaucoups of Blues/Coochy-Coochy 1970 ....40.00
—*Sleeve with wrong catalog number (actually 2969)*

1827   Lennon, John Mother/Why ....1970............8.00
—*As "John Lennon/Plastic Ono Band";
B-side by "Yoko Ono/Plastic Ono Band"*

1827   Lennon, John Mother/Why ....1970..........12.00
—*As "John Lennon/Plastic Ono Band"; star on A-side label*

1827   Lennon, John Mother/Why ....1970..........40.00
—*As "John Lennon/Plastic Ono Band"; "MONO" on A-side label*

1827 [PS] Lennon, John Mother/Why ....1970........120.00
—*As "John Lennon/Plastic Ono Band";
B-side by "Yoko Ono/Plastic Ono Band"*

1828   Harrison, George What Is Life/Apple Scruffs ..1971..........15.00
—*With star on A-side label*

1828   Harrison, George What Is Life/Apple Scruffs ..1971............8.00
—*Without star on A-side label*

1828 [PS] Harrison, George
What Is Life/Apple Scruffs ....1971..........40.00

1829   McCartney, Paul
Another Day/Oh Woman, Oh Why....................1971..........12.00
—*With star on A-side label*

1829   McCartney, Paul
Another Day/Oh Woman, Oh Why....................1971............8.00

1830   Lennon, John Power to the People/Touch Me ..1971............8.00
—*As "John Lennon/Plastic Ono Band";
B-side by "Yoko Ono/Plastic Ono Band"*

1830   Lennon, John Power to the People/Touch Me ..1971............8.00
—*As "John Lennon/Plastic Ono Band";
with star on A-side label*

1830 [PS] Lennon, John Power to the People/Touch Me ..1971..........30.00
—*As "John Lennon/Plastic Ono Band";
B-side by "Yoko Ono/Plastic Ono Band"*

1831   Starr, Ringo It Don't Come Easy/Early 1970 .....1971............8.00

1831   Starr, Ringo It Don't Come Easy/Early 1970 .....1971..........12.00
—*With star on A-side label*

1831 [PS] Starr, Ringo It Don't Come Easy/Early 1970 .....1971..........30.00

1831   Starr, Ringo It Don't Come Easy/Early 1970 .....1975..........30.00
—*With "All rights reserved" on label*

1832   Spector, Ronnie
Try Some, Buy Some/Tandoori Chicken ....1971............7.00

1832   Spector, Ronnie
Try Some, Buy Some/Tandoori Chicken ....1971............8.00
—*With star on A-side label*

1832 [PS] Spector, Ronnie
Try Some, Buy Some/Tandoori Chicken ....1971..........10.00

1834   Lomax, Jackie
Sour Milk Sea/(I) Fall Inside Your Eyes.............1971............8.00

1835   Elliott, Bill, and the Elastic Oz Band
God Save Us/Do the Oz....................................1971............8.00

1835 [PS] Elliott, Bill, and the Elastic Oz Band
God Save Us/Do the Oz....................................1971..........10.00

P-1835 [DJ] Elliott, Bill, and the Elastic Oz Band
God Save Us/Do the Oz....................................1971..........25.00
—*Has black star on A-side and unsliced apple on both sides*

1836   Harrison, George Bangla-Desh/Deep Blue ......1971..........25.00
—*With star on A-side label*

1836   Harrison, George Bangla-Desh/Deep Blue ......1971............8.00
—*Without star on A-side label*

1836 [PS] Harrison, George Bangla-Desh/Deep Blue ......1971..........20.00

1837   McCartney, Paul Uncle Albert/
Admiral Halsey//Too Many People ....1971..........15.00
—*Paul and Linda McCartney; with "Pual" misspelling on producer credit*

1837   McCartney, Paul Uncle Albert/
Admiral Halsey//Too Many People ....1971............8.00
—*Paul and Linda McCartney; with no misspelling*

1837   McCartney, Paul Uncle Albert/Admiral Halsey/
Too Many People ....1971..........50.00
—*Paul and Linda McCartney; with unsliced apple on B-side label*

1837   McCartney, Paul Uncle Albert/Admiral Halsey//
Too Many People ....1975..........30.00
—*Paul and Linda McCartney; with "All rights reserved" on label*

1838   Shankar, Ravi Joi Bangla-Oh Bhaugowan/
Raga Mishra-Jhinjhoti......................................1971............8.00
—*By Ravi Shankar & Ali Akbar with Alla Rakah*

1838 [PS] Shankar, Ravi Joi Bangla-Oh Bhaugowan/
Raga Mishra-Jhinjhoti......................................1971..........20.00

1839   Ono, Yoko Mrs. Lennon/Midsummer New York1971............7.00
—*As "Yoko Ono/Plastic Ono Band"*

1840   Lennon, John Imagine/It's So Hard ....1971............8.00
—*As "John Lennon Plastic Ono Band"; tan label*

1840   Lennon, John Imagine/It's So Hard ....1975..........12.00
—*As "John Lennon Plastic Ono Band"; green label with "All Rights Reserved"*

1841   Badfinger Day After Day/Money ....1971..........20.00
—*With star on A-side label*

1841   Badfinger Day After Day/Money ....1971............6.00

1841 [DJ] Badfinger Day After Day/Money ....1971........120.00
—*White label*

1842   Lennon, John Happy Xmas (War Is Over)/
Listen, the Snow Is Falling................................1971..........15.00
—*As "John & Yoko/Plastic Ono Band with the Harlem Community Choir"; green vinyl, faces label*

1842   Lennon, John Happy Xmas (War Is Over)/
Listen, the Snow Is Falling................................1971..........10.00
—*As "John & Yoko/Plastic Ono Band with the Harlem Community Choir"; green vinyl, Apple label*

1842 [PS] Lennon, John Happy Xmas (War Is Over)/
Listen, the Snow Is Falling................................1971..........20.00
—*As "John & Yoko/Plastic Ono Band with the Harlem Community Choir"*

1843   Hopkin, Mary Water, Paper and Clay/
Streets of London ....1972............8.00

1843   Hopkin, Mary Water, Paper and Clay/
Streets of London ....1972..........12.00
—*With star on A-side label*

1844   Badfinger Baby Blue/Flying ....1972............6.00

1844 [DJ] Badfinger Baby Blue/Flying ....1972........120.00
—*White label*

1844 [PS] Badfinger Baby Blue/Flying ....1972..........15.00

1845   Van Eaten, Lon and Derrek
Sweet Music/Song of Songs...........................1972............8.00

1845 [PS] Van Eaten, Lon and Derrek
Sweet Music/Song of Songs...........................1972..........10.00

1847   McCartney, Paul Give Ireland Back to the Irish/
Give Ireland Back to the Irish (Version)............1972..........10.00
—*Wings*

1847 [PS] McCartney, Paul Give Ireland Back to the Irish/
Give Ireland Back to the Irish (Version)............1972..........30.00
—*Wings; title sleeve with large center hole*

1848   Lennon, John Woman Is the Nigger of the World/
Sisters O Sisters ....1972............8.00
—*As "John Lennon/Plastic Ono Band...";
B-side by "Yoko Ono/Plastic Ono Band..."*

1848 [PS] Lennon, John Woman Is the Nigger of the World/
Sisters O Sisters ....1972..........25.00
—*As "John Lennon/Plastic Ono Band...";
B-side by "Yoko Ono/Plastic Ono Band..."
—As "Yoko Ono/Plastic Ono Band...";
B-side by "John Lennon/Plastic Ono Band..."*

263

1849	Starr, Ringo Back Off Boogaloo/Blindman	1972	8.00	
	—Green-background label			
1849	Starr, Ringo Back Off Boogaloo/Blindman	1972	75.00	
	—Blue-background label			
1849 [DJ]	Starr, Ringo Back Off Boogaloo/Blindman	1972	150.00	
	—White label			
1849 [PS]	Starr, Ringo Back Off Boogaloo/Blindman	1972	15.00	
	—Black paper with flat finish			
1849 [PS]	Starr, Ringo Back Off Boogaloo/Blindman	1972	40.00	
	—Glossy black paper on both sides			
1849 [PS]	Starr, Ringo Back Off Boogaloo/Blindman	1972	40.00	
	—Glossy black on one side, gray on the other			
1850	Hodge, Chris We're On Our Way/Supersoul	1972	8.00	
1850 [PS]	Hodge, Chris We're On Our Way/Supersoul	1972	10.00	
1851	McCartney, Paul Mary Had a Little Lamb/ Little Woman Love	1972	10.00	
	—Wings			
1851 [DJ]	McCartney, Paul Mary Had a Little Lamb/ Little Woman Love	1972	300.00	
	—White label promo, lists artist as Paul McCartney			
1851 [PS]	McCartney, Paul Mary Had a Little Lamb/ Little Woman Love	1972	25.00	
	—Wings; without "Little Woman Love" on sleeve			
1851 [PS]	McCartney, Paul Mary Had a Little Lamb/ Little Woman Love	1972	40.00	
	—Wings; with "Little Woman Love" on sleeve			
1852	Sundown Playboys, The Saturday Night Special/ Valse De Soleil Coucher	1972	15.00	
1853	Ono, Yoko Now or Never/Move On Fast	1972	7.00	
1853 [PS]	Ono, Yoko Now or Never/Move On Fast	1972	8.00	
1854	Elephants Memory Liberation Special/Madness	1972	8.00	
1854	Elephants Memory Liberation Special/Power Boogie	1972	400.00	
1854 [PS]	Elephants Memory Liberation Special/Madness	1972	10.00	
1855	Hopkin, Mary Knock Knock Who's There/ International	1972	8.00	
1857	McCartney, Paul Hi Hi Hi/C Moon	1972	10.00	
	—Wings; red label			
1858	Hodge, Chris Goodnight Sweet Lorraine/Contact Love	1973	8.00	
1859	Ono, Yoko Death of Samantha/Yang Yang	1973	7.00	
1861	McCartney, Paul My Love/The Mess	1973	8.00	
	—Paul McCartney and Wings; custom "Red Rose Speedway" label			
1861 [DJ]	McCartney, Paul My Love/The Mess	1973	200.00	
	—Paul McCartney and Wings; white label			
1862	Harrison, George Give Me Love (Give Me Peace on Earth)/Miss O'Dell (2:30)	1973	8.00	
	—With incorrect time for B-side listed			
1862	Harrison, George Give Me Love (Give Me Peace on Earth)/Miss O'Dell (2:20)	1973	8.00	
	—B-side playing time corrected			
P-1862 [DJ]	Harrison, George Give Me Love (Give Me Peace on Earth) (mono/stereo)	1973	50.00	
1863	McCartney, Paul Live and Let Die/I Lie Around	1973	8.00	
	—Wings			
1864	Badfinger Apple of My Eye/Blind Owl	1973	6.00	
P-1864 [DJ]	Badfinger Apple of My Eye (mono/stereo)	1973	25.00	
1865	Starr, Ringo Photograph/Down and Out	1973	6.00	
	—Custom star label			
1865 [PS]	Starr, Ringo Photograph/Down and Out	1973	20.00	
P-1865 [DJ]	Starr, Ringo Photograph (mono/stereo)	1973	50.00	
1867	Ono, Yoko Woman Power/Men, Men, Men	1973	7.00	

1868	Lennon, John Mind Games/Meat City	1973	6.00	
1868 [PS]	Lennon, John Mind Games/Meat City	1973	15.00	
P-1868 [DJ]	Lennon, John Mind Games (mono/stereo)	1973	50.00	
1869	McCartney, Paul Helen Wheels/Country Dreamer	1973	8.00	
P-1869 [DJ]	McCartney, Paul Helen Wheels/ Country Dreamer	1973	2000.00	
	—Paul McCartney and Wings; a very rare promo, as most promos have the same song on both sides (see 6786 and 6787 below)			
1870	Starr, Ringo You're Sixteen/Devil Woman	1973	6.00	
	—Custom star label			
1870	Starr, Ringo You're Sixteen/Devil Woman	1973	25.00	
	—Regular Apple label			
1870 [PS]	Starr, Ringo You're Sixteen/Devil Woman	1973	25.00	
P-1870 [DJ]	Starr, Ringo You're Sixteen (mono/stereo)	1973	50.00	
1871	McCartney, Paul Jet/Mamunia	1974	10.00	
	—Paul McCartney and Wings			
1871	McCartney, Paul Jet/Mamunia	1974	100.00	
	—Paul McCartney and Wings; A-side incorrectly listed as playing for 2:49			
1871	McCartney, Paul Jet/Let Me Roll It	1974	8.00	
	—Paul McCartney and Wings			
P-1871 [DJ]	McCartney, Paul Jet (Edited Mono)/Jet (Stereo)	1974	50.00	
	—Paul McCartney and Wings			
1872	Starr, Ringo Oh My My/Step Lightly	1974	6.00	
	—Custom star label			
1872	Starr, Ringo Oh My My/Step Lightly	1974	8.00	
	—Regular Apple label			
P-1872 [DJ]	Starr, Ringo Oh My My (Edited Mono)/ Oh My My (Long Stereo)	1974	50.00	
1873	McCartney, Paul Band on the Run/ Nineteen Hundred and Eighty-Five	1974	8.00	
	—Paul McCartney and Wings			
P-1873 [DJ]	McCartney, Paul Band on the Run (Edited Mono)/ Band on the Run (Full-length Stereo)	1974	40.00	
	—Paul McCartney and Wings			
P-1873 [DJ]	McCartney, Paul Band on the Run (mono/stereo, both edits)	1974	100.00	
	—Paul McCartney and Wings			
1874	Lennon, John Whatever Gets You Thru the Night/ Beef Jerky	1974	6.00	
	—As "John Lennon and the Plastic Ono Nuclear Band"			
P-1874 [DJ]	Lennon, John Whatever Gets You Thru the Night (mono/stereo)	1974	50.00	
	—As "John Lennon and the Plastic Ono Nuclear Band"			
1875	McCartney, Paul Junior's Farm/Sally G	1974	8.00	
	—Paul McCartney and Wings			
P-1875 [DJ]	McCartney, Paul Junior's Farm (Edited Mono)/ Junior's Farm (Full-length Stereo)	1974	50.00	
	—Paul McCartney and Wings			
P-1875 [DJ]	McCartney, Paul Sally G (mono/stereo)	1974	80.00	
	—Paul McCartney and Wings			
1875	McCartney, Paul Junior's Farm/Sally G	1975	80.00	
	—Paul McCartney and Wings; with "All Rights Reserved" on label			
1876	Starr, Ringo Only You/Call Me	1974	6.00	
	—Custom nebula label			
1876	Starr, Ringo Only You/Call Me	1974	8.00	
	—Regular Apple label			
1876 [PS]	Starr, Ringo Only You/Call Me	1974	20.00	
P-1876 [DJ]	Starr, Ringo Only You (mono/stereo)	1974	40.00	
1877	Harrison, George Dark Horse/ I Don't Care Anymore	1974	8.00	
	—Light blue and white custom photo label			

1877	Harrison, George Dark Horse/ I Don't Care Anymore ....1974..........10.00 —*White label; NOT a promo*	
1877 [PS]	Harrison, George Dark Horse/ I Don't Care Anymore ....1974..........80.00	
P-1877 [DJ]	Harrison, George Dark Horse (full length mono/stereo) ....1974..........40.00	
P-1877 [DJ]	Harrison, George Dark Horse (edited mono/stereo) ....1974..........60.00	
1878	Lennon, John #9 Dream/What You Got ....1974............8.00	
P-1878 [DJ]	Lennon, John #9 Dream (edited mono/stereo)..1974..........50.00	
P-1878 [DJ]	Lennon, John What You Got (mono/stereo) ...1974........100.00	
1879	Harrison, George Ding Dong, Ding Dong/ Hari's on Tour (Express) ....1974..........20.00 —*Black and white custom photo label*	
1879	Harrison, George Ding Dong, Ding Dong/ Hari's on Tour (Express) ....1974........250.00 —*Blue and white custon photo label*	
1879 [PS]	Harrison, George Ding Dong, Ding Dong/ Hari's on Tour (Express) ....1974..........20.00	
P-1879 [DJ]	Harrison, George Ding Dong, Ding Dong (remixed mono/edited stereo).................1974..........40.00	
1880	Starr, Ringo No No Song/Snookeroo ....1975............6.00 —*Custom nebula label*	
P-1880 [DJ]	Starr, Ringo No No Song/Snookeroo (both mono) ....1975..........40.00	
P-1880 [DJ]	Starr, Ringo No No Song/Snookeroo (both stereo) ....1975..........40.00	
1881	Lennon, John Stand By Me/Move Over Ms. L. ..1975............8.00	
P-1881 [DJ]	Lennon, John Stand By Me (mono/stereo) ....1975..........50.00	
1882	Starr, Ringo It's All Down to Goodnight Vienna/Oo-Wee ......1975............6.00 —*Custom nebula label*	
1882 [PS]	Starr, Ringo It's All Down to Goodnight Vienna/Oo-Wee ......1975..........20.00	
P-1882 [DJ]	Starr, Ringo It's All Down to Goodnight Vienna (mono/stereo) ....1975..........40.00	
P-1882 [DJ]	Starr, Ringo Oo-Wee/Oo-Wee ....1975..........70.00	
P-1883 [DJ]	Lennon, John Ain't That a Shame (mono/stereo) 1975........200.00 —*No stock copies issued*	
P-1883 [DJ]	Lennon, John Slippin' and Slidin' (mono/stereo).1975........200.00 —*No stock copies issued*	
1884	Harrison, George You/World of Stone ....1975............6.00	
1884 [PS]	Harrison, George You/World of Stone ....1975..........15.00	
P-1884 [DJ]	Harrison, George You (mono/stereo)..............1975..........40.00	
1885	Harrison, George This Guitar (Can't Keep from Crying)/Maya Love 1975..........25.00 —*The last Apple 45 until 1995*	
P-1885 [DJ]	Harrison, George This Guitar (Can't Keep from Crying) (mono/stereo) ....1975..........50.00	
Promo-1970 [DJ]	Beatles, The Dialogue from the Beatles' Motion Picture "Let It Be"...............1970..........60.00	
2056	Beatles, The Hello Goodbye/I Am the Walrus .1971..........30.00 —*With star on A-side label*	
2056	Beatles, The Hello Goodbye/I Am the Walrus .1971..........10.00 —*Without star on A-side label*	
2056	Beatles, The Hello Goodbye/I Am the Walrus ...1975..........20.00 —*With "All Rights Reserved" disclaimer*	
2138	Beatles, The Lady Madonna/The Inner Light.....1971..........30.00 —*With star on A-side label*	
2138	Beatles, The Lady Madonna/The Inner Light.....1971..........10.00 —*Without star on A-side label*	
2138	Beatles, The Lady Madonna/The Inner Light.....1975..........20.00 —*With "All Rights Reserved" disclaimer*	
2276	Beatles, The Hey Jude/Revolution....................1968..........15.00 —*Original: With small Capitol logo on bottom of B-side label*	
2276	Beatles, The Hey Jude/Revolution....................1968..........10.00 —*With "Mfd. by Apple" on label*	
2276	Beatles, The Hey Jude/Revolution....................1975..........20.00 —*With "All Rights Reserved" disclaimer*	
2490	Beatles, The Get Back/Don't Let Me Down........1969..........10.00 —*Original: With small Capitol logo on bottom of B-side label*	
2490	Beatles, The Get Back/Don't Let Me Down........1969..........10.00 —*With "Mfd. by Apple" on label*	
2490	Beatles, The Get Back/Don't Let Me Down........1975..........20.00 —*With "All Rights Reserved" disclaimer*	
2531	Beatles, The The Ballad of John and Yoko/Old Brown Shoe .1969..........10.00 —*Original: With small Capitol logo on bottom of B-side label*	
2531	Beatles, The The Ballad of John and Yoko/Old Brown Shoe .1969..........10.00 —*With "Mfd. by Apple" on label*	
2531 [PS]	Beatles, The The Ballad of John and Yoko/Old Brown Shoe .1969........100.00	
2531	Beatles, The The Ballad of John and Yoko/Old Brown Shoe .1975..........20.00 —*With "All Rights Reserved" disclaimer*	
2654	Beatles, The Something/Come Together ....1969........100.00 —*Original: With small Capitol logo on bottom of B-side label*	
2654	Beatles, The Something/Come Together ....1969..........10.00 —*With "Mfd. by Apple" on label*	
2654	Beatles, The Something/Come Together ....1975..........20.00 —*With "All Rights Reserved" disclaimer*	
2764	Beatles, The Let It Be/You Know My Name (Look Up My Number).....................................1970..........12.00 —*Original: With small Capitol logo on bottom of B-side label*	
2764	Beatles, The Let It Be/You Know My Name (Look Up My Number).....................................1970..........10.00 —*With "Mfd. by Apple" on label*	
2764 [PS]	Beatles, The Let It Be/You Know My Name (Look Up the Number).....................................1970........100.00	
2764	Beatles, The Let It Be/You Know My Name (Look Up My Number).....................................1975..........20.00 —*With "All Rights Reserved" disclaimer*	
2832	Beatles, The The Long and Winding Road/For You Blue ....1970..........20.00 —*Original: With small Capitol logo on bottom of B-side label*	
2832	Beatles, The The Long and Winding Road/For You Blue ....1970..........10.00 —*With "Mfd. by Apple" on label*	
2832 [PS]	Beatles, The The Long and Winding Road/For You Blue ....1970........100.00	
2832	Beatles, The The Long and Winding Road/For You Blue ....1975..........20.00 —*With "All Rights Reserved" disclaimer*	
2969	Starr, Ringo Beaucoups of Blues/Coochy-Coochy ....1970..........25.00 —*With small Capitol logo on bottom of B-side label and star on A-side label*	
2969	Starr, Ringo Beaucoups of Blues/Coochy-Coochy...................1970..........40.00 —*With "Mfd. by Apple" on label and star on A-side label*	
2969	Starr, Ringo Beaucoups of Blues/Coochy-Coochy ....1970............8.00 —*With "Mfd. by Apple" on label and no star on A-side label*	
2969 [PS]	Starr, Ringo Beaucoups of Blues/Coochy-Coochy ....1970..........50.00 —*Sleeve with correct catalog number*	
2995	Harrison, George My Sweet Lord/Isn't It a Pity .1970..........40.00 —*With black star on label*	

2995   Harrison, George   My Sweet Lord/Isn't It a Pity .1970.............8.00
        —With "Mfd. by Apple" on label

2995 [PS]   Harrison, George   My Sweet Lord/Isn't It a Pity .1970...........40.00

2995   Harrison, George   My Sweet Lord/Isn't It a Pity .1975...........25.00
        —With "All Rights Reserved" disclaimer

PRO-4671/2   Trash Road to Nowhere (Edit)/Road to Nowhere.1969...........80.00

PRO-5013/4 [DJ]Radha Krishna Temple   Govinda/Govinda Jai Jai1970.....25.00
        —With an edit of the A-side

SPRO-5067/8 [DJ]Radha Krishna Temple   Govinda (Edit)/Govinda1970....40.00

5112   Beatles, The
        I Want to Hold Your Hand/
        I Saw Her Standing There.....................1971...........30.00
        —With star on label

5112   Beatles, The   I Want to Hold Your Hand/
        I Saw Her Standing There ....1971...........10.00
        —Without star on label

5112   Beatles, The   I Want to Hold Your Hand/
        I Saw Her Standing There ....1975...........20.00
        —With "All Rights Reserved" disclaimer on label

5150   Beatles, The
        Can't Buy Me Love/You Can't Do That.................1971...........30.00
        —With star on A-side label

5150   Beatles, The
        Can't Buy Me Love/You Can't Do That ....1971...........10.00
        —Without star on A-side label

5150   Beatles, The
        Can't Buy Me Love/You Can't Do That ....1975...........15.00
        —With "All Rights Reserved" disclaimer on label

5222   Beatles, The
        A Hard Day's Night/I Should Have Known Better.1971...........30.00
        —With star on A-side label

5222   Beatles, The
        A Hard Day's Night/I Should Have Known Better.1971...........10.00
        —Without star on A-side label

5222   Beatles, The
        A Hard Day's Night/I Should Have Known Better.1975...........15.00
        —With "All Rights Reserved" disclaimer

5234   Beatles, The   I'll Cry Instead/
        I'm Happy Just to Dance with You ....1971...........30.00
        —With star on A-side label

5234   Beatles, The   I'll Cry Instead/
        I'm Happy Just to Dance with You...................1971...........10.00
        —Without star on A-side label

5234   Beatles, The   I'll Cry Instead/
        I'm Happy Just to Dance with You...................1975...........15.00
        —With "All Rights Reserved" disclaimer

5235   Beatles, The And I Love Her/If I Fell.................1971...........30.00
        —With star on A-side label

5235   Beatles, The And I Love Her/If I Fell.................1971...........10.00
        —Without star on A-side label

5235   Beatles, The And I Love Her/If I Fell.................1975...........15.00
        —With "All Rights Reserved" disclaimer

5255   Beatles, The Matchbox/Slow Down.................1971...........30.00
        —With star on A-side label

5255   Beatles, The Matchbox/Slow Down.................1971...........10.00
        —Without star on A-side label

5255   Beatles, The Matchbox/Slow Down.................1975...........15.00
        —With "All Rights Reserved" disclaimer

5327   Beatles, TheI Feel Fine/She's a Woman.............1971...........30.00
        —With star on A-side label

5327   Beatles, TheI Feel Fine/She's a Woman.............1971...........10.00
        —Without star on A-side label

5327   Beatles, TheI Feel Fine/She's a Woman.............1975...........15.00
        —With "All Rights Reserved" disclaimer

5371   Beatles, The   Eight Days a Week/
        I Don't Want to Spoil the Party ....1971...........30.00
        —With star on A-side label

5371   Beatles, The   Eight Days a Week/
        I Don't Want to Spoil the Party ....1971...........10.00
        —Without star on A-side label

5371   Beatles, The   Eight Days a Week/
        I Don't Want to Spoil the Party ....1975...........15.00
        —With "All Rights Reserved" disclaimer

5407   Beatles, The   Ticket to Ride/Yes It Is ....1971...........30.00
        —With star on A-side label

5407   Beatles, The   Ticket to Ride/Yes It Is ....1971...........10.00
        —Without star on A-side label

5407   Beatles, The   Ticket to Ride/Yes It Is ....1975...........15.00
        —With "All Rights Reserved" disclaimer

5476   Beatles, The Help!/I'm Down ....1971...........30.00
        —With star on A-side label

5476   Beatles, The Help!/I'm Down ....1971...........10.00
        —Without star on A-side label

5476   Beatles, The Help!/I'm Down ....1975...........15.00
        —With "All Rights Reserved" disclaimer

5498   Beatles, The Yesterday/Act Naturally.................1971...........30.00
        —With star on A-side label

5498   Beatles, The Yesterday/Act Naturally.................1971...........10.00
        —Without star on A-side label

5498   Beatles, The Yesterday/Act Naturally.................1975...........15.00
        —With "All Rights Reserved" disclaimer

5555   Beatles, The We Can Work It Out/Day Tripper...1971...........30.00
        —With star on A-side label

5555   Beatles, The We Can Work It Out/Day Tripper...1971...........10.00
        —Without star on A-side label

5555   Beatles, TheWe Can Work It Out/Day Tripper....1975...........15.00
        —With "All Rights Reserved" disclaimer

5587   Beatles, The Nowhere Man/What Goes On ....1971...........30.00
        —With star on A-side label

5587   Beatles, The Nowhere Man/What Goes On ....1971...........10.00
        —Without star on A-side label

5587   Beatles, The Nowhere Man/What Goes On ....1975...........15.00
        —With "All Rights Reserved" disclaimer

5651   Beatles, The Paperback Writer/Rain.................1971...........30.00
        —With star on A-side label

5651   Beatles, The Paperback Writer/Rain.................1971...........10.00
        —Without star on A-side label

5651   Beatles, The Paperback Writer/Rain.................1975...........15.00
        —With "All Rights Reserved" disclaimer

5715   Beatles, The Yellow Submarine/Eleanor Rigby..1971...........30.00
        —With star on A-side label

5715   Beatles, The Yellow Submarine/Eleanor Rigby..1971...........10.00
        —Without star on A-side label

5715   Beatles, The Yellow Submarine/Eleanor Rigby..1975...........15.00
        —With "All Rights Reserved" disclaimer

5810   Beatles, The Penny Lane/
        Strawberry Fields Forever ....1971...........30.00
        —With star on A-side label

5810   Beatles, The Penny Lane/
        Strawberry Fields Forever ....1971...........10.00
        —Without star on A-side label

5810   Beatles, The Penny Lane/
        Strawberry Fields Forever ....1975...........15.00
        —With "All Rights Reserved" disclaimer

5964   Beatles, The All You Need Is Love/
        Baby, You're a Rich Man...............................1971...........30.00
        —With star on A-side label

5964   Beatles, The All You Need Is Love/
        Baby, You're a Rich Man...............................1971...........10.00
        —Without star on A-side label

5964   Beatles, The All You Need Is Love/
        Baby, You're a Rich Man...............................1975...........15.00
        —With "All Rights Reserved" disclaimer

PRO-6193/4 [DJ]McCartney, Paul
    Another Day/Oh Woman, Oh Why ....1971...........80.00

PRO-6240/1 [DJ]Lomax, Jackie Sour Milk Sea/(I)
    Fall Inside Your Eyes...1971...........30.00

PRO-6498/9 [DJ] Peel, David F Is Not a Dirty Word/
    The Ballad of New York City ....1972.........120.00

PRO-6545/6 [DJ] Peel, David Hippie from New York City/
    The Ballad of New York City...............................1972.........120.00

PRO-6786 [DJ] McCartney, Paul Helen Wheels (mono/stereo).1973...........50.00
    —*Paul McCartney and Wings*

PRO-6787 [DJ] McCartney, Paul
    Country Dreamer (mono/stereo).......................1973.........400.00
    —*Paul McCartney and Wings*

S45X-47663/4 [DJ]Lennon, John Happy Xmas
    (War Is Over)/Listen, the Snow Is Falling ....1971........800.00
    —*As "John & Yoko/Plastic Ono Band with the Harlem
    Community Choir"; white label on styrene*

58348   Beatles, The Baby It's You/I'll Follow the Sun/
    Devil in Her Heart/Boys......................................1995............4.00
    —*All 4 tracks from BBC sessions*

58348 [PS]   Beatles, The Baby It's You/I'll Follow the Sun/
    Devil in Her Heart/Boys......................................1995............4.00

58497   Beatles, The Free as a Bird/Christmas Time
    (Is Here Again)..1995............4.00
    —*Small center hole; all with large hole were "dinked"
    somewhere other than when manufactured and have little,
    if any, value*

58497 [PS]   Beatles, The Free as a Bird/Christmas Time
    (Is Here Again)..1995............4.00

58544   Beatles, The Real Love/Baby's in Black (Live)....1996............3.00
    —*Small center hole; all with large hole were "dinked"
    somewhere other than when manufactured and have little,
    if any, value*

58544 [PS]   Beatles, TheReal Love/Baby's in Black (Live)....1996............3.00

Albums

SBC-100 [M]   Beatles, The The Beatles' Christmas Album....1970........400.00
    —*Fan club issue of the seven Christmas messages;
    very good counterfeits exist*

SWBO-101 [(2)]Beatles, The The Beatles...................................1968.........200.00
    —*Numbered copy; includes four individual photos and large
    poster (included in value); because the white cover shows ring
    wear so readily, this is an EXTREMELY difficult album to find in
    near-mint condition*

SWBO-101 [(2)]Beatles, The The Beatles...................................1975...........70.00
    —*With "All Rights Reserved" on labels; title in black on cover;
    photos and poster of thinner stock than originals*

SWBO-101 [(2)]Beatles, The The Beatles ....197?..........60.00
    —*Un-numbered copy; includes four individual photos and large
    poster (included in value)*

SW-153 [P]   Beatles, The Yellow Submarine.......................1969..........50.00
    —*With Capitol logo on Side 2 bottom. "Only a Northern Song"
    is rechanneled.*

SW-153 [P]   Beatles, The Yellow Submarine.......................1971..........20.00
    —*With "Mfd. by Apple" on label*

SW-153 [P]   Beatles, The Yellow Submarine.......................1975..........25.00
    —*With "All Rights Reserved" on label*

SO-383   Beatles, The Abbey Road ....1969..........75.00
    —*With Capitol logo on Side 2 bottom; "Her Majesty" is NOT .
    listed on either the jacket or the label*

SO-383   Beatles, The Abbey Road ....1969..........40.00
    —*With Capitol logo on Side 2 bottom; "Her Majesty" IS listed
    on both the jacket and the label*

SO-383   Beatles, The Abbey Road ....1969..........20.00
    —*With "Mfd. by Apple" on label; "Her Majesty" is NOT listed
    on the label*

SO-383   Beatles, The Abbey Road ....1969..........20.00
    —*With "Mfd. by Apple" on label; "Her Majesty" IS listed
    on the label*

SO-383   Beatles, The Abbey Road ....1975..........25.00
    —*With "All Rights Reserved" on label, either in black print or
    in light print along label edge (both versions exist)*

SO-385 [DJ]   Beatles, The The Beatles Again ....1970......8000.00
    —*Prototype covers with "The Beatles Again" on cover; not ...
    released to the general public. This is NOT a standard issue!*

SW-385   Beatles, The Hey Jude ....1970..........40.00
    —*Label calls the LP "The Beatles Again"; record is "SO-385"
    (this could be found in retail stores as late as 1973)*

SW-385   Beatles, The Hey Jude ....1970..........25.00
    —*Label calls the LP "The Beatles Again"; record is "SW-385"*

SW-385   Beatles, The Hey Jude ....1970..........75.00
    —*With Capitol logo on Side 2 bottom; label calls the LP
    "Hey Jude"*

SW-385   Beatles, The Hey Jude.....................................1970..........20.00
    —*With "Mfd. by Apple" on label; label calls the LP "Hey Jude"*

SW-385   Beatles, The Hey Jude.....................................1975..........25.00
    —*With "All Rights Reserved" on label; label calls the LP "Hey Jude"*

STCH-639 [(3)]Harrison, George All Things Must Pass..........1970..........40.00
    —*Apple labels on first two records and "Apple Jam" labels on
    third; includes poster and lyric innersleeves*

ST-3350   Harrison, George Wonderwall Music ....1968..........25.00
    —*With "Mfd. by Apple" on label*

ST-3350   Harrison, George Wonderwall Music ....1968........150.00
    —*With Capitol logo on Side 2 bottom*

ST-3350   Harrison, George
    Wonderwall Music Bonus Photo......................1968..........5.00

ST-3351   Hopkin, Mary Post Card...............................1969..........25.00

ST-5-3351   Hopkin, Mary Post Card...............................1969..........30.00
    —*Capitol Record Club edition*

SKAO 3352   Taylor, James James Taylor ....1969..........25.00
    —*With title in black print*

SKAO 3352   Taylor, James James Taylor ....1970..........20.00
    —*With title in orange print*

ST-3353   Modern Jazz Quartet, The
    Under the Jasmine Tree ....1969..........25.00

ST-5-3353   Modern Jazz Quartet, The
    Under the Jasmine Tree ....1969..........40.00
    —*Capitol Record Club edition*

ST-3354   Lomax, JackieIs This What You Want?.............1969..........25.00

ST-3355   BadfingerMaybe Tomorrow...............................1969......2000.00
    —*As "The Iveys"; album not released in US; price is for an LP
    slick, which does exist*

ST-3359   Preston, Billy That's the Way God Planned It .1969..........50.00
    —*Cover has close-up of Billy Preston*

ST-3359   Preston, Billy That's the Way God Planned It .1972..........20.00
    —*Cover has multiple images of Billy Preston*

STAO-3360   Modern Jazz Quartet, The Space ....1970..........25.00

STAO-5-3360   Modern Jazz Quartet, The Space ....1970..........40.00
    —*Capitol Record Club edition*

SMAX-3361   Lennon, John Wedding Album ....1969........150.00
    —*With photo strip, postcard, poster of wedding photos, poster
    of lithographs, "Bagism" bag, booklet, photo of slice of
    wedding cake. Missing inserts reduce the value.*

SW-3362   Lennon, John Live Peace in Toronto 1969 .....1970..........15.00
    —*By "The Plastic Ono Band" — without calendar*

SW-3362   Lennon, John Live Peace in Toronto 1969 .....1970..........20.00
    —*By "The Plastic Ono Band"; with calendar*

STAO-3363   McCartney, Paul McCartney...........................1970..........25.00
    —*"McCartney" and "Paul McCartney" on separate lines on ...
    label; New York address on back cover*

STAO-3363   McCartney, Paul McCartney...........................1970..........30.00
    —*"McCartney" and "Paul McCartney" on separate lines on ...
    label; California address on back cover*

Catalog No.	Artist	Title	Year	Value	Notes
STAO-3363	McCartney, Paul	McCartney	1970	80.00	—Apple label with small Capitol logo on B-side
STAO-3363	McCartney, Paul	McCartney	1970	20.00	—Only "McCartney" on label; back cover does NOT say "An Abkco managed company"
STAO-3363	McCartney, Paul	McCartney	1970	25.00	—Only "McCartney" on label; back cover says "An Abkco managed company"
SMAS-3363	McCartney, Paul	McCartney	1975	100.00	—With "All Rights Reserved" on label
SMAS-3363	McCartney, Paul	McCartney	197?	20.00	—New prefix on label
ST 3364	BadfingerMagic	Christian Music	1970	30.00	—With Capitol logo on Side 2 bottom
ST 3364	BadfingerMagic	Christian Music	1970	20.00	
SW-3365	Starr, Ringo	Sentimental Journey	1970	20.00	
SKAO 3367	Badfinger	No Dice	1970	30.00	
SMAS-3368	Starr, Ringo	Beaucoups of Blues	1970	20.00	
SMAS-3369	Tavener, John	The Whale	1972	20.00	
ST-3370	Preston, Billy	Encouraging Words	1970	20.00	
ST-3371	Troy, Doris	Doris Troy	1970	25.00	
SW-3372	Lennon, John	John Lennon Plastic Ono Band	1970	20.00	
SW-3373	Ono, Yoko	Yoko Ono Plastic Ono Band	1970	20.00	
MAS-3375 [M]	McCartney, Paul	Ram	1971	4000.00	—Credited to "Paul and Linda McCartney"; mono record in stereo cover for radio station use only
SMAS-3375	McCartney, Paul	Ram	1971	15.00	—Credited to "Paul and Linda McCartney"; unsliced apple on one label, sliced apple on other
SMAS-3375	McCartney, Paul	Ram	1971	30.00	—Credited to "Paul and Linda McCartney"; unsliced apple on both labels
SMAS-3375	McCartney, Paul	Ram	1971	50.00	—Credited to "Paul and Linda McCartney"; Apple label with small Capitol logo on B-side
SMAS-3375	McCartney, Paul	Ram	1975	100.00	—Credited to "Paul and Linda McCartney"; with "All Rights Reserved" on label
SKAO-3376	Radha Krishna Temple	The Radha Krishna Temple	1971	20.00	
SW-3377	Soundtrack	Come together	1971	20.00	
SW-3379	Lennon, John	Imagine	1971	20.00	—With either of two postcard inserts, lyric sleeve, poster
SW-3379	Lennon, John	Imagine	1975	20.00	—"All Rights Reserved" label
SVBB-3380 [(2)]	Ono, Yoko	Fly	1971	25.00	
SMAS-3381	Hopkin, Mary	Earth Song/Ocean Song	1970	25.00	
SWAO-3384	Shankar, Ravi	Raga	1971	25.00	
STCX-3385 [(3)]	Harrison, George, and Friends	The Concert for Bangla Desh	1971	40.00	—With 64-page booklet and custom innersleeves
STCX-3385 [(3)]	Harrison, George, and Friends	The Concert for Bangla Desh	1975	50.00	—As above, but with "All Rights Reserved" on labels
SW-3386	McCartney, Paul	Wild Life	1971	15.00	—Credited to "Wings"
SW 3387	Badfinger	Straight Up	1971	60.00	
SWAO-3388	Soundtrack	El Topo	1972	40.00	
SMAS-3389	Elephants Memory	Elephants Memory	1972	25.00	
SMAS-3390	Van Eaten, Lon and Derrek	Brother	1972	15.00	
SW-3391	Peel, David	The Pope Smokes Dope	1972	75.00	
SVBB-3392 [(2)]	Lennon, John	Some Time in New York City	1972	30.00	—By John and Yoko; with photo card and petition
SVBB-3392 [(2) DJ]	Lennon, John	Some Time in New York City	1972	1000.00	—White label promo
SVBB-3392 [(2)]	Ono, Yoko	Some Time in New York City	1972	0.00	—By John and Yoko
SW-3395	Hopkin, Mary	Those Were the Days	1972	40.00	
SVBB-3396 [(2)]	Shankar, Ravi	Ravi Shankar In Concert	1973	40.00	
SVBB-3399 [(2)]	Ono, Yoko	Approximately Infinite Universe	1973	25.00	
SW 3400 [M]	Various Artists	Phil Spector's Christmas Album	1972	30.00	
SKBO-3403 [P]	Beatles, The	The Beatles 1962-1966	1973	30.00	—Custom red Apple labels. "Love Me Do" and "I Want to Hold Your Hand" are rechanneled; "She Loves You," "A Hard Day's Night," "I Feel Fine" and "Ticket to Ride" are mono; "From Me to You," "Can't Buy Me Love" and everything else is stereo.
SKBO-3403 [P]	Beatles, The	The Beatles 1962-1966	1975	50.00	—Custom red Apple labels with "All Rights Reserved" on labels
SKBO-3404 [B]	Beatles, The	The Beatles 1967-1970	1973	30.00	—Custom blue Apple labels. "Hello Goodbye" and "Penny Lane" are mono, all others stereo.
SKBO-3404 [B]	Beatles, The	The Beatles 1967-1970	1975	50.00	—Custom blue Apple labels with "All Rights Reserved" on labels
SMAL-3409	McCartney, Paul	Red Rose Speedway	1973	20.00	—Credited to "Paul McCartney and Wings"; with bound-in booklet
SMAS-3410	Harrison, George	Living in the Material World	1973	15.00	
SW 3411	Badfinger	Ass	1973	20.00	
SW-3412	Ono, Yoko	Feeling the Space	1973	20.00	
SWAL-3413	Starr, Ringo	Ringo	1973	20.00	—Standard issue with booklet; Side 1, Song 2 identified on cover as "Hold On"
SWAL-3413	Starr, Ringo	Ringo	1973	400.00	—With a 5:26 version of "Six O'Clock." On later copies, the song is shortened to 4:05 though the label still says 5:26. All known copies have a promo punch-hole in top corner of jacket; on Side 2 record, "Six O'Clock" will be the widest track.
SWAL-3413	Starr, Ringo	Ringo	1974	25.00	—Later issue with booklet; Side 1, Song 2 identified on cover as "Have You Seen My Baby"
SW-3414	Lennon, John	Mind Games	1973	20.00	
SO-3415	McCartney, Paul	Band on the Run	1973	20.00	—Credited to "Paul McCartney and Wings"; with photo innersleeve and poster
SW-3416	Lennon, John	Walls and Bridges	1974	20.00	—With fold-open segmented front cover
SW-3417	Starr, Ringo	Goodnight Vienna	1974	12.00	
SMAS-3418	Harrison, George	Dark Horse	1974	15.00	
SK-3419	Lennon, John	Rock 'n' Roll	1975	20.00	
SW-3420	Harrison, George	Extra Texture (Read All About It)	1975	15.00	
SW-3421	Lennon, John	Shaved Fish	1975	20.00	
SW-3422	Starr, Ringo	Blast from Your Past	1975	15.00	
T-5001	Lennon, John	Two Virgins — Unfinished Music No. 1	1968	50.00	—With Yoko Ono; without brown bag
T-5001	Lennon, John	Two Virgins — Unfinished Music No. 1	1968	150.00	—With Yoko Ono; price with brown bag
T-5001	Lennon, John	Two Virgins — Unfinished Music No. 1	1968	150.00	—With Yoko Ono; with die-cut bag

T-5001   Lennon, John
Two Virgins — Unfinished Music No. 1 ....1985..........15.00
—*With Yoko Ono; reissue, flat label*

SPRO-6210 [DJ]McCartney, Paul Brung to Ewe By................1971......400.00
—*Promo-only radio spots for "Ram"; counterfeits have uneven spacing between tracks*

SPRO 11206/7 [EP]Beatles, The Anthology 2 Sampler ....1996........150.00
—*Promo-only collection sent to college radio stations*

C1-8-31796 [(2)]Beatles, The Live at the BBC........................1994..........50.00

AR-34001   Beatles, The Let It Be.....................................1970..........25.00
—*Red Apple label; originals have "Bell Sound" stamped in trail-off area, counterfeits do not*

C1-8-34445 [(3)]Beatles, The Anthology 1 ....1995..........40.00
—*All copies distributed in the U.S. were manufactured in the U.K. with no distinguishing marks (some LPs imported directly from the U.K. have "Made in England" stickers, which can be removed easily)*

C1-8-34448 [(3)]Beatles, The Anthology 2 ....1996..........40.00

C1-8-34451 [(3)]Beatles, The Anthology 3 ....1996..........30.00

C1-97036 [B] Beatles, The The Beatles 1962-1966 ....1993..........25.00
—*Custom red Apple labels; red vinyl; all copies pressed in U.K; U.S. versions have a bar-code sticker over the international bar code on back cover. "Love Me Do," "Please Please Me," "From Me to You" and "She Loves You" are mono; all others are stereo.*

C1-97039   Beatles, The The Beatles 1967-1970 ....1993..........25.00
—*Custom blue Apple labels; blue vinyl; all copies pressed in U.K.; U.S. versions have a bar-code sticker over the international bar code on back cover*

Apple/Capitol
Albums

(no #) [(10)] Beatles, The
The Beatles Special Limited Edition ....1974.....1200.00

(no #) [(17)] Beatles, The
The Beatles 10th Anniversary Box Set ....1974.....2000.00

ST 2047 [P] Beatles, The Meet the Beatles!...................1968..........40.00
—*With Capitol logo on Side 2 bottom*

ST 2047 [P] Beatles, The Meet the Beatles!...................1971..........20.00
—*With "Mfd. by Apple" on label*

ST 2047 [P] Beatles, The Meet the Beatles!...................1975..........25.00
—*With "All Rights Reserved" on label*

ST 2080 [P] Beatles, The The Beatles' Second Album........1968..........40.00
—*With Capitol logo on Side 2 bottom*

ST 2080 [P] Beatles, The The Beatles' Second Album........1971..........20.00
—*With "Mfd. by Apple" on label*

ST 2080 [P] Beatles, The The Beatles' Second Album........1975..........25.00
—*With "All Rights Reserved" on label*

ST 2108 [S] Beatles, The Something New ....1968..........40.00
—*With Capitol logo on Side 2 bottom*

ST 2108 [S] Beatles, The Something New ....1971..........20.00
—*With "Mfd. by Apple" on label*

ST 2108 [S] Beatles, The Something New ....1975..........25.00
—*With "All Rights Reserved" on label*

STBO 2222 [(2) P]Beatles, The The Beatles' Story.................1968..........50.00
—*With Capitol logo on bottom of B-side of both records*

STBO 2222 [(2) P]Beatles, The The Beatles' Story.................1971..........30.00
—*With "Mfd. by Apple" on labels*

STBO 2222 [(2) P]Beatles, The The Beatles' Story.................1975..........40.00
—*With "All Rights Reserved" on labels*

ST 2228 [P] Beatles, The Beatles '65.................................1968..........40.00
—*With Capitol logo on Side 2 bottom*

ST 2228 [P] Beatles, The Beatles '65.................................1971..........20.00
—*With "Mfd. by Apple" on label*

ST 2228 [P] Beatles, The Beatles '65.................................1975..........25.00
—*With "All Rights Reserved" on label*

ST 2309 [P] Beatles, The The Early Beatles ....1969..........40.00
—*With Capitol logo on Side 2 bottom*

ST 2309 [P] Beatles, The The Early Beatles ....1971..........20.00
—*With "Mfd. by Apple" on label*

ST 2309 [P] Beatles, The The Early Beatles ....1975..........25.00
—*With "All Rights Reserved" on label*

ST 2358 [P] Beatles, The Beatles VI ....1969..........40.00
—*With Capitol logo on Side 2 bottom*

ST 2358 [P] Beatles, The Beatles VI ....1971..........20.00
—*With "Mfd. by Apple" on label*

ST 2358 [P] Beatles, The Beatles VI ....1975..........25.00
—*With "All Rights Reserved" on label*

SMAS 2386 [P]Beatles, The Help!...1969..........40.00
—*With Capitol logo on Side 2 bottom*

SMAS 2386 [P]Beatles, The Help!...1971..........20.00
—*With "Mfd. by Apple" on label*

SMAS 2386 [P]Beatles, The Help!...1975..........25.00
—*With "All Rights Reserved" on label*

ST 2442 [S] Beatles, The Rubber Soul ....1969..........40.00
—*With Capitol logo on Side 2 bottom*

ST 2442 [S] Beatles, The Rubber Soul ....1971..........20.00
—*With "Mfd. by Apple" on label*

ST 2442 [S] Beatles, The Rubber Soul ....1975..........25.00
—*With "All Rights Reserved" on label*

ST 2553 [P] Beatles, The Yesterday and Today..................1969..........40.00
—*With Capitol logo on Side 2 bottom*

ST 2553 [P] Beatles, The Yesterday and Today..................1971..........20.00
—*With "Mfd. by Apple" on label*

ST 2553 [S] Beatles, The Yesterday and Today..................1971..........25.00
—*With "Mfd. by Apple" on label; all 11 tracks are in true stereo. Check for a triangle in the record's trail-off area.*

ST 2553 [P] Beatles, The Yesterday and Today..................1975..........25.00
—*With "All Rights Reserved" on label*

ST 2576 [S] Beatles, The Revolver ....1969..........40.00
—*With Capitol logo on Side 2 bottom*

ST 2576 [S] Beatles, The Revolver ....1971..........20.00
—*With "Mfd. by Apple" on label*

ST 2576 [S] Beatles, The Revolver ....1975..........25.00
—*With "All Rights Reserved" on label*

SMAS 2653 [S]Beatles, The
Sgt. Pepper's Lonely Hearts Club Band ....1969..........40.00
—*With Capitol logo on Side 2 bottom*

SMAS 2653 [S]Beatles, The
Sgt. Pepper's Lonely Hearts Club Band ....1971..........25.00
—*With "Mfd. by Apple" on label*

SMAS 2653 [S]Beatles, The
Sgt. Pepper's Lonely Hearts Club Band ....1975..........25.00
—*With "All Rights Reserved" on label*

SMAL 2835 [P] Beatles, The Magical Mystery Tour ....1969..........40.00
—*With Capitol logo on Side 2 bottom; with 24-page booklet*

SMAL 2835 [P] Beatles, The Magical Mystery Tour ....1971..........20.00
—*With "Mfd. by Apple" on label; with 24-page booklet*

SMAL 2835 [P] Beatles, The Magical Mystery Tour ....1975..........25.00
—*With "All Rights Reserved" on label; with 24-page booklet*

Zapple
Albums

ST-3357   Lennon, John
Life with the Lions — Unfinished Music No. 2 ....1969..........20.00
—*With Yoko Ono*

ST-3358   Harrison, George Electronic Sound ....1969..........40.00 ■

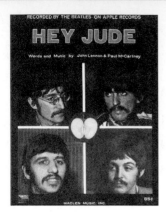

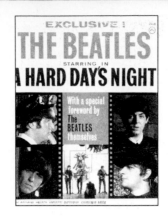

BEATLES, THE
12-Inch Singles
(NO LABEL)

Number	Title (A Side/B Side)	Yr	VG	VG+	NM
(no #) [DJ]	Merry Christmas and Happy New Year	1965	125.00	250.00	500.00

—*Promo item from KYA Radio, San Francisco; B-side is blank*

45s
APPLE

Number	Title (A Side/B Side)	Yr	VG	VG+	NM
Promo-1970[DJ]	Dialogue from the Beatles' Motion Picture "Let It Be"	1970	15.00	30.00	60.00
2056	Hello Goodbye/I Am the Walrus	1971	7.50	15.00	30.00

—*With star on A-side label*

2056	Hello Goodbye/I Am the Walrus	1971	2.50	5.00	10.00

—*Without star on A-side label*

2056	Hello Goodbye/I Am the Walrus	1975	5.00	10.00	20.00

—*With "All Rights Reserved" disclaimer*

2138	Lady Madonna/The Inner Light	1971	7.50	15.00	30.00

—*With star on A-side label*

2138	Lady Madonna/The Inner Light	1971	2.50	5.00	10.00

—*Without star on A-side label*

2138	Lady Madonna/The Inner Light	1975	5.00	10.00	20.00

—*With "All Rights Reserved" disclaimer*

2276	Hey Jude/Revolution	1968	3.75	7.50	15.00

—*Original: With small Capitol logo on bottom of B-side label*

2276	Hey Jude/Revolution	1968	2.50	5.00	10.00

—*With "Mfd. by Apple" on label*

2276	Hey Jude/Revolution	1975	5.00	10.00	20.00

—*With "All Rights Reserved" disclaimer*

2490	Get Back/Don't Let Me Down	1969	2.50	5.00	10.00

—*Original: With small Capitol logo on bottom of B-side label*

2490	Get Back/Don't Let Me Down	1969	2.50	5.00	10.00

—*With "Mfd. by Apple" on label*

2490	Get Back/Don't Let Me Down	1975	5.00	10.00	20.00

—*With "All Rights Reserved" disclaimer*

2531	The Ballad of John and Yoko/Old Brown Shoe	1969	2.50	5.00	10.00

—*Original: With small Capitol logo on bottom of B-side label*

2531	The Ballad of John and Yoko/Old Brown Shoe	1969	2.50	5.00	10.00

—*With "Mfd. by Apple" on label*

2531 [PS]	The Ballad of John and Yoko/Old Brown Shoe	1969	25.00	50.00	100.00

2531	The Ballad of John and Yoko/Old Brown Shoe	1975	5.00	10.00	20.00

—*With "All Rights Reserved" disclaimer*

2654	Something/Come Together	1969	25.00	50.00	100.00

—*Original: With small Capitol logo on bottom of B-side label*

2654	Something/Come Together	1969	2.50	5.00	10.00

—*With "Mfd. by Apple" on label*

2654	Something/Come Together	1975	5.00	10.00	20.00

—*With "All Rights Reserved" disclaimer*

2764	Let It Be/You Know My Name (Look Up My Number)	1970	3.00	6.00	12.00

—*Original: With small Capitol logo on bottom of B-side label*

2764	Let It Be/You Know My Name (Look Up My Number)	1970	2.50	5.00	10.00

—*With "Mfd. by Apple" on label*

2764	Let It Be/You Know My Name (Look Up My Number)	1975	5.00	10.00	20.00

—*With "All Rights Reserved" disclaimer*

2764 [PS]	Let It Be/You Know My Name (Look Up the Number)	1970	25.00	50.00	100.00

2832	The Long and Winding Road/For You Blue	1970	5.00	10.00	20.00

—*Original: With small Capitol logo on bottom of B-side label*

2832	The Long and Winding Road/For You Blue	1970	2.50	5.00	10.00

—*With "Mfd. by Apple" on label*

2832 [PS]	The Long and Winding Road/For You Blue	1970	25.00	50.00	100.00

2832	The Long and Winding Road/For You Blue	1975	5.00	10.00	20.00

—*With "All Rights Reserved" disclaimer*

5112	I Want to Hold Your Hand/I Saw Her Standing There	1971	7.50	15.00	30.00

—*With star on label*

5112	I Want to Hold Your Hand/I Saw Her Standing There	1971	2.50	5.00	10.00

—*Without star on label*

5112	I Want to Hold Your Hand/I Saw Her Standing There	1975	5.00	10.00	20.00

—*With "All Rights Reserved" disclaimer on label*

5150	Can't Buy Me Love/You Can't Do That	1971	7.50	15.00	30.00

—*With star on A-side label*

5150	Can't Buy Me Love/You Can't Do That	1971	2.50	5.00	10.00

—*Without star on A-side label*

5150	Can't Buy Me Love/You Can't Do That	1975	3.75	7.50	15.00

—*With "All Rights Reserved" disclaimer on label*

5222	A Hard Day's Night/I Should Have Known Better	1971	7.50	15.00	30.00

—*With star on A-side label*

5222	A Hard Day's Night/I Should Have Known Better	1971	2.50	5.00	10.00

—*Without star on A-side label*

5222	A Hard Day's Night/I Should Have Known Better	1975	3.75	7.50	15.00

—*With "All Rights Reserved" disclaimer*

5234	I'll Cry Instead/I'm Happy Just to Dance with You	1971	7.50	15.00	30.00

—*With star on A-side label*

5234	I'll Cry Instead/I'm Happy Just to Dance with You	1971	2.50	5.00	10.00

—*Without star on A-side label*

5234	I'll Cry Instead/I'm Happy Just to Dance with You	1975	3.75	7.50	15.00

—*With "All Rights Reserved" disclaimer*

5235	And I Love Her/If I Fell	1971	7.50	15.00	30.00

—With star on A-side label

5235	And I Love Her/If I Fell	1971	2.50	5.00	10.00

—Without star on A-side label

5235	And I Love Her/If I Fell	1975	3.75	7.50	15.00

—With "All Rights Reserved" disclaimer

5255	Matchbox/Slow Down	1971	7.50	15.00	30.00

—With star on A-side label

5255	Matchbox/Slow Down	1971	2.50	5.00	10.00

—Without star on A-side label

5255	Matchbox/Slow Down	1975	3.75	7.50	15.00

—With "All Rights Reserved" disclaimer

5327	I Feel Fine/She's a Woman	1971	7.50	15.00	30.00

—With star on A-side label

5327	I Feel Fine/She's a Woman	1971	2.50	5.00	10.00

—Without star on A-side label

5327	I Feel Fine/She's a Woman	1975	3.75	7.50	15.00

—With "All Rights Reserved" disclaimer

5371	Eight Days a Week/I Don't Want to Spoil the Party	1971	7.50	15.00	30.00

—With star on A-side label

5371	Eight Days a Week/ I Don't Want to Spoil the Party	1971	2.50	5.00	10.00

—Without star on A-side label

5371	Eight Days a Week/ I Don't Want to Spoil the Party	1975	3.75	7.50	15.00

—With "All Rights Reserved" disclaimer

5407	Ticket to Ride/Yes It Is	1971	7.50	15.00	30.00

—With star on A-side label

5407	Ticket to Ride/Yes It Is	1971	2.50	5.00	10.00

—Without star on A-side label

5407	Ticket to Ride/Yes It Is	1975	3.75	7.50	15.00

—With "All Rights Reserved" disclaimer

5476	Help!/I'm Down	1971	7.50	15.00	30.00

—With star on A-side label

5476	Help!/I'm Down	1971	2.50	5.00	10.00

—Without star on A-side label

5476	Help!/I'm Down	1975	3.75	7.50	15.00

—With "All Rights Reserved" disclaimer

5498	Yesterday/Act Naturally	1971	7.50	15.00	30.00

—With star on A-side label

5498	Yesterday/Act Naturally	1971	2.50	5.00	10.00

—Without star on A-side label

5498	Yesterday/Act Naturally	1975	3.75	7.50	15.00

—With "All Rights Reserved" disclaimer

5555	We Can Work It Out/Day Tripper	1971	7.50	15.00	30.00

—With star on A-side label

5555	We Can Work It Out/Day Tripper	1971	2.50	5.00	10.00

—Without star on A-side label

5555	We Can Work It Out/Day Tripper	1975	3.75	7.50	15.00

—With "All Rights Reserved" disclaimer

5587	Nowhere Man/What Goes On	1971	7.50	15.00	30.00

—With star on A-side label

5587	Nowhere Man/What Goes On	1971	2.50	5.00	10.00

—Without star on A-side label

5587	Nowhere Man/What Goes On	1975	3.75	7.50	15.00

—With "All Rights Reserved" disclaimer

5651	Paperback Writer/Rain	1971	7.50	15.00	30.00

—With star on A-side label

5651	Paperback Writer/Rain	1971	2.50	5.00	10.00

—Without star on A-side label

5651	Paperback Writer/Rain	1975	3.75	7.50	15.00

—With "All Rights Reserved" disclaimer

5715	Yellow Submarine/Eleanor Rigby	1971	7.50	15.00	30.00

—With star on A-side label

5715	Yellow Submarine/Eleanor Rigby	1971	2.50	5.00	10.00

—Without star on A-side label

5715	Yellow Submarine/Eleanor Rigby	1975	3.75	7.50	15.00

—With "All Rights Reserved" disclaimer

5810	Penny Lane/Strawberry Fields Forever	1971	7.50	15.00	30.00

—With star on A-side label

5810	Penny Lane/Strawberry Fields Forever	1971	2.50	5.00	10.00

—Without star on A-side label

5810	Penny Lane/Strawberry Fields Forever	1975	3.75	7.50	15.00

—With "All Rights Reserved" disclaimer

5964	All You Need Is Love/Baby, You're a Rich Man	1971	7.50	15.00	30.00

—With star on A-side label

5964	All You Need Is Love/Baby, You're a Rich Man	1971	2.50	5.00	10.00

—Without star on A-side label

5964	All You Need Is Love/Baby, You're a Rich Man	1975	3.75	7.50	15.00

—With "All Rights Reserved" disclaimer

58348	Baby It's You/I'll Follow the Sun/ Devil in Her Heart/Boys	1995	—	2.00	4.00

—All 4 tracks from BBC sessions

58348 [PS]	Baby It's You/I'll Follow the Sun/ Devil in Her Heart/Boys	1995	—	2.00	4.00

58497	Free as a Bird/Christmas Time (Is Here Again)	1995	—	—	2.00 4.00

—Small center hole; all with large hole were "dinked" somewhere other than when manufactured and have little, if any, value

58497 [PS]	Free as a Bird/Christmas Time (Is Here Again)	1995	—	—	2.00 4.00

58544	Real Love/Baby's in Black (Live)	1996	—	—	3.00

—Small center hole; all with large hole were "dinked" somewhere other than when manufactured and have little, if any, value

Catalog	Title	Year	VG	VG+	NM
58544 [PS]	Real Love/Baby's in Black (Live)	1996	—	—	3.00

APPLE/AMERICOM

Catalog	Title	Year	VG	VG+	NM
2276/M-221	Hey Jude/Revolution	1969	75.00	150.00	300.00
	—Four-inch flexi-disc sold in vending machines; "Hey Jude" is edited to 3:25				
2490/M-335	Get Back/Don't Let Me Down	1969	250.00	500.00	1000.00
	—Four-inch flexi-disc sold in vending machines				
2531/M-382	The Ballad of John and Yoko/ Old Brown Shoe	1969	200.00	400.00	800.00
	—Four-inch flexi-disc sold in vending machines				
5715	Yellow Submarine/Eleanor Rigby	1969	1000.00	1500.00	2000.00
	—Four-inch flexi-disc sold in vending machines				

ATCO

Catalog	Title	Year	VG	VG+	NM
6302	Sweet Georgia Brown/ Take Out Some Insurance On Me Baby	1964	50.00	100.00	200.00
6308	Ain't She Sweet/Nobody's Child	1964	12.50	25.00	50.00
	—With "Vocal by John Lennon" on left of label				
6308 [PS]	Ain't She Sweet/Nobody's Child	1964	125.00	250.00	500.00
	—Sleeves with black and green print are reproductions				
6308	Ain't She Sweet/Nobody's Child	1964	15.00	30.00	60.00
	—With "Vocal by John Lennon" under "The Beatles"				

ATLANTIC

Catalog	Title	Year	VG	VG+	NM
OS-13243	Ain't She Sweet/Sweet Georgia Brown	1983	2.50	5.00	10.00
	—"Oldies Series"				

BACKSTAGE

Catalog	Title	Year	VG	VG+	NM
1112 [DJ]	Like Dreamers Do/Love of the Loved	1982	6.25	12.50	25.00
	—Promotional 45 from "Oui" magazine				
1122 [DJ]	Love of the Loved/Memphis	1983	6.25	12.50	25.00
	—Promotional picture disc				
1133 [DJ]	Like Dreamers Do/Three Cool Cats	1983	6.25	12.50	25.00
	—Promotional picture disc				
1155 [DJ]	Crying, Waiting, Hoping/ Take Good Care of My Baby	1983	6.25	12.50	25.00

BEATLES FAN CLUB

Catalog	Title	Year	VG	VG+	NM
(1964)	Season's Greetings from the Beatles	1964	75.00	150.00	300.00
	—Tri-fold soundcard				
(1965)	The Beatles Third Christmas Record	1965	20.00	40.00	80.00
	—Flexi-disc				
(1965) [PS]	The Beatles Third Christmas Record	1965	25.00	50.00	100.00
(1966)	Everywhere It's Christmas	1966	37.50	75.00	150.00
	—Postcard				
(1967)	Christmastime Is Here Again	1967	37.50	75.00	150.00
	—Postcard				
(1968) H-2041	The Beatles 1968 Christmas Record	1968	15.00	30.00	60.00
	—Flexi-disc				
(1968) H-2041 [PS]	The Beatles 1968 Christmas Record	1968	17.50	35.00	70.00
(1969) H-2565	Happy Christmas 1969	1969	10.00	20.00	40.00
	—Flexi-disc				
(1969) H-2565 [PS]	Happy Christmas 1969	1969	15.00	30.00	60.00

CAPITOL

Catalog	Title	Year	VG	VG+	NM
2056	Hello Goodbye/I Am the Walrus	1967	7.50	15.00	30.00
	—Original: Orange and yellow swirl, without "A Subsidiary Of"... in perimeter label print; publishing credited to "Maclen" (we're not sure which came first)				
2056	Hello Goodbye/I Am the Walrus	1967	7.50	15.00	30.00
	—Original: Orange and yellow swirl, without "A Subsidiary Of"... in perimeter label print; publishing credited to "Comet" (we're not sure which came first)				
P 2056 [DJ]	Hello Goodbye/I Am the Walrus	1967	62.50	125.00	250.00
	—Light green label promo				
2056 [PS]	Hello Goodbye/I Am the Walrus	1967	25.00	50.00	100.00
2056	Hello Goodbye/I Am the Walrus	1968	12.50	25.00	50.00
	—Orange and yellow swirl label with "A Subsidiary Of" in perimeter print				
2056	Hello Goodbye/I Am the Walrus	1969	15.00	30.00	60.00
	—Red and orange "target" label with Capitol dome logo				

Catalog	Title	Year	VG	VG+	NM
2056	Hello Goodbye/I Am the Walrus	1969	5.00	10.00	20.00
	—Red and orange "target" label with Capitol round logo				
2056	Hello Goodbye/I Am the Walrus	1976	—	3.00	6.00
	—Orange label with "Capitol" at bottom				
2056	Hello Goodbye/I Am the Walrus	1978	2.00	4.00	8.00
	—Purple label label has reeded edge				
2056	Hello Goodbye/I Am the Walrus	1983	—	3.00	6.00
	—Black label with colorband				
2056	Hello Goodbye/I Am the Walrus	1988	—	2.50	5.00
	—Purple label; label has smooth edge				
2138	Lady Madonna/The Inner Light	1968	7.50	15.00	30.00
	—Original: Orange and yellow swirl, without "A Subsidiary Of"... in perimeter label print				
2138	Lady Madonna/The Inner Light	1968	12.50	25.00	50.00
	—Orange and yellow swirl label with "A Subsidiary Of" in perimeter print				
P 2138 [DJ]	Lady Madonna/The Inner Light	1968	50.00	100.00	200.00
	—Light green label promo				
2138 [PS]	Lady Madonna/The Inner Light	1968	25.00	50.00	100.00
2138 [PS]	Lady Madonna/The Inner Light	1968	5.00	10.00	20.00
	—"Beatles Fan Club" insert that was issued with above sleeve. Originals are glossy.				
2138	Lady Madonna/The Inner Light	1969	15.00	30.00	60.00
	—Red and orange "target" label with Capitol dome logo				
2138	Lady Madonna/The Inner Light	1969	5.00	10.00	20.00
	—Red and orange "target" label with Capitol round logo				
2138	Lady Madonna/The Inner Light	1976	—	3.00	6.00
	—Orange label with "Capitol" at bottom				
2138	Lady Madonna/The Inner Light	1978	2.00	4.00	8.00
	—Purple label; label has reeded edge				
2138	Lady Madonna/The Inner Light	1983	—	3.00	6.00
	—Black label with colorband				
2138	Lady Madonna/The Inner Light	1988	—	2.50	5.00
	—Purple label; label has smooth edge				
2276	Hey Jude/Revolution	1976	—	3.00	6.00
	—Orange label with "Capitol" at bottom				
2276	Hey Jude/Revolution	1978	2.00	4.00	8.00
	—Purple label; label has reeded edge				
2276	Hey Jude/Revolution	1983	—	3.00	6.00
	—Black label with colorband				
2276	Hey Jude/Revolution	1988	—	2.50	5.00
	—Purple label; label has smooth edge				
2490	Get Back/Don't Let Me Down	1976	—	3.00	6.00
	—Orange label with "Capitol" at bottom				
2490	Get Back/Don't Let Me Down	1978	2.00	4.00	8.00
	—Purple label; label has reeded edge				
2490	Get Back/Don't Let Me Down	1983	—	3.00	6.00
	—Black label with colorband; "Get Back" replaced by LP version as on Let It Be				
2490	Get Back/Don't Let Me Down	1988	—	2.50	5.00
	—Purple label; label has smooth edge; "Get Back" replaced by LP version as on Let It Be				
2531	The Ballad of John and Yoko/Old Brown Shoe	1976	—	—	—
	—Orange label with "Capitol" at bottom; should exist, but not known to exist				
2531	The Ballad of John and Yoko/ Old Brown Shoe	1978	—	3.00	6.00
	—Purple label; label has reeded edge				
2531	The Ballad of John and Yoko/ Old Brown Shoe	1983	—	3.50	7.00
	—Black label with colorband				
2531	The Ballad of John and Yoko/ Old Brown Shoe	1988	—	3.00	6.00
	—Purple label; label has smooth edge				
2654	Something/Come Together	1976	—	3.00	6.00
	—Orange label with "Capitol" at bottom				
2654	Something/Come Together	1978	—	3.00	6.00
	—Purple label; label has reeded edge				
2654	Something/Come Together	1983	—	3.00	6.00
	—Black label with colorband				

Cat.	Title	Year			
2654	Something/Come Together	1988	—	2.50	5.00

—*Purple label; label has smooth edge*

| 2764 | Let It Be/You Know My Name (Look Up My Number) | 1976 | — | 3.00 | 6.00 |

—*Orange label with "Capitol" at bottom*

| 2764 | Let It Be/You Know My Name (Look Up My Number) | 1978 | 2.00 | 4.00 | 8.00 |

—*Purple label; label has reeded edge*

| 2764 | Let It Be/You Know My Name (Look Up My Number) | 1983 | — | 3.00 | 6.00 |

—*Black label with colorband*

| 2764 | Let It Be/You Know My Name (Look Up My Number) | 1988 | — | 2.50 | 5.00 |

—*Purple label; label has smooth edge*

| 2832 | The Long and Winding Road/For You Blue | 1976 | — | 3.00 | 6.00 |

—*Orange label with "Capitol" at bottom*

| 2832 | The Long and Winding Road/For You Blue | 1978 | 2.00 | 4.00 | 8.00 |

—*Purple label; label has reeded edge*

| 2832 | The Long and Winding Road/For You Blue | 1983 | — | 3.00 | 6.00 |

—*Black label with colorband*

| 2832 | The Long and Winding Road/For You Blue | 1988 | — | 2.50 | 5.00 |

—*Purple label; label has smooth edge*

| P-4274 [DJ] | Got to Get You Into My Life (mono/stereo) | 1976 | 10.00 | 20.00 | 40.00 |

| 4274 | Got to Get You Into My Life/Helter Skelter | 1976 | — | 3.00 | 6.00 |

—*Original: Orange label with "Capitol" at bottom, George Martin's name not on label*

| 4274 [PS] | Got to Get You Into My Life/Helter Skelter | 1976 | — | 2.50 | 5.00 |

| 4274 | Got to Get You Into My Life/Helter Skelter | 1976 | 2.50 | 5.00 | 10.00 |

—*Orange label with "Capitol" at bottom, George Martin's name is on label*

| 4274 | Got to Get You Into My Life/Helter Skelter | 1978 | — | 3.00 | 6.00 |

—*Purple label; label has reeded edge*

| 4274 | Got to Get You Into My Life/Helter Skelter | 1983 | — | 3.00 | 6.00 |

—*Black label with colorband*

| 4274 | Got to Get You Into My Life/Helter Skelter | 1988 | — | 2.50 | 5.00 |

—*Purple label; label has smooth edge*

| P-4274 [DJ] | Helter Skelter (mono/stereo) | 1976 | 10.00 | 20.00 | 40.00 |

| P-4347 [DJ] | Ob-La-Di, Ob-La-Da (mono/stereo) | 1976 | 10.00 | 20.00 | 40.00 |

| 4347 | Ob-La-Di, Ob-La-Da/Julia | 1976 | 2.00 | 4.00 | 8.00 |

—*Original: Orange label with "Capitol" at bottom*

| 4347 [PS] | Ob-La-Di, Ob-La-Da/Julia | 1976 | 2.00 | 4.00 | 8.00 |

—*Sleeves are individually numbered; very low numbers (under 1000) can fetch premium prices*

| 4347 | Ob-La-Di, Ob-La-Da/Julia | 1978 | 2.00 | 4.00 | 8.00 |

—*Purple label; label has reeded edge*

| 4347 | Ob-La-Di, Ob-La-Da/Julia | 1983 | — | 3.00 | 6.00 |

—*Black label with colorband*

| 4347 | Ob-La-Di, Ob-La-Da/Julia | 1988 | — | 2.50 | 5.00 |

—*Purple label; label has smooth edge*

| P-4506 [DJ] | Girl (mono/stereo) | 1977 | 50.00 | 100.00 | 200.00 |

—*Promo only; all colored vinyl versions are counterfeits*

| 4506 [PS] | Girl/You're Going to Lose That Girl | 1977 | 3.75 | 7.50 | 15.00 |

—*Sleeve for a single that was never pressed*

| P-4612 [DJ] | Sgt. Pepper's Lonely Hearts Club Band-With a Little Help from My Friends (mono/stereo) | 1978 | 10.00 | 20.00 | 40.00 |

| 4612 | Sgt. Pepper's Lonely Hearts Club Band-With a Little Help from My Friends/A Day in the Life | 1978 | 2.00 | 4.00 | 8.00 |

—*Original: Purple label; label has reeded edge*

| 4612 [PS] | Sgt. Pepper's Lonely Hearts Club Band-With a Little Help from My Friends/A Day in the Life | 1978 | 5.00 | 10.00 | 20.00 |

| 4612 | Sgt. Pepper's Lonely Hearts Club Band-With a Little Help from My Friends/A Day in the Life | 1983 | — | 3.00 | 6.00 |

—*Black label with colorband*

| 4612 | Sgt. Pepper's Lonely Hearts Club Band-With a Little Help from My Friends/A Day in the Life | 1988 | — | 2.50 | 5.00 |

—*Purple label; label has smooth edge*

| B-5100 | The Beatles' Movie Medley/Fab Four on Film | 1982 | 12.50 | 25.00 | 50.00 |

—*Stock copy; not officially released, but some got out by mistake*

| PB-5100 [DJ] | The Beatles' Movie Medley /Fab Four on Film | 1982 | 6.25 | 12.50 | 25.00 |

| B-5100 [PS] | The Beatles' Movie Medley/Fab Four on Film | 1982 | 5.00 | 10.00 | 20.00 |

| B-5107 | The Beatles' Movie Medley/I'm Happy Just to Dance with You | 1982 | — | 2.50 | 5.00 |

| B-5107 [PS] | The Beatles' Movie Medley/I'm Happy Just to Dance with You | 1982 | — | 2.50 | 5.00 |

| 5112 | I Want to Hold Your Hand/I Saw Her Standing There | 1964 | 10.00 | 20.00 | 40.00 |

—*First pressing credits "Walter Hofer" as B-side publisher*

| 5112 | I Want to Hold Your Hand/I Saw Her Standing There | 1964 | 8.75 | 17.50 | 35.00 |

—*Second pressing credits "George Pincus and Sons" as B-side publisher*

| 5112 | I Want to Hold Your Hand/I Saw Her Standing There | 1964 | 7.50 | 15.00 | 30.00 |

—*Third pressings credit "Gil Music" as B-side publisher*

| 5112 [PS] | I Want to Hold Your Hand/I Saw Her Standing There | 1964 | 25.00 | 50.00 | 100.00 |

—*Die-cut, crops George Harrison's head in photo*

| 5112 [PS] | I Want to Hold Your Hand/I Saw Her Standing There | 1964 | 25.00 | 50.00 | 100.00 |

—*Straight cut, shows all of George Harrison's head*

| 5112 | I Want to Hold Your Hand/I Saw Her Standing There | 1968 | 15.00 | 30.00 | 60.00 |

—*Orange and yellow swirl label with "A Subsidiary Of" in perimeter print*

| 5112 | I Want to Hold Your Hand/I Saw Her Standing There | 1969 | 6.25 | 12.50 | 25.00 |

—*Red and orange "target" label, round logo*

| 5112 | I Want to Hold Your Hand/I Saw Her Standing There | 1969 | 15.00 | 30.00 | 60.00 |

—*Red and orange "target" label, dome logo*

| 5112 | I Want to Hold Your Hand/I Saw Her Standing There | 1976 | 2.50 | 5.00 | 10.00 |

—*Orange label, "Capitol" logo on bottom*

| 5112 | I Want to Hold Your Hand/I Saw Her Standing There | 1978 | 3.75 | 7.50 | 15.00 |

—*Purple label*

| 5112 | I Want to Hold Your Hand/I Saw Her Standing There | 1984 | — | 2.50 | 5.00 |

—*20th anniversary reissue; black print on perimeter of label (1964 pressings are white)*

| 5112 [PS] | I Want to Hold Your Hand/I Saw Her Standing There | 1984 | — | 3.00 | 6.00 |

—*Same as 1964 sleeve except has "1984" in small print, and Paul McCartney's cigarette is airbrushed out*

| 5112 | I Want to Hold Your Hand/I Saw Her Standing There | 1994 | — | 2.50 | 5.00 |

—*30th anniversary reissue; has "7243-8-58123-7-8" engraved in record's trail-off area*

| 5112 [PS] | I Want to Hold Your Hand/I Saw Her Standing There | 1994 | — | 2.00 | 4.00 |

—*Same as 1964 sleeve except "Reg. U.S. Pat. Off." has periods (1964s do not). Also came with a plastic sleeve with a "30th Anniversary" and UPC stickers (add 25%)*

| 5112 [PS] | I Want to Hold Your Hand/WMCA Good Guys | 1964 | 500.00 | 1000.00 | 2000.00 |

—*Giveaway from New York radio station with photo of WMCA DJs on rear*

| 5150 | Can't Buy Me Love/You Can't Do That | 1964 | 7.50 | 15.00 | 30.00 |

—*Original: Orange and yellow swirl, without "A Subsidiary Of"... in perimeter label print*

| 5150 | Can't Buy Me Love/You Can't Do That | 1964 | 2000. | 3000. | 4000. |

—*Yellow vinyl (unauthorized); value is conjecture*

| 5150 | Can't Buy Me Love/You Can't Do That | 1964 | 1000. | 1500. | 2000. |

—*Yellow and black vinyl (unauthorized); value is conjecture*

| 5150 [PS] | Can't Buy Me Love/You Can't Do That | 1964 | 200.00 | 400.00 | 800.00 |

—*One of the rarest Beatles picture sleeves. Numerous counterfeits exist; if in doubt, see an expert.*

| 5150 | Can't Buy Me Love/You Can't Do That | 1968 | 12.50 | 25.00 | 50.00 |

—*Orange and yellow swirl label with "A Subsidiary Of" in perimeter print*

| 5150 | Can't Buy Me Love/You Can't Do That | 1969 | 6.25 | 12.50 | 25.00 |

—*Red and orange "target" label, dome logo*

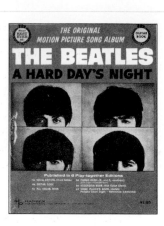

| 5150 | Can't Buy Me Love/You Can't Do That | 1969 | 15.00 | 30.00 | 60.00 |
—*Red and orange "target" label, round logo*

| 5150 | Can't Buy Me Love/You Can't Do That | 1976 | — | 3.00 | 6.00 |
—*Orange label with "Capitol" at bottom*

| 5150 | Can't Buy Me Love/You Can't Do That | 1978 | 3.75 | 7.50 | 15.00 |
—*Purple label*

| PB-5189 [DJ] | Love Me Do (same on both sides) | 1982 | 3.75 | 7.50 | 15.00 |

| B-5189 | Love Me Do/P.S. I Love You | 1982 | — | 2.50 | 5.00 |
—*Original: Orange and yellow swirl label, black print*

| B-5189 [PS] | Love Me Do/P.S. I Love You | 1982 | — | 2.50 | 5.00 |

| B-5189 | Love Me Do/P.S. I Love You | 1983 | — | 3.00 | 6.00 |
—*Black label with colorband*

| B-5189 | Love Me Do/P.S. I Love You | 1988 | — | 2.00 | 4.00 |
—*Purple label; label has smooth edge*

| 5222 | A Hard Day's Night/I Should Have Known Better | 1964 | 7.50 | 15.00 | 30.00 |
—*Original: Orange and yellow swirl, without "A Subsidiary Of"... in perimeter label print; first version credited both "Unart" and "Maclen" as publishers*

| 5222 | A Hard Day's Night/I Should Have Known Better | 1964 | 7.50 | 15.00 | 30.00 |
—*Orange and yellow swirl, without "A Subsidiary Of"... in perimeter label print; second version credited only "Maclen" as publishers*

| 5222 [PS] | A Hard Day's Night/I Should Have Known Better | 1964 | 25.00 | 50.00 | 100.00 |

| 5222 | A Hard Day's Night/I Should Have Known Better | 1968 | 12.50 | 25.00 | 50.00 |
—*Orange and yellow swirl with "A Subsidiary Of"... on perimeter print in white*

| 5222 | A Hard Day's Night/I Should Have Known Better | 1968 | 25.00 | 50.00 | 100.00 |
—*Orange and yellow swirl with "A Subsidiary Of"... on perimeter print in black*

| 5222 | A Hard Day's Night/I Should Have Known Better | 1969 | 15.00 | 30.00 | 60.00 |
—*Red and orange "target" label with Capitol dome logo*

| 5222 | A Hard Day's Night/I Should Have Known Better | 1969 | 5.00 | 10.00 | 20.00 |
—*Red and orange "target" label with Capitol round logo*

| 5222 | A Hard Day's Night/I Should Have Known Better | 1976 | — | 3.00 | 6.00 |
—*Orange label with "Capitol" at bottom*

| 5222 | A Hard Day's Night/I Should Have Known Better | 1978 | 3.75 | 7.50 | 15.00 |
—*Purple label*

| 5234 | I'll Cry Instead/I'm Happy Just to Dance with You | 1964 | 10.00 | 20.00 | 40.00 |
—*Original: Orange and yellow swirl, without "A Subsidiary Of"... in perimeter label print*

| 5234 [PS] | I'll Cry Instead/I'm Happy Just to Dance with You | 1964 | 37.50 | 75.00 | 150.00 |

| 5234 | I'll Cry Instead/I'm Happy Just to Dance with You | 1968 | 15.00 | 30.00 | 60.00 |
—*Orange and yellow swirl label with "A Subsidiary Of" in perimeter print*

| 5234 | I'll Cry Instead/I'm Happy Just to Dance with You | 1969 | 17.50 | 35.00 | 70.00 |
—*Red and orange "target" label with Capitol dome logo*

| 5234 | I'll Cry Instead/I'm Happy Just to Dance with You | 1969 | 5.00 | 10.00 | 20.00 |
—*Red and orange "target" label with Capitol round logo*

| 5234 | I'll Cry Instead/I'm Happy Just to Dance with You | 1976 | — | 3.00 | 6.00 |
—*Orange label with "Capitol" at bottom*

| 5234 | I'll Cry Instead/I'm Happy Just to Dance with You | 1978 | 3.75 | 7.50 | 15.00 |
—*Purple label*

| 5235 | And I Love Her/If I Fell | 1964 | 7.50 | 15.00 | 30.00 |
—*Original: Orange and yellow swirl, without "A Subsidiary Of"... in perimeter label print; publishers listed as "Unart" and "Maclen"*

| 5235 | And I Love Her/If I Fell | 1964 | 7.50 | 15.00 | 30.00 |
—*Original: Orange and yellow swirl, without "A Subsidiary Of"... in perimeter label print; publishers listed as "Maclen" only*

| 5235 [PS] | And I Love Her/If I Fell | 1964 | 30.00 | 60.00 | 120.00 |

| 5235 | And I Love Her/If I Fell | 1968 | 12.50 | 25.00 | 50.00 |
—*Orange and yellow swirl with "A Subsidiary Of"... on perimeter print in white*

| 5235 | And I Love Her/If I Fell | 1968 | 18.75 | 37.50 | 75.00 |
—*Orange and yellow swirl with "A Subsidiary Of"... on perimeter print in black*

| 5235 | And I Love Her/If I Fell | 1969 | 5.00 | 10.00 | 20.00 |
—*Red and orange "target" label with Capitol dome logo*

| 5235 | And I Love Her/If I Fell | 1969 | 15.00 | 30.00 | 60.00 |
—*Red and orange "target" label with Capitol round logo*

| 5235 | And I Love Her/If I Fell | 1976 | — | 3.00 | 6.00 |
—*Orange label with "Capitol" at bottom*

| 5235 | And I Love Her/If I Fell | 1978 | 3.75 | 7.50 | 15.00 |
—*Purple label*

| 5255 | Matchbox/Slow Down | 1964 | 7.50 | 15.00 | 30.00 |
—*Original: Orange and yellow swirl, without "A Subsidiary Of"... in perimeter label print*

| 5255 [PS] | Matchbox/Slow Down | 1964 | 37.50 | 75.00 | 150.00 |

| 5255 | Matchbox/Slow Down | 1968 | 12.50 | 25.00 | 50.00 |
—*Orange and yellow swirl label with "A Subsidiary Of" in perimeter print*

| 5255 | Matchbox/Slow Down | 1969 | 15.00 | 30.00 | 60.00 |
—*Red and orange "target" label with Capitol dome logo*

| 5255 | Matchbox/Slow Down | 1969 | 5.00 | 10.00 | 20.00 |
—*Red and orange "target" label with Capitol round logo*

| 5255 | Matchbox/Slow Down | 1976 | — | 3.00 | 6.00 |
—*Orange label with "Capitol" at bottom*

| 5255 | Matchbox/Slow Down | 1978 | 3.75 | 7.50 | 15.00 |
—*Purple label*

| 5327 | I Feel Fine/She's a Woman | 1964 | 7.50 | 15.00 | 30.00 |
—*Original: Orange and yellow swirl, without "A Subsidiary Of"... in perimeter label print*

| 5327 [PS] | I Feel Fine/She's a Woman | 1964 | 20.00 | 40.00 | 80.00 |

| 5327 | I Feel Fine/She's a Woman | 1968 | 12.50 | 25.00 | 50.00 |
—*Orange and yellow swirl label "A Subsidiary Of" in perimeter print*

| 5327 | I Feel Fine/She's a Woman | 1969 | 5.00 | 10.00 | 20.00 |
—*Red and orange "target" label with Capitol dome logo*

| 5327 | I Feel Fine/She's a Woman | 1969 | 15.00 | 30.00 | 60.00 |
—*Red and orange "target" label with Capitol round logo*

| 5327 | I Feel Fine/She's a Woman | 1976 | — | 3.00 | 6.00 |
—*Orange label with "Capitol" at bottom*

| 5327 | I Feel Fine/She's a Woman | 1978 | 3.75 | 7.50 | 15.00 |
—*Purple label*

| 5371 | Eight Days a Week/I Don't Want to Spoil the Party | 1965 | 7.50 | 15.00 | 30.00 |
—*Original: Orange and yellow swirl, without "A Subsidiary Of"... in perimeter label print*

| 5371 [PS] | Eight Days a Week/I Don't Want to Spoil the Party | 1965 | 6.25 | 12.50 | 25.00 |
—*Die-cut sleeve*

| 5371 [PS] | Eight Days a Week/I Don't Want to Spoil the Party | 1965 | 18.75 | 37.50 | 75.00 |
—*Straight-cut sleeve*

| 5371 | Eight Days a Week/I Don't Want to Spoil the Party | 1968 | 12.50 | 25.00 | 50.00 |
—*Orange and yellow swirl label with "A Subsidiary Of" in perimeter print*

| 5371 | Eight Days a Week/I Don't Want to Spoil the Party | 1969 | 15.00 | 30.00 | 60.00 |
—*Red and orange "target" label with Capitol dome logo*

| 5371 | Eight Days a Week/I Don't Want to Spoil |

Number	Title	Year			
	the Party	1969	5.00	10.00	20.00
—Red and orange "target" label with Capitol round logo					
5371	Eight Days a Week/I Don't Want to Spoil the Party	1976	—	3.00	6.00
—Orange label with "Capitol" at bottom					
5371	Eight Days a Week/I Don't Want to Spoil the Party	1978	3.75	7.50	15.00
—Purple label					
5407	Ticket to Ride/Yes It Is	1965	7.50	15.00	30.00
—Original: Orange and yellow swirl, without "A Subsidiary Of"... in perimeter label print					
5407 [PS]	Ticket to Ride/Yes It Is	1965	25.00	50.00	100.00
5407	Ticket to Ride/Yes It Is	1968	12.50	25.00	50.00
—Orange and yellow swirl with "A Subsidiary Of"... on perimeter print in white					
5407	Ticket to Ride/Yes It Is	1968	25.00	50.00	100.00
—Orange and yellow swirl with "A Subsidiary Of"... on perimeter print in black					
5407	Ticket to Ride/Yes It Is	1969	15.00	30.00	60.00
—Red and orange "target" label with Capitol dome logo					
5407	Ticket to Ride/Yes It Is	1969	5.00	10.00	20.00
—Red and orange "target" label with Capitol round logo					
5407	Ticket to Ride/Yes It Is	1976	—	3.00	6.00
—Orange label with "Capitol" at bottom					
5407	Ticket to Ride/Yes It Is	1978	3.75	7.50	15.00
—Purple label					
B-5439 [PS]	Leave My Kitten Alone/Ob-La-Di, Ob-La-Da	1985	12.50	25.00	50.00
—Sleeve for a record that was never released, not even as a promo					
5476	Help!/I'm Down	1965	7.50	15.00	30.00
—Original: Orange and yellow swirl, without "A Subsidiary Of"... in perimeter label print					
5476 [PS]	Help!/I'm Down	1965	18.75	37.50	75.00
5476	Help!/I'm Down	1968	12.50	25.00	50.00
—Orange and yellow swirl with "A Subsidiary Of"... on perimeter print in white					
5476	Help!/I'm Down	1968	25.00	50.00	100.00
—Orange and yellow swirl with "A Subsidiary Of"... on perimeter print in black					
5476	Help!/I'm Down	1969	15.00	30.00	60.00
—Red and orange "target" label with Capitol dome logo					
5476	Help!/I'm Down	1969	5.00	10.00	20.00
—Red and orange "target" label with Capitol round logo					
5476	Help!/I'm Down	1976	—	3.00	6.00
—Orange label with "Capitol" at bottom					
5476	Help!/I'm Down	1978	3.75	7.50	15.00
—Purple label					
5498	Yesterday/Act Naturally	1965	7.50	15.00	30.00
—Original: Orange and yellow swirl, without "A Subsidiary Of"... in perimeter label print					
5498 [PS]	Yesterday/Act Naturally	1965	25.00	50.00	100.00
5498	Yesterday/Act Naturally	1968	12.50	25.00	50.00
—Orange and yellow swirl with "A Subsidiary Of"... on perimeter print in white					
5498	Yesterday/Act Naturally	1968	25.00	50.00	100.00
—Orange and yellow swirl with "A Subsidiary Of"... on perimeter print in black					
5498	Yesterday/Act Naturally	1969	15.00	30.00	60.00
—Red and orange "target" label with Capitol dome logo					
5498	Yesterday/Act Naturally	1969	5.00	10.00	20.00
—Red and orange "target" label with Capitol round logo					
5498	Yesterday/Act Naturally	1976	—	3.00	6.00
—Orange label with "Capitol" at bottom					
5498	Yesterday/Act Naturally	1978	3.75	7.50	15.00
—Purple label					
5555	We Can Work It Out/Day Tripper	1965	7.50	15.00	30.00
—Original: Orange and yellow swirl, without "A Subsidiary Of"... in perimeter label print					
5555	We Can Work It Out/Day Tripper	1968	12.50	25.00	50.00
—Orange and yellow swirl label with "A Subsidiary Of" in perimeter print					
5555	We Can Work It Out/Day Tripper	1969	15.00	30.00	60.00
—Red and orange "target" label with Capitol dome logo					
5555	We Can Work It Out/Day Tripper	1969	5.00	10.00	20.00
—Red and orange "target" label with Capitol round logo					
5555	We Can Work It Out/Day Tripper	1969	500.00	1000.	1500.
—Red and white "Starline" label (mispress)					
5555	We Can Work It Out/Day Tripper	1976	—	3.00	6.00
—Orange label with "Capitol" at bottom					
5555	We Can Work It Out/Day Tripper	1978	3.75	7.50	15.00
—Purple label					
5555 [PS]	We Can Work It Out/Day Tripper	1978	15.00	30.00	60.00
5587	Nowhere Man/What Goes On	1966	6.25	12.50	25.00
—Original: Orange and yellow swirl, without "A Subsidiary Of"... in perimeter label print; composers of B-side listed as "John Lennon-Paul McCartney"					
5587	Nowhere Man/What Goes On	1966	12.50	25.00	50.00
—Orange and yellow swirl, without "A Subsidiary Of"... in perimeter label print, B-side composers listed as "Lennon-McCartney-Starkey"					
5587 [PS]	Nowhere Man/What Goes On	1966	10.00	20.00	40.00
5587	Nowhere Man/What Goes On	1968	12.50	25.00	50.00
—Orange and yellow swirl label with "A Subsidiary Of" in perimeter print					
5587	Nowhere Man/What Goes On	1969	15.00	30.00	60.00
—Red and orange "target" label with Capitol dome logo					
5587	Nowhere Man/What Goes On	1969	5.00	10.00	20.00
—Red and orange "target" label with Capitol round logo					
5587	Nowhere Man/What Goes On	1976	—	3.00	6.00
—Orange label with "Capitol" at bottom					
5587	Nowhere Man/What Goes On	1978	3.75	7.50	15.00
—Purple label					
P-B-5624 [DJ]	Twist and Shout (same on both sides)	1986	3.75	7.50	15.00
B-5624	Twist and Shout/There's a Place	1986	—	2.50	5.00
—Black label with colorband					
B-5624	Twist and Shout/There's a Place	1988	—	2.50	5.00
—Purple label; label has smooth edge					
5651	Paperback Writer/Rain	1966	6.25	12.50	25.00
—Original: Orange and yellow swirl, without "A Subsidiary Of"... in perimeter label print					
5651 [PS]	Paperback Writer/Rain	1966	18.75	37.50	75.00
5651	Paperback Writer/Rain	1968	12.50	25.00	50.00
—Orange and yellow swirl with "A Subsidiary Of"... on perimeter print in white					
5651	Paperback Writer/Rain	1968	25.00	50.00	100.00
—Orange and yellow swirl with "A Subsidiary Of"... on perimeter print in black					
5651	Paperback Writer/Rain	1969	15.00	30.00	60.00
—Red and orange "target" label with Capitol dome logo					
5651	Paperback Writer/Rain	1969	5.00	10.00	20.00
—Red and orange "target" label with Capitol round logo					
5651	Paperback Writer/Rain	1976	—	3.00	6.00
—Orange label with "Capitol" at bottom					
5651	Paperback Writer/Rain	1978	3.75	7.50	15.00
—Purple label					
5715	Yellow Submarine/Eleanor Rigby	1966	6.25	12.50	25.00
—Original: Orange and yellow swirl, without "A Subsidiary Of"... in perimeter label print; print on perimeter is white					
5715	Yellow Submarine/Eleanor Rigby	1966	12.50	25.00	50.00
—Orange and yellow swirl, without "A Subsidiary Of"... in perimeter label print; print on perimeter is yellow (mispress)					
5715 [PS]	Yellow Submarine/Eleanor Rigby	1966	25.00	50.00	100.00
5715	Yellow Submarine/Eleanor Rigby	1968	12.50	25.00	50.00
—Orange and yellow swirl label with "A Subsidiary Of" in perimeter print					
5715	Yellow Submarine/Eleanor Rigby	1969	5.00	10.00	20.00
—Red and orange "target" label with Capitol dome logo					
5715	Yellow Submarine/Eleanor Rigby	1969	15.00	30.00	60.00
—Red and orange "target" label with Capitol round logo					
5715	Yellow Submarine/Eleanor Rigby	1976	—	3.00	6.00
—Orange label with "Capitol" at bottom					
5715	Yellow Submarine/Eleanor Rigby	1978	3.75	7.50	15.00
—Purple label					
5810	Penny Lane/Strawberry Fields Forever	1967	6.25	12.50	25.00
—Original: Orange and yellow swirl, without "A Subsidiary Of"... in perimeter label print; "Penny Lane" time listed as 3:00					
5810	Penny Lane/Strawberry Fields Forever	1967	7.50	15.00	30.00
—Orange and yellow swirl, without "A Subsidiary Of"... in perimeter label print; "Penny Lane" time listed as 2:57					

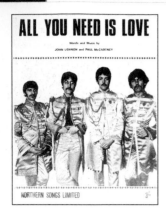

P 5810 [DJ] Penny Lane/Strawberry Fields Forever 1967 75.00 150.00 300.00
—Light green promo; most copies have an extra trumpet solo at the end of "Penny Lane"

P 5810 [DJ] Penny Lane/Strawberry Fields Forever 1967 150.00 300.00 600.00
—Light green promo; a few copies have no trumpet solo at the end of "Penny Lane"

5810 [PS] Penny Lane/Strawberry Fields Forever 1967 25.00 50.00 100.00

5810 Penny Lane/Strawberry Fields Forever 1968 12.50 25.00 50.00
—Orange and yellow swirl label with "A Subsidiary Of" in perimeter print

5810 Penny Lane/Strawberry Fields Forever 1969 15.00 30.00 60.00
—Red and orange "target" label with Capitol dome logo

5810 Penny Lane/Strawberry Fields Forever 1969 5.00 10.00 20.00
—Red and orange "target" label with Capitol round logo

5810 Penny Lane/Strawberry Fields Forever 1976 — 3.00 6.00
—Orange label with "Capitol" at bottom

5810 Penny Lane/Strawberry Fields Forever 1978 3.75 7.50 15.00
—Purple label

5964 All You Need Is Love/Baby, You're a Rich Man 1967 6.25 12.50 25.00
—Original: Orange and yellow swirl, without "A Subsidiary Of"... in perimeter label print

P 5964 [DJ] All You Need Is Love/Baby, You're a Rich Man 1967 62.50 125.00 250.00
—Light green label promo

5964 [PS] All You Need Is Love/Baby, You're a Rich Man 1967 10.00 20.00 40.00

5964 All You Need Is Love/Baby, You're a Rich Man 1968 12.50 25.00 50.00
—Orange and yellow swirl label with "A Subsidiary Of" in perimeter print

5964 All You Need Is Love/Baby, You're a Rich Man 1969 18.75 37.50 75.00
—Red and orange "target" label with Capitol dome logo

5964 All You Need Is Love/Baby, You're a Rich Man 1969 5.00 10.00 20.00
—Red and orange "target" label with Capitol round logo

5964 All You Need Is Love/Baby, You're a Rich Man 1976 — 3.00 6.00
—Orange label with "Capitol" at bottom

5964 All You Need Is Love/Baby, You're a Rich Man 1978 3.75 7.50 15.00
—Purple label

S7-17488 Birthday/Taxman 1994 12.50 25.00 50.00
—Black vinyl "error" pressing

S7-17488 Birthday/Taxman 1994 — 2.00 4.00
—Green vinyl

S7-17688 She Loves You/I'll Get You 1994 — 2.00 4.00
—Red vinyl

S7-17689 I Want to Hold Your Hand/This Boy 1994 — 2.00 4.00
—Clear vinyl

S7-17690 Can't Buy Me Love/You Can't Do That 1994 — 2.00 4.00
—Gren vinyl

S7-17691 Help!/I'm Down 1994 — 2.00 4.00
—White vinyl

S7-17692 A Hard Day's Night/Things We Said Today 1994 — 2.00 4.00
—White vinyl

S7-17693 All You Need Is Love/Baby You're a Rich Man 1994 — 2.00 4.00
—Pink vinyl

S7-17694 Hey Jude/Revolution 1994 — 2.00 4.00
—Blue vinyl

S7-17695 Let It Be/You Know My Name (Look Up My Number) 1994 — 2.00 4.00
—Yellow vinyl

S7-17696 Yellow Submarine/Eleanor Rigby 1994 — 2.00 4.00
—Yellow vinyl

S7-17697 Strawberry Fields Forever/Penny Lane 1994 — 2.00 4.00
—Red vinyl

S7-17698 Something/Come Together 1994 — 2.00 4.00
—Blue vinyl

S7-17699 Twist and Shout/There's a Place 1994 — 2.00 4.00
—Pink vinyl

S7-17700 Here Comes the Sun/Octopus's Garden 1994 — 2.00 4.00
—Gold/orange vinyl

S7-17701 Sgt. Pepper's Lonely Hearts Club Band-With a Little Help from My Friends/A Day in the Life 1994 — 2.00 4.00
—Clear vinyl

S7-18888 Norwegian Wood/If I Needed Someone 1995 37.50 75.00 150.00
—Green vinyl; 1,000 pressed, given by Collectors' Choice Music to buyers of Beatles reissue LPs

S7-18889 You've Got to Hide Your Love Away/I've Just Seen a Face 1996 — 2.00 4.00
—Gold/orange vinyl

S7-18890 Magical Mystery Tour/The Fool on the Hill 1996 — 2.00 4.00
—Yellow vinyl

S7-18891 Across the Universe/Two of Us 1996 — 2.00 4.00
—Clear vinyl

S7-18892 While My Guitar Gently Weeps/Blackbird 1996 — 2.00 4.00
—Blue vinyl

S7-18893 It's All Too Much/Only a Northern Song 1996 — 2.00 4.00
—Blue vinyl

S7-18894 Nowhere Man/What Goes On 1996 — 2.00 4.00
—Green vinyl

S7-18895 We Can Work It Out/Day Tripper 1996 — 2.00 4.00
—Pink vinyl

S7-18896 Lucy in the Sky with Diamonds/When I'm 64 1996 — 2.00 4.00
—Red vinyl

S7-18897 Here, There and Everywhere/Good Day Sunshine 1996 — 2.00 4.00
—Yellow vinyl

S7-18898 The Long and Winding Road/For You Blue 1996 — 2.00 4.00
—Blue vinyl

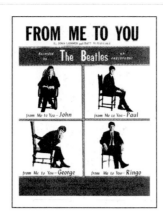

S7-18899	Got to Get You Into My Life/Helter Skelter	1996	—	2.00	4.00

—Gold/orange vinyl

S7-18900	Ob-La-Di, Ob-La-Da/Julia	1996	—	2.00	4.00

—Clear vinyl

S7-18901	Yesterday/Act Naturally	1996	—	2.00	4.00

—Pink vinyl

S7-18902	Paperback Writer/Rain	1996	—	2.00	4.00

—Red vinyl

S7-19341	Norwegian Wood (This Bird Has Flown)/ If I Needed Someone	1996	—	—	3.00

S7-56785	Love Me Do/P.S. I Love You	1992	—	2.00	4.00

S7-56785	Love Me Do/P.S. I Love You	1992	7.50	15.00	30.00

—Small pressing on red vinyl "by mistake"

72133	Roll Over Beethoven/Please Mister Postman	1964	12.50	25.00	50.00

—Orange and yellow swirl; Canadian release that was heavily imported to the U.S.

72144	All My Loving/This Boy	1964	12.50	25.00	50.00

—Orange and yellow swirl; Canadian release that was heavily imported to the U.S.

72144	All My Loving/This Boy	1971	25.00	50.00	100.00

—Canadian number with U.S. labels (red and orange "target" label)

7PRO-79551/2 [DJ]Love Me Do/P.S. I Love You	1992	6.25	12.50	25.00

7PRO-79551/2 [PS]Love Me Do/P.S. I Love You	1992	6.25	12.50	25.00

CAPITOL STARLINE

6061	Twist and Shout/There's a Place	1965	30.00	60.00	120.00

—Green swirl label

6062	Love Me Do/P.S. I Love You	1965	30.00	60.00	120.00

—Green swirl label

6063	Please Please Me/From Me to You	1965	30.00	60.00	120.00

—Green swirl label

6064	Do You Want to Know a Secret/ Thank You Girl	1965	30.00	60.00	120.00

—Green swirl label

6065	Roll Over Beethoven/Misery	1965	30.00	60.00	120.00

—Green swirl label

6065	Roll Over Beethoven/Misery	1971	7.50	15.00	30.00

—Red and orange "target" label

6066	Boys/Kansas City	1965	20.00	40.00	80.00

—Green swirl label

6066	Boys/Kansas City	1971	7.50	15.00	30.00

—Red and orange "target" label

6278	I Want to Hold Your Hand/I Saw Her Standing There	1981	5.00	10.00	20.00

—Originals have blue labels

6279	Can't Buy Me Love/You Can't Do That	1981	2.00	4.00	8.00

—Originals have blue labels

6281	A Hard Day's Night/I Should Have Known Better	1981	2.00	4.00	8.00

—Originals have blue labels

6282	I'll Cry Instead/I'm Happy Just to Dance

	with You	1981	2.00	4.00	8.00

—Originals have blue labels

6283	And I Love Her/If I Fell	1981	2.00	4.00	8.00

—Originals have blue labels

6284	Matchbox/Slow Down	1981	2.00	4.00	8.00

—Originals have blue labels

6286	I Feel Fine/She's a Woman	1981	2.00	4.00	8.00

—Originals have blue labels

6287	Eight Days a Week/I Don't Want to Spoil the Party	1981	2.00	4.00	8.00

—Originals have blue labels

6288	Ticket to Ride/Yes It Is	1981	2.00	4.00	8.00

—Originals have blue labels

6290	Help!/I'm Down	1981	2.00	4.00	8.00

—Originals have blue labels

6291	Yesterday/Act Naturally	1981	2.00	4.00	8.00

—Originals have blue labels

6293	We Can Work It Out/Day Tripper	1981	2.00	4.00	8.00

—Originals have blue labels

6294	Nowhere Man/What Goes On	1981	2.00	4.00	8.00

—Originals have blue labels

6296	Paperback Writer/Rain	1981	2.00	4.00	8.00

—Originals have blue labels

6297	Yellow Submarine/Eleanor Rigby	1981	2.00	4.00	8.00

—Originals have blue labels

6299	Penny Lane/Strawberry Fields Forever	1981	2.00	4.00	8.00

—Originals have blue labels

6300	All You Need Is Love/Baby You're a Rich Man	1981	2.00	4.00	8.00

—Originals have blue labels

CAPITOL/EVATONE

420826cs	All My Loving/You've Got to Hide Your Love Away	1982	2.50	5.00	10.00

—Flexi-disc issued as giveaway by The Musicland Group; "Musicland" version

420826cs	All My Loving/You've Got to Hide Your Love Away	1982	5.00	10.00	20.00

—Flexi-disc issued as giveaway by The Musicland Group; "Discount" version

420826cs	All My Loving/You've Got to Hide Your Love Away	1982	6.25	12.50	25.00

—Flexi-disc issued as giveaway by The Musicland Group; "Sam Goody" version

420827cs	Magical Mystery Tour/Here Comes the Sun	1982	2.50	5.00	10.00

—Flexi-disc issued as giveaway by The Musicland Group; "Musicland" version

420827cs	Magical Mystery Tour/Here Comes the Sun	1982	5.00	10.00	20.00

—Flexi-disc issued as giveaway by The Musicland Group; "Discount" version

420827cs	Magical Mystery Tour/Here Comes the Sun	1982	6.25	12.50	25.00

—Flexi-disc issued as giveaway by The Musicland Group; "Sam Goody" version

420828cs	Rocky Raccoon/Why Don't We Do It in the Road?	1982	2.50	5.00	10.00

—Flexi-disc issued as giveaway by The Musicland Group; "Musicland" version

420828cs	Rocky Raccoon/Why Don't We Do It in the Road?	1982	5.00	10.00	20.00

—Flexi-disc issued as giveaway by The Musicland Group; "Discount" version

420828cs	Rocky Raccoon/Why Don't We Do It in the Road?	1982	6.25	12.50	25.00

—Flexi-disc issued as giveaway by The Musicland Group; "Sam Goody" version

830771 X	Till There Was You/Three Cool Cats	1983	—	3.00	6.00

—*Flexi-disc issued as giveaway with a book*

| 1214825cs | German Medley | 1983 | 15.00 | 30.00 | 60.00 |

—*Flexi-disc given away by House of Guitars in New York*

CICADELIC/BIODISC

| 001 | A Hard Day's Night Open End Interview | 1990 | 3.75 | 7.50 | 15.00 |

—*Limited edition of 700; lower numbers increase value substantially*

| 001 | A Hard Day's Night Open End Interview | 1990 | 7.50 | 15.00 | 30.00 |

—*"Records Etc." pressing*

| 002 | Help! Open End Interview | 1990 | — | 2.50 | 5.00 |
| 002 [PS] | Help! Open End Interview | 1990 | — | 2.50 | 5.00 |

COLLECTABLES

1501	I'm Gonna Sit Right Down and Cry Over You/Roll Over Beethoven	1982	—	—	3.00
1501 [PS]	I'm Gonna Sit Right Down and Cry Over You/Roll Over Beethoven	1982	—	—	3.00
1502	Hippy Hippy Shake/Sweet Little Sixteen	1982	—	—	3.00
1502 [PS]	Hippy Hippy Shake/Sweet Little Sixteen	1982	—	—	3.00
1503	Lend Me Your Comb/Your Feets Too Big	1982	—	—	3.00
1503 [PS]	Lend Me Your Comb/Your Feets Too Big	1982	—	—	3.00
1504	Where Have You Been All My Life/Mr. Moonlight	1982	—	—	3.00
1504 [PS]	Where Have You Been All My Life/Mr. Moonlight	1982	—	—	3.00
1505	A Taste of Honey/Besame Mucho	1982	—	—	3.00
1505 [PS]	A Taste of Honey/Besame Mucho	1982	—	—	3.00
1506	Till There Was You/Everybody's Trying to Be My Baby	1982	—	—	3.00
1506 [PS]	Till There Was You/Everybody's Trying to Be My Baby	1982	—	—	3.00
1507	Kansas City-Hey Hey Hey Hey/Ain't Nothing Shakin Like the Leaves on a Tree	1982	—	—	3.00
1507 [PS]	Kansas City-Hey Hey Hey Hey/Ain't Nothing Shakin Like the Leaves on a Tree	1982	—	—	3.00
1508	To Know Her Is To Love Her/Little Queenie	1982	—	—	3.00
1508 [PS]	To Know Her Is To Love Her/Little Queenie	1982	—	—	3.00
1509	Falling in Love Again/Sheila	1982	—	—	3.00
1509 [PS]	Falling in Love Again/Sheila	1982	—	—	3.00
1510	Be-Bop-a-Lula/Hallelujah I Love Her So	1982	—	—	3.00
1510 [PS]	Be-Bop-a-Lula/Hallelujah I Love Her So	1982	—	—	3.00
1511	Red Sails in the Sunset/Matchbox	1982	—	—	3.00
1511 [PS]	Red Sails in the Sunset/Matchbox	1982	—	—	3.00
1512	Talkin' Bout You/Shimmy Shake	1982	—	—	3.00
1512 [PS]	Talkin' Bout You/Shimmy Shake	1982	—	—	3.00
1513	Long Tall Sally/I Remember You	1982	—	—	3.00
1513 [PS]	Long Tall Sally/I Remember You	1982	—	—	3.00
1514	Ask Me Why/Twist and Shout	1982	—	—	3.00
1514 [PS]	Ask Me Why/Twist and Shout	1982	—	—	3.00
1515	I Saw Her Standing There/Can't Help It "Blue Angel"	1982	—	—	3.00

—*B-side is actually "Reminiscing"*

| 1515 [PS] | I Saw Her Standing There/Can't Help It "Blue Angel" | 1982 | — | — | 3.00 |
| 1516 | I'll Try Anyway/I Don't Know Why I Do (I Just Do) | 1987 | 2.50 | 5.00 | 10.00 |

—*Despite label credit to The Beatles, both are Peter Best recordings*

| 1517 | She's Not the Only Girl in Town/More Than I Need Myself | 1987 | 2.50 | 5.00 | 10.00 |

—*Despite label credit to The Beatles, both are Peter Best recordings*

| 1518 | I'll Have Everything Too/I'm Checking Out Now Baby | 1987 | 2.50 | 5.00 | 10.00 |

—*Despite label credit to The Beatles, both are Peter Best recordings*

| 1519 | How'd You Get to Know Her Name/If You Can't Get Her | 1987 | 2.50 | 5.00 | 10.00 |

—*Despite label credit to The Beatles, both are Peter Best recordings*

| 1520 | Cry for a Shadow/Rock and Roll Music | 1987 | — | 2.50 | 5.00 |

—*Despite label credit to The Beatles, B-side is a Peter Best recording*

| 1521 | Let's Dance/If You Love Me Baby | 1987 | — | 3.00 | 6.00 |

—*Despite label credit to The Beatles, A-side is a Tony Sheridan solo recording*

| 1522 | What'd I Say/Sweet Georgia Brown | 1987 | — | 3.00 | 6.00 |

—*Despite label credit to The Beatles, A-side is a Tony Sheridan solo recording*

| 1523 | Ruby Baby/Ya Ya | 1987 | — | 3.00 | 6.00 |

—*Despite label credit to The Beatles, both are by Tony Sheridan without the Fab Four*

| 1524 | Why/I'll Try Anyway | 1987 | — | 3.00 | 6.00 |

—*Despite label credit to The Beatles, B-side is a Peter Best recording*

EVA-TONE

| 830771X [DJ] | Til There Was You/Three Cool Cats (both on same side) | 1983 | — | 3.00 | 6.00 |

—*Red plastic flexidisc; issued as giveaway with a Beatles price guide*

MGM

| 13213 | My Bonnie (My Bonnie Lies Over the Ocean)/ The Saints (When the Saints Go Marching In) | 1964 | 10.00 | 20.00 | 40.00 |

—*The Beatles with Tony Sheridan; no reference to LP on label*

| 13213 | My Bonnie (My Bonnie Lies Over the Ocean)/The Saints (When the Saints Go Marching In) | 1964 | 12.50 | 25.00 | 50.00 |

—*The Beatles with Tony Sheridan; LP number on label*

| 13213 [DJ] | My Bonnie (My Bonnie Lies Over the Ocean)/The Saints (When the Saints Go Marching In) | 1964 | 75.00 | 150.00 | 300.00 |

—*The Beatles with Tony Sheridan*

| 13213 [PS] | My Bonnie (My Bonnie Lies Over the Ocean) /The Saints (When the Saints Go Marching In) | 1964 | 30.00 | 60.00 | 120.00 |

—*The Beatles with Tony Sheridan*

| 13227 | Why/Cry for a Shadow | 1964 | 37.50 | 75.00 | 150.00 |

—*The Beatles with Tony Sheridan*

| 13227 [DJ] | Why/Cry for a Shadow | 1964 | 62.50 | 125.00 | 250.00 |

—*The Beatles with Tony Sheridan*

| 13227 [PS] | Why/Cry for a Shadow | 1964 | 100.00 | 200.00 | 400.00 |

—*The Beatles with Tony Sheridan*

OLDIES 45

#149	Do You Want to Know a Secret/Thank You Girl	1965	3.75	7.50	15.00
#150	Please Please Me/From Me to You	1965	3.75	7.50	15.00
#151	Love Me Do/P.S. I Love You	1965	3.75	7.50	15.00
#152	Twist and Shout/There's a Place	1965	3.75	7.50	15.00

SWAN

| 4152 [DJ] | I'll Get You (one-sided) | 1964 | 200.00 | 400.00 | 600.00 |
| 4152 | She Loves You/I'll Get You | 1963 | 150.00 | 300.00 | 600.00 |

—*Semi-glossy white label/red print; "Don't Drop Out" not on label*

| 4152 | She Loves You/I'll Get You | 1963 | 162.50 | 325.00 | 650.00 |

—*Flat white label/red print, "Don't Drop Out" not on label*

| 4152 | She Loves You/I'll Get You | 1963 | 162.50 | 325.00 | 650.00 |

—*Semi-glossy white label/red print, "Don't Drop Out" on label*

| 4152 | She Loves You/I'll Get You | 1963 | 150.00 | 300.00 | 600.00 |

—*Semi-glossy white label/blue printing*

| 4152 [DJ] | She Loves You/I'll Get You | 1963 | 125.00 | 250.00 | 500.00 |

—*Thick print, no "Don't Drop Out" on label*

| 4152 [DJ] | She Loves You/I'll Get You | 1963 | 112.50 | 225.00 | 450.00 |

—*Thin print, "Don't Drop Out" on label*

| 4152 [DJ] | She Loves You/I'll Get You | 1963 | 125.00 | 250.00 | 500.00 |

—*Flat white label, no "Don't Drop Out" on label*

| 4152 | She Loves You/I'll Get You | 1964 | 10.00 | 20.00 | 40.00 |

—*Black label, silver print, "Don't Drop Out" not on label*

| 4152 | She Loves You/I'll Get You | 1964 | 7.50 | 15.00 | 30.00 |

—*Black label, silver print, "Don't Drop Out" on label*

4152	She Loves You/I'll Get You	1964	12.50	25.00	50.00

—Black label, silver print, "Produced by George Martin" on both labels

4152	She Loves You/I'll Get You	1964	12.50	25.00	50.00

—Black label, silver print, "Produced by George Martin" on only one label

4152 [PS]	She Loves You/I'll Get You	1964	30.00	60.00	120.00

4152	She Loves You/I'll Get You	196?	5.00	10.00	20.00

—Black label, silver print, "Don't Drop Out" not on label, smaller numbers in trailoff area

4152	She Loves You/I'll Get You	196?	12.50	25.00	50.00

—White label, red or maroon print, same as above

4182	Sie Liebt Dich (She Loves You)/I'll Get You	1964	37.50	75.00	150.00

—White label, "Sie Liebt Dich (She Loves You)" on one line

4182	Sie Liebt Dich (She Loves You)/I'll Get You	1964	37.50	75.00	150.00

—White label, "(She Loves You)" under "Sie Liebt Dich," narrow print

4182	Sie Liebt Dich (She Loves You)/I'll Get You	1964	37.50	75.00	150.00

—White label, "(She Loves You)" under "Sie Liebt Dich," wide red print

4182	Sie Liebt Dich (She Loves You)/I'll Get You	1964	43.75	87.50	175.00

—White label, "(She Loves You)" under "Sie Liebt Dich," wide orange print

4182 [DJ]	Sie Liebt Dich (She Loves You)/I'll Get You	1964	100.00	200.00	400.00

—White label, "(She Loves You)" under "Sie Liebt Dich"

4182 [DJ]	Sie Liebt Dich (She Loves You)/I'll Get You	1964	112.50	225.00	450.00

—White label, "Sie Liebt Dich (She Loves You)" on one line

TOLLIE

9001	Twist and Shout/There's a Place	1964	12.50	25.00	50.00

—Yellow label, green print, "tollie" lowercase

9001	Twist and Shout/There's a Place	1964	12.50	25.00	50.00

—Yellow label, black print, "TOLLIE" stands alone

9001	Twist and Shout/There's a Place	1964	12.50	25.00	50.00

—Yellow label, black print, black "tollie" in box

9001	Twist and Shout/There's a Place	1964	15.00	30.00	60.00

—Yellow label, black print, purple "tollie" in box

9001	Twist and Shout/There's a Place	1964	12.50	25.00	50.00

—Yellow label, black print, black "TOLLIE" in thin box

9001	Twist and Shout/There's a Place	1964	18.75	37.50	75.00

—Yellow label, black print, "TOLLIE" in brackets

9001	Twist and Shout/There's a Place	1964	15.00	30.00	60.00

—Yellow label, blue print

9001	Twist and Shout/There's a Place	1964	20.00	40.00	80.00

—Yellow label, purple print

9001	Twist and Shout/There's a Place	1964	20.00	40.00	80.00

—Yellow label, green print, "TOLLIE" uppercase

9001	Twist and Shout/There's a Place	1964	15.00	30.00	60.00

—Black label, silver print

9008 [DJ]	Love Me Do/P.S. I Love You	1964	100.00	200.00	400.00

9008	Love Me Do/P.S. I Love You	1964	12.50	25.00	50.00

—Yellow label, black print (any logo or print variation)

9008	Love Me Do/P.S. I Love You	1964	12.50	25.00	50.00

—Yellow label, blue/green print

9008	Love Me Do/P.S. I Love You	1964	15.00	30.00	60.00

—Black label, silver print

9008 [PS]	Love Me Do/P.S. I Love You	1964	37.50	75.00	150.00

UNITED ARTISTS

SP-2357 [DJ]	A Hard Day's Night Theatre Lobby Spot	1964	500.00	1000.00	1500.00
UAEP 10029 [DJ]	A Hard Day's Night Open End Interview	1964	500.00	1000.00	1500.00
ULP-42370	Let It Be Radio Spots	1970	400.00	800.00	1200.00

VEE JAY

(no #) [PS]	We Wish You a Merry Christmas and a Happy New Year	1964	20.00	40.00	80.00

—Used with any Vee Jay or Tollie Beatles single in 1964-65 holiday season

Spec. DJ No. 8	Ask Me Why/Anna	1964	5000.	7500.	10000.

—Though it doesn't fit into any known Vee Jay numbering system (other "Spec. DJ No." records are rumored, but none are confirmed), this is an authentic 1964 promotional release

498	Please Please Me/Ask Me Why	1963	800.00	1200.00	1600.00

—Misspelled "The Beattles"; number is "#498"

498	Please Please Me/Ask Me Why	1963	750.00	1125.00	1500.00

—Misspelled "The Beattles"; number is "VJ 498"

498	Please Please Me/Ask Me Why	1963	800.00	1200.00	1600.00

—Correct spelling; number is "#498"

498	Please Please Me/Ask Me Why	1963	300.00	600.00	900.00

—Correct spelling; number is "VJ 498"; thick print

498	Please Please Me/Ask Me Why	1963	1000.00	1500.00	2000.00

—Correct spelling; number is "VJ 498"; brackets label

498 [DJ]	Please Please Me/Ask Me Why	1963	550.00	825.00	1100.00

—Misspelled "The Beattles"

522	From Me to You/Thank You Girl	1963	150.00	300.00	600.00

—Black rainbow label; "Vee Jay" in oval

522	From Me to You/Thank You Girl	1963	300.00	600.00	900.00

—Black rainbow label; "VJ" in brackets

522	From Me to You/Thank You Girl	1963	200.00	400.00	800.00

—Plain black label

522 [DJ]	From Me to You/Thank You Girl	1963	125.00	250.00	500.00

581 [DJ]	Please Please Me/From Me to You	1964	200.00	400.00	600.00

—White label, blue print; "Promotional Copy" on label

581 [DJ]	Please Please Me/From Me to You	1964	300.00	600.00	900.00

—White label, blue print; no "Promotional Copy" on label

581 [PS]	Please Please Me/From Me to You	1964	1250.	1875.	2500.

—Special "The Record That Started Beatlemania" promo-only sleeve

581	Please Please Me/From Me to You	1964	12.50	25.00	50.00

—Black rainbow label, oval logo

581	Please Please Me/From Me to You	1964	11.25	22.50	45.00

—Plain black label with two horizontal lines

581	Please Please Me/From Me to You	1964	18.75	37.50	75.00

—Plain black label, brackets logo

581	Please Please Me/From Me to You	1964	18.75	37.50	75.00

—Yellow label

581	Please Please Me/From Me to You	1964	40.00	80.00	160.00

—White label

581	Please Please Me/From Me to You	1964	62.50	125.00	250.00

—Purple label

581 [PS]	Please Please Me/From Me to You	1964	125.00	250.00	500.00

581	Please Please Me/From Me to You	1964	15.00	30.00	60.00

—Plain black label, "VEE JAY" stands alone

581	Please Please Me/From Me to You	1964	16.25	32.50	65.00

—Plain black label, "VJ" stands alone

581	Please Please Me/From Me to You	1964	15.00	30.00	60.00

—Black rainbow label, brackets logo

581	Please Please Me/From Me to You	1964	15.00	30.00	60.00

—Plain black label, oval logo

587 [DJ]	Do You Want to Know a Secret/Thank You Girl	1964	150.00	300.00	600.00

587	Do You Want to Know a Secret/Thank You Girl	1964	12.50	25.00	50.00

—Black rainbow label, oval logo

587	Do You Want to Know a Secret/Thank You Girl	1964	16.25	32.50	65.00

—Plain black label; "Vee Jay" in oval

587	Do You Want to Know a Secret/Thank You Girl	1964	16.25	32.50	65.00

—Plain black label; "VJ" in brackets

587	Do You Want to Know a Secret/Thank You Girl	1964	16.25	32.50	65.00

—Plain black label; "VJ" stands alone

587	Do You Want to Know a Secret/Thank You Girl	1964	12.50	25.00	50.00

—Plain black label; "VEE JAY" stands alone

587	Do You Want to Know a Secret/Thank You Girl	1964	11.25	22.50	45.00

—Plain black label with two horizontal lines; "VJ" in brackets

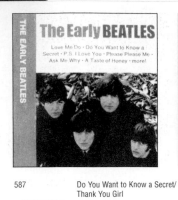

587	Do You Want to Know a Secret/ Thank You Girl	1964	16.25	32.50	65.00

—Yellow label

587 [PS]	Do You Want to Know a Secret/ Thank You Girl	1964	30.00	60.00	120.00

587	Do You Want to Know a Secret/ Thank You Girl	1964	10.00	20.00	40.00

—Black rainbow label, brackets logo

(NO LABEL)

MBRF-55551	Decade	1974	—	—	—

—A clever bootleg of radio spots for the Beatles' back catalog, compiled without authorization by two former Capitol employees.

7-Inch Extended Plays
CAPITOL

SXA-2047 [PS]	Meet the Beatles				
1964	150.00		300.00	600.00	

—With all jukebox title strips intact (deduct 33 percent if missing, deduct less if material is there but not intact)

SXA-2047 [S]	(contents unknown)	1964	100.00	200.00	400.00

—33 1/3 rpm, small hole jukebox edition

SXA-2080 [PS]	The Beatles' Second Album	1964	150.00	300.00	600.00

—With all jukebox title strips intact (deduct 33 percent if missing, deduct less if material is there but not intact)

SXA-2080 [S]	(contents unknown)	1964	100.00	200.00	400.00

—33 1/3 rpm, small hole jukebox edition

SXA-2108 [PS]	Something New	1964	150.00	300.00	600.00

—With all jukebox title strips intact (deduct 33 percent if missing, deduct less if material is there but not intact)

SXA-2108 [S]	(contents unknown)	1964	100.00	200.00	400.00

—33 1/3 rpm, small hole jukebox edition

EAP 1-2121 [PS]	Four by the Beatles	1964	75.00	150.00	300.00

EAP 1-2121	Roll Over Beethoven/This Boy//All My Loving/ Please Mr. Postman	1964	25.00	50.00	100.00

PRO-2548/9 [DJ]	Open End Interview with the Beatles	1964	200.00	400.00	800.00

—33 1/3 rpm, small hole. Authentic copies have colorband along outside of label.

PRO-2548/9 [PS]	Open End Interview with the Beatles	1964	250.00	500.00	1000.00

—Contains script for interview. Authentic copies are glossy and have a die-cut thumb tab.

PRO-2598/9 [DJ]	The Beatles Second Album Open End Interview	1964	200.00	400.00	800.00

—33 1/3 rpm, small hole; interview plus three songs from the LP

PRO-2598/9 [PS]	The Beatles Second Album Open End Interview	1964	250.00	500.00	1000.

—Contains script for interview

R-5365 [PS]	4-By the Beatles	1965	50.00	100.00	200.00

R-5365	Honey Don't/I'm a Loser//Mr. Moonlight/ Everybody's Trying to Be My Baby	1965	20.00	40.00	80.00

POLYDOR

PRO 1113-7 [DJ]	Ain't She Sweet/Cry for a Shadow// My Bonnie/ The Saints	1994	6.25	12.50	25.00

PRO 1113-7 [PS]	Backbeat	1994	6.25	12.50	25.00

—Picture sleeve for above sampler
VEE JAY

1-903	Misery/Taste of Honey//Ask Me Why/Anna	1964	10.00	20.00	40.00

—Black rainbow label, oval logo

1-903	Misery/Taste of Honey//Ask Me Why/Anna	1964	31.25	62.50	125.00

—Plain black label, oval logo

1-903	Misery/Taste of Honey//Ask Me Why/Anna	1964	31.25	62.50	125.00

—Black rainbow label, brackets logo, "Ask Me Why" in much larger print

1-903	Misery/Taste of Honey//Ask Me Why/Anna	1964	22.50	45.00	90.00

—Black rainbow label, brackets logo, all titles the same size

1-903	Misery/Taste of Honey//Ask Me Why/Anna	1964	50.00	100.00	200.00

—Plain black label, brackets logo

1-903	Misery/Taste of Honey//Ask Me Why/Anna	1964	37.50	75.00	150.00

—Plain black label, "VEE JAY" stands alone

1-903 [DJ]	Misery/Taste of Honey//Ask Me Why/Anna	1964	100.00	200.00	400.00

—White and blue label, all titles the same size

1-903 [DJ]	Misery/Taste of Honey//Ask Me Why/Anna	1964	75.00	150.00	300.00

—White and blue label, "Ask Me Why" in much larger print

1-903 [PS]	Souvenir of Their Visit to America	1964	15.00	30.00	60.00

—Cardboard sleeve

1-903 [PS]	Souvenir of Their Visit to America	1964	4000.	6000.	8000.

—"Ask Me Why/The Beatles" plugged on promo-only sleeve

Albums
APPLE

SBC-100 [M]	The Beatles' Christmas Album	1970	100.00	200.00	400.00

—Fan club issue of the seven Christmas messages; very good counterfeits exist

SWBO-101 [(2)]	The Beatles	1968	37.50	75.00	200.00

—Numbered copy; includes four individual photos and large poster (included in value); because the white cover shows ring wear so readily, this is an EXTREMELY difficult album to find in near-mint condition

SWBO-101 [(2)]	The Beatles	1975	17.50	35.00	70.00

—With "All Rights Reserved" on labels; title in black on cover; photos and poster of thinner stock than originals

SWBO-101 [(2)]	The Beatles	197?	15.00	30.00	60.00

—Un-numbered copy; includes four individual photos and large poster (included in value)

SW-153 [P]	Yellow Submarine	1969	12.50	25.00	50.00

—With Capitol logo on Side 2 bottom. "Only a Northern Song" is rechanneled.

SW-153 [P]	Yellow Submarine	1971	5.00	10.00	20.00

—With "Mfd. by Apple" on label

SW-153 [P]	Yellow Submarine	1975	6.25	12.50	25.00

—With "All Rights Reserved" on label

SO-383	Abbey Road	q1969	18.75	37.50	75.00

—With Capitol logo on Side 2 bottom; "Her Majesty" is NOT listed on either the jacket or the label

SO-383	Abbey Road	1969	10.00	20.00	40.00

—With Capitol logo on Side 2 bottom; "Her Majesty" IS listed on both the jacket and the label

SO-383	Abbey Road	1969	5.00	10.00	20.00

—With "Mfd. by Apple" on label; "Her Majesty" is NOT listed on the label

SO-383	Abbey Road	1969	5.00	10.00	20.00

—With "Mfd. by Apple" on label; "Her Majesty" IS listed on the label

SO-383	Abbey Road	1975	6.25	12.50	25.00

—With "All Rights Reserved" on label, either in black print or in light print along label edge (both versions exist)

SW-385	Hey Jude	1970	10.00	20.00	40.00

—Label calls the LP "The Beatles Again"; record is "SO-385" (this could be found in retail stores as late as 1973)

Beatles *Price Guide*

SW-385   Hey Jude   1970   6.25   12.50   25.00
—Label calls the LP "The Beatles Again"; record is "SW-385"

SW-385   Hey Jude   1970   18.75   37.50   75.00
—With Capitol logo on Side 2 bottom; label calls the LP "Hey Jude"

SW-385   Hey Jude   1970   5.00   10.00   20.00
—With "Mfd. by Apple" on label; label calls the LP "Hey Jude"

SW-385   Hey Jude   1975   6.25   12.50   25.00
—With "All Rights Reserved" on label; label calls the LP "Hey Jude"

SO-385 [DJ]   The Beatles Again   1970   4000.   6000.   8000.
—Prototype covers with "The Beatles Again" on cover; not released to the general public. This is NOT a standard issue!

SKBO-3403 [P]   The Beatles 1962-1966   1973   7.50   15.00   30.00
—Custom red Apple labels. "Love Me Do" and "I Want to Hold Your Hand" are rechanneled; "She Loves You," "A Hard Day's Night," "I Feel Fine" and "Ticket to Ride" are mono; "From Me to You," "Can't Buy Me Love" and everything else is stereo.

SKBO-3403 [P]   The Beatles 1962-1966   1975   12.50   25.00   50.00
—Custom red Apple labels with "All Rights Reserved" on labels

SKBO-3404 [B]   The Beatles 1967-1970   1973   7.50   15.00   30.00
—Custom blue Apple labels. "Hello Goodbye" and "Penny Lane" are mono, all others stereo.

SKBO-3404 [B]   The Beatles 1967-1970   1975   12.50   25.00   50.00
—Custom blue Apple labels with "All Rights Reserved" on labels

SPRO 11206/7 [EP] Anthology 2 Sampler   1996   37.50   75.00   150.00
—Promo-only collection sent to college radio stations

C1-8-31796 [(2)]   Live at the BBC   1994   12.50   25.00   50.00

AR-34001   Let It Be   1970   6.25   12.50   25.00
—Red Apple label; originals have "Bell Sound" stamped in trail-off area, counterfeits do not

C1-8-34445 [(3)]   Anthology 1   1995   10.00   20.00   40.00
—All copies distributed in the U.S. were manufactured in the U.K. with no distinguishing marks (some LPs imported directly from the U.K. have "Made in England" stickers, which can be removed easily)

C1-8-34448 [(3)]   Anthology 2   1996   10.00   20.00   40.00

C1-8-34451 [(3)]   Anthology 3   1996   7.50   15.00   30.00

C1-97036 [B]   The Beatles 1962-1966   1993   6.25   12.50   25.00
—Custom red Apple labels; red vinyl; all copies pressed in U.K; U.S. versions have a bar-code sticker over the international bar code on back cover. "Love Me Do," "Please Please Me," "From Me to You" and "She Loves You" are mono; all others are stereo.

C1-97039   The Beatles 1967-1970   1993   6.25   12.50   25.00
—Custom blue Apple labels; blue vinyl; all copies pressed in U.K.; U.S. versions have a bar-code sticker over the international bar code on back cover.

APPLE FILMS

KAL 004 [DJ]   The Yellow Submarine (A United Artists Release) 1969   1000.   1500.   2000.
—One-sided LP with radio spots for movie

APPLE/CAPITOL

(no #) [(17)]   The Beatles 10th Anniversary Box Set   1974   1000.00   1500.00   2000.00

(no #) [(10)]   The Beatles Special Limited Edition   1974   300.00   600.00   1200.00

ST 2047 [P]   Meet the Beatles!   1968   10.00   20.00   40.00
—With Capitol logo on Side 2 bottom

ST 2047 [P]   Meet the Beatles!   1971   5.00   10.00   20.00
—With "Mfd. by Apple" on label

ST 2047 [P]   Meet the Beatles!   1975   6.25   12.50   25.00
—With "All Rights Reserved" on label

ST 2080 [P]   The Beatles' Second Album   1968   10.00   20.00   40.00
—With Capitol logo on Side 2 bottom

ST 2080 [P]   The Beatles' Second Album   1971   5.00   10.00   20.00
—With "Mfd. by Apple" on label

ST 2080 [P]   The Beatles' Second Album   1975   6.25   12.50   25.00
—With "All Rights Reserved" on label

ST 2108 [S]   Something New   1968   10.00   20.00   40.00
—With Capitol logo on Side 2 bottom

ST 2108 [S]   Something New   1971   5.00   10.00   20.00
—With "Mfd. by Apple" on label

ST 2108 [S]   Something New   1975   6.25   2.50   25.00
—With "All Rights Reserved" on label

STBO 2222 [(2) P] The Beatles' Story   1968   12.50   25.00   50.00
—With Capitol logo on bottom of B-side of both records

STBO 2222 [(2) P] The Beatles' Story   1971   7.50   15.00   30.00
—With "Mfd. by Apple" on labels

STBO 2222 [(2) P] The Beatles' Story   1975   10.00   20.00   40.00
—With "All Rights Reserved" on labels

ST 2228 [P]   Beatles '65   1968   10.00   20.00   40.00
—With Capitol logo on Side 2 bottom

ST 2228 [P]   Beatles '65   1971   5.00   10.00   20.00
—With "Mfd. by Apple" on label

ST 2228 [P]   Beatles '65   1975   6.25   12.50   25.00
—With "All Rights Reserved" on label

ST 2309 [P]   The Early Beatles   1969   10.00   20.00   40.00
—With Capitol logo on Side 2 bottom

ST 2309 [P]   The Early Beatles   1971   5.00   10.00   20.00
—With "Mfd. by Apple" on label

ST 2309 [P]   The Early Beatles   1975   6.25   12.50   25.00
—With "All Rights Reserved" on label

ST 2358 [P]   Beatles VI   1969   10.00   20.00   40.00
—With Capitol logo on Side 2 bottom

ST 2358 [P]   Beatles VI   1971   5.00   10.00   20.00
—With "Mfd. by Apple" on label

ST 2358 [P]   Beatles VI   1975   6.25   12.50   25.00
—With "All Rights Reserved" on label

SMAS 2386 [P]   Help!   1969   10.00   20.00   40.00
—With Capitol logo on Side 2 bottom

SMAS 2386 [P]   Help!   1971   5.00   10.00   20.00
—With "Mfd. by Apple" on label

SMAS 2386 [P]   Help!   1975   6.25   12.50   25.00
—With "All Rights Reserved" on label

ST 2442 [S]   Rubber Soul   1969   10.00   20.00   40.00
—With Capitol logo on Side 2 bottom

ST 2442 [S]   Rubber Soul   1971   5.00   10.00   20.00
—With "Mfd. by Apple" on label

ST 2442 [S]   Rubber Soul   1975   6.25   12.50   25.00
—With "All Rights Reserved" on label

ST 2553 [P]   Yesterday and Today   1969   10.00   20.00   40.00
—With Capitol logo on Side 2 bottom

ST 2553 [P]	Yesterday and Today	1971	5.00	10.00	20.00

—With "Mfd. by Apple" on label

ST 2553 [S]	Yesterday and Today	1971	6.25	12.50	25.00

—With "Mfd. by Apple" on label; all 11 tracks are in true stereo. Check for a triangle in the record's trail-off area.

ST 2553 [P]	Yesterday and Today	1975	6.25	12.50	25.00

—With "All Rights Reserved" on label

ST 2576 [S]	Revolver	1969	10.00	20.00	40.00

—With Capitol logo on Side 2 bottom

ST 2576 [S]	Revolver	1971	5.00	10.00	20.00

—With "Mfd. by Apple" on label

ST 2576 [S]	Revolver	1975	6.25	12.50	25.00

—With "All Rights Reserved" on label

SMAS 2653 [S]	Sgt. Pepper's Lonely Hearts Club Band	1969	10.00	20.00	40.00

—With Capitol logo on Side 2 bottom

SMAS 2653 [S]	Sgt. Pepper's Lonely Hearts Club Band	1971	6.25	12.50	25.00

—With "Mfd. by Apple" on label

SMAS 2653 [S]	Sgt. Pepper's Lonely Hearts Club Band	1975	6.25	12.50	25.00

—With "All Rights Reserved" on label

SMAL 2835 [P]	Magical Mystery Tour	1969	10.00	20.00	40.00

—With Capitol logo on Side 2 bottom; with 24-page booklet

SMAL 2835 [P]	Magical Mystery Tour	1971	5.00	10.00	20.00

—With "Mfd. by Apple" on label; with 24-page booklet

SMAL 2835 [P]	Magical Mystery Tour	1975	6.25	12.50	25.00

—With "All Rights Reserved" on label; with 24-page booklet

ATCO

33-169 [M]	Ain't She Sweet	1964	50.00	100.00	200.00
33-169 [M]	Ain't She Sweet	1964	250.00	500.00	1000.

—White label promo

SD 33-169 [P]	Ain't She Sweet	1964	100.00	200.00	400.00

—Tan and purple label; all four Beatles tracks are rechanneled

SD 33-169 [P]	Ain't She Sweet	1969	125.00	250.00	500.00

—Yellow label

AUDIO RARITIES

AR-2452 [M]	The Complete Silver Beatles	1982	3.75	7.50	15.00

—Contains 12 Decca audition tracks

AUDIOFIDELITY

PHX-339 [M]	First Movement	1982	3.00	6.00	12.00

—Contains eight Decca audition tracks

PD-339 [M]	First Movement	1982	7.50	15.00	30.00

—Contains eight Decca audition tracks; picture disc

BACKSTAGE

2-201 [(2) M]	Like Dreamers Do	1982	10.00	20.00	40.00

—Gatefold package, individually numbered (numbers under 100 increase value significantly)

2-201 [(2) M]	Like Dreamers Do	1982	12.50	25.00	50.00

—Non-gatefold package

BSR-1111 [(3) M]	Like Dreamers Do	1982	15.00	30.00	60.00

—Two picture discs (10 of 15 Decca audition tracks on one, interviews on the other) and one white- vinyl record (same contests as musical picture disc)

BSR-1111 [(3) M]	Like Dreamers Do	1982	25.00	50.00	100.00

—Same as above, except colored-vinyl LP is gray

BSR-1111 [DJ]	Like Dreamers Do	1982	12.50	25.00	50.00

—White vinyl promo in white sleeve

BSR-1111 [DJ]	Like Dreamers Do	1982	12.50	25.00	50.00

—Gray vinyl promo in white sleeve

BSR-1165 [PD]	The Beatles Talk with Jerry G.	1982	6.25	12.50	25.00

—Picture disc

BSR-1175 [PD]	The Beatles Talk with Jerry G., Vol. 2	1983	6.25	12.50	25.00

—Picture disc0

CAPITOL

(no #) [(18)]	The Beatles Collection Platinum Series	1984	200.00	400.00	800.00
BC-13 [(14)]	The Beatles Collection	1978	62.50	125.00	250.00

—American versions have "EMI" and "BC-13" on box spine; imports go for less

SWBO-101 [(2)]	The Beatles	1976	7.50	15.00	30.00

—Orange label; with photos and poster

SWBO-101 [(2)]	The Beatles	1978	7.50	15.00	30.00

—Purple label, large Capitol logo; with photos and poster (some copies have four photos as one perforated sheet)

SWBO-101 [(2)]	The Beatles	1983	10.00	20.00	40.00

—Black label, print in colorband; with photos and poster (some copies have four photos as one perforated sheet)

SW-153 [P]	Yellow Submarine	1976	3.00	6.00	12.00

—Orange label

SW-153 [P]	Yellow Submarine	1978	2.50	5.00	10.00

—Purple label, large Capitol logo

SW-153 [P]	Yellow Submarine	1983	3.75	7.50	15.00

—Black label, print in colorband

SO-383	Abbey Road	1976	3.00	6.00	12.00

—Orange label

SO-383	Abbey Road	1978	2.50	5.00	10.00

—Purple label, large Capitol logo

SO-383	Abbey Road	1983	3.75	7.50	15.00

—Black label, print in colorband

SJ-383	Abbey Road	1984	7.50	15.00	30.00

—New prefix; black label, print in colorband

SW-385	Hey Jude	1976	3.00	6.00	12.00

—Orange label (all Capitol label versions call the LP "Hey Jude")

SW-385	Hey Jude	1978	2.50	5.00	10.00

—Purple label, large Capitol logo

SW-385	Hey Jude	1983	12.50	25.00	50.00

—Black label, print in colorband

SJ-385	Hey Jude	1984	7.50	15.00	30.00

—New prefix; black label, print in colorband

T 2047 [M]	Meet the Beatles!	1964	50.00	100.00	200.00

—Black label with colorband; "Beatles!" on cover in tan to brown print; label has "ASCAP" after every title except "I Want to Hold Your Hand" (BMI); no producer credit on back cover (this is the second edition of this LP)

ST 2047 [P]	Meet the Beatles!	1964	37.50	75.00	150.00

—Black label with colorband; "Beatles!" on cover in tan to brown print; label has "ASCAP" after every title except "I Want to Hold Your Hand" (BMI); no producer credit on back cover (this is the second edition of this LP)

T 2047 [M]	Meet the Beatles!	1964	100.00	200.00	400.00

—Black label with colorband; "Beatles!" on cover in tan to brown print; no producer credit on back cover; "ASCAP" and "BMI" credits are missing on the label (this is the first edition of the LP)

ST 2047 [P]	Meet the Beatles!	1964	100.00	200.00	400.00

—Black label with colorband; "Beatles!" on cover in tan to brown print; "ASCAP" and "BMI" credits are missing on the label; no producer credit on back cover (this is the first edition of the LP)

T 2047 [M]	Meet the Beatles!	1964	37.50	75.00	150.00

—Black label with colorband; "Beatles!" on cover in tan to brown print; some labels have "ASCAP" after every title except "I Want to Hold Your Hand"; other labels have "ASCAP" after every title except "I Want to Hold Your Hand," "I Saw Her Standing There" and "I Wanna Be Your Man"; still other labels have "ASCAP" after every title except "I Want to Hold Your Hand" and "I Wanna Be Your Man"; back cover adds "Produced by George Martin" to lower left

ST 2047 [P]	Meet the Beatles!	1964	30.00	60.00	120.00

—Black label with colorband; "Beatles!" on cover in tan to brown print; some labels have "ASCAP" after every title except "I Want to Hold Your Hand"; other labels have "ASCAP" after every title except "I Want to Hold Your Hand," "I Saw Her Standing There" and "I Wanna Be Your Man"; still other labels have "ASCAP" after every title except "I Want to Hold Your Hand" and "I Wanna Be Your Man"; back cover adds "Produced by George Martin" to lower left

T 2047 [M]	Meet the Beatles!	1965	25.00	50.00	100.00

—Black label with colorband; "Beatles!" on cover in green print; most of these have "Produced by George Martin" on lower left of back cover; many of these have a label giving "BMI" credit to every song except "Don't Bother Me" and "Till There Was You"

ST 2047 [P]	Meet the Beatles!	1965	18.75	37.50	75.00

—Black label with colorband; "Beatles!" on cover in green print; most of these have "Produced by George Martin" on lower left of back cover; many of these have a label giving "BMI" credit to every song except "Don't Bother Me" and "Till There Was You"

ST 2047 [P]	Meet the Beatles!	1968	12.50	25.00	50.00

—Black colorband label; border print adds "A Subsidiary of Capitol Industries Inc."

ST-8-2047 [P]	Meet the Beatles!	1969	125.00	250.00	500.00

—Capitol Record Club edition; black label with colorband

ST-8-2047 [P]	Meet the Beatles!	1969	50.00	100.00	200.00
—*Capitol Record Club edition; lime green label*					
ST 2047 [P]	Meet the Beatles!	1969	10.00	20.00	40.00
—*Lime green label*					
ST 2047 [P]	Meet the Beatles!	1976	3.00	6.00	12.00
—*Orange label*					
ST 2047 [P]	Meet the Beatles!	1978	2.50	5.00	10.00
—*Purple label, large Capitol logo*					
ST 2047 [P]	Meet the Beatles!	1983	3.75	7.50	15.00
—*Black label, print in colorband*					
T 2080 [M]	The Beatles' Second Album	1964	45.00	90.00	180.00
ST 2080 [P]	The Beatles' Second Album	1964	25.00	50.00	100.00
—*Black label with colorband. "She Loves You," "I'll Get You" and "You Can't Do That" are rechanneled*					
ST-8-2080 [P]	The Beatles' Second Album	1964	125.00	250.00	500.00
—*Capitol Record Club edition; black label with colorband*					
ST 2080 [P]	The Beatles' Second Album	1968	12.50	25.00	50.00
—*Black colorband label; border print adds "A Subsidiary of Capitol Industries Inc."*					
ST-8-2080 [P]	The Beatles' Second Album	1969	75.00	150.00	300.00
—*Capitol Record Club edition; lime green label*					
ST 2080 [P]	The Beatles' Second Album	1969	10.00	20.00	40.00
—*Lime green label*					
ST 2080 [P]	The Beatles' Second Album	1976	3.00	6.00	12.00
—*Orange label*					
ST 2080 [P]	The Beatles' Second Album	1978	2.50	5.00	10.00
—*Purple label, large Capitol logo*					
ST 2080 [P]	The Beatles' Second Album	1983	3.75	7.50	15.00
—*Black label, print in colorband*					
T 2108 [M]	Something New	1964	37.50	75.00	150.00
ST 2108 [S]	Something New	1964	20.00	40.00	80.00
—*Black label with colorband*					
ST-8-2108 [S]	Something New	1964	75.00	150.00	300.00
—*Capitol Record Club edition; black label with colorband*					
ST 2108 [S]	Something New	1968	12.50	25.00	50.00
—*Black colorband label; border print adds "A Subsidiary of Capitol Industries Inc."*					
ST-8-2108 [S]	Something New	1969	37.50	75.00	150.00
—*Capitol Record Club edition; lime green label*					
ST-8-2108 [S]	Something New	1969	75.00	150.00	300.00
—*Longines Symphonette edition (will be stated on label); lime green label*					
ST 2108 [S]	Something New	1969	10.00	20.00	40.00
—*Lime green label*					
ST 2108 [S]	Something New	1976	3.00	6.00	12.00
—*Orange label*					
ST 2108 [S]	Something New	1978	2.50	5.00	10.00
—*Purple label, large Capitol logo*					
ST 2108 [S]	Something New	1983	3.75	7.50	15.00
—*Black label, print in colorband*					
TBO 2222 [(2) M]	The Beatles' Story	1964	50.00	100.00	200.00
STBO 2222 [(2) P]	The Beatles' Story	1964	37.50	75.00	150.00
—*Black label with colorband. Some of the musical snippets are rechanneled.*					
STBO 2222 [(2) P]	The Beatles' Story	1968	20.00	40.00	80.00
—*Black colorband label; border print adds "A Subsidiary of Capitol Industries Inc."*					
STBO 2222 [(2) P]	The Beatles' Story	1969	12.50	25.00	50.00
—*Lime green label*					
STBO 2222 [(2) P]	The Beatles' Story	1976	5.00	10.00	20.00
—*Orange label*					
STBO 2222 [(2) P]	The Beatles' Story	1978	5.00	10.00	20.00
—*Purple label, large Capitol logo*					
STBO 2222 [(2) P]	The Beatles' Story	1983	10.00	20.00	40.00
—*Black label, print in colorband*					
T 2228 [M]	Beatles '65	1964	30.00	60.00	120.00
ST 2228 [P]	Beatles '65	1964	20.00	40.00	80.00
—*Black label with colorband. "She's a Woman" and "I Feel Fine" are rechanneled.*					
ST 2228 [P]	Beatles '65	1968	12.50	25.00	50.00
—*Black colorband label; border print adds "A Subsidiary of Capitol Industries Inc."*					

ST 2228 [P]	Beatles '65	1960	10.00	20.00	40.00
—*Lime green label*					
ST 2228 [P]	Beatles '65	1976	3.00	6.00	12.00
—*Orange label*					
ST 2228 [P]	Beatles '65	1978	2.50	5.00	10.00
—*Purple label, large Capitol logo*					
ST 2228 [P]	Beatles '65	1983	3.75	7.50	15.00
—*Black label, print in colorband*					
T 2309 [M]	The Early Beatles	1965	50.00	100.00	200.00
ST 2309 [P]	The Early Beatles	1965	25.00	50.00	100.00
—*Black label with colorband. "Love Me Do" and "P.S. I Love You" are rechanneled.*					
ST 2309 [P]	The Early Beatles	1968	12.50	25.00	50.00
—*Black colorband label; border print adds "A Subsidiary of Capitol Industries Inc."*					
ST 2309 [P]	The Early Beatles	1969	10.00	20.00	40.00
—*Lime green label*					
ST 2309 [P]	The Early Beatles	1976	3.00	6.00	12.00
—*Orange label*					
ST 2309 [P]	The Early Beatles	1978	2.50	5.00	10.00
—*Purple label, large Capitol logo*					
ST 2309 [P]	The Early Beatles	1983	6.25	12.50	25.00
—*Black label, print in colorband*					
T 2358 [M]	Beatles VI	1965	30.00	60.00	120.00
—*With "See label for correct playing order" on back cover*					
T 2358 [M]	Beatles VI	1965	25.00	50.00	100.00
—*With song titles listed in correct order on back cover*					
ST 2358 [P]	Beatles VI	1965	20.00	40.00	80.00
—*Black label with colorband; with "See label for correct playing order" on back cover*					
ST 2358 [P]	Beatles VI	1965	18.75	37.50	75.00
—*Black label with colorband; with song titles listed in correct order on back cover. "Yes It Is" is rechanneled.*					
ST-8-2358 [P]	Beatles VI	1965	125.00	250.00	500.00
—*Capitol Record Club edition; black label with colorband*					
ST 2358 [P]	Beatles VI	1968	12.50	25.00	50.00
—*Black colorband label; border print adds "A Subsidiary of Capitol Industries Inc."*					
ST-8-2358 [P]	Beatles VI	1969	100.00	200.00	400.00
—*Capitol Record Club edition; lime green label*					
ST 2358 [P]	Beatles VI	1969	10.00	20.00	40.00
—*Lime green label*					
ST 2358 [P]	Beatles VI	1976	3.00	6.00	12.00
—*Orange label*					
ST 2358 [P]	Beatles VI	1978	2.50	5.00	10.00
—*Purple label, large Capitol logo*					
ST 2358 [M]	Beatles VI	1983	3.75	7.50	15.00
—*Black label, print in colorband; plays in mono despite label designation*					
ST 2358 [M]	Beatles VI	1988	20.00	40.00	80.00
—*Purple label, small Capitol logo; plays in mono despite label designation*					
MAS 2386 [M]	Help!	1965	37.50	75.00	150.00
SMAS 2386 [P]	Help!	1965	18.75	37.50	75.00
—*Black label with colorband. Has incidental music by George Martin. "Ticket to Ride" is rechanneled.*					
SMAS-8-2386 [P]	Help!	1965	100.00	200.00	400.00
—*Capitol Record Club edition; black label with colorband; no "8" on cover*					
SMAS-8-2386 [P]	Help!	1965	150.00	300.00	600.00
—*Capitol Record Club edition; black label with colorband; with "8" on cover*					
SMAS 2386 [P]	Help!	1968	12.50	25.00	50.00
—*Black colorband label; border print adds "A Subsidiary of Capitol Industries Inc."*					
SMAS-8-2386 [P]	Help!	1969	50.00	100.00	200.00
—*Capitol Record Club edition; lime green label; no "8" on cover*					
SMAS-8-2386 [P]	Help!	1969	100.00	200.00	400.00
—*Capitol Record Club edition; lime green label; with "8" on cover*					
SMAS 2386 [P]	Help!	1969	10.00	20.00	40.00
—*Lime green label*					
SMAS 2386 [P]	Help!	1976	3.00	6.00	12.00
—*Orange label*					
SMAS 2386 [P]	Help!	1978	2.50	5.00	10.00
—*Purple label, large Capitol logo*					

SMAS-8-2386 [P]	Help!	197?	175.00	350.00	700.00

—Longines Symphonette edition; with "Mfd. by Longines" and "8" on cover

SMAS 2386 [P]	Help!	1983	3.75	7.50	15.00

—Black label, print in colorband

T 2442 [M]	Rubber Soul	1965	30.00	60.00	120.00
ST 2442 [S]	Rubber Soul	1965	15.00	30.00	60.00

—Black label with colorband

ST-8-2442 [S]	Rubber Soul	1965	75.00	150.00	300.00

—Capitol Record Club edition; black label with colorband

ST 2442 [S]	Rubber Soul	1968	12.50	25.00	50.00

—Black colorband label; border print adds "A Subsidiary of Capitol Industries Inc."

ST-8-2442 [S]	Rubber Soul	1969	50.00	100.00	200.00

—Capitol Record Club edition; lime green label

ST-8-2442 [S]	Rubber Soul	1969	62.50	125.00	250.00

—Longines Symphonette edition (will be stated on label); lime green label

ST 2442 [S]	Rubber Soul	1969	10.00	20.00	40.00

—Lime green label

ST 2442 [S]	Rubber Soul	1976	3.00	6.00	12.00

—Orange label

SW 2442 [S]	Rubber Soul	1978	2.50	5.00	10.00

—Purple label, large Capitol logo

SW 2442 [S]	Rubber Soul	1983	3.75	7.50	15.00

—Black label, print in colorband

T 2553 [M]	Yesterday and Today	1966	2000.00	3000.00	4000.00

—"First state" butcher cover (never had other cover on top); cover will be the same size as other Capitol Beatles LPs

T 2553 [M]	Yesterday and Today	1966	250.00	500.00	1000.00

—"Second state" butcher cover (trunk cover pasted over original cover)

T 2553 [M]	Yesterday and Today	1966	400.00	800.00	1200.

—"Third state" butcher cover (trunk cover removed, leaving butcher cover intact); cover will be about 3/16-inch narrower than other Capitol Beatles LPs; value is highly negotiable depending upon the success of removing the paste-over

T 2553 [M]	Yesterday and Today	1966	37.50	75.00	150.00

—Trunk cover

ST 2553 [P]	Yesterday and Today	1966	4000.	6000.	8000.

—"First state" butcher cover (never had other cover on top); cover will be the same size as other Capitol Beatles LPs

ST 2553 [P]	Yesterday and Today	1966	500.00	750.00	1000.

—"Second state" butcher cover (trunk cover pasted over original cover)

ST 2553 [P]	Yesterday and Today	1966	375.00	750.00	1500.

—"Third state" butcher cover (trunk cover removed, leaving butcher cover intact); cover will be about 3/16-inch narrower than other Capitol Beatles LPs; value is highly negotiable depending upon the success of removing the paste-over

ST 2553 [P]	Yesterday and Today	1966	20.00	40.00	80.00

—Trunk cover; black label with colorband (all later variations have the trunk cover). "I'm Only Sleeping," "Dr. Robert" and "And Your Bird Can Sing" are rechanneled.

ST-8-2553 [P]	Yesterday and Today	1966	75.00	150.00	300.00

—Capitol Record Club edition; black label with colorband

ST 2553 [P]	Yesterday and Today	1968	12.50	25.00	50.00

—Black colorband label; border print adds "A Subsidiary of Capitol Industries Inc."

ST-8-2553 [S]	Yesterday and Today	1969	37.50	75.00	150.00

—Capitol Record Club edition; lime green label; all 11 tracks are in true stereo! (We don't know if the same is true of the black label version.)

ST 2553 [P]	Yesterday and Today	1969	10.00	20.00	40.00

—Lime green label

ST 2553 [P]	Yesterday and Today	1976	3.00	6.00	12.00

—Orange label; it's possible that this and all future pressings have all 11 tracks in true stereo, but we don't know.

ST 2553 [P]	Yesterday and Today	1978	2.50	5.00	10.00

—Purple label, large Capitol logo

ST 2553 [P]	Yesterday and Today	1983	3.75	7.50	15.00

—Black label, print in colorband

T 2576 [M]	Revolver	1966	50.00	100.00	200.00
ST 2576 [S]	Revolver	1966	25.00	50.00	100.00

—Black label with colorband

ST-8-2576 [S]	Revolver	1966	100.00	200.00	400.00

—Capitol Record Club edition; black label with colorband

ST 2576 [S]	Revolver	1968	12.50	25.00	50.00

—Black colorband label; border print adds "A Subsidiary of Capitol Industries Inc."

ST-8-2576 [S]	Revolver	1969	30.00	60.00	120.00

—Capitol Record Club edition; lime green label

ST 2576 [S]	Revolver	1969	10.00	20.00	40.00

—Lime green label

ST 2576 [S]	Revolver	1970	75.00	150.00	300.00

—Red label with "target" Capitol at top (same design as lime green label)

ST-8-2576 [S]	Revolver	1973?	50.00	100.00	200.00

—Capitol Record Club edition; orange label (a very late issue, as Capitol Record Club closed in 1973)

ST 2576 [S]	Revolver	1976	3.00	6.00	12.00

—Orange label

SW 2576 [S]	Revolver	1978	2.50	5.00	10.00

—Purple label, large Capitol logo

SW 2576 [S]	Revolver	1983	3.75	7.50	15.00

—Black label, print in colorband

MAS 2653 [M]	Sgt. Pepper's Lonely Hearts Club Band	1967	75.00	150.00	300.00
SMAS 2653 [S]	Sgt. Pepper's Lonely Hearts Club Band	1967	25.00	50.00	100.00

—Black label with colorband

SMAS 2653 [S]	Sgt. Pepper's Lonely Hearts Club Band	1968	15.00	30.00	60.00

—Black colorband label; border print adds "A Subsidiary of Capitol Industries Inc."

SMAS 2653 [S]	Sgt. Pepper's Lonely Hearts Club Band	1969	12.50	25.00	50.00

—Lime green label

SMAS 2653 [S]	Sgt. Pepper's Lonely Hearts Club Band	1976	3.00	6.00	12.00

—Orange label

SMAS 2653 [S]	Sgt. Pepper's Lonely Hearts Club Band	1978	2.50	5.00	10.00

—Purple label, large Capitol logo. Many copies from 1978 had a "The Original Classic" sticker on shrink wrap; it was added at the time of the release of the bomb movie version of Sgt. Pepper. Double the value if the sticker is still there.

SMAS 2653 [S]	Sgt. Pepper's Lonely Hearts Club Band	1983	3.75	7.50	15.00

—Black label, print in colorband; some of these had "The Original Classic" stickers, too. Add $10 to value if it is there.

2653	Sgt. Pepper's Lonely Hearts Club Band Cut-Out Inserts	1967	—	—	3.00
2653	Sgt. Pepper's Lonely Hearts Club Band Special Inner Sleeve	1967	3.75	7.50	15.00

—Red-pink psychedelic sleeve only issued with 1967 (mono and stereo) editions

MAL 2835 [M]	Magical Mystery Tour	1967	75.00	150.00	300.00

—With 24-page book bound into center of gatefold

SMAL 2835 [P]	Magical Mystery Tour	1967	25.00	50.00	100.00

—Black label with colorband; with 24-page booklet. "Penny Lane," "Baby You're a Rich Man" and "All You Need Is Love" is rechanneled, as is the second half of "I Am the Walrus" (every "stereo" version of "Walrus" is this way)

SMAL 2835 [P]	Magical Mystery Tour	1968	15.00	30.00	60.00

—Black colorband label; border print adds "A Subsidiary of Capitol Industries Inc."; with 24-page booklet

SMAL 2835 [P]	Magical Mystery Tour	1969	12.50	25.00	50.00

—Lime green label; with 24-page booklet

SMAL 2835 [P]	Magical Mystery Tour	1976	3.00	6.00	12.00

—Orange label; with 24-page booklet

SMAL 2835 [P]	Magical Mystery Tour	1978	2.50	5.00	10.00

—Purple label, large Capitol logo; this edition did not come with booklet

SMAL 2835 [P]	Magical Mystery Tour	1983	3.75	7.50	15.00

—Black label, print in colorband; no booklet

SKBO-3403 [P]	The Beatles 1962-1966	1976	5.00	10.00	20.00

—Red labels

SKBO-3403 [P]	The Beatles 1962-1966	1976	7.50	15.00	30.00

—Blue labels (error pressing)

SKBO-3404 [B]	The Beatles 1967-1970	1976	5.00	10.00	20.00

—Blue labels

SPRO-8969	Rarities	1978	12.50	25.00	50.00

—Purple label, large Capitol logo; part of the U.S. box set The Beatles Collection (BC-13)

SKBO-11537 [(2)]	Rock 'n' Roll Music	1976	6.25	12.50	25.00
SMAS-11638	The Beatles at the Hollywood Bowl	1977	5.00	10.00	20.00

—Originals with embossed title and ticket on front cover

SMAS-11638 [DJ] The Beatles at the Hollywood Bowl 1977 125.00 250.00 500.00
—Advance tan label promo in plain white jacket

SMAS 11638 The Beatles at the Hollywood Bowl 1980 3.75 7.50 15.00
—Second pressing without embossed title and ticket

SMAS-11638 The Beatles at the Hollywood Bowl 1989 10.00 20.00 40.00
—With UPC code on back cover

SKBL-11711 [(2) P]Love Songs 1977 5.00 10.00 20.00
—With booklet and embossed, leather-like cover. "P.S. I Love You" and "Yes It Is" are rechanneled.

SKBL-11711 [(2) P] Love Songs 1988 7.50 15.00 30.00
—With booklet, but without embossed cover

SEAX-11840 [PD] Sgt. Pepper's Lonely Hearts Club Band 1978 5.00 10.00 20.00
—Picture disc; deduct 25% for cut-outs

SEBX-11841 [(2)] The Beatles 1978 12.50 25.00 50.00
—White vinyl; with photos and poster (with number "SEBX-11841" on each)

SEBX-11842 [P] The Beatles 1962-1966 1978 10.00 20.00 40.00
—Red vinyl

SEBX-11843 [B] The Beatles 1967-1970 1978 10.00 20.00 40.00
—Blue vinyl

SEAX-11900 [PD] Abbey Road 1978 10.00 20.00 40.00
—Picture disc; deduct 25% for cut-outs

SW-11921 [P] A Hard Day's Night 1979 3.00 6.00 12.00
—Purple label, large Capitol logo

SW-11921 [P] A Hard Day's Night 1983 3.75 7.50 15.00
—Black label, print in colorband

SW-11921 [P] A Hard Day's Night 1988 6.25 12.50 25.00
—Purple label, small Capitol logo

SW-11922 Let It Be 1979 3.75 7.50 15.00
—Purple label, large Capitol logo; with poster and custom innersleeve

SW-11922 Let It Be 1983 3.75 7.50 15.00
—Black label, print in colorband; add 33% if poster is included

SW-11922 Let It Be 1988 6.25 12.50 25.00
—Purple label, small Capitol logo; add 20% if poster and custom innersleeve are included

SN-12009 [DJ] Rarities 1979 75.00 150.00 300.00
—Green label; withdrawn before official release; all known copies have a plain white sleeve

SHAL-12060 [B] Rarities 1980 5.00 10.00 20.00
—Black label with colorband. First pressing says that "There's a Place" debuts in stereo (false) and that the screaming at the end of "Helter Skelter" was a "classic Lennon statement" (it's actually Ringo).

SHAL-12060 [B] Rarities 1980 3.75 7.50 15.00
—Same as above, with errors deleted and "Produced by George Martin" added to back cover

SV-12199 [DJ] Reel Music 1982 10.00 20.00 40.00
—Yellow vinyl promo; numbered back cover with 12-page booklet

SV-12199 [DJ] Reel Music 1982 5.00 10.00 20.00
—Yellow vinyl promo; plain white cover with 12-page booklet

SV-12199 Reel Music 1982 2.50 5.00 10.00
—Standard issue with 12-page booklet

SV-12245 [P] 20 Greatest Hits 1982 5.00 10.00 20.00
—Purple label, large Capitol logo. "Love Me Do" and "She Loves You" are rechanneled, the other 18 tracks are stereo

SV-12245 [P] 20 Greatest Hits 1983 5.00 10.00 20.00
—Black label, print in colorband

SV-12245 [P] 20 Greatest Hits 1988 6.25 12.50 25.00
—Purple label, small Capitol logo

SN-16020 Rock 'n' Roll Music, Volume 1 1980 2.50 5.00 10.00

SN-16021 Rock 'n' Roll Music, Volume 2 1980 2.50 5.00 10.00

CLJ-46435 [M] Please Please Me 1987 5.00 10.00 20.00
—Black label, print in colorband; first Capitol version of original British LP

CLJ-46435 [M] Please Please Me 1988 6.25 12.50 25.00
—Purple label, small Capitol logo

C1-46435 [M] Please Please Me 1995 3.00 6.00 12.00
—New prefix; Apple logo on back cover

CLJ-46436 [M] With the Beatles 1987 5.00 10.00 20.00
—Black label, print in colorband; first Capitol version of original British LP

CLJ-46436 [M] With the Beatles 1988 6.25 12.50 25.00
—Purple label, small Capitol logo

C1-46436 [M] With the Beatles 1995 3.00 6.00 12.00
—New prefix; Apple logo on back cover

CLJ-46437 [M] A Hard Day's Night 1987 5.00 10.00 20.00
—Black label, print in colorband; first Capitol version of original British LP

CLJ-46437 [M] A Hard Day's Night 1988 6.25 12.50 25.00
—Purple label, small Capitol logo

C1-46437 [M] A Hard Day's Night 1995 3.00 6.00 12.00
—New prefix; Apple logo on back cover

CLJ-46438 [M] Beatles for Sale 1987 5.00 10.00 20.00
—Black label, print in colorband; first Capitol version of original British LP

CLJ-46438 [M] Beatles for Sale 1988 6.25 12.50 25.00
—Purple label, small Capitol logo

C1-46438 [M] Beatles for Sale 1995 3.00 6.00 12.00
—New prefix; Apple logo on back cover

CLJ-46439 [S] Help! 1987 5.00 10.00 20.00
—Black label, print in colorband; first Capitol version of original British LP

CLJ-46439 [S] Help! 1988 6.25 12.50 25.00
—Purple label, small Capitol logo

C1-46439 [S] Help! 1995 3.00 6.00 12.00
—New prefix; Apple logo on back cover

CLJ-46440 [S] Rubber Soul 1987 5.00 10.00 20.00
—Black label, print in colorband; first Capitol version of original British LP

CLJ-46440 [S] Rubber Soul 1988 6.25 12.50 25.00
—Purple label, small Capitol logo

C1-46440 [S] Rubber Soul 1995 3.00 6.00 12.00
—New prefix; Apple logo on back cover

CLJ-46441 [S] Revolver 1987 5.00 10.00 20.00
—Black label, print in colorband; first Capitol version of original British LP

CLJ-46441 [S] Revolver 1988 6.25 12.50 25.00
—Purple label, small Capitol logo

C1-46441 [S] Revolver 1995 3.00 6.00 12.00
—New prefix; Apple logo on back cover

C1-46442 [S] Sgt. Pepper's Lonely Hearts Club Band 1988 6.25 12.50 25.00
—New number; purple label, small Capitol logo

C1-46442 [S] Sgt. Pepper's Lonely Hearts Club Band 1995 3.00 6.00 12.00
—With Apple logo on back cover

C1-46443 [(2)] The Beatles 1988 12.50 25.00 50.00
—New number; purple label, small Capitol logo; with photos and poster (some copies have four photos as one perforated sheet)

C1-46443 [(2)] The Beatles 1995 5.00 10.00 20.00
—With Apple logo on back cover

C1-46445 [P] Yellow Submarine 1988 6.25 12.50 25.00
—New number; purple label, small Capitol logo

C1-46445 [P] Yellow Submarine 1995 3.00 6.00 12.00
—Reissue has the British liner notes, which include a review of the White Album.

C1-46446 Abbey Road 1988 6.25 12.50 25.00
—New number; purple label, small Capitol logo

C1-46446 Abbey Road 1995 3.00 6.00 12.00
—Apple logo restored to back cover on reissue

C1-46447 Let It Be 1995 3.00 6.00 12.00
—New number (the only 1995 reissue with a completely new number)

C1-48062 [P] Magical Mystery Tour 1988 6.25 12.50 25.00
—New number; purple label, small Capitol logo; no booklet

C1-48062 [P] Magical Mystery Tour 1992 3.00 6.00 12.00
—With Apple logo on back cover; reissue restores booklet to package

C1-90435 [P] The Beatles 1962-1966 1988 7.50 15.00 30.00
—New number; purple labels, small Capitol logo

C1-90438 [B] The Beatles 1967-1970 1988 7.50 15.00 30.00
—New number; purple label, small Capitol logo

C1-90441 [P] Meet the Beatles! 1988 6.25 12.50 25.00
—New number; purple label, small Capitol logo

C1-90442 Hey Jude 1988 6.25 12.50 25.00
—New number; purple label, small Capitol logo

C1-90443 [S]	Something New	1988	6.25	12.50	25.00

—*New number; purple label, small Capitol logo*

C1-90444 [P]	The Beatles' Second Album	1988	6.25	12.50	25.00

—*New number; purple label, small Capitol logo*

C1-90445 [M]	Beatles VI	1988	6.25	12.50	25.00

—*New number; purple label, small Capitol logo; plays in mono despite label designation*

C1-90446 [P]	Beatles '65	1988	6.25	12.50	25.00

—*New number; purple label, small Capitol logo*

C1-90447 [P]	Yesterday and Today	1988	6.25	12.50	25.00

—*New number; purple label, small Capitol logo; stereo content uncertain*

C1-90452 [S]	Revolver	1988	6.25	12.50	25.00

—*New number; purple label, small Capitol logo*

C1-90453 [S]	Rubber Soul	1988	6.25	12.50	25.00

—*New number; purple label, small Capitol logo*

C1-90454 [P]	Help!	1988	6.25	12.50	25.00

—*New number; purple label, small Capitol logo*

C1-91135 [(2) B]	Past Masters Volume 1 and 2	1988	6.25	12.50	25.00

—*Some early tracks are in mono, but "This Boy," "She's a Woman." "Yes It Is," and "The Inner Light" are in stereo.*

BBX1-91302 [(14)]	The Beatles Deluxe Box Set	1988	75.00	150.00	300.00

CICADELIC

1960	Moviemania	1987	3.00	6.00	12.00
1961	Not a Second Time	1987	3.00	6.00	12.00
1962	Things We Said Today	1986	3.00	6.00	12.00
1963	All Our Loving	1986	3.00	6.00	12.00
1964	East Coast Invasion	1985	3.00	6.00	12.00
1965	Round the World	1986	3.00	6.00	12.00
1966	West Coast Invasion	1985	3.00	6.00	12.00
1967	From Britain with Beat!	1987	3.00	6.00	12.00
1968	Here, There and Everywhere	1988	3.00	6.00	12.00

CLARION

601 [M]	The Amazing Beatles and Other Great English Group Sounds	1966	25.00	50.00	100.00
SD 601 [P]	The Amazing Beatles and Other Great English Group Sounds	1966	50.00	100.00	200.00

—*All four Beatles tracks are rechaneled*

GREAT NORTHWEST

GNW 4007	Beatle Talk	1978	2.50	5.00	10.00
GNW 4007	Beatle Talk	1978	12.50	25.00	50.00

—*Columbia Record Club edition; "CRC" on spine*

HALL OF MUSIC

HM-1-2200 [(2) M]	Live 1962, Hamburg, Germany	1981	12.50	25.00	50.00

—*Only American LP with the original Eurpoean contents — "I Saw Her Standing There," "Twist and Shout," "Ask Me Why" and "Reminiscing" replace the four songs listed with the Lingasong issue*

I-N-S RADIO NEWS

DOC-1 [DJ]	Beatlemania Tour Coverage	1964	750.00	1125.	1500.

—*Promo-only open-end interview with script in plain white jacket*

LINGASONG

LS-2-7001 [(2) R]	Live at the Star Club in Hamburg, Germany, 1962	1977	5.00	10.00	20.00

—*American version contains "I'm Gonna Sit Right Down and Cry," "Where Have You Been All My Life," "Till There Was You," and "Sheila," not on imports*

LS-2-7001 [(2) DJ]	Live at the Star Club in Hamburg, Germany, 1962	1977	75.00	150.00	300.00

—*Promo only on blue vinyl*

LS-2-7001 [(2) DJ]	Live at the Star Club in Hamburg, Germany, 1962	1977	50.00	100.00	200.00

—*Promo only on red vinyl*

LS-2-7001 [(2) DJ]	Live at the Star Club in Hamburg, Germany, 1962	1977	10.00	20.00	40.00

—*Promo on black vinyl; "D.J. Copy Not for Sale" on labels*

LLOYDS

ER-MC-LTD	The Great American Tour — 1965 Live Beatlemania Concert	1965	150.00	300.00	600.00

—*Another interview album from the Ed Rudy people, with a live Beatles show in the background and the songs poorly overdubbed by the Liverpool Lads*

METRO

M-563 [M]	This Is Where It Started	1966	25.00	50.00	100.00

—*Reissue of MGM album with two of the "others" tracks deleted*

MS-563 [R]	This Is Where It Started	1966	37.50	75.00	150.00

—*In stereo cover*

MS-563 [R]	This Is Where It Started	1966	50.00	100.00	200.00

—*In mono cover with "Stereo" sticker*

MGM

E-4215 [M]	The Beatles with Tony Sheridan and Their Guests	1964	50.00	100.00	200.00

—*Without "And Guests" on cover*

E-4215 [M]	The Beatles with Tony Sheridan and Their Guests	1964	62.50	125.00	250.00

—*With "And Guests" on cover*

SE-4215 [R]	The Beatles with Tony Sheridan and Their Guests	1964	150.00	300.00	600.00

—*With "And Guests" on cover*

SE-4215 [R]	The Beatles with Tony Sheridan and Their Guests	1964	200.00	400.00	800.00

—*Without "And Guests" on cover*

MOBILE FIDELITY

BC-1 [(13)]	The Beatles Collection	1982	125.00	250.00	500.00
1-023	Abbey Road	1979	12.50	25.00	50.00

—*Audiophile vinyl*

1-047 [P]	Magical Mystery Tour	1980	15.00	30.00	60.00

—*Audiophile vinyl; yes, this contains the rechanneled stereo versions of "Penny Lane," "Baby You're a Rich Man" and "All You Need Is Love"*

2-072 [(2)]	The Beatles	1982	12.50	25.00	50.00

—*Audiophile vinyl; not issued with photos or poster*

UHQR 1-100 [S]	Sgt. Pepper's Lonely Hearts Club Band	1982	75.00	150.00	300.00

—*Ultra High Quality release with special cover; numbered edition of 5,000; numbers under 100 fetch even more*

1-100 [S]	Sgt. Pepper's Lonely Hearts Club Band	1985	10.00	20.00	40.00

—*Audiophile vinyl*

1-101 [P]	Please Please Me	1986	10.00	20.00	40.00

—*Audiophile vinyl; British version of album. "Love Me Do" and "P.S. I Love You" are rechanneled.*

1-102 [S]	With the Beatles	1986	37.50	75.00	150.00

—*Audiophile vinyl; British version of album. Limited run because of a damaged stamper that was not replaced.*

1-103 [S]	A Hard Day's Night	1987	10.00	20.00	40.00

—*Audiophile vinyl; British version of album*

1-104 [S]	Beatles for Sale	1986	10.00	20.00	40.00

—*Audiophile vinyl; British version of album*

1-105 [S]	Help!	1985	10.00	20.00	40.00

—*Audiophile vinyl; British version of album*

1-106 [S]	Rubber Soul	1985	10.00	20.00	40.00

—*Audiophile vinyl; British version of album*

1-107 [S]	Revolver	1986	10.00	20.00	40.00

—*Audiophile vinyl; British version of album*

1-108 [P]	Yellow Submarine	1987	15.00	30.00	60.00

—*Audiophile vinyl*

1-109	Let It Be	1987	10.00	20.00	40.00

—*Audiophile vinyl; gatefold cover*

1-109	Let It Be	1987	50.00	100.00	200.00

—*Audiophile vinyl; regular cover*

ORANGE

ORC-12880 [DJ]	The Silver Beatles	1985	75.00	150.00	300.00

—*Test pressing; white cover with title sticker*

ORC-12880 [DJ]   The Silver Beatles   1985   100.00   200.00   400.00
—*Test pressing; full cover cover slick folded around a white cover. Both contain all 15 Decca audition tracks*

PBR INTERNATIONAL

7005/6 [(2)]   The David Wigg Interviews (The Beatles Tapes)   1978   20.00   40.00
80.00
—*Blue vinyl*

7005/6 [(2)]   The David Wigg Interviews (The Beatles Tapes)1980   15.00   30.00   60.00
—*Black vinyl*

PHOENIX

PHX-352 [M]   Silver Beatles, Volume 1   1982   3.00   6.00   12.00
—*Contains seven Decca audition tracks*

PHX-353 [M]   Silver Beatles, Volume 2   1982   3.00   6.00   12.00
—*Contains seven Decca audition tracks (different seven than Phoenix 352)*

P20-623   20 Hits, Beatles   1983   5.00   10.00   20.00
—*With 12 Decca audition tracks, four Beatles/Tony Sheridan tracks, and four Tony Sheridan solo tracks*

P20-629   20 Hits, Beatles   1983   5.00   10.00   20.00
—*With 20 live Hamburg tracks*

PICKWICK

PTP-2098 [(2) M] The Historic First Live Recordings   1980   4.50   9.00   18.00
—*Same contents as Lingasong LP, plus "Hully Gully"*

SPC-3661 [M]   The Beatles' First Live Recordings, Volume 1   1979   3.00   6.00
12.00

SPC-3662 [M]   The Beatles' First Live
                 Recordings, Volume 2   1979   3.00   6.00   12.00

BAN-90051 [M]   Recorded Live in Hamburg, Vol. 1   1978   7.50   15.00   30.00

BAN-90061 [M]   Recorded Live in Hamburg, Vol. 2   1978   7.50   15.00   30.00

BAN-90071 [M]   Recorded Live in Hamburg, Vol. 3   1978   10.00   20.00   40.00

POLYDOR

24-4504 [P]   The Beatles — Circa 1960 — In the Beginning
                 Featuring Tony Sheridan   1970   6.25   12.50   25.00
—*Originals have gatefold cover*

24-4504 [P]   The Beatles — Circa 1960 — In the Beginning
                 Featuring Tony Sheridan   197?   10.00   20.00   40.00
—*Some copies of the record contain only the title "The Beatles — In the Beginning"*

PD-4504 [P]   The Beatles — Circa 1960 — In the Beginning
                 Featuring Tony Sheridan   1981   3.00   6.00   12.00
—*Reissue without gatefold cover*

SKAO-93199 [P]   The Beatles — Circa 1960 —
                 In the Beginning Featuring Tony Sheridan   1970   10.00   20.00   40.00
—*Capitol Record Club edition*

825073-1 [P]   The Beatles — Circa 1960 —
                 In the Beginning Featuring Tony Sheridan   1988   5.00   10.00   20.00
—*Reissue with new number*

RADIO PULSEBEAT NEWS

2   The American Tour with Ed Rudy   1964   25.00   50.00   100.00
—*Yellow label; some copies came with a special edition of Teen Talk magazine (add 50%)*

2   The American Tour with Ed Rudy   1980   6.25   12.50   25.00
—*Blue label; authorized reissue with Beatles' photo on cover*

3   1965 Talk Album — Ed Rudy with
                 New U.S. Tour   1965   37.50   75.00   150.00
—*"The Beatles" in black print under front cover photo (other versions appear to be bootlegs)*

RAVEN/PVC

8911   Talk Downunder   1981   2.50   5.00   10.00

8911 [DJ]   Talk Downunder   1981   20.00   40.00   80.00
—*Promo only in white cover with title sticker. Label reads "For Radio Play Only"*

SAVAGE

BM-69 [M]   The Savage Young Beatles   1964   37.50   75.00   150.00
—*Orange label; no legitimate copy says "Stereo" on cover*

BM-69 [M]   The Savage Young Beatles   1964   375.00   750.00   1500.
—*Yellow label, glossy orange cover*

SILHOUETTE

SM-10004 [PD]   Timeless   1981   5.00   10.00   20.00
—*Picture disc with all interviews*

SM-10004 [PD]   Timeless   1981   6.25   12.50   25.00
—*Picture disc with interviews plus remakes of "Imagine" and "Let It Be" (by non-Beatles)*

SM-10010 [PD]   Timeless II   1982   5.00   10.00   20.00
—*Picture disc with mostly interviews*

SM-10013   The British Are Coming   1984   3.75   7.50   15.00
—*Interview album with numbered sticker (very low numbers increase the value)*

SM-10013   The British Are Coming   1984   20.00   40.00   80.00
—*Same as above, but on red vinyl*

SM-10013 [DJ]   The British Are Coming   1984   10.00   20.00   40.00
—*White label promo; no numbered sticker*

SM-10015   Golden Beatles   1985   3.75   7.50   15.00

SM-10015   Golden Beatles   1985   20.00   40.00   80.00
—*Gold vinyl*

PD-83010 [PD]   The British Are Coming   1985   7.50   15.00   30.00
—*Picture disc*

STERLING

8895-6481   I Apologize   1966   100.00   200.00   400.00
—*One-sided LP with John Lennon's "apology" for supposed anti-Christian remarks; includes photo*

8895-6481   I Apologize   1966   75.00   150.00   300.00
—*Same as above, but without photo*

UNITED ARTISTS

UA-Help-A/B [DJ]   United Artists Presents Help!   1965   500.00   1000.00 1500.00
—*Radio spots for movie*

UA-Help-INT [DJ]   United Artists Presents Help!   1965   1000.00 1500.00 2000.00
—*Open-end interview with script (red label)*

UA-Help-Show [DJ]United Artists Presents Help!   1965   1500.00 2250.00 3000.00
—*One-sided interview with script (blue label)*

SP-2359/60 [DJ]   United Artists Presents A Hard Day's Night 1964   1000.00 1500.00 2000.00
—*Open-end interview with script*

SP-2362/3 [DJ]   United Artists Presents A Hard Day's Night 1964   375.00   750.00   1500.00
—*Radio spots for movie*

UAL 3366 [M]   A Hard Day's Night   1964   750.00   1500.00 3000.00
—*White label promo*

UAL 3366 [M]   A Hard Day's Night   1964   50.00   100.00   200.00
—*With "I Cry Instead" listing*

UAL 3366 [M]   A Hard Day's Night   1964   62.50   125.00   250.00

—*With "I'll Cry Instead" listing*

UAS 6366 [P]   A Hard Day's Night   1964   50.00   100.00   200.00
—*With "I Cry Instead" listing*

UAS 6366 [P]   A Hard Day's Night   1964   62.50   125.00   250.00
—*With "I'll Cry Instead" listing. Has incidental music by George Martin. All eight Beatles tracks are rechanneled; Martin's are in true stereo.*

UAS 6366 [P]   A Hard Day's Night   1964   6000.   9000.   12000.
—*Pink vinyl; only one copy known, probably privately (and secretly) done by a pressing-plant employee*

UAS 6366 [P]   A Hard Day's Night   1968   12.50   25.00   50.00
—*Pink and orange label*

UAS 6366 [P]   A Hard Day's Night   1970   12.50   25.00   50.00
—*Black and orange label*

UAS 6366 [P]   A Hard Day's Night   1971   5.00   10.00   20.00
—*Tan label*

UAS 6366 [P]   A Hard Day's Night   1975   5.00   10.00   20.00
—*Tan label with "All Rights Reserved" in perimeter print*

UAS 6366 [P]   A Hard Day's Night   1977   5.00   10.00   20.00
—*Sunrise label. Note: Any of the variations from 1968 on can have titles of songs incorrectly listed as "I Cry Instead" and "Tell Me Who," or only one can be wrong, or neither can be wrong. No difference in value at this time.*

T-90828 [M]   A Hard Day's Night   1964   750.00   1125.00 1500.00
—*Capitol Record Club edition*

ST-90828 [P]	A Hard Day's Night	1964	187.50	375.00	750.00

—Capitol Record Club edition

UNITED DISTRIBUTORS

UDL-2333 [M]	Dawn of the Silver Beatles	1981	15.00	30.00	60.00

—Hand-stamped numbers on back cover and label; contains 10 Decca audition tracks

UDL-2333 [M]	Dawn of the Silver Beatles	1981	12.50	25.00	50.00

—With numbered registration card (deduct 20% if missing)

UDL-2382 [M]	Lightning Strikes Twice	1981	15.00	30.00	60.00

—Side 1 has five Beatles' Decca audition tracks; Side 2 has live Elvis Presley performances from 1955

VEE JAY

DX-30 [(2) M]	The Beatles vs. The Four Seasons	1964	200.00	400.00	800.00

—Combines "Introducing the Beatles" with "Golden Hits of the Four Seasons" (Vee Jay 1065)

DXS-30 [(2) S]	The Beatles vs. The Four Seasons	1964	1500.00	2250.00	3000.00

—Combines "Introducing the Beatles" with "Golden Hits of the Four Seasons" (Vee Jay 1065)

DX(S)-30	The Beatles vs. The Four Seasons Poster	1964	75.00	150.00	300.00
PRO 202 [M]	Hear the Beatles Tell All	1964	50.00	100.00	200.00

—With "PRO" prefix on label

202 [M]	Hear the Beatles Tell All	1964	75.00	150.00	300.00

—Without "PRO" prefix on label

PRO 202 [DJ]	Hear the Beatles Tell All	1964	6000.	12000.	18000.

—White label promo with blue print

PRO 202 [S]	Hear the Beatles Tell All	1979	2.50	5.00	10.00

—Authorized reissue in stereo

PRO 202 [PD]	Hear the Beatles Tell All	1987	5.00	10.00	20.00

—Shaped picture disc with same recordings as the black vinyl versions

LP 1062 [M]	Introducing the Beatles	1964	1500.00	2750.00	4000.00

—"Ad back" cover; with "Love Me Do" and "P.S. I Love You"; oval Vee Jay logo with colorband only!

SR 1062 [B]	Introducing the Beatles	1964	4000.00	8000.00	12000.00

—"Ad back" cover; with "Love Me Do" and "P.S. I Love You" (both mono); oval Vee Jay logo with colorband only!

LP 1062 [M]	Introducing the Beatles	1964	400.00	800.00	1200.00

—Blank back cover; with "Love Me Do" and "P.S. I Love You"; oval Vee Jay logo with colorband only!

SR 1062 [B]	Introducing the Beatles	1964	625.00	1250.00	2500.00

—Blank back cover; with "Love Me Do" and "P.S. I Love You"; oval Vee Jay logo with colorband only!

LP 1062 [M]	Introducing the Beatles	1964	250.00	500.00	1000.00

—Blank back cover; with "Please Please Me" and "Ask Me Why"; oval Vee Jay logo with colorband only!

LP 1062 [M]	Introducing the Beatles	1964	200.00	400.00	800.00

—Song titles cover; with "Love Me Do" and "P.S. I Love You"; oval Vee Jay logo with colorband only!

SR 1062 [B]	Introducing the Beatles	1964	3000.00	5500.00	8000.00

—Song titles cover; with "Love Me Do" and "P.S. I Love You"; oval Vee Jay logo with colorband only! Only two dozen or so authentic copies are known, with hundreds of thousands of counterfeits

LP 1062 [M]	Introducing the Beatles	1964	75.00	150.00	300.00

—Song titles cover; with "Please Please Me" and "Ask Me Why"; oval Vee Jay logo with colorband

LP 1062 [M]	Introducing the Beatles	1964	62.50	125.00	250.00

—Song titles cover; with "Please Please Me" and "Ask Me Why"; brackets Vee Jay logo with colorband (most common authentic version)

LP 1062 [M]	Introducing the Beatles	1964	62.50	125.00	250.00

—Song titles cover; with "Please Please Me" and "Ask Me Why"; plain Vee Jay logo on solid black label

LP 1062 [M]	Introducing the Beatles	1964	75.00	150.00	300.00

—Song titles cover; with "Please Please Me" and "Ask Me Why"; oval Vee Jay logo on solid black label

LP 1062 [M]	Introducing the Beatles	1964	250.00	500.00	1000.00

—Song titles cover; with "Please Please Me" and "Ask Me Why"; brackets Vee Jay logo on solid black label

SR 1062 [S]	Introducing the Beatles	1964	400.00	800.00	1600.00

—Song titles cover; with "Please Please Me" and "Ask Me Why"; oval Vee Jay logo with colorband

SR 1062 [S]	Introducing the Beatles	1964	375.00	750.00	1500.00

—Song titles cover; with "Please Please Me" and "Ask Me Why"; brackets Vee Jay logo with colorband

SR 1062 [S]	Introducing the Beatles	1964	400.00	800.00	1600.00

—Song titles cover; with "Please Please Me" and "Ask Me Why"; plain Vee Jay logo on solid black label

LP 1085 [M]	Jolly What! The Beatles and Frank Ifield on Stage	1964	62.50	125.00	250.00

—Man in Beatle wig cover; originals have printing on spine and a dark blue/purple background (counterfeits have a black background and no spine print)

SR 1085 [M]	Jolly What! The Beatles and Frank Ifield on Stage	1964	125.00	250.00	500.00

—Man in Beatle wig cover; "Stereo" on both cover and label. "From Me to You" is mono.

LP 1085 [M]	The Beatles and Frank Ifield on Stage	1964	2000.00	3500.00	5000.00

—Portrait of Beatles cover; counterfeits are poorly reproduced and have no spine print

SR 1085 [B]	The Beatles and Frank Ifield on Stage	1964	4000.00	8000.00	12000.00

—Portrait of Beatles cover; "Stereo" on both cover and label

LP 1092 [M]	Songs, Pictures and Stories of the Fabulous Beatles	1964	125.00	250.00	500.00

—All copies have gatefold cover with 2/3 width on front; also, all copies have "Introducing the Beatles" records. Oval Vee Jay logo with colorband.

LP 1092 [M]	Songs, Pictures and Stories of the Fabulous Beatles	1964	125.00	250.00	500.00

—See above; brackets Vee Jay logo with colorband

LP 1092 [M]	Songs, Pictures and Stories of the Fabulous Beatles	1964	125.00	250.00	500.00

—See above; plain Vee Jay logo on solid black label

LP 1092 [M]	Songs, Pictures and Stories of the Fabulous Beatles	1964	125.00	250.00	500.00

—See above; oval Vee Jay logo on solid black label

VJS 1092 [S]	Songs, Pictures and Stories of the Fabulous Beatles	1964	800.00	1600.00	2400.00

—All copies have gatefold cover with 2/3 width on front; also, all copies have "Introducing the Beatles" records. Oval Vee Jay logo with colorband.

VJS 1092 [S]	Songs, Pictures and Stories of the Fabulous Beatles	1964	800.00	1600.00	2400.00

—See above; brackets Vee Jay logo with colorband

VJS 1092 [S]	Songs, Pictures and Stories of the Fabulous Beatles	1964	800.00	1600.00	2400.00

—See above; plain Vee Jay logo on solid black label. NOTE: Any non-gatefold copy or any copy called "Songs and Pictures of the Fabulous Beatles" is a counterfeit.

BEST, PETER
45s
CAMEO

391	Boys/Kansas City	1965	20.00	40.00	80.00
391 [PS]	Boys/Kansas City	1965	25.00	50.00	100.00

HAPPENING

405	If You Can't Get Her/Don't Play with Me	1964	45.00	90.00	180.00
1117/8	If You Can't Get Her/The Way I Feel About You	1966	37.50	75.00	150.00

—Label credit: "Best of the Beatles (Peter Best)"

MR. MAESTRO

711	I Can't Do Without You Now/Keys to My Heart	1965	50.00	100.00	200.00

—Label credit: "Best of the Beatles"; black vinyl

711	I Can't Do Without You Now/Keys to My Heart	1965	37.50	75.00	150.00

—Label credit: "Best of the Beatles"; blue vinyl

712	Casting My Spell/I'm Blue	1965	37.50	75.00	150.00

—Black vinyl

712	Casting My Spell/I'm Blue	1965	50.00	100.00	200.00

—Blue vinyl

ORIGINAL BEATLES DRUMMER

800	(I'll Try) Anyway/I Wanna Be There	1964	45.00	90.00	180.00

Albums
PHOENIX

PHX-340	The Beatle That Time Forgot	1982	3.00	6.00	12.00

SAVAGE

BM-71	Best of the Beatles	1966	50.00	100.00	200.00

—Authentic copies have white circle around the word "Savage" and white circle around

Pete Best's head on the album cover.

HARRISON, GEORGE
12-Inch Singles
COLUMBIA

CAS 2085 [DJ]	I Don't Want to Do It (same on both sides)	1985	5.00	10.00	20.00

DARK HORSE

PRO-A-949 [DJ]	All Those Years Ago (same on both sides)	1981	6.25	12.50	25.00
PRO-A-1075 [DJ]	Wake Up My Love (same on both sides)	1982	6.25	12.50	25.00
PRO-A-2845 [DJ]	Got My Mind Set on You (same on both sides)	1987	6.25	12.50	25.00
PRO-A-2885 [DJ]	When We Was Fab (same on both sides)	1987	6.25	12.50	25.00
PRO-A-2889 [DJ]	Devil's Radio (Gossip) (same on both sides)	1987	7.50	15.00	30.00

45s
APPLE

1828	What Is Life/Apple Scruffs	1971	3.75	7.50	15.00
—With star on A-side label					
1828	What Is Life/Apple Scruffs	1971	2.00	4.00	8.00
—Without star on A-side label					
1828 [PS]	What Is Life/Apple Scruffs	1971	10.00	20.00	40.00
1836	Bangla-Desh/Deep Blue	1971	6.25	12.50	25.00
—With star on A-side label					
1836	Bangla-Desh/Deep Blue	1971	2.00	4.00	8.00
—Without star on A-side label					
1836 [PS]	Bangla-Desh/Deep Blue	1971	5.00	10.00	20.00
P-1862 [DJ]	Give Me Love (Give Me Peace on Earth) (mono/ stereo)	1973	12.50	25.00	50.00
1862	Give Me Love (Give Me Peace on Earth) /Miss O'Dell (2:20)	1973	2.00	4.00	8.00
—B-side playing time corrected					
1862	Give Me Love (Give Me Peace on Earth) /Miss O'Dell (2:30)	1973	2.00	4.00	8.00
—With incorrect time for B-side listed					
P-1877 [DJ]	Dark Horse (edited mono/stereo)	1974	15.00	30.00	60.00
P-1877 [DJ]	Dark Horse (full length mono/stereo)	1974	10.00	20.00	40.00
1877	Dark Horse/I Don't Care Anymore	1974	2.00	4.00	8.00
—Light blue and white custom photo label					
1877	Dark Horse/I Don't Care Anymore	1974	2.50	5.00	10.00
—White label; NOT a promo					
1877 [PS]	Dark Horse/I Don't Care Anymore	1974	20.00	40.00	80.00
P-1879 [DJ]	Ding Dong, Ding Dong (remixed mono/edited stereo)	1974	10.00	20.00	40.00
1879	Ding Dong, Ding Dong/ Hari's on Tour (Express)	1974	5.00	10.00	20.00
—Black and white custom photo label					
1879	Ding Dong, Ding Dong/ Hari's on Tour (Express)	1974	62.50	125.00	250.00
—Blue and white custom photo label					
1879 [PS]	Ding Dong, Ding Dong/ Hari's on Tour (Express)	1974	5.00	10.00	20.00
P-1884 [DJ]	You (mono/stereo)	1975	10.00	20.00	40.00
1884	You/World of Stone	1975	—	3.00	6.00
1884 [PS]	You/World of Stone	1975	3.75	7.50	15.00
P-1885 [DJ]	This Guitar (Can't Keep from Crying) (mono/ stereo)	1975	12.50	25.00	50.00
1885	This Guitar (Can't Keep from Crying)/ Maya Love	1975	6.25	12.50	25.00
—The last Apple 45 until 1995					
2995	My Sweet Lord/Isn't It a Pity	1970	10.00	20.00	40.00
—With black star on label					
2995	My Sweet Lord/Isn't It a Pity	1970	2.00	4.00	8.00
—With "Mfd. by Apple" on label					

2995 [PS]	My Sweet Lord/Isn't It a Pity	1970	10.00	20.00	40.00
2995	My Sweet Lord/Isn't It a Pity	1975	6.25	12.50	25.00
—With "All Rights Reserved" disclaimer					

CAPITOL

1828	What Is Life/Apple Scruffs	1976	7.50	15.00	30.00
—Orange label					
1828	What Is Life/Apple Scruffs	1978	—	3.00	6.00
—Purple late-1970s label					
1836	Bangla-Desh/Deep Blue	1976	7.50	15.00	30.00
—Orange label					
1836	Bangla-Desh/Deep Blue	1978	—	3.00	6.00
—Purple late-1970s label					
1836	Bangla-Desh/Deep Blue	1983	3.75	7.50	15.00
—Black colorband label					
1862	Give Me Love (Give Me Peace on Earth) /Miss O'Dell	1978	2.00	4.00	8.00
—Purple late-1970s label					
1862	Give Me Love (Give Me Peace on Earth) /Miss O'Dell	1978	3.75	7.50	15.00
—Black colorband label					
1879	Ding Dong, Ding Dong/ Hari's on Tour (Express)	1978	2.00	4.00	8.00
—Purple late-1970s label					
2995	My Sweet Lord/Isn't It a Pity	1976	5.00	10.00	20.00
—Orange label with "Capitol" at bottom					
2995	My Sweet Lord/Isn't It a Pity	1978	—	3.00	6.00
—Purple label; label has reeded edge					
2995	My Sweet Lord/Isn't It a Pity	1983	—	3.00	6.00
—Black label with colorband					
2995	My Sweet Lord/Isn't It a Pity	1988	—	2.50	5.00
—Purple label; label has smooth edge					
15930 [DJ]	My Sweet Lord/My Sweet Lord 2000	2001	2.50	5.00	10.00
—White label, small hole					
15930 [PS]	My Sweet Lord/My Sweet Lord 2000	2001	3.75	7.50	15.00
—Promo item for the re-release of the All Things Must Pass CD					
58983	My Sweet Lord (2000)/ All Things Must Pass	2001	—	2.50	5.00
—Green vinyl					

COLUMBIA

04887	I Don't Want to Do It/Queen of the Hop	1985	6.25	12.50	25.00
—B-side by Dave Edmunds					

DARK HORSE

8294 [DJ]	This Song (mono/stereo)	1976	6.25	12.50	25.00
8294 [PS]	This Song (mono/stereo)	1976	10.00	20.00	40.00
—Promotional only sleeve, different from stock sleeve					
8294 [PS]	This Song (mono/stereo)	1976	10.00	20.00	40.00
—Flyer with "The Story Behind This Song"					
8294	This Song/Learning How to Love You	1976	2.50	5.00	10.00
—Tan label					
8294	This Song/Learning How to Love You	1976	2.00	4.00	8.00
—White label, NOT a promo					
8294 [PS]	This Song/Learning How to Love You	1976	7.50	15.00	30.00
8313	Crackerbox Palace/ Learning How to Love You	1977	—	2.50	5.00
8763	Blow Away/Soft-Hearted Hana	1979	—	2.50	5.00
—With "RE-1" on label					
8763	Blow Away/Soft-Hearted Hana	1979	5.00	10.00	20.00
—Without "RE-1" on label (no "Loka Productions S.A." on label)					
8763 [PS]	Blow Away/Soft-Hearted Hana	1979	—	2.50	5.00
8844	Love Comes to Everyone/Soft Touch	1979	2.50	5.00	10.00
8844 [PS]	Love Comes to Everyone/Soft Touch	1979	250.00	500.00	750.00
21891	Got My Mind Set on You/ When We Was Fab	198?	—	2.00	4.00
—"Back to Back Hits" series					

Number	Title	Year			
27913	This Is Love/Breath Away from Heaven	1988	—	2.50	5.00
27913 [PS]	This Is Love/Breath Away from Heaven	1988	—	2.50	5.00
28131	When We Was Fab/Zig Zag	1988	—	2.50	5.00
28131 [PS]	When We Was Fab/Zig Zag	1988	—	2.50	5.00
28178	Got My Mind Set on You/Lay His Head	1987	—	2.00	4.00
28178 [PS]	Got My Mind Set on You/Lay His Head	1987	—	2.00	4.00
29744	I Really Love You/Circles	1983	6.25	12.50	25.00
29864	Wake Up My Love/Greece	1982	2.50	5.00	10.00
49725	All Those Years Ago/Writing's on the Wall	1981	—	2.50	5.00
49725 [PS]	All Those Years Ago/Writing's on the Wall	1981	—	2.50	5.00
49785	Teardrops/Save the World	1981	2.50	5.00	10.00

WARNER BROS.

22807 [DJ]	Cheer Down (same on both sides)	1989	50.00	100.00	200.00
22807	Cheer Down/That's What It Takes	1989	3.75	7.50	15.00
22807 [PS]	Cheer Down/That's What It Takes	1989	3.75	7.50	15.00

Albums
APPLE

| STCH-639 [(3)] | All Things Must Pass | 1970 | 10.00 | 20.00 | 40.00 |

—Apple labels on first two records and "Apple Jam" labels on third; includes poster and lyric innersleeves

| ST-3350 | Wonderwall Music | 1968 | 6.25 | 12.50 | 25.00 |

—With "Mfd. by Apple" on label

| ST-3350 | Wonderwall Music | 1968 | 37.50 | 75.00 | 150.00 |

—With Capitol logo on Side 2 bottom

ST-3350	Wonderwall Music Bonus Photo	1968	—	2.50	5.00
SMAS-3410	Living in the Material World	1973	3.75	7.50	15.00
SMAS-3418	Dark Horse	1974	3.75	7.50	15.00
SW-3420	Extra Texture (Read All About It)	1975	3.75	7.50	15.00

CAPITOL

| STCH-639 [(3)] | All Things Must Pass | 1976 | 7.50 | 15.00 | 30.00 |

—Orange labels with poster and lyric innersleeves

| STCH-639 [(3)] | All Things Must Pass | 1978 | 6.25 | 12.50 | 25.00 |

—Purple labels with poster and lyric innersleeves

| STCH-639 [(3)] | All Things Must Pass | 1983 | 25.00 | 50.00 | 100.00 |

—Black labels, print in colorband, with poster and lyric innersleeves

| ST-11578 | The Best of George Harrison | 1976 | 3.75 | 7.50 | 15.00 |

—Custom label, no bar code on back

| ST-11578 | The Best of George Harrison | 1976 | 45.00 | 90.00 | 180.00 |

—Orange label

| ST-11578 | The Best of George Harrison | 1978 | 2.50 | 5.00 | 10.00 |

—Purple label, large Capitol logo

| ST-11578 | The Best of George Harrison | 1983 | 6.25 | 12.50 | 25.00 |

—Black label, print in colorband

| ST-11578 | The Best of George Harrison | 1988 | 6.25 | 12.50 | 25.00 |

—Odd reissue with custom label; large stand-alone "S" in trail-off area; bar code on cover

| ST-11578 | The Best of George Harrison | 1989 | 20.00 | 40.00 | 80.00 |

—Purple label, small Capitol logo

| SN-16055 | Dark Horse | 1980 | 3.75 | 7.50 | 15.00 |

—Budget-line reissue; reverses front and back covers

| SN-16216 | Living in the Material World | 1980 | 5.00 | 10.00 | 20.00 |

—Budget-line reissue

| SN-16217 | Extra Texture (Read All About It) | 1980 | 6.25 | 12.50 | 25.00 |

—Budget-line reissue

CAPITOL/APPLE

| STCH-639 [(3)] | All Things Must Pass | 1988 | 20.00 | 40.00 | 80.00 |

—Odd pressing with Apple labels and Capitol cover (look for stand-alone "S" in trail-off wax); with large sticker on back cover

DARK HORSE

| (no #) [DJ] | Dark Horse Radio Special | 1974 | 100.00 | 200.00 | 400.00 |

—Promo-only; George Harrison introduces his new record label and artists

| PRO 649 [DJ] | A Personal Music Dialogue at Thirty Three and 1/3 | 1976 | 12.50 | 25.00 | 50.00 |
| DH 3005 | Thirty Three and 1/3 | 1976 | 2.50 | 5.00 | 10.00 |

   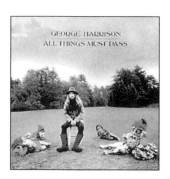

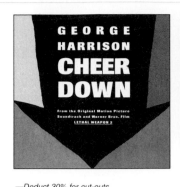

—Deduct 30% for cut-outs

DHK 3255	George Harrison	1979	2.50	5.00	10.00

—Deduct 30% for cut-outs

DHK 3255	George Harrison	1979	10.00	20.00	40.00

—Columbia House edition (back cover says "Manufactured by Columbia House Under License"

DHK 3492	Somewhere in England	1981	2.50	5.00	10.00

—Deduct 30% for cut-outs

23724	Gone Troppo	1982	2.50	5.00	10.00

—Deduct 30% for cut-outs

23724 [DJ]	Gone Troppo	1982	6.25	12.50	25.00

—Promo on Quiex II vinyl

25643	Cloud Nine	1987	2.50	5.00	10.00
W1-25643	Cloud Nine	1987	3.00	6.00	12.00

—Columbia House edition

25726	Best of Dark Horse 1976-1989	1989	6.25	12.50	25.00
W1-25726	Best of Dark Horse 1976-1989	1989	3.75	7.50	15.00

—Columbia House edition

R 174328	Cloud Nine	1987	3.75	7.50	15.00

—BMG Direct Marketing edition

R 180307	Best of Dark Horse 1976-1989	1989	3.75	7.50	15.00

—BMG Direct Marketing edition

ZAPPLE

ST-3358	Electronic Sound	1969	10.00	20.00	40.00

HARRISON, GEORGE, AND FRIENDS
Albums
APPLE

STCX-3385 [(3)]	The Concert for Bangla Desh	1971	10.00	20.00	40.00

—With 64-page booklet and custom innersleeves

STCX-3385 [(3)]	The Concert for Bangla Desh	1975	12.50	25.00	50.00

—As above, but with "All Rights Reserved" on labels

CAPITOL

SABB-12248 [(2)]	The Concert for Bangla Desh	1982	75.00	150.00	300.00

—Scheduled reissue that was never officially released, though a few copies got out by mistake

HARRISON, GEORGE/JEFF BECK/DAVE EDMUNDS
12-Inch Singles
COLUMBIA

CAS 2034 [DJ]	I Don't Want to Do It/Sleepwalk/Queen of the Hop	1985	5.00	10.00	20.00

—Promo sampler from movie "Porky's Revenge"

LENNON, JOHN
12-Inch Singles
CAPITOL

SPRO-9585/6 [DJ]	Imagine/Come Together	1986	10.00	20.00	40.00
SPRO-9894 [DJ]	Happy Xmas (War Is Over) (same on both sides)	1986	50.00	100.00	200.00

—Limited edition for the Central Virginia Food Bank

SPRO-9917 [DJ]	Rock and Roll People (same on both sides)	1986	15.00	30.00	60.00

SPRO-9929 [DJ]	Happy Xmas (War Is Over)/Listen, the Snow Is Falling	1986	12.50	25.00	50.00

—Custom silver label, plastic sleeve with sticker

SPRO-79463 [DJ]	Stand By Me (same on both sides)	1988	10.00	20.00	40.00

GEFFEN

PRO-A-919 [DJ]	(Just Like) Starting Over/Kiss Kiss Kiss	1980	20.00	40.00	80.00

—A-side is slightly longer (4:17) than any other release of this song

PRO-A-1079 [DJ]	Happy Xmas (War Is Over) Beautiful Boy (Darling Boy)	1982	7.50	15.00	30.00

POLYDOR

PRO 250-1 [DJ]	Nobody Told Me/O' Sanity	1983	7.50	15.00	30.00

45s
APPLE

1809	Give Peace a Chance/Remember Love	1969	—	2.50	5.00

—As "Plastic Ono Band"

1809 [PS]	Give Peace a Chance/Remember Love	1969	3.75	7.50	15.00

—As "Plastic Ono Band"

1813	Cold Turkey/Don't Worry Kyoko (Mummy's Only Looking for a Hand in the Snow)	1969	—	2.50	5.00

—As "Plastic Ono Band"; most copies skip on A-side on the third chorus because of a pressing defect

1813 [PS]	Cold Turkey/Don't Worry Kyoko (Mummy's Only Looking for a Hand in the Snow)	1969	10.00	20.00	40.00

—As "Plastic Ono Band"

1813	Cold Turkey/Don't Worry Kyoko (Mummy's Only Looking for a Hand in the Snow)	1969	2.50	5.00	10.00

—As "Plastic Ono Band"; some copies don't skip on A-side. They tend to have wider, bolder print than those that do.

1818 [DJ]	Instant Karma! (We All Shine On)	1970	50.00	100.00	200.00

—As "John Ono Lennon"; one-sided promo

1818	Instant Karma! (We All Shine On)/Who Has Seen the Wind?	1970	—	2.00	4.00

—As "John Ono Lennon"; B-side by "Yoko Ono Lennon"

1818 [PS]	Instant Karma! (We All Shine On)/Who Has Seen the Wind?	1970	3.75	7.50	15.00

—As "John Ono Lennon"; B-side by "Yoko Ono Lennon"

1827	Mother/Why	1970	2.00	4.00	8.00

—As "John Lennon/Plastic Ono Band"; B-side by "Yoko Ono/Plastic Ono Band"

1827 [PS]	Mother/Why	1970	30.00	60.00	120.00

—As "John Lennon/Plastic Ono Band"; B-side by "Yoko Ono/Plastic Ono Band"

1827	Mother/Why	1970	3.00	6.00	12.00

—As "John Lennon/Plastic Ono Band"; star on A-side label

1827	Mother/Why	1970	10.00	20.00	40.00

—As "John Lennon/Plastic Ono Band"; "MONO" on A-side label

1830	Power to the People/Touch Me	1971	2.00	4.00	8.00

—As "John Lennon/Plastic Ono Band"; B-side by "Yoko Ono/Plastic Ono Band"

1830 [PS]	Power to the People/Touch Me	1971	7.50	15.00	30.00

—As "John Lennon/Plastic Ono Band"; B-side by "Yoko Ono/Plastic Ono Band"

1830	Power to the People/Touch Me	1971	2.00	4.00	8.00

—As "John Lennon/Plastic Ono Band"; with star on A-side label

1840	Imagine/It's So Hard	1971	2.00	4.00	8.00

—As "John Lennon Plastic Ono Band"; tan label

1840	Imagine/It's So Hard	1975	3.00	6.00	12.00

—As "John Lennon Plastic Ono Band"; green label with "All Rights Reserved"

1842	Happy Xmas (War Is Over)/Listen, the Snow Is Falling	1971	3.75	7.50	15.00

—As "John & Yoko/Plastic Ono Band with the Harlem Community Choir"; green vinyl, faces label

1842	Happy Xmas (War Is Over)/Listen, the Snow Is Falling	1971	2.50	5.00	10.00

—As "John & Yoko/Plastic Ono Band with the Harlem Community Choir"; green vinyl, Apple label

1842 [PS]	Happy Xmas (War Is Over)/Listen, the Snow Is Falling	1971	5.00	10.00	20.00

—As "John & Yoko/Plastic Ono Band with the Harlem Community Choir"

1848	Woman Is the Nigger of the World/Sisters O Sisters	1972	2.00	4.00	8.00

—As "John Lennon/Plastic Ono Band..."; B-side by "Yoko Ono/Plastic Ono Band..."

1848 [PS]	Woman Is the Nigger of the World/Sisters O Sisters	1972	6.25	12.50	25.00

—As "John Lennon/Plastic Ono Band..."; B-side by "Yoko Ono/Plastic Ono Band..."

P-1868 [DJ]	Mind Games (mono/stereo)	1973	12.50	25.00	50.00
1868	Mind Games/Meat City	1973	—	3.00	6.00
1868 [PS]	Mind Games/Meat City	1973	3.75	7.50	15.00
P-1874 [DJ]	Whatever Gets You Thru the Night (mono/stereo)	1974	12.50	25.00	50.00

—As "John Lennon and the Plastic Ono Nuclear Band"

1874	Whatever Gets You Thru the Night/Beef Jerky	1974	—	3.00	6.00

—As "John Lennon and the Plastic Ono Nuclear Band"

P-1878 [DJ]	What You Got (mono/stereo)	1974	25.00	50.00	100.00
P-1878 [DJ]	#9 Dream (edited mono/stereo)	1974	12.50	25.00	50.00
1878	#9 Dream/What You Got	1974	2.00	4.00	8.00
P-1881 [DJ]	Stand By Me (mono/stereo)	1975	12.50	25.00	50.00
1881	Stand By Me/Move Over Ms. L.	1975	2.00	4.00	8.00
P-1883 [DJ]	Ain't That a Shame (mono/stereo)	1975	50.00	100.00	200.00

—No stock copies issued

P-1883 [DJ]	Slippin' and Slidin' (mono/stereo)	1975	50.00	100.00	200.00

—No stock copies issued

S45X-47663/4 [DJ]	Happy Xmas (War Is Over)/Listen, the Snow Is Falling	1971	200.00	400.00	800.00

—As "John & Yoko/Plastic Ono Band with the Harlem Community Choir"; white label on styrene

APPLE/AMERICOM

1809P/M-435	Give Peace a Chance/Remember Love	1969	187.50	375.00	750.00

—As "Plastic Ono Band"; four-inch flexi-disc sold in vending machines

ATLANTIC

PR-104/5 [DJ]	John Lennon on Ronnie Hawkins: The Short Rap/ The Long Rap	1970	25.00	50.00	100.00

CAPITOL

1840	Imagine/It's So Hard	1978	—	3.00	6.00

—As "John Lennon Plastic Ono Band"; purple late 1970s label

1840	Imagine/It's So Hard	1983	—	3.00	6.00

—As "John Lennon Plastic Ono Band"; black colorband label

1840	Imagine/It's So Hard	1988	—	2.50	5.00

—As "John Lennon Plastic Ono Band"; purple late-1980s label (wider)

1842	Happy Xmas (War Is Over)/Listen, the Snow Is Falling	1976	12.50	25.00	50.00

—As "John & Yoko/Plastic Ono Band with the Harlem Community Choir"; orange label

1842	Happy Xmas (War Is Over)/Listen, the Snow Is Falling	1978	—	3.00	6.00

—As "John & Yoko/Plastic Ono Band with the Harlem Community Choir"; purple late-1970s label

1842	Happy Xmas (War Is Over)/Listen, the Snow Is Falling	1983	—	3.00	6.00

—As "John & Yoko/Plastic Ono Band with the Harlem Community Choir"; black colorband label

1842	Happy Xmas (War Is Over)/Listen, the Snow Is Falling	1988	5.00	10.00	20.00

—As "John & Yoko/Plastic Ono Band with the Harlem Community Choir"; purple late-1980s label (wider)

1868	Mind Games/Meat City	1978	—	3.00	6.00

—Purple late-1970s label

1868	Mind Games/Meat City	1983	3.00	6.00	12.00

—Black colorband label

1874	Whatever Gets You Thru the Night/Beef Jerky	1978	—	3.00	6.00

—Purple late-1970s label

1874	Whatever Gets You Thru the Night/Beef Jerky	1983	—	3.00	6.00

—Black colorband label

1874	Whatever Gets You Thru the Night/Beef Jerky	1988	—	3.00	6.00

—Purple late-1980s label

1878	#9 Dream/What You Got	1976	10.00	20.00	40.00

—Orange label

1878	#9 Dream/What You Got	1978	—	3.00	6.00

—Purple late-1970s label

1878	#9 Dream/What You Got	1983	2.50	5.00	10.00

—Black colorband label

S7-17644	Happy Xmas (War Is Over)/Listen, the Snow Is Falling	1993	—	2.00	4.00

—John & Yoko/The Plastic Ono Band; green vinyl

S7-17783	Give Peace a Chance/Remember Love	1994	25.00	50.00	100.00

—CEMA Special Markets issue; meant for gold-plating in a special plaque. About 100 were not.

B-44230	Jealous Guy/Give Peace a Chance	1988	—	2.50	5.00
B-44230 [PS]	Jealous Guy/Give Peace a Chance	1988	—	2.50	5.00
S7-57849	Imagine/It's So Hard	1992	12.50	25.00	50.00

—CEMA Special Markets issue; meant for gold-plating in a special plaque. About 1,000 were not.

58894	(Just Like) Starting Over/Watching the Wheels	2000	—	2.50	5.00

—Blue vinyl

58895	Woman/Walking on Thin Ice	2000	—	2.50	5.00

—*Clear vinyl; B-side as "John Lennon and Yoko Ono" though originally issued as a Yoko Ono solo single*

COTILLION

PR-104/5 [DJ]	John Lennon on Ronnie Hawkins: The Short Rap/ The Long Rap	1970	20.00	40.00	80.00

—*White label with promo markings*

PR-104/5 [DJ]	John Lennon on Ronnie Hawkins: The Short Rap/ The Long Rap	1970	22.50	45.00	90.00

—*No promo markings on white label*

GEFFEN

29855	Happy Xmas (War Is Over)/ Beautiful Boy (Darling Boy)	1982	—	2.50	5.00
29855 [PS]	Happy Xmas (War Is Over)/ Beautiful Boy (Darling Boy)	1982	—	2.50	5.00
49604	(Just Like) Starting Over/Kiss Kiss Kiss	1980	—	2.00	4.00

—*B-side by Yoko Ono*

49604 [PS]	(Just Like) Starting Over/Kiss Kiss Kiss	1980	—	2.00	4.00

—*B-side by Yoko Ono*

49644	Woman/Beautiful Boys	1980	—	2.00	4.00

—*B-side by Yoko Ono*

49644 [PS]	Woman/Beautiful Boys	1980	—	2.00	4.00

—*B-side by Yoko Ono*

49695	Watching the Wheels/ Yes, I'm Your Angel	1981	—	2.00	4.00

—*B-side by Yoko Ono*

49695 [PS]	Watching the Wheels/ Yes, I'm Your Angel	1981	—	2.00	4.00

—*B-side by Yoko Ono*

KYA

1260 [DJ]	The KYA 1969 Peace Talk	1969	50.00	100.00	200.00

NOISEVILLE

43	John Lennon Talks About David Peel	199?	10.00	20.00	40.00

—*Red vinyl, signed by David Peel*

43	John Lennon Talks About David Peel	199?	2.50	5.00	10.00

—*Black vinyl*

43 [PS]	John Lennon Talks About David Peel	199?	2.50	5.00	10.00

POLYDOR

817254-7	Nobody Told Me/O' Sanity	1983	2.50	5.00	10.00

—*With "Manufactured by Polydor Incorporated..." on label; B-side by Yoko Ono*

817254-7	Nobody Told Me/O' Sanity	1983	—	2.50	5.00

—*With "Manufactured and Marketed by Polygram..." on label; B-side by Yoko Ono*

817254-7 [PS]	Nobody Told Me/O' Sanity	1983	—	2.50	5.00
821107-7	I'm Stepping Out/Sleepless Night	1984	—	2.00	4.00

—*B-side by Yoko Ono*

821107-7 [PS]	I'm Stepping Out/Sleepless Night	1984	—	2.00	4.00
821204-7	Borrowed Time/Your Hands	1984	—	2.50	5.00

—*B-side by Yoko Ono*

821204-7 [PS]	Borrowed Time/Your Hands	1984	—	2.50	5.00
881378-7	Every Man Has a Woman Who Loves Him /It's Alright	1984	2.00	4.00	8.00

—*B-side by Sean Ono Lennon*

881378-7 [PS]	Every Man Has a Woman Who Loves Him /It's Alright	1984	2.00	4.00	8.00

QUAKER GRANOLA DIPPS

(no #)	A Tribute to John Lennon	1986	3.75	7.50	15.00

—*Cardboard record included in specially marked boxes of Quaker Granola Dipps*

QUAYE/TRIDENT

SK 3419 [DJ]	Rock 'N' Roll	1975	125.00	250.00	500.00

—*Radio spot to promote the album Rock 'N' Roll*

Albums
ADAM VIII

A-8018	John Lennon Sings the Great Rock & Roll Hits (Roots)	1975	250.00	500.00	1000.

—*Counterfeits abound. On authentic copies, cover is posterboard (not slicks); labels are normal size (not overly large); printing on cover is sharp, not blurry; the word "Greatest" does NOT appear on the spine. Authentic copies usually have ad sleeve also.*

APPLE

SMAX-3361	Wedding Album	1969	37.50	75.00	150.00

—*With photo strip, postcard, poster of wedding photos, poster of lithographs, "Bagism" bag, booklet, photo of slice of wedding cake. Missing inserts reduce the value.*

SW-3362	Live Peace in Toronto 1969	1970	3.75	7.50	15.00

—*By "The Plastic Ono Band" — without calendar*

SW-3362	Live Peace in Toronto 1969	1970	5.00	10.00	20.00

—*By "The Plastic Ono Band"; with calendar*

SW-3372	John Lennon Plastic Ono Band	1970	5.00	10.00	20.00
SW-3379	Imagine	1971	5.00	10.00	20.00

—*With either of two postcard inserts, lyric sleeve, poster*

SW-3379	Imagine	1975	5.00	10.00	20.00

—*"All Rights Reserved" label*

SVBB-3392 [(2)]	Some Time in New York City	1972	7.50	15.00	30.00

—*By John and Yoko; with photo card and petition*

SVBB-3392 [(2) DJ]	Some Time in New York City	1972	250.00	500.00	1000.00

—*White label promo*

SW-3414	Mind Games	1973	5.00	10.00	20.00
SW-3416	Walls and Bridges	1974	5.00	10.00	20.00

—*With fold-open segmented front cover*

Cat. No.	Title	Year			
SK-3419	Rock 'n' Roll	1975	5.00	10.00	20.00
SW-3421	Shaved Fish	1975	5.00	10.00	20.00
T-5001	Two Virgins — Unfinished Music No. 1	1968	12.50	25.00	50.00
—With Yoko Ono; without brown bag					
T-5001	Two Virgins — Unfinished Music No. 1	1968	37.50	75.00	150.00
—With Yoko Ono; price with brown bag					
T-5001	Two Virgins — Unfinished Music No. 1	1968	37.50	75.00	150.00
—With Yoko Ono; with die-cut bag					
T-5001	Two Virgins — Unfinished Music No. 1	1985	3.75	7.50	15.00
—With Yoko Ono; reissue, flat label					

CAPITOL

Cat. No.	Title	Year			
SW-3372	John Lennon Plastic Ono Band	1978	3.00	6.00	12.00
—Purple label, large Capitol logo					
SW-3372	John Lennon Plastic Ono Band	1982	5.00	10.00	20.00
—Black label, print in colorband					
SW-3372	John Lennon Plastic Ono Band	1988	7.50	15.00	30.00
—Purple label, small Capitol logo					
SW-3379	Imagine	1978	2.50	5.00	10.00
—Purple label, large Capitol logo					
SW-3379	Imagine	1986	7.50	15.00	30.00
—Black label, print in colorband					
SW-3379	Imagine	1987	6.25	12.50	25.00
—Black label, print in colorband; "Digitally Re-Mastered" at top of front cover					
SW-3379	Imagine	1988	7.50	15.00	30.00
—Purple label, small Capitol logo					
SVBB-3392 [(2)]	Some Time in New York City	197?	6.25	12.50	25.00
—By John and Yoko; purple label, large Capitol logo					
SVBB-3392 [(2)]	Some Time in New York City	197?	25.00	50.00	100.00
—Both discs in single-pocket gatefold (the other pocket is glued shut)					
SW-3414	Mind Games	1978	10.00	20.00	40.00
—Purple label, large Capitol logo					
SW-3416	Walls and Bridges	1978	3.75	7.50	15.00
—Purple label, large Capitol logo; standard front cover					
SW-3416	Walls and Bridges	1982	7.50	15.00	30.00
—Black label, print in colorband					
SW-3416	Walls and Bridges	1989	7.50	15.00	30.00
—Purple label, small Capitol logo					
SK-3419	Rock 'n' Roll	1978	10.00	20.00	40.00
—Purple label, large Capitol logo					
SW-3421	Shaved Fish	1978	3.00	6.00	12.00
—Purple Capitol label with Apple logo on cover					
SW-3421	Shaved Fish	1978	10.00	20.00	40.00
—Purple Capitol label with Capitol logo on cover					
SW-3421	Shaved Fish	1983	5.00	10.00	20.00
—Black Capitol label with Apple logo on cover					
SW-3421	Shaved Fish	1983	10.00	20.00	40.00
—Black Capitol label with Capitol logo on cover					
SW-3421	Shaved Fish	1989	10.00	20.00	40.00
—Purple Capitol label (small logo) with Capitol logo on cover					
ST-12239	Live Peace in Toronto 1969	1982	2.50	5.00	10.00
—By "The Plastic Ono Band"; reissue, purple Capitol label					
ST-12239	Live Peace in Toronto 1969	1983	12.50	25.00	50.00
—By "The Plastic Ono Band"; reissue, black Capitol label					
SV-12451	Live in New York City	1986	3.00	6.00	12.00
SJ-12533	Menlove Ave.	1986	3.75	7.50	15.00
SN-16068	Mind Games	1980	3.00	6.00	12.00
—Budget-line reissue					
SN-16069	Rock 'n' Roll	1980	3.00	6.00	12.00
—Budget-line reissue					
C1-90803 [(2)]	Imagine: Music from the Motion Picture	1988	5.00	10.00	20.00
C1-91425	Double Fantasy	1989	5.00	10.00	20.00
—Very briefly available reissue					
R 144136	Menlove Ave.	1986	12.50	25.00	50.00
—RCA Music Service edition					
R 144136	Menlove Ave.	198?	12.50	25.00	50.00
—BMG Direct Marketing edition					
R 144497	Live in New York City	1986	3.75	7.50	15.00
—RCA Music Service edition					
SV-512451	Live in New York City	1986	3.75	7.50	15.00
—Columbia House edition					
C1-591425	Double Fantasy	1989	15.00	30.00	60.00
—Columbia House edition of reissue					

GEFFEN

Cat. No.	Title	Year			
GHS 2001	Double Fantasy	1980	2.50	5.00	10.00
—Seven tracks by John, seven by Yoko; off-white label; titles on back cover out of order					
GHS 2001	Double Fantasy	1981	18.75	37.50	75.00
—Columbia House edition (all have corrected back cover) with "CH" on label					
GHS 2001	Double Fantasy	1981	3.00	6.00	12.00
—Off-white label, titles in order on the back cover					
GHS 2001	Double Fantasy	1981	3.00	6.00	12.00
—Columbia House edition (all have corrected back cover) without "CH" on label					
GHS 2001	Double Fantasy	1986	12.50	25.00	50.00
—Same as above, but with black Geffen label					
GHSP 2023	The John Lennon Collection	1982	5.00	10.00	20.00
GHSP 2023 [DJ]	The John Lennon Collection	1982	12.50	25.00	50.00
—Promo only on Quiex II audiophile vinyl					
R 104689	Double Fantasy	1981	10.00	20.00	40.00
—RCA Music Service edition					

MOBILE FIDELITY

Cat. No.	Title	Year			
1-153	Imagine	1984	12.50	25.00	50.00
—Audiophile vinyl					

NAUTILUS

Cat. No.	Title	Year			
NR-47	Double Fantasy	1982	20.00	40.00	80.00
—Half-speed master					
NR-47	Double Fantasy	1982	500.00	1000.	2000.
—Half-speed master; alternate experimental cover with yellow and red added to black and white front					

PARLOPHONE

Cat. No.	Title	Year			
21954 [(2)]	Lennon Legend	1998	5.00	10.00	20.00
—"Made in U.S.A." on back cover					

POLYDOR

Cat. No.	Title	Year			
817160-1	Milk and Honey	1983	2.50	5.00	10.00
—Six tracks by John, six by Yoko					
817160-1	Milk and Honey	1984	37.50	75.00	150.00
—Yellow or green vinyl; unauthorized "inside jobs"					
817238-1	Heart Play (Unfinished Dialogue)	1983	3.00	6.00	12.00
—Interviews with John Lennon and Yoko Ono					

SILHOUETTE

Cat. No.	Title	Year			
SM-10012 [(2)]	Reflections and Poetry	1984	6.25	12.50	25.00

ZAPPLE

Cat. No.	Title	Year			
ST-3357	Life with the Lions — Unfinished Music No. 2	1969	5.00	10.00	20.00
—With Yoko Ono					

MCCARTNEY, PAUL
12-Inch Singles
ATLANTIC

PR 388 [DJ]	Every Night/Lucille	1981	62.50	125.00	250.00

CAPITOL

SPRO-8574 [DJ] —As "Wings"	Maybe I'm Amazed (mono/stereo)	1976	20.00	40.00	80.00
SPRO-9556/7 [DJ]	Spies Like Us (4:40) (3:46)	1985	7.50	15.00	30.00
SPRO-9763 [DJ]	Press (same on both sides)	1986	5.00	10.00	20.00
SPRO-9797 [DJ]	Angry (same on both sides)	1986	7.50	15.00	30.00
SPRO-9860/1 [DJ]	Stranglehold/Angry	1986	6.25	12.50	25.00
SPRO-9928 [DJ]	Pretty Little Head (same on both sides)	1986	12.50	25.00	50.00
V-15212 —"MPL" correct on label	Spies Like Us (Party Mix)/(Alternative Mix) /(DJ Version)/My Carnival	1985	5.00	10.00	20.00
V-15212 (DJ Version) —"MLP" on label instead of "MPL"	Spies Like Us (Party Mix)/(Alternative Mix) /My Carnival	1985	3.75	7.50	15.00
V-15235	Press (Video Mix 4:41)/It's Not True (5:51) Hanglide (5:18)/Press (Dub Mix 6:28)	1986	3.00	6.00	12.00
V-15499	Ou Est Le Soleil? (7:10)/(Tub Dub Mix 4:27) (Instrumental 4:25)	1989	3.00	6.00	12.00

COLUMBIA

AS 775 [DJ] —Red label	Coming Up/Coming Up (Live at Glasgow)	1980	15.00	30.00	60.00
AS 775 [DJ] —White label	Coming Up/Coming Up (Live at Glasgow)	1980	12.50	25.00	50.00
AS 1444 [DJ]	Ebony and Ivory//Ballroom Dancing/ The Pound Is Sinking	1982	7.50	15.00	30.00
AS 1940 [DJ]	No More Lonely Nights (Ballad) (same on both sides)	1984	5.00	10.00	20.00
AS 1990 [DJ]	No More Lonely Nights (Special Dance Mix) (same on both sides)	1984	5.00	10.00	20.00
44-03019	Take It Away//I'll Give You a Ring/ Dress Me Up as a Robber	1982	3.00	6.00	12.00
44-05077	No More Lonely Nights (Playout Version)//Silly Love Songs/ No More Lonely Nights (Ballad)	1984	3.00	6.00	12.00
44-05077	No More Lonely Nights (Special Dance Mix)//Silly Love Songs /No More Lonely Nights (Ballad)	1984	7.50	15.00	30.00
23-10940 —Credited to "Wings"; generic white cover, no picture cover or sticker	Goodnight Tonight (7:25)/Daytime Nighttime Suffering	1979	2.50	5.00	10.00
23-10940 —Credited to "Wings"; generic white cover with large blue and white sticker	Goodnight Tonight (7:25)/Daytime Nighttime Suffering	1979	20.00	40.00	80.00
23-10940 —Credited to "Wings"; with picture cover	Goodnight Tonight (7:25)/Daytime Nighttime Suffering	1979	3.75	7.50	15.00
23-10940 [DJ] —Credited to "Wings"; promo issue with two versions of the A-side	Goodnight Tonight (7:25)/(4:18)	1979	6.25	12.50	25.00
8C8 39927 [PD]	No More Lonely Nights (Extended Version)//Silly Love Songs/ No More Lonely Nights (Ballad)	1984	5.00	10.00	20.00

—Picture disc; despite having only the above three tracks, its number is in the CBS album (not singles) numbering system

45s
APPLE

1829 —With star on A-side label	Another Day/Oh Woman, Oh Why	1971	3.00	6.00	12.00
1829	Another Day/Oh Woman, Oh Why	1971	2.00	4.00	8.00
1837 —Paul and Linda McCartney; with "Pual" misspelling on producer credit	Uncle Albert/Admiral Halsey// Too Many People	1971	3.75	7.50	15.00
1837 —Paul and Linda McCartney; with no misspelling	Uncle Albert/Admiral Halsey// Too Many People	1971	2.00	4.00	8.00

Mary Had A Little Lamb
1851

1837 —Paul and Linda McCartney; with unsliced apple on B-side label	Uncle Albert/Admiral Halsey// Too Many People	1971	12.50	25.00	50.00
1837 —Paul and Linda McCartney; with "All rights reserved" on label	Uncle Albert/Admiral Halsey// Too Many People	1975	7.50	15.00	30.00
1847 —Wings	Give Ireland Back to the Irish/ Give Ireland Back to the Irish (Version)	1972	2.50	5.00	10.00
1847 [PS] —Wings; title sleeve with large center hole	Give Ireland Back to the Irish/Give Ireland Back to the Irish (Version)	1972	7.50	15.00	30.00
1851 —Wings	Mary Had a Little Lamb/Little Woman Love	1972	2.50	5.00	10.00
1851 [PS] —Wings; without "Little Woman Love" on sleeve	Mary Had a Little Lamb/Little Woman Love	1972	6.25	12.50	25.00
1851 [PS] —Wings; with "Little Woman Love" on sleeve	Mary Had a Little Lamb/Little Woman Love	1972	10.00	20.00	40.00
1851 [DJ] —White label promo, lists artist as Paul McCartney	Mary Had a Little Lamb/Little Woman Love	1972	75.00	150.00	300.00
1857 —Wings; red label	Hi Hi Hi/C Moon	1972	2.50	5.00	10.00
1861 —Paul McCartney and Wings; custom "Red Rose Speedway" label	My Love/The Mess	1973	2.00	4.00	8.00
1861 [DJ] —Paul McCartney and Wings; white label	My Love/The Mess	1973	50.00	100.00	200.00
1863 —Wings	Live and Let Die/I Lie Around	1973	2.00	4.00	8.00
1869 —Paul McCartney and Wings	Helen Wheels/Country Dreamer	1973	2.00	4.00	8.00
P-1869 [DJ] —Paul McCartney and Wings; a very rare promo, as most promos have the same song on both sides (see 6786 and 6787 below)	Helen Wheels/Country Dreamer	1973	500.00	1000.00	2000.00
P-1871 [DJ] —Paul McCartney and Wings	Jet (Edited Mono)/Jet (Stereo)	1974	12.50	25.00	50.00
1871 —Paul McCartney and Wings	Jet/Let Me Roll It	1974	2.00	4.00	8.00
1871 —Paul McCartney and Wings	Jet/Mamunia	1974	2.50	5.00	10.00
1871 —Paul McCartney and Wings; A-side incorrectly listed as playing for 2:49	Jet/Mamunia	1974	25.00	50.00	100.00
P-1873 [DJ] —Paul McCartney and Wings	Band on the Run (Edited Mono)/ Band on the Run (Full-length Stereo)	1974	10.00	20.00	40.00
P-1873 [DJ] —Paul McCartney and Wings	Band on the Run (mono/stereo, both edits)	1974	25.00	50.00	100.00
1873 —Paul McCartney and Wings	Band on the Run/Nineteen Hundred and Eighty- Five	1974	2.00	4.00	8.00
P-1875 [DJ] —Paul McCartney and Wings	Junior's Farm (Edited Mono)/Junior's Farm (Full- length Stereo)	1974	12.50	25.00	50.00
1875 —Paul McCartney and Wings	Junior's Farm/Sally G	1974	2.00	4.00	8.00

1875	Junior's Farm/Sally G	1975	20.00	40.00	80.00
—Paul McCartney and Wings; with "All Rights Reserved" on label					
P-1875 [DJ]	Sally G (mono/stereo)	1974	20.00	40.00	80.00
—Paul McCartney and Wings					
PRO-6193/4 [DJ]	Another Day/Oh Woman, Oh Why	1971	20.00	40.00	80.00
PRO-6786 [DJ]	Helen Wheels (mono/stereo)	1973	12.50	25.00	50.00
—Paul McCartney and Wings					
PRO-6787 [DJ]	Country Dreamer (mono/stereo)	1973	100.00	200.00	400.00
—Paul McCartney and Wings					

CAPITOL

1829	Another Day/Oh Woman, Oh Why	1976	3.75	7.50	15.00
—Black label					
1837	Uncle Albert/Admiral Halsey//Too Many People	1976		3.75	7.50
15.00					
—Credited to "Paul and Linda McCartney"; black label					
1847	Give Ireland Back to the Irish/Give Ireland Back to the Irish	1976	5.00	10.00	20.00
—Credited to "Wings"; black label					
1851	Mary Had a Little Lamb/Little Woman Love	1976	3.00	6.00	12.00
—Credited to "Wings"; black label					
1857	Hi Hi Hi/C Moon	1976	3.75	7.50	15.00
—Credited to "Wings"; black label					
1861	My Love/The Mess	1976	5.00	10.00	20.00
—Credited to "Paul McCartney and Wings"; black label; "The Mess" plays too fast					
1861	My Love/The Mess	1976	5.00	10.00	20.00
—Credited to "Paul McCartney and Wings"; black label; "The Mess" plays normally					
1863	Live and Let Die/I Lie Around	1976	3.00	6.00	12.00
—Credited to "Wings"; black label					
1869	Helen Wheels/Country Dreamer	1976	3.75	7.50	15.00
—Credited to "Paul McCartney and Wings"; black label					
1871	Jet/Let Me Roll It	1976	3.75	7.50	15.00
—Credited to "Paul McCartney and Wings"; black label					
1873	Band on the Run/Nineteen Hundred and Eighty- Five	1976	3.75	7.50	15.00
—Credited to "Paul McCartney and Wings"; black label					
1875	Junior's Farm/Sally G	1976	3.75	7.50	15.00
—Credited to "Paul McCartney and Wings"; black label					
4091	Listen to What the Man Said/Love in Song	1975	—	2.50	5.00
—Credited to "Wings"					
4091 [PS]	Listen to What the Man Said/Love in Song	1975	3.00	6.00	12.00
4145	Letting Go/You Gave Me the Answer	1975	—	2.50	5.00
—Credited to "Wings"					
4175	Venus and Mars Rock Show/Magneto and Titanium Man	1975	—	2.50	5.00
—Credited to "Wings"					
4256	Silly Love Songs/Cook of the House	1976	2.00	4.00	8.00
—Credited to "Wings"; black label					
4256	Silly Love Songs/Cook of the House	1976	—	2.00	4.00
—Credited to "Wings"; "Speed of Sound" label (more common version)					

4293	Let 'Em In/Beware My Love	1976	—	3.00	6.00
—Credited to "Wings"; black label (more common version)					
4293	Let 'Em In/Beware My Love	1976	—	2.00	4.00
—Credited to "Wings"; "Speed of Sound" label					
4385	Maybe I'm Amazed/Soily	1976	—	2.00	4.00
—Credited to "Wings"; custom label (more common version)					
4385	Maybe I'm Amazed/Soily	1976	5.00	10.00	20.00
—Credited to "Wings"; black label					
4504	Girls' School/Mull of Kintyre	1977	—	2.50	5.00
—Credited to "Wings"; black label (more common version)					
4504 [PS]	Girls' School/Mull of Kintyre	1977	3.00	6.00	12.00
4504	Girls' School/Mull of Kintyre	1978	30.00	60.00	120.00
—Credited to "Wings"; purple label, label has reeded edge					
4559	With a Little Luck/Backwards Traveller-Cuff Link	1978	—		2.00
4.00					
—Credited to "Wings"					
4594	I've Had Enough/Deliver Your Children	1978	—	2.00	4.00
—Credited to "Wings"					
4625	London Town/I'm Carrying	1978	—	2.00	4.00
—Credited to "Wings"					
B-5537	Spies Like Us/My Carnival	1985	—	—	3.00
B-5537 [PS]	Spies Like Us/My Carnival	1985	—	3.00	6.00
B-5597	Press/It's Not True	1986	—	2.50	5.00
B-5597 [PS]	Press/It's Not True	1986	—	2.50	5.00
B-5636	Stranglehold/Angry	1986	—	2.50	5.00
B-5636 [PS]	Stranglehold/Angry	1986	—	2.50	5.00
B-5672	Only Love Remains/Tough on a Tightrope	1987	—	2.50	5.00
B-5672 [PS]	Only Love Remains/Tough on a Tightrope	1987	—	2.50	5.00
SPRO-8570/1 [DJ]	Maybe I'm Amazed (3:43) (stereo/mono)	1977	7.50	15.00	30.00
—As "Wings"					
7PRO-9552/3 [DJ]	Spies Like Us (4:40)/(3:46)	1985	5.00	10.00	20.00
S7-17318	Off the Ground/Cosmically Conscious	1993	—	3.00	6.00
—White vinyl standard issue					
S7-17318	Off the Ground/Cosmically Conscious	1993	—	3.00	6.00
—Black vinyl "error" issue					
S7-17319	Biker Like an Icon/Things We Said Today	1993	—	3.00	6.00
—Black vinyl "error" issue					
S7-17319	Biker Like an Icon/Things We Said Today	1993	—	3.00	6.00
—White vinyl standard issue					
S7-17489	C'mon People/Down to the River	1993	2.00	4.00	8.00
—All copies on white vinyl					
S7-17643	Wonderful Christmastime/Rudolph, the Red- Nosed Reggae	1993	—	3.00	6.00
—Credited to "Paul McCartney & Wings"; red vinyl					
B-44367	My Brave Face/Flying to My Home	1989	2.50	5.00	10.00
—Version 1: Both title and artist in block print, time of A-side is "3:17"					
B-44367	My Brave Face/Flying to My Home	1989	2.00	4.00	8.00
—Version 2: Artist in custom print, title in block print, time of A-side is "3:17"					

 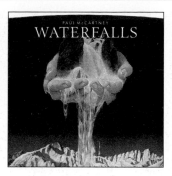  

B-44367	My Brave Face/Flying to My Home	1989	—	2.50	5.00

—*Version 3: Same as Version 2, time of A-side is "3:16"*

B-44367 [PS]	My Brave Face/Flying to My Home	1989	—	2.50	5.00
50291	Freedom/From a Lover to a Friend	2001	—	2.00	4.00
S7-56946	Hope of Deliverance/Long Leather Coat	1993	—	3.00	6.00
58823	No Other Baby/Try Not to Cry	1999	—	2.00	4.00
58995	Maybe I'm Amazed/Band on the Run	2001	—	2.50	5.00

—*Credited to "Wings"; gold vinyl; both sides feature spoken introductions by Paul*

77730	Your Loving Flame/Lonely Road	2002	—	2.00	4.00
7PRO-79700 [DJ]	This One (same on both sides)	1989	100.00	200.00	400.00

—*Vinyl is promo only*

7PRO-79889 [DJ]	Figure of Eight (same on both sides)	1989	25.00	50.00	100.00

—*Test pressings with blank label; most known copies come in a Capitol sleeve; number taken from dead wax*

COLUMBIA

AE7 1204 [DJ]	Coming Up (Live at Glasgow)/ (B-side blank)	1980	2.00	4.00	8.00

—*Small hole, plays at 33 1/3 rpm; this was the bonus single included with most early pressings of the "McCartney II" LP (Columbia FC 36511) and was not distributed separately*

18-02171	Silly Love Songs/Cook of the House	1981	6.25	12.50	25.00

—*Credited to "Wings"; despite label information, this has an edited version of A-side*

18-03018	Take It Away/I'll Give You a Ring	1982	—	—	3.00
18-03018 [PS]	Take It Away/I'll Give You a Ring	1982	—	—	3.00
38-03235	Tug of War/Get It	1982	3.00	6.00	12.00
38-04127	Wonderful Christmastime/Rudolph the Red- Nosed Reggae	1983	7.50	15.00	30.00

—*Scarce reissue with B-side in stereo*

38-04296	So Bad/Pipes of Peace	1983	—	2.50	5.00
38-04296 [PS]	So Bad/Pipes of Peace	1983	—	2.50	5.00
38-04581	No More Lonely Nights/(playout version)	1984	—	2.00	4.00
38-04581 [PS]	No More Lonely Nights/(playout version)	1984	7.50	15.00	30.00

—*Title print in gray, credit print in white*

38-04581 [PS]	No More Lonely Nights/(playout version)	1984	—	2.50	5.00

—*Title print in white, credit print in gray*

38-04581	No More Lonely Nights/ (Special Dance Version)	1984	10.00	20.00	40.00
3-10939	Goodnight Tonight/ Daytime Nighttime Suffering	1979	—	3.00	6.00

—*Credited to "Wings"*

3-11020	Getting Closer/Spin It On	1979	—	3.00	6.00

—*Credited to "Wings"*

3-11020 [PS]	Getting Closer/Spin It On	1979	7.50	15.00	30.00

—*Title sleeve with large center hole*

1-11070	Arrow Through Me/Old Siam, Sir	1979	—	3.00	6.00

—*Credited to "Wings"*

1-11162	Wonderful Christmastime/Rudolph the Red- Nosed Reggae	1979	2.50	5.00	10.00
1-11162 [PS]	Wonderful Christmastime/Rudolph the				

	Red- Nosed Reggae	1979	3.75	7.50	15.00
1-11263	Coming Up//Coming Up (Live at Glasgow)/Lunch Box-Odd Sox	1980	—	2.00	4.00

—*The first song on side 2 is credited to "Paul McCartney & Wings"*

1-11263 [PS]	Coming Up//Coming Up (Live at Glasgow)/Lunch Box-Odd Sox	1980	—	2.50	5.00
1-11335	Waterfalls/Check My Machine	1980	—	3.00	6.00
1-11335 [PS]	Waterfalls/Check My Machine	1980	5.00	10.00	20.00
13-33405	Goodnight Tonight/Getting Closer	1980	2.50	5.00	10.00

—*Credited to "Wings"; red label "Hall of Fame" series*

13-33407	My Love/Maybe I'm Amazed	1980	2.50	5.00	10.00

—*Credited to "Paul McCartney and Wings"; red label "Hall of Fame" series; B-side is the studio version, making its first appearance on U.S. 45 here*

13-33407	My Love/Maybe I'm Amazed	1985	7.50	15.00	30.00

—*Credited to "Paul McCartney and Wings"; briefly available grayish label reissue*

13-33408	Jet//Uncle Albert/Admiral Halsey	1980	2.50	5.00	10.00

—*Credited to "Paul McCartney and Wings"; red label "Hall of Fame" series*

13-33408	Jet//Uncle Albert/Admiral Halsey	1985	7.50	15.00	30.00

—*Credited to "Paul McCartney and Wings"; briefly available grayish label reissue*

13-33409	Band on the Run/Helen Wheels	1980	2.50	5.00	10.00

—*Credited to "Paul McCartney and Wings"; red label "Hall of Fame" series*

13-33409	Band on the Run/Helen Wheels	1985	7.50	15.00	30.00

—*Credited to "Paul McCartney and Wings"; briefly available grayish label reissue*

EMI

3977	Walking in the Park with Eloise/ Bridge on the River Suite	1974	15.00	30.00	60.00
3977 [PS]	Walking in the Park with Eloise/Bridge on the River Suite	1974	20.00	40.00	80.00

—*As "The Country Hams"*

Albums
APPLE

STAO-3363	McCartney	1970	6.25	12.50	25.00

—*"McCartney" and "Paul McCartney" on separate lines on label; New York address on back cover*

STAO-3363	McCartney	1970	7.50	15.00	30.00

—*"McCartney" and "Paul McCartney" on separate lines on label; California address on back cover*

STAO-3363	McCartney	1970	20.00	40.00	80.00

—*Apple label with small Capitol logo on B-side*

STAO-3363	McCartney	1970	5.00	10.00	20.00

—*Only "McCartney" on label; back cover does NOT say "An Abkco managed company"*

STAO-3363	McCartney	1970	6.25	12.50	25.00

—*Only "McCartney" on label; back cover says "An Abkco managed company"*

SMAS-3363	McCartney	1975	25.00	50.00	100.00

—*With "All Rights Reserved" on label*

SMAS-3363	McCartney	197?	5.00	10.00	20.00

—*New prefix on label*

MAS-3375 [M]	Ram	1971	1000.00	2000.00	4000.00

—*Credited to "Paul and Linda McCartney"; mono record in stereo cover for radio station use only*

SMAS-3375	Ram	1971	3.75	7.50	15.00

—*Credited to "Paul and Linda McCartney"; unsliced apple on one label, sliced apple on other*

■ Pictorial Press U.K. 1963 left, 1965 right

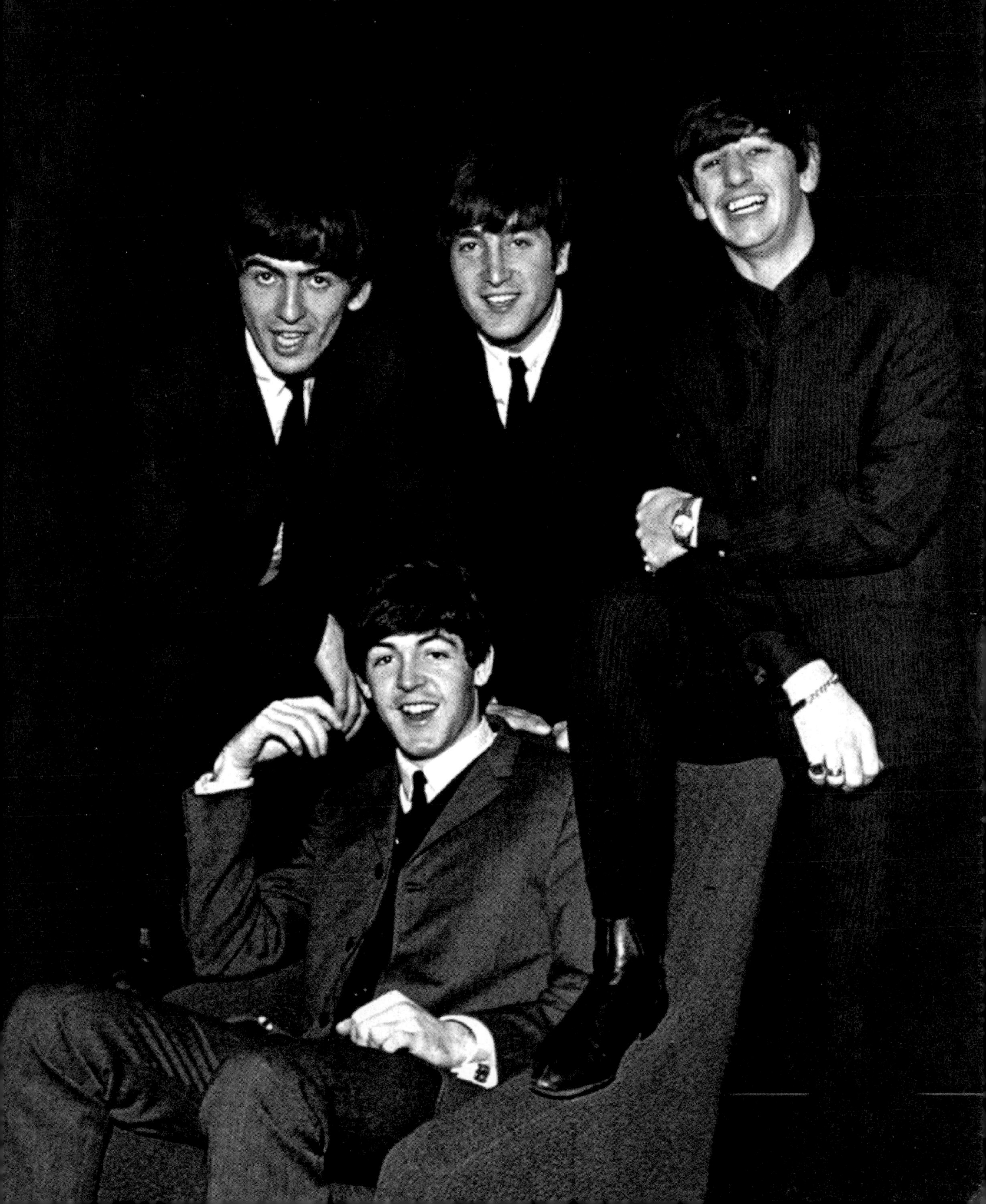

SMAS-3375   Ram   1971   7.50   15.00   30.00
—Credited to "Paul and Linda McCartney"; unsliced apple on both labels

SMAS-3375   Ram   1971   12.50 25.00   50.00
—Credited to "Paul and Linda McCartney"; Apple label with small Capitol logo on B-side

SMAS-3375   Ram   1975   25.00 50.00   100.00
—Credited to "Paul and Linda McCartney"; with "All Rights Reserved" on label

SW-3386   Wild Life   1971   3.75   7.50   15.00
—Credited to "Wings"

SMAL-3409   Red Rose Speedway   1973   5.00   10.00   20.00
—Credited to "Paul McCartney and Wings"; with bound-in booklet

SO-3415   Band on the Run   1973   5.00   10.00   20.00
—Credited to "Paul McCartney and Wings"; with photo innersleeve and poster

SPRO-6210 [DJ] Brung to Ewe By   1971   100.00 200.00 400.00
—Promo-only radio spots for "Ram"; counterfeits have uneven spacing between tracks

CAPITOL

SMAS-3363   McCartney   1976   6.25   12.50   25.00
—Black label, "Manufactured by McCartney Music Inc" at top

SMAS-3363   McCartney   1976   5.00   10.00   20.00
—Black label, "Manufactured by MPL Communications Inc" at top

SMAS-3375   Ram   1976   7.50   15.00   30.00
—Credited to "Paul and Linda McCartney"; black label, "Manufactured by McCartney Music Inc" at top

SMAS-3375   Ram   197?   5.00   10.00   20.00
—Credited to "Paul and Linda McCartney"; black label, "Manufactured by MPL Communications Inc" at top

SMAS-3375   Ram   197?   10.00 20.00   40.00
—Credited to "Paul and Linda McCartney"; black label, "Manufactured by Capitol Records" on label

SW-3386   Wild Life   1976   7.50   15.00   30.00
—Credited to "Wings"; black label, "Manufactured by McCartney Music Inc" at top

SW-3386   Wild Life   197?   5.00   10.00   20.00
—Credited to "Wings"; black label, "Manufactured by MPL Communications Inc" at top

SMAL-3409   Red Rose Speedway   1976   7.50   15.00   30.00
—Credited to "Paul McCartney and Wings"; black label, "Manufactured by McCartney Music Inc" at top

SMAL-3409   Red Rose Speedway   197?   6.25   12.50   25.00
—Credited to "Paul McCartney and Wings"; black label, "Manufactured by MPL Communications Inc" at top

SO-3415   Band on the Run   1975   5.00   10.00   20.00
—Credited to "Paul McCartney and Wings"; custom label with MPL logo

SO-3415   Band on the Run   197?   12.50 25.00   50.00
—Credited to "Paul McCartney and Wings"; black label, "Manufactured by Capitol Records..."

SO-3415   Band on the Run   197?   5.00   10.00   20.00
—Credited to "Paul McCartney and Wings"; black label, "Maunfactured by MPL Communications Inc." at top

SMAS-11419   Venus and Mars   1975   3.75   7.50   15.00
—Credited to "Wings"; with two posters and two stickers

SW-11525   Wings at the Speed of Sound   1976   2.50   5.00   10.00
—Credited to "Wings"; custom label

SW-11525 [DJ] Wings at the Speed of Sound   1976   75.00 150.00 300.00
—Credited to "Wings"; white label advance promo

SWCO-11593 [(3)] Wings Over America   1976   6.25   12.50   25.00
—Credited to "Wings"; custom labels with poster

ST-11642   Thrillington   1977   25.00 50.00   100.00
—Credited to "Percy 'Thrills' Thrillington"; instrumental versions of songs from Ram LP

SW-11777   London Town   1978   3.75   7.50   15.00
—Credited to "Wings"; custom label with poster

SEAX-11901 [PD] Band on the Run   1978   10.00 20.00   40.00
—Credited to "Paul McCartney and Wings"; picture disc

SOO-11905   Wings Greatest   1978   3.75   7.50   15.00
—Credited to "Wings"; custom label with poster

SOO-11905 [DJ] Wings Greatest   1978   100.00 200.00 400.00
—Credited to "Wings"; white label advance promo/test pressing

PJAS-12475   Press to Play   1986   3.00   6.00   12.00

CLW-48287 [(2)] All the Best!   1987   5.00   10.00   20.00

C1-56500   Flaming Pie   1997   3.75   7.50   15.00

C1-91653   Flowers in the Dirt   1989   5.00   10.00   20.00

C1-94778 [(3)] Tripping the Live Fantastic   1990   15.00 30.00   60.00

99176 [(2)] Band on the Run   1999   10.00 20.00   40.00
—Limited-edition 180-gram reissue with original LP on one record and interviews and "The Making of.." on the second

C1-595379   Tripping the Live Fantastic — Highlights! 1990 6.25   12.50   25.00
—Released on vinyl only through Columbia House; with U.S. address on back cover

C1-595379   Tripping the Live Fantastic — Highlights! 1990 6.25   12.50   25.00
—Released on vinyl only through Columbia House; with Canada address on back cover, this was sold in the U.S. by Columbia House

COLUMBIA

A2S 821 [(2) DJ] The McCartney Interview   1980   10.00 20.00   40.00
—Promo-only set; one LP is the entire interview, the other is banded for airplay; white labels with black print; counterfeits have blank white labels

FC 36057   Back to the Egg   1979   2.50   5.00   10.00
—Credited to "Wings"; custom label

FC 36057 [DJ] Back to the Egg   1979   10.00 20.00   40.00
—Credited to "Wings"; "Demonstration — Not for Sale" on custom label

PC 36057   Back to the Egg   1984   7.50   15.00   30.00
—Credited to "Wings"; "PC" cover with "FC" label

PC 36057   Back to the Egg   1984   10.00 20.00   40.00
—Credited to "Wings"; "PC" cover with "PC" label

JC 36478   McCartney   1979   3.75   7.50   15.00

PC 36478   McCartney   1984   3.75   7.50   15.00
—Budget-line reissue

JC 36479   Ram   1980   3.75   7.50   15.00
—Credited to "Paul and Linda McCartney"

PC 36479   Ram   1984   3.75   7.50   15.00
—Credited to "Paul and Linda McCartney"; budget-line reissue

JC 36480   Wild Life   1980   3.75   7.50   15.00
—Credited to "Wings"

PC 36480   Wild Life   1982   3.75   7.50   15.00
—Credited to "Wings"; budget-line reissue

JC 36481   Red Rose Speedway   1980   3.75   7.50   15.00
—Credited to "Paul McCartney and Wings"; flat or glossy cover

PC 36481   Red Rose Speedway   198?   3.75   7.50   15.00
—Credited to "Paul McCartney and Wings"; not issued with booklet

JC 36482   Band on the Run   1980   3.75   7.50   15.00
—Credited to "Paul McCartney and Wings"; custom label

JC 36482   Band on the Run   198?   25.00 50.00   100.00
—Credited to "Paul McCartney and Wings"; white "MPL" logo on lower left front cover

PC 36482   Band on the Run   198?   5.00   10.00   20.00
—Credited to "Paul McCartney and Wings"; "PC" cover with "JC" label

PC 36482   Band on the Run   198?   7.50   15.00   30.00
—Credited to "Paul McCartney and Wings"; "PC" cover with "PC" label

FC 36511   McCartney II   1980   2.50   5.00   10.00
—Add 80% if bonus single of "Coming Up (Live at Glasgow)" (AE7 1204) is with package

FC 36511 [DJ]	McCartney II		1980	7.50	15.00	30.00
—White label promo						
PC 36511	McCartney II		1984	6.25	12.50	25.00
—"PC" cover with "FC" label						
PC 36511	McCartney II		1984	25.00	50.00	100.00
—"PC" cover with "PC" label						
JC 36801	Venus and Mars		1980	3.75	7.50	15.00
—Credited to "Wings"; with one poster and two stickers						
PC 36801	Venus and Mars		1982	3.75	7.50	15.00
—Credited to "Wings"; budget-line reissue, not issued with inserts						
PC 36987	The McCartney Interview		1980	3.00	6.00	12.00
—Stock release of interview originally intended for promotional use only						
FC 37409	Wings at the Speed of Sound		1981	3.75	7.50	15.00
—Credited to "Wings"; custom label						
PC 37409	Wings at the Speed of Sound		1982	3.75	7.50	15.00
—Credited to "Wings"; regular Columbia label, budget-line reissue						
TC 37462	Tug of War		1982	2.50	5.00	10.00
PC 37462	Tug of War		1984	7.50	15.00	30.00
—Custom label; "PC" cover with "TC" label						
PC 37462	Tug of War		1984	25.00	50.00	100.00
—Regular Columbia label; "PC" cover with "PC" label						
C3X 37990 [(3)]	Wings Over America		1982	12.50	25.00	50.00
—Credited to "Wings"; custom labels, no poster						
QC 39149	Pipes of Peace		1983	3.00	6.00	12.00
SC 39613	Give My Regards to Broad Street		1984	3.75	7.50	15.00
HC 46382	Band on the Run		1981	12.50	25.00	50.00
—Credited to "Paul McCartney and Wings"; half-speed mastered edition						

MPL/PARLOPHONE

96413	Unplugged (The Official Bootleg)		1991	18.75	37.50	75.00
—No U.S. pressings; "American" copies were U.K. imports with liner notes in Spanish!						

NATIONAL FEATURES CORP.

2955/6	Band on the Run Radio Interview Special	1973	375.00	750.00	1500.00
—Promo-only interview disc					

MCCARTNEY, PAUL, AND STEVIE WONDER
12-Inch Singles
COLUMBIA

44-02878	Ebony and Ivory//Rainclouds/Ebony and Ivory (Solo)		1982	3.00	6.00	12.00
—B-side by McCartney solo						

45s
COLUMBIA

18-02860	Ebony and Ivory/Rainclouds		1982	—	2.00	4.00
—B-side by McCartney solo						
18-02860 [PS]	Ebony and Ivory/Rainclouds		1982	—	2.00	4.00

ONO, YOKO
12-Inch Singles
GEFFEN

PRO-A-934 [DJ]	Walking on Thin Ice (3:23) (5:58)		1981	3.75	7.50	15.00
PRO-A-975 [DJ]	No, No, No/Dogtown/I Don't Know Why /She Gets Down on Her Knees		1981	5.00	10.00	20.00

POLYDOR

PRO 192 [DJ]	My Man/Let the Tears Dry		1982	2.50	5.00	10.00
810575-1	Never Say Goodbye (Remix)/Loneliness (Remix)	1983	3.75	7.50	15.00
883455-1	Hell in Paradise (Club Version) (Dub Version) (Single Version)		1985	2.00	4.00	8.00
883872-1 [DJ]	Walking on Thin Ice (Remix 7:17)/ Cape Clear (2 versions)		1986	3.75	7.50	15.00

45s
APPLE

GM/OYB-1 [DJ]	Greenfield Morning/Open Your Box	1971	200.00	400.00	800.00
—Exactly six copies made for the personal use of Yoko Ono.					
1839	Mrs. Lennon/Midsummer New York		1971	—	3.50	7.00
—As "Yoko Ono/Plastic Ono Band"						

1853	Now or Never/Move On Fast		1972	—	3.50	7.00
1853 [PS]	Now or Never/Move On Fast		1972	2.00	4.00	8.00
1859	Death of Samantha/Yang Yang		1973	—	3.50	7.00
1867	Woman Power/Men, Men, Men		1973	—	3.50	7.00

CAPITOL

S7-18550	Never Say Goodbye/We're All Water		1995	—	2.00	4.00

GEFFEN

PRO-S-935 [DJ]	Walking on Thin Ice (3:23) (5:58)		1981	3.00	6.00	12.00
49683	Walking on Thin Ice/It Happened		1981	—	2.50	5.00
49683 [PS]	Walking on Thin Ice/It Happened		1981	—	2.50	5.00
—Includes picture sleeve and lyric insert						
49802	No, No, No/Will You Touch Me		1981	—	2.50	5.00
49802 [PS]	No, No, No/Will You Touch Me		1981	—	2.50	5.00
49849	Goodbye Sadness/I Don't Know Why		1981	—	2.50	5.00

POLYDOR

2224	My Man/Let the Tears Dry		1982	—	2.00	4.00
2224 [PS]	My Man/Let the Tears Dry		1982	—	2.00	4.00
883455-7	Hell in Paradise/(Instrumental)		1985	—	2.00	4.00
883455-7 [PS]	Hell in Paradise/(Instrumental)		1985	—	2.00	4.00

Albums
APPLE

SW-3373	Yoko Ono Plastic Ono Band		1970	5.00	10.00	20.00
SVBB-3380 [(2)]	Fly 1971			6.50	12.50	25.00
SVBB-3399 [(2)]	Approximately Infinite Universe		1973	6.25	12.50	25.00
SW-3412	Feeling the Space		1973	5.00	10.00	20.00

CAPITOL

SPRO-11219 [DJ]	Rising Mixes		1996	3.00	6.00	12.00
—Promo-only vinyl EP of six remixes from the CD "Rising"						

GEFFEN

GHS 2004	Season of Glass		1981	3.00	6.00	12.00

POLYDOR

PD-1-6364	It's Alright (I See Rainbows)		1982	2.50	5.00	10.00
823289-1	It's Alright (I See Rainbows)		1984	2.00	4.00	8.00
—Reissue						
827530-1	Starpeace		1985	3.00	6.00	12.00

STARR, RINGO
12-Inch Singles
ATLANTIC

DSKO 93 [DJ]	Drowning in the Sea of Love (5:08) (same on both sides)		1977	7.50	15.00	30.00

45s
APPLE

1826 [PS]	Beaucoups of Blues/Coochy-Coochy		1970	10.00	20.00	40.00
—Sleeve with wrong catalog number (actually 2969)						
1831	It Don't Come Easy/Early 1970		1971	2.00	4.00	8.00
1831	It Don't Come Easy/Early 1970		1971	3.00	6.00	12.00
—With star on A-side label						
1831 [PS]	It Don't Come Easy/Early 1970		1971	7.50	15.00	30.00
1831	It Don't Come Easy/Early 1970		1975	7.50	15.00	30.00
—With "All rights reserved" on label						
1849	Back Off Boogaloo/Blindman		1972	2.00	4.00	8.00
—Green-background label						
1849	Back Off Boogaloo/Blindman		1972	18.75	37.50	75.00
—Blue-background label						
1849 [PS]	Back Off Boogaloo/Blindman		1972	3.75	7.50	15.00
—Black paper with flat finish						

   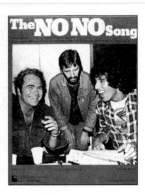

1849 [PS]	Back Off Boogaloo/Blindman	1972	10.00	20.00	40.00
—Glossy black paper on both sides						
1849 [PS]	Back Off Boogaloo/Blindman	1972	10.00	20.00	40.00
—Glossy black on one side, gray on the other						
1849 [DJ]	Back Off Boogaloo/Blindman	1972	37.50	75.00	150.00
—White label						
P-1865 [DJ]	Photograph (mono/stereo)	1973	12.50	25.00	50.00
1865	Photograph/Down and Out	1973	—	3.00	6.00
—Custom star label						
1865 [PS]	Photograph/Down and Out	1973	5.00	10.00	20.00
P-1870 [DJ]	You're Sixteen (mono/stereo)	1973	12.50	25.00	50.00
1870	You're Sixteen/Devil Woman	1973	—	3.00	6.00
—Custom star label						
1870	You're Sixteen/Devil Woman	1973	6.25	12.50	25.00
—Regular Apple label						
1870 [PS]	You're Sixteen/Devil Woman	1973	6.25	12.50	25.00
P-1872 [DJ]	Oh My My (Edited Mono)/Oh My My (Long Stereo)	1974	12.50	25.00	50.00
1872	Oh My My/Step Lightly	1974	—	3.00	6.00
—Custom star label						
1872	Oh My My/Step Lightly	1974	2.00	4.00	8.00
—Regular Apple label						
P-1876 [DJ]	Only You (mono/stereo)	1974	10.00	20.00	40.00
1876	Only You/Call Me	1974	—	3.00	6.00
—Custom nebula label						
1876	Only You/Call Me	1974	2.00	4.00	8.00
—Regular Apple label						
1876 [PS]	Only You/Call Me	1974	5.00	10.00	20.00
1880	No No Song/Snookeroo	1975	—	3.00	6.00
—Custom nebula label						
P-1880 [DJ]	No No Song/Snookeroo (both mono)	1975	10.00	20.00	40.00
P-1880 [DJ]	No No Song/Snookeroo (both stereo)	1975	10.00	20.00	40.00
P-1882 [DJ]	It's All Down to Goodnight Vienna (mono/stereo)	1975	10.00	20.00	40.00
1882	It's All Down to Goodnight Vienna/Oo-Wee	1975	—	3.00	6.00
—Custom nebula label						
1882 [PS]	It's All Down to Goodnight Vienna/Oo-Wee	1975	5.00	10.00	20.00
P-1882 [DJ]	Oo-Wee/Oo-Wee	1975	17.50	35.00	70.00
2969	Beaucoups of Blues/Coochy-Coochy	1970	6.25	12.50	25.00
—With small Capitol logo on bottom of B-side label and star on A-side label						
2969	Beaucoups of Blues/Coochy-Coochy	1970	10.00	20.00	40.00
—With "Mfd. by Apple" on label and star on A-side label						
2969	Beaucoups of Blues/Coochy-Coochy	1970	2.00	4.00	8.00
—With "Mfd. by Apple" on label and no star on A-side label						
2969 [PS]	Beaucoups of Blues/Coochy-Coochy	1970	12.50	25.00	50.00
—Sleeve with correct catalog number						

ATLANTIC

3361	A Dose of Rock 'N' Roll/Cryin'	1976	2.50	5.00	10.00
3371	Hey Baby/Lady Gaye	1976	7.50	15.00	30.00
3412	Drowning in the Sea of Love/Just a Dream	1977	30.00	60.00	120.00
3429	Wings/Just a Dream	1977	7.50	15.00	30.00

BOARDWALK

NB7-11-130	Wrack My Brain/Drumming Is My Madness	1981	—	2.50	5.00
NB7-11-130 [PS]	Wrack My Brain/Drumming Is My Madness	1981	—	2.50	5.00
NB7-11-134	Private Property/Stop and Take the Time to Smell the Roses	1982	3.00	6.00	12.00

CAPITOL

1831	It Don't Come Easy/Early 1970	1976	6.25	12.50	25.00
—Orange label						
1831	It Don't Come Easy/Early 1970	1978	—	3.00	6.00
—Purple late-1970s label						
1831	It Don't Come Easy/Early 1970	1983	—	3.00	6.00
—Black colorband label						
1831	It Don't Come Easy/Early 1970	1988	—	2.50	5.00
—Purple late-1980s label (wider)						
1849	Back Off Boogaloo/Blindman	1976	7.50	15.00	30.00
—Orange label						
1849	Back Off Boogaloo/Blindman	1978	2.00	4.00	8.00
—Purple late-1970s label						
1865	Photograph/Down and Out	1978	2.00	4.00	8.00
—Purple late-1970s label						
1865	Photograph/Down and Out	1983	2.00	4.00	8.00
—Black colorband label						
1865	Photograph/Down and Out	1988	—	3.00	6.00
—Purple late-1980s label (wider)						
1870	You're Sixteen/Devil Woman	1976	15.00	30.00	60.00
—Orange label						
1870	You're Sixteen/Devil Woman	1978	2.00	4.00	8.00
—Purple late-1970s label						
1870	You're Sixteen/Devil Woman	1983	2.00	4.00	8.00
—Black colorband label						
1870	You're Sixteen/Devil Woman	1988	—	2.50	5.00
—Purple late-1980s label (wider)						
1876	Only You/Call Me	1978	2.00	4.00	8.00
—Purple late-1970s label						
1876	Only You/Call Me	1983	25.00	50.00	100.00
—Black colorband label						
1880	No No Song/Snookeroo	1978	2.00	4.00	8.00
—Purple late-1970s label						
1880	No No Song/Snookeroo	1983	2.00	4.00	8.00
—Black colorband label						
1880	No No Song/Snookeroo	1988	7.50	15.00	30.00
—Purple late-1980s label (wider)						
1882	It's All Down to Goodnight Vienna/Oo-Wee	1978	2.00	4.00	8.00
—Purple late-1970s label						
2969	Beaucoups of Blues/Coochy-Coochy	1976	10.00	20.00	40.00
—Orange label						

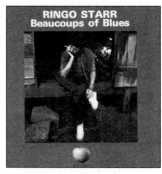   

B-44409	Act Naturally/Key's in the Mailbox	1989	3.75	7.50	15.00

—A-side with Buck Owens; B-side is Owens solo

MERCURY

MELP-195 [DJ]	La De Da/Everyday	1998	3.75	7.50	15.00

—Number only in the dead wax

MELP-195 [PS]	La De Da/Everyday	1998	3.75	7.50	15.00

—The above record and sleeve were a giveaway from Beatlefest and J&R's Music World with advance purchase of the CD "Vertical Man" and later from Beatlefest with any Ringo Starr Mercury CD.

PORTRAIT

70015	Lipstick Traces (On a Cigarette)/Old Time Relovin'	1978	3.75	7.50	15.00
70018	Heart on My Sleeve/Who Needs a Heart	1978	3.75	7.50	15.00

THE RIGHT STUFF

S7-18178	In My Car/She's About a Mover	1994	2.00	4.00	8.00

—Gold/orange vinyl

S7-18179	Wrack My Brain/Private Property	1994	2.00	4.00	8.00

—Red vinyl

Albums
APPLE

SW-3365	Sentimental Journey	1970	5.00	10.00	20.00
SMAS-3368	Beaucoups of Blues	1970	5.00	10.00	20.00
SWAL-3413	Ringo	1973	5.00	10.00	20.00

—Standard issue with booklet; Side 1, Song 2 identified on cover as "Hold On"

SWAL-3413	Ringo	1973	100.00	200.00	400.00

—With a 5:26 version of "Six O'Clock." On later copies, the song is shortened to 4:05 though the label still says 5:26. All known copies have a promo punch-hole in top corner of jacket; on Side 2 record, "Six O'Clock" will be the widest track.

SWAL-3413	Ringo	1974	6.25	12.50	25.00

—Later issue with booklet; Side 1, Song 2 identified on cover as "Have You Seen My Baby"

SW-3417	Goodnight Vienna	1974	3.00	6.00	12.00
SW-3422	Blast from Your Past	1975	3.75	7.50	15.00

ATLANTIC

SD 18193	Ringo's Rotogravure	1976	3.75	7.50	15.00

—Deduct 2/3 for cut-outs

SD 18193 [DJ]	Ringo's Rotogravure	1976	7.50	15.00	30.00

—With "DJ Only" scrawled into trail-off area

SD 19108	Ringo the 4th	1977	3.75	7.50	15.00

—Deduct 1/2 for cut-outs

SD 19108 [DJ]	Ringo the 4th	1977	7.50	15.00	30.00

—With "DJ Only" scrawled into trail-off area

BOARDWALK

NB1-33246	Stop and Smell the Roses	1981	2.50	5.00	10.00

—Deduct 1/2 for cut-outs

CAPITOL

SW-3365	Sentimental Journey	197?	10.00	20.00	40.00

—Purple label, large Capitol logo

SN-16114	Ringo	198?	3.75	7.50	15.00

—Green label budget-line reissue with all errors corrected

SN-16218	Sentimental Journey	198?	6.25	12.50	25.00

—Green label budget-line reissue

SN-16219	Goodnight Vienna	198?	6.25	12.50	25.00

—Green label budget-line reissue

SN-16235	Beaucoups of Blues	198?	5.00	10.00	20.00

—Green label budget-line reissue

SN-16236	Blast from Your Past	198?	3.75	7.50	15.00

—Green label budget-line reissue

PORTRAIT

JR 35378	Bad Boy	1978	3.75	7.50	15.00

—Deduct 1/3 for cut-outs

JR 35378 [DJ]	Bad Boy	1978	25.00	50.00	100.00

—White label promo with "Advance Promotion" on label; in plain white cover

JR 35378 [DJ]	Bad Boy	1978	7.50	15.00	30.00

—Regular white-label promo in standard jacket

RHINO

R1 70199	Starr Struck: Ringo's Best 1976-1983	1989	6.25	12.50	25.00

RYKODISC

RALP 0190	Ringo Starr and His All-Starr Band	1990	7.50	15.00	30.00

—With limited, numbered obi (deduct $5 if missing)

SUZY AND THE RED STRIPES
12-Inch Singles
CAPITOL

V-15244	Seaside Woman/B-Side to Seaside	1986	10.00	20.00	40.00

EPIC

ASF 361 [DJ]	Seaside Woman (same on both sides)	1977	7.50	15.00	30.00

45s
CAPITOL

B-5608	Seaside Woman/B-Side to Seaside	1986	7.50	15.00	30.00

EPIC

50403 [DJ]	Seaside Woman (mono/stereo)	1977	25.00	50.00	100.00

—"Advance Promotion" label, black vinyl

50403 [DJ]	Seaside Woman (mono/stereo)	1977	6.25	12.50	25.00

—Red vinyl, orange label on one side, white on the other

50403 [DJ]	Seaside Woman (mono/stereo)	1977	25.00	50.00	100.00

—Black vinyl, orange label on one side, white on the other

50403	Seaside Woman/B-Side to Seaside	1977	2.50	5.00	10.00

TRAVELING WILBURYS
45s
WILBURY

21867	Handle with Care/End of the Line	1990	3.75	7.50	15.00

—"Back to Back Hits" series

27637 [DJ]	End of the Line (same on both sides)	1989	5.00	10.00	20.00
27637	End of the Line/Congratulations	1989	3.75	7.50	15.00
27637 [PS]	End of the Line/Congratulations	1989	5.00	10.00	20.00
27732 [DJ]	Handle with Care (same on both sides)	1988	3.75	7.50	15.00
27732	Handle with Care/Margarita	1988	2.00	4.00	8.00
27732 [PS]	Handle with Care/Margarita	1988	2.00	4.00	8.00

Albums
WILBURY

25796	Traveling Wilburys (Volume One)	1988	5.00	10.00	20.00
26324	Traveling Wilburys, Vol. 3	1990	5.00	10.00	20.00

or more information about the clubs listed below, most require a self-addressed stamped envelope. For more information on these clubs, contact the National Association of Fan Clubs at 818-763-3280. The information contained in this section is provided by the fan clubs and is subject to change.

Beatlefan

P.O. Box 33515

Decatur GA 30033

Phone: 770-492-0444

Fax: 404-321-3109

Best time to call: 9 a.m. to noon, Mon.-Fri. EST

Web: beatlefan.com

beatlefan@mindspring.com

Cost: Cost: $22 ($25 first class) USA; $33 printed matter airmail UK, Western Europe, Latin America; $35 printed matter airmail overseas; credit card orders accepted

Frequency: Six issues per year

Special features: Exclusive interviews, photo-packed tour issues, retrospectives; sample issue $4 USA; $5.50 overseas; back issues also available

Description: Been around 24 years; readership of 15,000+.

Year Updated: 2002

Beatlefan/Extra!

P.O. Box 33515

Decatur GA 30033

Phone: 770-492-0444

Fax: 404-321-3109

Best time to call: 9 a.m. to noon EST Mon.-Fri.

Web: beatlefan.com

E-mail: beatlefan@mindspring.com

Cost: $36 USA; $37.50 North America; $38 overseas; SASE for sample

Frequency: 18 issues per year

Special features: Fax subscriptions available for additional charge

Description: Our subscribers get the news while it's still news!

Year Updated: 2002

Beatles Fan Club "Next Generation"

Attention: Roger Bruneel

Address: 63 Whiteside Road, Haydock, Merseyside WA11 OJB, England

Phone: 00-44-1744-24511 & 00-44-7730-813979 (mobile)

Fax: 00-44-1744-24511.

Web: www.beatlesfannext.com

E-mail: beatlesfannext@aol.com, beatlesfannext@hotmail.com

Cost: £28.00 first year, £23.00 second year

Special features: album specials, bootleg reviews, readers letters and for sale and wants as from Issue 8.

Description: We only talk about John, Paul, George and Ringo and about their music.

Beatlology

Attention: Subscriptions

PO Box 90 260 Adelaide Street East

Toronto ONTARIO

CANADA M5A 1N1

Phone: 416-360-8902

Fax: 416-360-0588

Best time to call: 9 a.m. to 5 p.m. EST M-F

Web: www.beatlology.com

E-mail: orders@beatlology.com

Cost: $30 North America; $45 overseas

Frequency: Six times per year

Special features: Exclusive articles on the history of The Beatles, their music and collectibles

Description: Full color magazine dedicated to collectors of Beatles memorabilia and fans alike around the world.

Come Together - Southern California Beatles Fan Club

Attention: Carmen Salmon, president
PO Box 1793
Lakeside CA 92040
Hotline: 619-687-3687
Best time to call: Anytime
Web: http://members.cox.net/beatlefair
E-mail: ctclub@msn.com

Cost: $10

Frequency: Quarterly

Special features: Club news, Beatles news, fan club directory

Description: We are a nonprofit organization in existence for seven years. Our members "come together" to share memories and news about the greatest musical band ever, The Beatles. We meet regularly throughout the year for social events. Our biggest event is our annual Beatlefair. This is an opportunity for Beatles fans to come together for a day of fun and music. Guests have included Pete Best, Tony Sheridan, Joey Molland, Gordon Waller, Laurence Juber, Denny Laine, and Walter Shenson. Charities we have donated to in the past include: The American Cancer Society, Joe Pope Memorial Fund, and the San Diego Youth Symphony. We collected more than 5,000 signatures to get The Beatles' star on the Hollywood Walk Of Fame and are also involved with the petition to keep John Lennon's killer from being released from prison.

Daytrippin'

Attention: Trina Yannicos, editor and publisher
23A Beverly Place
Edgewater NJ 07020
Phone: 201-224-5214
Fax: 201-224-5214
Web: www.daytrippin.com
E-mail: editor@daytrippin.com

Cost: $16

Frequency: Quarterly

Special features: The most Fab magazine for Beatles fans!

Description: From the fresh perspective of rock journalists, celebrate The Beatles with exclusive interviews and in-depth articles on the latest Beatles news, events and people, as well as columns by Martin Lewis and our own auction and memorabilia experts. Plus, book/CD/video reviews, calendar of events, artwork, convention info, contests and reader contributions.

Liverpool Beatlescene International Fan Club

Cavern Walks, Mathew Street
Liverpool
UK L2 6RE
Phone: 0151-207-0148
Fax: Fax: 0151-207-0148
Web: http://come.to/Liverpoolbeatlescene
E-mail: Jcatha1@aol.com

Cost: £12 UK; £15 Europe; £17 worldwide

Frequency: Quarterly

Special features: Membership pack containing postcards, membership card, letter, other information, pen pal service, reports on Liverpool Beatles convention, regular articles by Alistair Taylor

Description: The only fan club in Liverpool since the early 1960s. Our aim is to bring together those who enjoy the music of the world's greatest musical phenomenon, The Beatles.

Octopus' Garden

Attention: Tom Aguiar, editor
PO Box 3683
Peabody MA 01961-3683
Web: http://members.home.net/hlnwheels
E-mail: beatles94@excite.com

Cost: $12 USA; $18 overseas

Frequency: Quarterly (March, June, Sept., Dec.)

Description: We are a quarterly fanzine registered with the National Association Of Fan Clubs. Weve been around for more than 10 years and are dedicated to putting out a fanzine for all age groups. Our readers keep us alive with their input, short stories, news, opinions, games, etc... Whatever our readers want is what they get!

Tokyo Beatles Fan Club

Attention: Kenji Maeda & Otohei Shima
4-6-14-304 Toyotama-Kita Nerima-ku
Tokyo JAPAN 176-0012
Phone: +81-48-773-6320 (24 hours)

Cost: $27

Frequency: Quarterly

Special features: Our magazine is written in English

Description: We are the largest nonprofit Beatles fan club in Japan, established in 1991 to celebrate The Beatles' 25th anniversary of their visit to Japan.

Beatles Unlimited

Attention: Rene' van Haarlem

PO Box 602

3430 AP Nieuwegein

Netherlands

Phone: 31-30-6063678

Fax: 31-30-2445292

Best time to call: Tuesdays 1-4 p.m. EST

Web: www.beatles-unlimited.com

E-mail: beatunl@knoware.nl

Cost: $31 or *insert euro symbol* 36,75

Frequency: Bimonthly

Special features: George Harrison tribute special

Description: 60 pages, in English, printed offset; size 215 mm by 162 mm. Established in Nov. 10, 1963

The World Beatles Forum

Attention: Brad Howard, editor

2440 Bank Street, PO Box 40081

Ottawa Ontario

Canada K1V 0W8

E-mail: beatles@happy.mondenet.com

Cost: $15 USA; $15CA Canada; $20 international

Frequency: Six times per year (always shipped first class air mail)

Special features: Beatles news, views, reviews and interviews

Description: We are a quarterly fanzine registered with the National Association Of Fan Clubs. We've been around for more than 10 years and are dedicated to putting out a fanzine for all age groups. Our readers keep us alive with their input, short stories, news, opinions, games, etc... Whatever our readers want is what they get!

Beatles Web Sites

http://incolor.inetnebr.com/sumaree/beatles/index.htm

Description: Recommended by Beatles publications as one of the best, all-round Beatles sites.

www.thebeatles.com

Desccription: Official site.

http://abbeyrd.best.vwh.net/

Description: Recommended by Beatles fan clubs as a news source.

www.music.indiana.edu/som/courses/rock/england.html

Desccription: The Beatles' England: Beatles sites in England, Hamburg, and more.

www.beatlefest.com

Desccription: Official site of nationwide Beatles conventions.

www.BeatleLinks.net

Description: Site contains hundreds and hundreds of categorized and ranked links to Beatles-related web sites from all across the universe.

Beatles Web Ring

Description: A great source for Beatles sites — just type Beatles Ring in yahoo.com. It's a service that lets you locate various Beatles sites on the Internet.

Albums and memorabilia

www.rarebeatles.com/whatsnew.htm

Description: Beatles memorabilia/records reference.

www.eskimo.com/~bpentium/butcher.html

Description: Everything you've always wanted to know about the Butcher Cover.

www.dermon.com/Beatles/Beatles.htm

Description: Site features photos of label variations used on Beatles and solo singles. Note: Address is case-sensitive.

http://users.telerama.com/~agp/

Description: Dedicated to Beatles worldwide 78s.

John Lennon

www.lennon.net/

Description: Official site of the Liverpool Lennons. Includes a family tree.

www.instantkarma.com/

Description: John, Yoko, Sean & Julian. Magazine since 1981.

http://foia.fbi.gov/lennon.htm

Description: FBI Files on John Lennon, courtesy of the Freedom Of Information Act. .pdf format.

www.taisei.co.jp/museum/index_e.html

Description: Japanese museum dedicated to preserving John Lennon's memory; approved by Yoko Ono.

http://johnlennonsociety.tripod.com/

Description: John Lennon Society Web site includes a petition to sign to keep Lennon's murderer in jail. He's up for parole in Oct. 2002.

http://abcnews.go.com/onair/lennon/

Description: ABC documentary about John Lennon's life in New York.

www.bagism.com/

Description: Extensive fan site.

http://www.john-lennon.com/

Note: Pop-up ads galore.

Paul McCartney

www.paulmccartney.com

Description: Official site. Note: Site starts with a flash intro that doesn't appear to be skip-able.

www.mplcommunications.com/index.asp

Description: Official site of MPL Communications.

www.siegen-wittgenstein.de/kultur/pmc/indexb.htm

Description: A gallery of Paul McCartney paintings.

www.macca-l.net/

Description: Paul McCartney e-mail list web site.

www.quipo.it/mccartney/nhome.htm

Description: In-depth fan site.

http://macca.inter-pc.com/index.cfm

Description: In-depth fan site.

www.quipo.it/mccartney/newsen.htm

Description: A Paul McCartney fan club site.

www.geocities.com/SunsetStrip/3674/pidsgt.html

Description: A site dedicated to the "Paul Is Dead" hoax.

George Harrison

www.georgeharrison.com

Description: Official site; at press time has information about Brainwashed.

www.hariscruffs.com/index2.html

Description: In-depth fan site.

www.bekkoame.ne.jp/~garp/index1.htm

Description: Fan site with information on releases, film, TV and radio show appearances, as well as recording session info.

Ringo Starr

www.ringotour.com

Description: The offical site of Ringo's tour dates, put together by David Fishof Presents. It appears to not have been updated past 2001.

www.klaus-voormann.com

Description: Grammy Award-winning artist's (Revolver) official site.

www.julianlennon.com

Description: Julian Lennon's official site. ∎